THE OTHER EUROPE

King's Court Communications, Inc.
Post Office Box 224
Brunswick, Ohio 44212
Library of Congress
Catalogue Card Number 76-3210
....
ISBN: 0-89139-013-8

PREFACE/PREVIEW

This project is a direct outgrowth of my experience teaching survey and intermediate level courses on European politics. Its conception is clearly the product of something less than blinding originality. It seemed obvious to me that the study of European politics was one of the few political science subfields for which reading material was not available which effectively challenged the more orthodox treatments. Over the years, I have assigned most of these texts and while each has merit, I have been alarmed by their remarkable uniformity of interpretation. Numerous conversations with colleagues and students convinced me that a need exists for another perspective, an antidote perhaps, not wedded to the status quo and willing to entertain a radical critique of the four systems usually "covered" in this course: Britain, France, West Germany and the Soviet Union. My purpose is to make some of this unconventional material more easily accessible to the student. In the absence of an integrated and coherent text on the subject, I hope this volume will partially suffice to remedy what I view as a glaring deficiency in the available teaching literature.

There is solid basis for doubting the usefulness of the traditional approach. The need for other viewpoints has been magnified recently by the growing political and economic crisis facing Britain and rapidly appearing elsewhere. Most texts provide little guidance for the student seeking to place these events in their proper context — in this case, Britain's liberal capitalist socio-economic system. Here one might object that it is unwise to study societies before exposing oneself to certain "nuts and bolts" as found in most textbooks. My reply is that one cannot begin to understand formal structures and political behavior without appreciating certain social and economic realities. Rarely in the orthodox text is a cause and effect relationship pursued that might reveal the class-based character of conventional wisdom regarding voting patterns, educational and legal systems, various parliamentary forms, and general decision-making processes. It is rarely if ever acknowledged that the nature of the political process in these societies is significantly influenced by economic considerations — most often by the desire to maintain ownership and control by a small class.

On Britain, the contributors to this volume examine a host of "givens" including "inherited traditions" of upper class "duty," "traditional working class deference," rejection of extra-Parliamentary politics, consensual social change, and the supposed impartiality of the State machine. Additionally, the British Labour Party's claim to be the leading force behind creating a socialist society is subjected to a withering critique.

On France, one could note the tendency in the literature to comment approvingly on the role of national planning and the concomitant failure to note the function of this state guidance — protecting the capitalist class from the chaos of the market. State planning in France should not be misconstrued as a stage of socialism since it does not serve the total society. As Ernest Mandel, the Belgian Marxist, maintains:

> Increasing state intervention in the economy, the growth of a "public" sector, and even nationalization of certain unprofitable branches do not amount to "socialism." An economy can no more be a "little bit socialist," than a woman can be a "little bit pregnant." State intervention, management of the economy, within the framework of capitalism in order to consolidate capitalist profits, or at least those of the decisive sections of the capitalist monopolies. . . . The idea of planning is accepted and applied by the bourgeoisie; indeed, one can even say that it is of bourgeois origin. But the bourgeoisie accept and adopt it only to the extent that it does not imperil the *profit motive,* does not embrace the whole of economic life, substituting production to meet need for production for profit.[1]

Massive doses of state aid in France go to big business while the broad goals and objectives of planning are once again taken as givens.

In the Federal Republic of Germany, if economic power is becoming increasingly concentrated in private hands, I believe a textbook author is derelict if he fails to examine the manner in which West German political institutions help to create, perpetuate, and legitimate that unequal distribution. Or, one could raise questions about the long-standing myth of United States "generosity" in extending substantial assistance to Germany under The Marshall Plan. In fact, this was a capitalist restoration in post-fascist Germany during a period when many Germans were interested in creating a socialist "new order." Further, a few authors concede that the Federal Republic's "miraculous" recovery was financed, in part, by low labor costs. That is, capitalists paid low wages to some 7 million destitute refugee workers and used the extraordinarily high profit margins for industrial expansion. The quiescent posture adopted by these workers, including a disinclination to engage in strikes, tends to be treated as a special blessing for the economy. One even receives the impression that workers fighting for their rights in this situation, as well as later on, would somehow have been acting irresponsibly and contrary to the "public interest." Surely this period could be given a different interpretation: the workers behavior could be analyzed as an indicator of retarded political consciousness, heavily reinforced by those groups favoring vested economic interest. In any case, once set in motion, a capitalist restoration ideology produced many features of contemporary West Germany that are now treated as a natural evolution of that system.

Moreover, while the standard approach to the three Western nations often misses the mark by accepting what *is* as *natural,* it just as often errs in other ways on the Soviet Union. At times, the USSR is found wanting in unstated comparisons with certain notions of liberal "democracy," or worse, one finds a strained effort to be sympathetic to the faults of an "alien" culture. One also notes a disturbing tendency to celebrate selected elements of the intelligentsia, primarily those dissident intellectuals who are anti-socialist, elitist, and hostile to the Soviet working class — the only force capable of fundamentally altering the system. These critics are embraced by some social scientists precisely because of their distance from the battle for socialist democracy, their disdain for the genuine revolutionary heirs of the 1920's and 1930's, and their occasional kind words for Western economic systems. In short, too many texts are colored by the author's implicit hopes for the Soviet Union's future evolution, usually some variation on pluralist theories of industrial society.

In fact, it can be asked whether any of the four countries deserve to be termed democratic. The workers do not control the material *conditions* of production, *what* is produced, how that product should be *distributed* and/or *invested;* and in none of the four societies are serious official efforts being undertaken to realize these essential ingredients of democracy.

This leads to another objection that might be raised about the conventional orientation. Too many social scientists have approached political democracy as if it were divorced from economic democracy. In the three Western nations, workers take political equality as a birthright and yet few would dream of extending this right to include the determination of how the wealth they produce should be apportioned. Because only this decision-making in the economic sphere can give political decision-making any real meaning, it might be fruitful for the student to ponder the possible sources of attitudes which hold people back (themselves included) from concretizing democracy in this fashion and also, why so little attention is given to this critical issue in most orthodox texts. Because society now can be organized in radically more productive and life-supportive ways, economic democracy would open the possibility for "freedom *from* the economy — from being controlled by economic forces and relationships; freedom from the daily struggle for existence, from earning a living."[2] Why isn't it?

The contributors to this book do not engage in the traditional and usually self-serving bow of obeisance in the direction of "scholarly neutrality." They seek to rise above intellectual puzzle solving and identify the negative consequences for individual lives that flow from current social arrangements. They recognize that existing power structures are inherently void of any possibility for creating humane polities and that various reformist schemes have invariably failed to ameliorate the situation. Furthermore, the authors maintain that these societies should not only be compared with *one another* but also with a vision of authentic democratic socialism — an idea that is feared by the dominant classes in each of the four nations. That is, the goal is one of qualitative changes in human existence whereby men and women can consciously control their own destinies — can become self-governing, self-managing people. This involves more than "participation." During the French student revolt of 1968, General de Gaulle offered the protestors limited participation in their universities and factories. A now famous poster appeared shortly thereafter which captured the primary reason for rejecting this substitute for a socialist democracy:

> I participate
> You participate
> He participates
> We participate
> You participate
> They profit!

Genuine participation cannot be equated with ritualistic visits to the voting booth, public acquisition of bankrupt industries, and co-optive workers' participation. Self-management is an alternative to social change imposed "from above," the latter leading to unresponsive, bureaucratic, hierarchical arrangements. A succinct statement on self-management was put forward by the French student revolutionaries in their tract "We Are Continuing to Struggle," which explained,

> Practically, self-management consists in the worker comrades operating their factories by and for themselves, and consequently, the suppression of the hierarchy of salaries as well as the notions of wage-earner and boss. It is for them to constitute the worker's councils, elected by themselves and executing the decisions of the whole.
>
> These councils must be in close relation with councils of other enterprises on the regional, national, and international plane.
>
> The members of these workers' councils are elected at a determinate time and their tasks are rotated. It is in fact necessary to avoid the re-creation of a bureaucracy which would tend to set up a leadership and re-create oppressive power.[3]

This process can be instituted at the workplace but has much broader implications since it challenges the very legitimacy of existing social regimentation. As Andre Gorz has observed, "The demand for self-management which arises out of productive praxis cannot be contained within the factory walls, the laboratories, and research bureaus. Men who cannot be ordered around in their work cannot indefinitely be ordered around in their life as citizens, nor can they submit to the rigid decision of central administration."[4]

In any event, I believe that most of the contributors to this book would agree that our comprehension of modern Europe can be enhanced only by jettisoning bourgeois social science outlooks on these systems. Conventional assumptions tend to mask and reify existing distributions of wealth and power by their seeming disinterestedness. The status quo is either challenged or supported by political analysis — it cannot remain unaffected any more than the analyst can remain neutral. The selections in this book adopt what I believe to be a more fruitful mode of analysis for consistently examining politics in the four nations.

These essays do not add up to a complete overview of the subject. But beyond that, for most students of European politics this reader can only begin to compete against a lifetime of pro-capitalist conditioning in the United States. Fortunately, the task of raising fundamental questions about these societies has been facilitated by parallel efforts in other areas. Introductory courses in American government, economics, and Third World studies have profited in recent years from radical critiques that have undermined a previously unchallenged ideological hegemony.* These heretical analyses often seem to strike students as more penetrating assessments of political reality. Because there is no analogous text for comparative politics courses in Europe it is my hope that this reader will provide an alternative and a companion to orthodox texts. The format is intended to correspond to most of them.

I anticipate that the readings will lead to speculation and lively class discussions on the meaning of "development" in modern industrial societies: Is the essence of man the striving for possessions and, correspondingly, is commodity accumulation the best definition of human well-being? What type of system would be most responsive to meeting human needs? Do the actual producers of a nation's wealth have any rights relating to that process? What forces in societies prevent human beings from questioning existing property and class divisions? Finally, a closely related theme in this book, why is it that masses of working men and women remain loyal to political parties which repeatedly fail to respond to their real interests?

I believe that approaching the subject matter of the course in this fashion can be extremely rewarding if at the same time somewhat troubling. I welcome reactions and criticisms from those teaching and studying in this area.

*From this rapidly proliferating literature one could cite: David Mermelstein (Editor), *The Economic Crisis Reader* (New York: Vintage, 1975); Michael Parenti, *Democracy for the Few* (New York: St. Martin's, 1974); Charles K. Wilber (Editor), *The Political Economy of Development and Underdevelopment* (New York: Random House, 1973); Ronald Chilcote and Joel C. Edelstein (Editors), *Latin America: The Struggle with Dependency and Beyond* (Cambridge: Schenkman, 1974); Richard C. Edwards, Michael Reich and Thomas E. Weisskopf, *The Capitalist System* (Englewood Cliffs: Prentice-Hall, 1972); Richard Harris (Editor), *The Political Economy of Africa* (Cambridge: Schenkman, 1975).

[1] As found in William K. Tabb, "We are All Socialists Now: Corporate Planning for America," *Social Policy* (March/April, 1975), p. 34.

[2] Herbert Marcuse, *One Dimensional Man* (Boston: Beacon Press, 1964), p. 4.

[3] As found in Andrew Feenberg, "Socialism in France? The Common Program and the Future of the French Left," *Socialist Revolution 4*, 1 (January-March, 1974), p. 17.

[4] Andre Gorz, *Strategy for Labour* (Boston: Beacon Press, 1967).

PERSONAL ACKNOWLEDGMENTS

I wish I could claim some credit for any merits to be found in this collection but I must limit my responsibility to problems relating to choice and organization of the readings and any other shortcomings that remain. I would like to thank several friends, colleagues, and students who have generously offered advice and aided my project in one way or another: Jim O'Connor, Alan Wolfe, Hugo Radice, Hwa Yol Jung, Walter Roettger, Hans Wuerth, Lewis Greenstein, Claus Offe, Jack Zipes, Ian Brichall, Wolf-Richard Grauhan, Kurt Tauber, Sue Ellen Charlton, Alberto Martinelli, Tony Sodroski, Laura Katz-Olson, Don Mastrodomenico and, especially, Peggy Stinson.

I am also indebted to the faculty research and development committee at Moravian College for their assistance and to Margie Boyer who provided invaluable typing assistance at several stages. Ruth D'Aleo was indefatigable in assisting my search of the literature. Without the kind cooperation and firm encouragement of Michael Sego at King's Court this book would not have materialized. I'm also extremely grateful to the authors who allowed me to include their work in this book; I hope their trust was not totally misplaced.

Concentrate on 1!

CONTENTS

The Other Europe
Radical Critiques of Britain, France, West Germany and the Soviet Union

Gary L. Olson
Moravian College

KING'S COURT COMMUNICATIONS, INC.
BRUNSWICK, OHIO

1. Great Britain

The central fact of a capitalist society is the power of a minority who own and control the means of production to regulate the lives of all other members of the society — the vast majority who must sell their labor power for wages. Of the total personal wealth in Britain, 10 percent of the people own 83 percent; the rest of the people, that is, the other 90 percent, must share the remainder. The weight assigned to such factors, when undertaking a political analysis, affects the conclusions about that society. For example, the authors of a recent text on comparative politics attribute the existence of a relatively monolithic value system or "consensus on the basic ends of society and politics" in Britain, in part, to the *presence* of mass communications.[1] By contrast, the first reading in this section, by Raymond Williams, draws attention to the implicit *message* transmitted by the media — the content of which reflects ownership in a few hands by those who accept, and benefit from, the existence of concentrated economic power and a message which subtly legitimates privileged social elites, widespread inequality of educational opportunity, and limited access. Thus, as Williams observes, when initiating a political analysis "your choice of a starting point is a choice of what you take to be decisively important." Williams proceeds to offer an overview of social reality in Britain and argues that these conditions are inexticably bound to British capitalism. Juliet Mitchell adds a brief summary on the situation of working women in British society. Both authors possess a profound commitment to realizing a qualitatively different society and yet both recognize the immense tasks involved in altering a manipulative social and political system.

It is a "mental police force" — a set of attitudes held by working people as to what constitutes authoritative principles of "normality" — that best explains why the masses of British citizens accept their subordinate position.[2] Tom Nairn, an editor of the *New Left Review,* offers a penetrating historical analysis of the upper-class origins of these enfeebling conceptions of proper behavior and, closely related, why British working people have not challenged the legitimacy of the existing order. His study can be fruitfully compared with the conventional text's tendency to celebrate Britain's "orderly" political development as evidence of some peculiar virtues within her people. Nairn contends that comprehending the peculiar social character of mid-Victorian England is essential in this regard. As the first modern proletariat, the British working class of 1848 was the largest in Europe. Nairn seeks to uncover factors which ensured bourgeoisie dominance over this emerging class. His account includes political institutions, social structures, cultural mores, working class ideologies, and the critical role played by British imperialism. This period's influence on the birth of the modern Labor Party in 1918, a party claiming to defy conservative hegemony, should not be discounted. One also discovers a partial explanation for the sizable working class vote consistently cast for the Conservative party in modern day British elections.

Nairn's discussion serves as an introduction for the contribution by David Coates, Lecturer in Politics at the University of York. Coates seeks to demonstrate why the Labor Party's radical promise to create a democratic socialist society in Britain can never be fulfilled under rules set up by corporate capital — rules generally accepted by Laborites. He contends that "the power of the Parliamentary state is apparently not open to those who seek fundamental social transformation of a socialist kind." In developing his thesis Coates offers a view of Parliament, special interest groups, voters, parties, and bureaucracy not often found in traditional explanations of British politics. He takes strong issue with the orthodox views that decision-making in Britain lacks an ideological component and a coherent long-range goal. Indeed, it requires tortured logic to attribute ideology only to those who reject capitalism and its assumptions, while characterizing leaders who promote and protect that system as somehow existing above and beyond ideology. Students of British politics who promote this superficial perspective tend to reveal more about their own ideological predilections than they do about British political reality.

An abbreviated piece by Chris Harmon, a member of the London-based International Socialists, is from his longer study *The Struggle in Ireland*. It is included here to raise questions about the prevailing and mostly charitable view of Britain's role in Northern Ireland. [For the interested reader the best book-length treatment is Eamonn McCann's *War and an Irish Town* (Penguin Books, 1972).] Finally, general failure to develop an effective program against advanced international capitalism and Britain's role within it. He calls for a transnational strategy in Western Europe that takes into account phenomena such as the Common Market.

[1]David Roth and Frank Wilson, *The Comparative Study of Politics* (Boston: Houghton Mifflin, 1976), pp. 73-4.
[2]Ken Coates and Tony Topham, *The New Unionism* (Middlesex: Penguin, 1974), pp. 231-234.

**The continuing personal poverty in our society
is not incidental; it is a matter of
conscious social policy, and of the structure of
the society itself.**

May-day Manifesto 1968
Raymond Williams

Consider first where a political analysis starts. You can start from an election, and what is necessary to win it. But if you do, you have taken as central a particular fact, which then affects or determines all the subsequent analysis. What you are most interested in, and what you want to happen, decides the things you discuss and the way you discuss them. Or you can start, alternatively, from the general condition of a country: its overall record, its total results. You can discuss the condition of Britain as if it were some single thing, to be amended by this percentage or improved by that average. But then the general figure can hide as much as it shows; it can show a national income, but not how it is distributed; or a total production, but not what things are produced. What looks like a neutral analysis has in fact been prejudiced by a political assumption: that we are all in the same situation, and have an equal stake and interest in it. Or again you can start from the state of an alliance, or the defense requirements of a particular region. You go on, in a realistic manner, to weigh political factors, to count friends and enemies and the leanings of neutrals. The argument flows, but you do not always notice that your choice of a starting point is a choice of what you take to be decisively important. If the state of an alliance is where you start, you do not look first at the war in Vietnam, but at the effect of the war on the relations between Britain and the United States. If defence is assumed, against a specified enemy, the first call on your resources is military expediture, and you discuss what is left over in relation to that. Or again, you can start an analysis from particular personal careers: the prospects of X in his new administration; the developing rivalry between Y and Z; the character factors, in this speech or that television appearance. And what is then supposed to matter, to the majority of men, is how these careers will work out. Policies, then, are an aspect of careers, and are judged accordingly.

We are all familiar with these kinds of analysis. In fact, between them, they dominate orthodox discussion, serious and popular. To be interested in politics is to be interested in these things and in these ways. It is often difficult to see how things might be otherwise, how you could start differently. This is how a particular culture imposes its orthodoxy, in a way before any of the detailed arguments start. You may go on to differ, at this or that point, but if you accept those starting points, you are certain things you can never find time to say, or say reasonably and relevantly. The key to a political analysis is always where it starts. . . .

We are asking what it means to live in Britain now, with the familiar political landmarks changing and disappearing, and with an urgent reality that we must try to understand, as particular people in a particular country. We believe we have lived too long under the domination of other starting points, and that the kind of politics which follows from them is destructive and pointless. We think we have to make the break to seeing the world in our own way, and then by analysis and description to offer this way to others, to see how far they can agree with it, how closely it connects with their lives.

Our starting point, then is where people are living. Not the abstract condition of a party or a government or a country, but the condition of life of the majority of ordinary people. . . .

Social Realities

We have to start with a paradox, in the real situation. There is now serious, widespread and avoidable poverty in Britain, but in another way of looking at the same country, there is high standard of living, especially by comparison with the years before the war. In the technical progress of the society, and supported by the long struggles of the unions and other reforming agencies, the post-war Labour government made real changes in the conditions of ordinary life: peace-time full employment; the extension of the social services; the expansion of public ownership. There was then not only a higher standard of living, increasingly apparent as the post-war shortages and reorganization were worked through by the fifties. There was also a substantial gain in the dignity, happiness and security of millions of working people. Conditions before and after the war became a familiar contrast, and an important one. This in its turn was interpreted as a contrast between poverty and affluence.

Full employment, undoubtedly, was a major real factor. If the society had simply got wealthier, in total, but left two or three million people out of work, the change would have been differently understood. But until 1967, the average unemployment rate in the society rarely rose above 2.5 per cent. It is true that in certain regions, and in certain industries and occupations, 'full employment' had a hollow ring. Yet memories of the mass unemployment of the thirties lived on, handed from father to son. With that depression as their reference point, most people were impressed by this particular aspect of a better society.

Moreover, although the serious periodic balance-of-payments crises typical of the post-war era slowed down and even at times stopped the growth of output, they did not cause those absolute declines in output which were so characteristic a feature of the pre-war trade cycle. Average earnings, except during periods of wage restrictions and wage freeze, rose fairly steadily. There was for many people a real prospect of improved living standards; and with the rapid expansion in the employment of married women, multi-earner families became very common.

So there was more money to spend, and also, with an economic system geared to the rapid production of consumer goods, a partial blurring of distinctions in patterns of consumption between social groups. Home ownership became a realizable goal for some working people; cars, washing machines and similar goods (scarcely 'luxuries' in any case especially for the old person or the large family) became more widely available. But these tangible improvements formed the basis of a myth, which, Labour intellectuals as much as anyone have helped to create and propagate. It is the myth that the basic problems of the distribution of wealth have been solved, that poverty has effectively ceased to exist or seriously matter, and that we are now comfortably set upon the smooth road to progress and greater equality. It is only ten years since the now President of the Board of Trade was writing:

> The essential fact remains that the rich are distinctly less rich and the poor are much less poor. The levelling process is a reality even in terms of consumption standards; and Britain has an appreciably more equal society after six years of Labour rule either than it had before the war or than it would otherwise have had.

Even when the hollowness of this argument became exposed by the progressive accumulation of research, a process of accommodation occured. There was no fundamental reassessment of the analysis. The view that poverty had been brought to an end was still complacently assumed, and is still the official rhetoric of British society. What poverty remained was seen as incidental, a matter of special cases which could be treated in isolation from wider, structural considerations. Inequality was similarly incidental, or alternatively was only of that kind essential for providing necessary incentives to make the economic system operate more effectively.

We reject these views. To move from the rhetoric to the reality is to see that not everyone has in fact shared equally in the benefits of economic growth and full employment: that the gap between the rich and poor has not, in fact, grown noticeably less. Two per cent of the British people still own 55 per cent of all private wealth. Ten per cent own 80 per cent. Differences of income are still very wide. When income from property is added to earnings, the top 1 per cent of the British people receive about as much income as the bottom 30 per cent put together. These are the ground-lines of all the other changes.

Our case then is: that there are still gross and intolerable areas of traditional poverty and inequality. Further, that post-war capitalism, even at its most successful, creates and ratifies new kinds of poverty. That the policies of the current Labour government, far from tackling these problems at their source have intensified them. And that it is possible, by a socialist analysis and programme, to reveal and to change those mechanisms inherent in British capitalist society which create the poverty and inequality which, with a shift of emphasis, have now plainly to be seen.

Poverty Today

The continuing personal poverty in our society is not incidental; it is a matter of social policy, and of the structures of society itself. Poverty not only remains substantial, but the prospect of the comprehensive legislative programme which could abolish it, at one stage promised, recedes with every turn of the economic crisis. Nor is it a question of ignorance. The scale of the problem of poverty is officially admitted, and much of the most important recent evidence comes from the government's own surveys.

The numbers subject to poverty, by any reasonable definitions, are very large indeed. Using the standard of 40 per cent above basic National Assistance rates, in 1964, Peter Townsend estimated that three million members of families whose head was in full-time work, two and a half million persons of pensionable age, three quarters of a million fatherless families, three quarters of a million chronic sick or disabled and over a half a million families of unemployed fathers were in poverty. This amounts to about 14 per cent of the population. By basic National Assistance standards, about a third of those groups were in acute poverty.

It has long been known that old age is accompanied by a descent into poverty for a large proportion of old people. The government's *Circumstances of Retirement Pensioners* report in 1966 estimated that three quarters of a million people lived below National Assistance level. Supplementary Pensions legislation has somewhat improved this position. But if one takes Supplementary Benefit levels as a new minimal definition of subsistence, since 1966, one still finds 1,670,000 old people in poverty; one must add to this figure 20 per cent or more dependants of these pensioners, and an unknown but significant number who would be entitled to Supplementary Benefit but do not receive it. About a third of old people, from official evidence, cannot live without a special supplementation of their income to subsistence level.

Widespread poverty is not confined to retired people, and there has been growing attention in recent years to the problem of poverty among wage earners and families. The Ministry of Social Security estimated that 280,000 families with two or more children lived, before November 1966, at or below National Assistance level. This included 910,000 children. By the newer Supplementary Benefit standards (amounting to 14s per week extra for a family with three children) there were 345,000 families in poverty, including 125,000 in full-time work, and 1,110,000 children. One-child families were excluded from this *Circumstances of Families* report, but if one adds them the Ministry estimates that out of a total of seven million families, approaching half a million, with up to one and a quarter million children, were in poverty.

These families in poverty include a large proportion of the chronic sick, the unemployed, and fatherless families. A third of families whose wage earner was sick or unemployed were receiving National Assistance in 1966, while a quarter were entitled to but not receiving it. Though large families are only a small minority of the total in poverty, nevertheless one in five of them with six or more children were in poverty by the still stringent Supplementary Benefit standards. Most families made fatherless by widowhood or separation had total incomes near to National Assistance level in 1966; half received National Assistance. Of the half million families the Ministry estimated to be in poverty 145,000 were fatherless. The wage-stop is an additional factor, keeping another 30,000 families in poverty by these standards. This regulation restricts the Supplementary Benefit payable to the sick and unemployed, where payment of the full rate would increase a man's income. By this rule, a family whose needs by the Supplementary Benefit scale amount to £15-20 a week can quite easily only get £10-12. The law thus confirms the below-subsistence incomes of men in work.

On top of the wage-stop, there are 140,000 families who could not be raised to Supplementary Benefit levels because they are in work. One recent survey which excluded some low-paid occupations such as agriculture, retail distribution, and catering, estimated that the earnings of nearly 16 per cent of men were below £15 per week. Of course women's earnings are much lower than this. In a number of industries, notably public employment and textiles of those investigated, more than 10 per cent of men earned less than £12 per week. The structure of incomes and employment is as important as the meanness of welfare provisions in the creation and perpetuation of poverty.

It should be stated clearly that these estimates are made by using conventional measures, and are in no case running ahead of what public opinion views as subsistence. A recent survey showed that the great majority of a national random sample of adults described a family with two children as needy if its income was £12 a week. Twelve pounds per week is what such a family would get on the Supplementary Benefit scale. In eleven months in 1967, 372,000 lump-sum payments for 'exceptional needs' were made on top of Supplementary Benefit payments, which indicates the extent to which the government is forced to reorganize the inadequacy of its own subsistence standards.

Moreover, although it is true that poverty has been pushed away from the daily experience of a majority of working people, it is also true that it has been removed to only a short distance — the distance of a few weekly pay packets. What distinguishes the poor from the rest of the working-class population is only, after all, a particular misfortune — illness or unemployment — or a customary phase of life — parenthood of young children, retirement. The population experiencing poverty is not static: most people grow old; many people in the next few years will be ill, will lose their jobs, or be widowed. Poverty is thus a condition to be anticipated by a much larger proportion of people than those who are poor at any one time, at some stage of their lives. Poverty is thus not merely a problem of special groups, or of other people, but an atmosphere in which large numbers of people live their lives, and which threatens at any time to assume a more concrete presence.

There are signs of a structural *increase* in the proportion of the population subject to poverty, in spite of the persistent myth that poverty is disappearing. There has been a disproportionate increase in the numbers of very old and very young people in the population. The Registrar-General's estimates suggest that in the next decade the number of children under 15 and persons of pensionable age will increase by 15 or 16 per cent, but the population aged 15 to 59 will increase by only 2 per cent. The value of important social benefits has fallen; Family Allowances are worth less in relation to real earnings than when they were first introduced in 1946. Welfare payments are still based on calculations of minimal subsistence, reluctantly raised to keep up, barely, with rising income levels, while tax reliefs and private insurance are in generous relation to earning for the better-off. High levels of 'permanent' unemployment, the displacement of skills, and a flagging demand for unskilled workers threaten to increase the proportion of workers thrown into poverty.

The poor are ill-organized, and their weakness is exploited. They are subject to humiliating treatment, for example at the hands of the Supplementary Benefits Commission who have discretionary powers to withhold benefits from sick or unemployed men, or fatherless families, without giving grounds. What are in fact legal rights are surrounded by a taint of charity and suspicion, denying self-respect, and so many rights go unclaimed. Nearly half the children entitled to free school meals pay for them. Very few families with fathers in full-time work are receiving free welfare milk, though 90,000 children are apparently eligible. A small proportion of poor families entitled to rent rebates receive them, and only a small proportion of private tenants who could expect reductions in rents from Rent Tribunals and Rent officers in fact apply to them. The machinery of the welfare system depends for its 'efficiency' on the fact that so many of those in the greatest need do not use it.

In part this is a matter of indifference, ignorance and a lack of political commitment to changing the priorities which perpetuate this situation. But the existence of poverty is more profoundly rooted in our society even than this. The poor, with the crucial conception of a 'minimum level', are preserved as the floor from which the competitive ladder can be raised. They still exist 'to encourage the others', as negative definition of failure against which the more fortunate can measure their success. Modern capitalist society, in generating such tension between desire and opportunity, expectation and fulfillment, creates and confirms this poverty as its own standards are raised.

We believe that a new definition of poverty, and of its connexions to fundamental social and political realities, needs urgently to be established. Because of conventional 'minimal' interpretations of what poverty actually is, the extent of deprivation is seriously underestimated: poverty has not lessened, relative to the common standard of life, for it is the felt absence of a standard of comfort and opportunity which is present in the society, but which is always beyond personal grasp. It can be ended only when the right is recognizable for all to share a rising standard of life, security and relationships in common.

The Facts of Inequality

But problems of poverty, in this primary sense, are only one aspect of the more fundamental problem of inequality. How much inequality in the command over resources are we prepared to tolerate? The myth that poverty has been effectively abolished in Britain is closely connected with the assumption that an 'affluent society' has cancelled serious inequalities.

The 'affluent society' in Britain was made possible by the successful management of post-war recovery. Yet as the affluence matured, it became obvious that still, underneath, there were radical inequalities of wealth and opportunity, and a starvation of the public sector to supply the demands of private consumption. In the 'affluent society', universal public services have not automatically conferred equality of access. More middle-class than working-class children gain university degrees at state expense. Seventy-nine per cent of schools in slum areas are gravely inadequate. National Health lists and school classes are larger in working-class areas. The poorest people seem not to qualify for subsidized council housing, or are obliged to leave it for far worse and usually more costly privately-rented housing.

The 'affluent society' has not, in fact, abolished fundamental inequalities in the structure of British society, and it is to this fact that the problem of poverty must be related. Affluence left the distribution of income and the ownership of property relatively untouched. It is unfashionable to begin a discussion of equality with references to the ownership of property. But this, after all, is the basic characteristic of capitalism, and wealth is still distributed fantastically unequally in British society. There may have been some trend towards a more equal distribution compared with pre-war, but problems of measurement are great. It has been said very aptly that 90 per cent of the population only have wealth when they die. That is when the life insurance policy becomes payable, or the owner-occupied house can be sold. This is wealth of a totally different character from that which can be disposed of by the top ten per cent of the population who own 80 per cent of all private property. Ownership of capital of this kind confers immense power, freeing the individual from the hazards of life which most ordinary people face: how to deal with the unexpected drop in income from sickness or change of work or unemployment. It also gives power to exploit the characteristics and chances of the capitalist system. To him that hath shall verily be given. In a managed capitalism which achieves some growth, and with rising price levels, capital gains become as important a source of increased purchasing power as income itself. And behind this concentration of private wealth lies the concentration of wealth in the hands of the large corporations, the investment trusts and the insurance companies.

As for the distribution of income, it is now clear that any trend towards greater equality was almost certainly temporary. The higher post-war levels of employment were reflected in such trends in income distribution in most capitalist countries. There was nothing particularly remarkable about Britain. The share of income after tax of top income-receivers in this country has remained very stable over the last few years. More significantly, the poorest of the population, the bottom 30 per cent in the income scale, have actually been receiving a declining proportion of total income. This poorest

30 per cent receive only 12 per cent of total income after tax. By comparison, the top 1½ per cent receive, even after tax, 7 per cent of the total.

These inequalities are underlined by other comparisons. In 1913 and 1914 the unskilled worker received approximately 19 per cent of the average earnings of 'higher' professional workers, and in 1960 26 per cent. In 1913 and 1914 he earned 31 per cent of the average income of managers, but in 1960 only 29 per cent. In 1938, the ratio of gross profits to all employment incomes (including directors' salaries) was 1 to 4.5; in 1962 it was 4.8. Perhaps one of the most striking facts of all is that when we turn to examine the effect of government measures via taxation, direct and indirect, and the provisions of benefits in cash and kind, we find, as one authority recently expressed it, that 'there appears to have been little increase in the amount of vertical redistribution [i.e. from rich to poor] between 1937 and 1959.' There is little reason to suppose that the picture has changed since then, except for the worse.

In Britain today, the odds against a manual worker's son achieving professional status, by comparison with the son of an established business or professional man, are very much as they were at the beginning of the century. In the distribution of educational opportunity, the social status of the child's father remains the single most important determinant of success. In the 1950s only ½ per cent of the children of unskilled and semi-skilled manual workers were reaching university, about the same proportion as in the late 1930s and the 1940s. About 14½ per cent of the children of professional, managerial and intermediate occupational groups were doing so, compared with 4 per cent in the 1930s. In recent years, one in every four of the middle-class children entering a grammar school course at the age of 11 have eventually gone on to university, but only one in every fifteen to twenty of the children of unskilled manual workers entering such a course have done so. Upper-middle-class children obtain three times as many selective school places as the children of unskilled manual workers, more than twice as many skilled manual workers' children, and one and a half times as many as lower-middle class children. This, as many studies have shown, is not because of some built-in and absolute relation between class and ability, but because of an effective and damaging relation between class and opportunity.

Underlying these general inequalities, there is a gross and continuing inequality between men and women: in rates of pay, most obviously, but also in legal status and educational opportunity, and in many aspects of the administration of social security. Like other inequalities, this is no more tolerable because it has become familiar and is rationalized as 'the way things are'.

Social Poverty

Poverty and inequality are then inherent in the present structures of British society. This is again clear if we look at those areas which most immediately affect the quality and substance of social life. The whole field of social welfare is one example. The Labour government can point to the increases in National Insurance benefits in 1965 and 1967, but these have already been largely eroded by price increases. National Assistance is now called Supplementary Benefit, but there has been no new look at the whole concept of 'subsistence', no search for a different conception of standards, in terms of what a decent society would give to its members rather than in terms of the minimum which can be safely got away with. There have been some changes in the regulations which allow people to qualify for Supplementary Benefits, but in other areas, as in the case of discretionary additions to basic benefit rates for the purpose of meeting special needs, there may well now be less flexibility.

It was the Labour government which published the report about poverty among families with children; yet the measures it produced to deal with this problem were ludicrously inadequate. Once again, increases in Family Allowance have been virtually wiped out both by the decision to increase the price of school meals and welfare milk and by the general increases in prices, particularly following devaluation. The Prime Minister had the effrontery at Scarborough to dwell upon the increases in social expenditure under the Labour government as an 'achievement'. Overall in four years under the Tories, social expenditures increased by 43 per cent, prices by 11 per cent; under four years of Labour social expenditures increased by 45 per cent, prices by 15 per cent. Much of even this social increase is accounted for by the growth of the number of people qualifying for benefits: more children to educate, more old people to provide pensions for, and so on. It does not represent an improvement in the standard of the services provided.

That this was taken for granted was underlined already even in the National Plan, when it was still hoped that a growth rate of 4 per cent would be achieved. It was also in the National Plan that the criteria for choosing items on which expenditure was to be concentrated were clearly spelled out. The criterion was to be not social need but 'contribution to economic growth'. We have also had clear statements from government spokesmen like Gordon Walker:

> In a democracy, it is very difficult to reduce private affluence. . . . All one
> can reasonably do is to take a larger share of any increase from them. . . .
> Those who advocate that we should simply take more and more money,
> whatever is happening to the economy, aren't on the whole people who have

to win votes and stay in office and try to get things done. Large increases in expenditure on the social services are just not possible unless economic growth is going happily forward.

This is a clear statement of acceptance of the values of capitalism. A clear statement, also, of an unpleasant and right-wing kind of political calculation: stay in office to get what things done? For it is wholly unrealistic as a solution of social problems. We have only to look at the United States, with a per capita income twice as high as in this country, to see that economic growth in no way automatically solves any of these difficulties. We need a clear identification of the mechanisms which in capitalist society generate this inequality which we so bitterly oppose. The problem must be tackled at its roots, and these are fundamentally in the ownership and control of the economic system. But there are certain mechanisms which relate specifically to the social services.

The first is the extent to which poverty as we have described it is the experience of relatively isolated groups. The poor do exist in 'pockets' (just as there are once again emerging pockets of rickets in Glasgow and among immigrant children). It is significant that the one group who command most popular support in their need for money are the old. Many people do have experience of the poverty of old age through their experiences of their parents. Far fewer have experience of the poverty of the long-term sick, the fatherless family, or of the unemployed or the low wage earner. Even among the employed there is not a common shared experience of low wages; particular groups of men with particular types of employer, in particular industries, or with particular backgrounds of ill health are the ones who suffer most. This presents an exceptionally difficult task for the trade unions to tackle, and this is the real importance of proposals for a national minimum wage. It is difficult for the poor in these situations to generate, on their own, any effective political pressure.

Then there is the failure to make any attempt to use the tax system to influence the distribution of wealth and income. Without a radical and far reaching attack on the distribution of private property through a wealth tax, very little progress can be made. But even marginal progress is unlikely while government insists upon viewing taxes and social benefits as virtually separate systems (except when it comes to paying increased National Insurance benefits when it is always thought legitimate to increase one of the most reactionary taxes of all, the National Insurance contribution).

The third mechanism of inequality is the acceptance of a continued and ever growing private sector in direct competition with the public sector in the provision of social services. The 'public' schools are the most obvious example. But such competition exists too in the field of sickness benefits, occupational pensions and, not least, the health service. The private sector, untrammelled by limitations put upon the public spending, can bid far more effectively for resources. It can then not only supply higher standards, giving advantage to those who have the money to pay; it also succeeds in a growing number of cases in giving the public service the flavour of a second-class service.

Social realities and social values interact. It is under the Labour government, and with its connivance, that the attack on the basic principle of the 'free' social services has reached its peak. Once again the battle cry is 'only to those who need it', and the terms 'universality' versus 'selectivity' are bandied about. Alternatively the cry goes up 'to each according to his abili͚ to pay'. Despite some elements of redistribution contained within it, this is tuͤ fundamental principle of the Labour party's own superannuation plan for wage-related pensions. The government has made an attempt to beat the market at its own game (i.e. private occupational pensions). But without control the market proves too strong.

In isolation from a general strategy for moving towards greater equality, the debate about 'universality' and 'selectivity' is meaningless. 'Selectivity' may be a useful way of rationing scarce resources; or it may be a way of stigmatizing second-class citizens. It depends on the context, on what other things are happening. And the other things that are now actually happening, in a whole social and economic policy, are in the interest of a persistent inequality.

Housing, Health and Education

Housing

The failure to make housing a social service and to break the speculative and bureaucratic interests which still stand between people and decent homes continues to outrage conscience.

It is not only the heartbreaking problem of the homeless. It is also the failure to prevent rents rising; to challenge what items can properly be included in a housing account which is all too glibly said to be in deficit; to stop the Tories selling off the social property of council housing. Aṛ ᵢin, the persistent ugliness of our cities brought a notable response from architects and planners, who have shown repeatedly, given the least chance, how a civilized modern environment can be created. But it is not only that they have to live, like the rest of us, in the shadow of a financial policy which, pushing up interest rates, has made the moneylenders the only effective planners. It is also that when the conflict comes, as it seems to come in every city and town, between community needs and established or speculative commercial interests, there is a scandalous absence of any real national lead, any public dramatization of the essential conflict, with all the facts in the open, so that we could fight the issue right through. Commercial and financial priorities have been learned too well, and many people are tired of fighting them. The weak and needy, without resources, have to put up with what they can get, at a still scandalous market price. Labour's attempts to assert a different policy have been slow and feeble; they have come from one part of the split mind of the party, its residual social objectives, and have been unable to prevail against the commercial run of the society which is elsewhere being actively protected and encouraged. No social policy can be carried through in isolation. All that happens, as now in housing, is that it declines to a marginal need.

When Labour came to power, it announced the need for the immediate reimposition of rent control and the acceleration of the building programme to an ultimate target of 500,000 houses a year. Its housing programme since 1964 has in fact suffered continually from the lack of any planned and consistent perspective, revealing at every point timidity, fragmentation and compromise.

One obvious field in which these qualities have dominated is that of subsidies to owner-occupiers and local authority tenants. It is preposterous that a Labour government is urging local authorities to charge its better-off tenants economic rents *before* abolishing the tax-relief subsidy for owner-occupiers, which increases as the owner-occupiers becomes more wealthy and can afford a more expensive home. The mortgage option scheme, in this context, can be nothing more than a sop to a socialist conscience; it is a curious kind of 'socialist' government which prides itself on giving for the first time to the poorer owner-occupiers some of the advantages which still accrue to the richer owner-occupiers. It will still remain the case that the subsidy for owner-occupiers will increase with their income.

The problem of high rents and insecurity of tenure, before the 1965 Rent Act, was overwhelmingly a problem of the 'twilight' areas of the large cities — Sparkbrook, Notting Hill and similar districts. Yet the form of the Rent Act, demanding as it does both knowledge and initiative from the tenant, is least appropriate for the immigrants, migrants, old people and social outcasts who largely compose the population of these districts. In order to 'take rents out of politics', by setting up a structure which involves 'agreements' on 'fair rents' between landlord and tenant, rather than the simple and rigid rent control related to rateable value which existed before 1957, the government has sacrificed many of those most in need of protection. Even when the tenant knows the Act (and there is evidence of widespread ignorance) the structure is weighted against him. There has been evidence of landlords offering revised rents which remain far above what a Rent Officer would consider suitable, and which the tenant gratefully accepts. There have been cases of new tenancies refused to people who show signs of familiarity with the Act. There is no legal aid available for tenants who appear before rent tribunals. Unlike his landlord, the tenant has no body of case-law which can aid him in his interpretation of what constitutes a fair rent.

In the field of subsidies for local authority building, the projected fifty-fifty spread between the public and private housing sectors will lead only to a continued misallocation of funds, unless the government confronts the need for price controls in the private sector. Mortgage option schemes, tax relief on the interest of mortgage repayments, subsidies to the tenants of private landlords will result in higher profit margins for the builder, seller and landlord of homes, and a waste of public funds which could have otherwise been channelled into the public sector.

The need for socialist priorities within housing, meeting the greater before the lesser need, remains imperative. In the present situation in British society, at least half the number of houses assessed as needed will be built where speculative builders find it most profitable. In a society of acutely unequal income distribution, these areas will not coincide with the areas of need. Coloured immigrants, large families, the elderly and problem families are offered only the decaying lodging houses of Sparkbrook, Islington, and Notting Hill. Here the landlords are typically the 'slumlord' successors of Rachman; the children are from the 'social priority' schools of Plowden; the 'Cathys' are the families evicted from their last despairing refuge. And here too flow the prostitutes, the drug-addicts, the small-time criminals: all the elements of our society clustering in the same anonymous gloom of deprivation.

Health

The National Health Service was a major attempt, by the post-war Labour government, to establish a new standard of civilized community care. From the outset, it was subjected to severe and damaging pressures; from the vested interests of private medicine, the narrow government policies mediated by the Ministry of Health, the patterns of influence exerted by a capitalist drugs industry. Its present condition is a sufficient commentary on what has since happened, in the recovery of capitalism, to that kind of socialist objective. Dilapidated hospitals; bad pay and conditions for staff; authoritarian institutions and attitudes; a class-biased selection of medical workers; a drastic shortage of specialist workers in the overlapping fields of medicine, psychiatric care and social work; the draining of the public sector for private medical provision: all these are evidence of the disintegration. What is now happening is a fight to keep even this service going, against powerful pressures to revert to a more primitive correlation of care and money.

It is only by asserting and developing the original principle that these pressures can be resisted. The present health service reveals a confict between two opposed attitudes: the private-enterprise conception of the individual doctor practising in his own home (to which the whole theory of private medical care is linked), and an emerging conception of community care and cooperative partnership centring on an inter-relation of medical and social needs, in which social and welfare services, public and preventive medicine, psychiatric and geriatric care could be coordinated into a common effort. To return the health service to its true status, at the centre of any humane society, is to demand the resources which would make possible not only the reconstruction of the most threadbare parts of the service, but also the radical remaking of existing structures in a new emphasis on community care.

Education

In education, poverty and inequality can be seen in two main ways: in the severely inadequate resources available for this fundamental social need; and in the gearing of the educational system to a narrow and restrictive conception of human intelligence which confirms and perpetuates the class structure of British society. The separation of an elitist education for the 'leaders' from a rigidly vocational training for the 'lower ranks'; the offering of false alternatives between education as liberal self-development for those not immediately vulnerable to the pressures of the economic system, and as the transmission of values and skills for a subordinate place within that system: these remain characteristic.

In 1963, 75 per cent of primary school children and 53 per cent of secondary school children were in classes whose average size exceeded thirty. In that year only 45 per cent of children aged 15 were at school, the enrollment ratio for 17-year-olds was 13 per cent (as against 74 per cent in the U.S.A.), and in full-time higher education the ratio was only 8 per cent (as against 30 per cent in the U.S.A.). Over half our primary schools were built before 1900; the Newsom Report noted that 40 per cent of all secondary modern schools were seriously inadequate, and that figure rose to 79 per cent in slum districts. In other branches of education, there is a continuing shortage of places. Qualified candidates are still turned away from training colleges and universities.

Inequalities between different levels of the state system, and between geographical regions, are also serious. The average grammar school child has 70 per cent more money expended on him than the child from the average secondary modern school. Some local authorities are spending £100 per child, while eight are spending less than £72. A comparison of local educational authorities reveals wide disparity in the conditions of slum schools, the pupil-teacher ratio, the provision of equipment. To compare the state system as a whole with the privileged private sector is to see even grosser inequality. What advances have been made, to unlock a damaging and impoverished educational structure, have been marginal and ineffective: only 8.7 per cent of our children are at present in comprehensive schools, and it is not expected, on any realistic estimate, that all the comprehensive schemes so far proposed can be fulfilled until at least 1980. The necessary extension of the school-leaving age is at once under-financed and postponed.

The socialist alternative, of education as a preparation for personal life, for democratic practice and for participation in a common and equal culture, involves several practical and urgent measures. We need to abolish a private educational provision which perpetuates social division. We need to create a genuinely comprehensive system of nursery, primary and secondary education which will be more than a matter of 'efficiency' or 'streamlining' but will break through the existing, self generating system of a class-structured inequality of expectancy and achievement. We need to shift emphasis, within what is actually taught, from the transmission of isolated academic disciplines, with marginal creative activities, to the centrality of creative self-expression and an organic inter-relation between subjects, between theory and practice. The existing curriculum, particularly at the secondary stage, is an expression in intellectual terms of our underlying structure of classes: specialized and unconnected disciplines for what are called academic — in fact professional — people; the fallout from these disciplines, in partial and grudging ways, for the remaining three out of four. There can be no comprehensive education until there is a genuinely basic common curriculum, which relates all learning to the centres of human need, rather than to prospective social and economic grades. The present comprehensive programme has to be defended against openly reactionary attempts to maintain a discredited selective system. But equally it will in its turn be absorbed, into a persistent class structure, if in substance and manner the actual education remains divisive. An immediate lead could be given, in the necessary expansion of higher education, by the creation of genuinely comprehensive universities. Instead of the present class structure of institutions, it would be possible to link colleges of technology, art, education, domestic science and adult education with each other and with the existing university departments: making them regional centres of learning of an open kind.

The Realities of Work

Education is now, increasingly, the deciding factor in kind and status of work. We move from one unequal world to another. Thus fringe benefits, which have mushroomed in the period of 'affluence', give the 'golden' handshake to top mangers and the 'copper' handshake to the man on the shop floor. Shift working has increased, so manual workers find themselves increasingly cut off from normal social life and enduring the increased health hazards imposed. Accident rates among manual workers are increasing. Certain skilled manual workers may achieve whitecollar living standards, but differences of work experience and social value keep the class divisions more or less intact. The man on the shop floor is still likely to remain there for all his working life; the middle-class man has a career before him, prospects of promotion, and a rising income. At the lower end of the whitecollar scale, promotion opportunities appear more restricted than in the past, and economic levels are relatively depressed. The gap between skilled and unskilled manual workers widened during this period of 'affluence', but with the routinization of office and administrative work, linked to the advance in skilled manual workers' income level, a parallel gap seems to have opened between controllers and supervisors on the one hand and routine black-coated operatives on the other.

Meanwhile, in certain advanced industries, other changes in working relations are coming clearly into view. New complex technologies and large-scale integrated patterns of production require higher levels of skill, which penetrate gradually downwards into the hierarchy of the work force. As industry becomes more intensively capitalist, so the reliability and loyal commitment of labour grows in significance. Advanced capitalism cannot afford to have its vast schemes of investment, its intricately planned and co-ordinated programme of production, thrown unpredictably out of gear by an insubordinate and unassimilated work force. The direct costs of labour matter less, in industries which are highly capitalized; these, in any case can be passed on in terms of managed prices. What matters, crucially, is that the work force should be reliable, sufficiently skilled, and at least compliant with the process of production. Advanced corporate organizations cannot afford relations of overt coercion, and the hostility and rebellion which these engender.

Thus we find the development, in industries which use developed technologies, of corporatism. Relatively high wages, guaranteed employment, occasionally a graded career structure, higher future expectations, fringe benefits, 'labour relations', the co-option of unions as agents of labour discipline: these are the strategies used to create the compliance which is technically and organizationally required. In return for these graded benefits, men are induced to 'belong to the firm.'

These are the emergent patterns of an advanced capitalist organization. While they come to include a larger proportion of workers — while-collar, technical and skilled — they create also, at the bottom of the system, a much poorer proletariat, composed both of those who are left behind by industrial change and of those performing the most menial social functions. These poorest workers tend not to be in unions; they are the long-term unemployed of declining regions and industries; they are a new population of immigrants imported to do jobs which indigenous workers will not do in sufficient numbers.

At the same time, the industrial changes which are now urged on working people in the name of modernization, in mines, railways and docks, are threatening traditional communities, discarding men after many years of work, devaluing old skills and destroying the whole life-experience of people as capitalism has done throughout its history. Those who resist and defend themselves, in the name of a continuing way of life and a whole social experience, are dismissed as irresponsible, the prey of 'agitators'. Men who are in the way of impersonal market forces — and they will include, over the years, a large proportion of working people — are simply disposable, to be shifted and disciplined as capital dictates. But it is not only in conditions of technological obsolescence that men are being dismissed. The economy has also institutionalized a periodic redundancy for what it calls the national good. In the winter of 1967-68, more than half a million people, and many more who have withdrawn from the labour market in the absence of work, were made unemployed by a cold-blooded exercise in capitalist economic planning: what is called, in the miserable jargon, deflation. It is the economy that is being deflated, but it is men and women — the exposed men and women who have to find work to live — who take the actual suffering, and tighten real belts.

It is not only conditions of work, in a general sense. One of the most bitter areas of poverty and inequality, in modern society, is our experience of what work means, giving and taking of human energy. It is characteristic that in modern capitalism, and in a diluted Labourism, the problem of meaning in work is hardly even discussed. What we get instead is the debased talk of human relations in industry: that is to say, the human relations that are possible after the crude economic relations have been laid down. What is now called man-management is an exact expression of this degraded technocracy; it means, quite openly, keeping people happy while they are working for you. Any other working relationship is now not even conceived.

At the centre of capitalism is the power of a minority, through ownership and control, to direct the energies of all other members of the society. It was to end this intolerable situation that socialists proposed public ownership, as in the Labour party's famous Clause Four. But as the struggle to retain Clause Four grew more desperate, the gradual erosion of its socialist content went largely unnoticed. The terms of the argument have been increasingly dictated by the opposition: nationalization has been offered as the answer to inefficiency, or as the remedy for industries hit by current crises of capitalism.

Clearly, a more rational use of limited resources is part of any socialist programme. But public ownership has always meant, too, the substitution of communal co-operation for the divisive forces of competition. It is concern for the actual social relations generated by capitalism, of inequality, mutual exploitation, mutual aggression, which has produced the socialist critique of contemporary socio-economic organization. It is this which should be our central concern in redefining the concept of public ownership.

For in a technically advancing economy, and in the extreme complication and impersonality of large-scale institutions, we are forced to choose between fitting men to systems and fitting systems to men. Against an advanced capitalism, only an advanced socialism offers any chance of the recovery of human controls. Men can gain more control, not less, when the kinds of work that have been, through generations, backbreaking, frustrating, or boring can quite practically be mechanized and automated. But if, as now, these technical developments are used mainly to reduce the cost of labour to the capitalist, there is no good future in them; only unemployment and loss of meaning in activity. If instead, they are used to reduce labour itself, under the democratic controls which will ensure that men are not simply discarded and that the released energy will be used in active ways — a more active care for people in need; the endless work of exploring ourselves and our world — they are the means of a liberation which the labour movement has always imagined and which is becoming possible. Modern capitalism, and a Labour government accepting its view of the world, are in nothing more poverty-stricken, more attached to the meanness and scarcity of a dying world, than in their attempts to rationalize the priorities of machines, and to reject all perspectives which offer the release of free human energy. In a jaded period, they can often communicate their cynicism, or transform into enemies the very men who in their places of work try to preserve a human priority and to assert a human will. We believe that in work, centrally, the quality of our society is decided and will go on being decided.

Poverty and inequality are material conditions, but they are also states of mind, states of being. In a class society, the majority of men are seen only as a work force, a labour market, and welfare is marginal to that, with some minimum provision for those who have dropped out, through age, sickness, disability, family care, or bereavement. We say, on the contrary, that we have first to see the human needs, and then the work necessary to provide for them. To tire a man out, to force disciplines on him, to separate the work from the meaning, which is always decided by priorities from elsewhere, is intolerable, yet it is what we are tolerating. Men are now poorer than they need be, in skills as much as in income, in hope as much as in security, in the desire to create as much as in the power to know. A transforming energy will only flow in our society — confident, co-operative, giving and taking in a necessary process of change — when we have got rid of a system which is fundamentally divisive, exploiting and frustrating in its basic structures, which has been so for a long period, and which in this central respect shows no signs of real change.

Communications

In any complicated society, social realities not only exist; they are formed and interpreted. For any actual people, including the most exposed, direct experience of the society is fragmentary and discontinuous. To get a sense of what is happening, at any given time, we depend on a system of extended communications. The technical means for this now exist in many new and effective forms. But it is then necessary to realize that the overwhelming majority of these means are firmly in capitalist hands.

It is true that most of our communications — for example newspapers and magazines — have always been in capitalist ownership. But in the present century, and with increasing effect in recent years, the relative variety of ownership and opinion which marked the earlier phase has been sharply restricted. Seven out of eight copies of all national morning papers are now controlled by three publishing combines, while seven out of eight copies of all national Sunday papers are controlled by two of these same groups and one other. Behind this concentration of the ownership of newspapers there has been a related development of combined ownership in the provincial press, in magazines and now increasingly in books. Similar combine ownership has developed to an extreme scale in cinemas and to an important extent in theatres. The important exception to ownership by a capitalist combine has been the broadcasting and television. But the introduction of commercial television, which is to an important extent in the hands of the press and entertainment combines, has radically modified this. There are increasing pressures to convert what remains of public communications into the familiar commercial pattern. Within this situation the B.B.C., which traditionally regarded itself as the voice of the old Establishment, is under constant pressure, which it by no means always resists, to function as part of the new Establishment: to be the organ of a new capitalist state and its official culture.

The economic pressures in every area of communications are severe and increasing. During the 1960s six national papers have been shut down, although five of them had circulations of well over a million. With rising costs, and with the ownership of the vital raw material — newsprint — in combine hands, we are likely to see still futher reductions in the range of the national press — perhaps to as few as two or three morning papers — while the survival of the Left press, already weakened by the loss of the *Sunday Citizen,* is bound to be problematical. It is a paradox of the modern means of communication, which are so essential if a complicated society is to know and speak to itself, that they are so expensive that their control passes inevitably, unless there is public intervention, into minority hands, which then use them to impose their own views of the world.

It is significant that the full elaboration of this system has coincided with the development of an electoral democracy. Of course, within a particular consensus, rival opinions, rival styles and rival facts are offered. Competition between established viewpoints gets full play. But it is then not only that minorities and emergent opinions find great difficulty in being heard on anything like equal terms. It is, even more crucially, that the continuous description of social reality is in what are clearly minority hands, with no possibility for effective majorities to articulate their own experience in their own terms. What life now is like, which can be only partly and unevenly verified from first-hand experience, is continually presented to us in a politically structured form, which it is very difficult to confront with any similarly total view. . . .

The higher the academic standard of education, the more likely it is to be segregated.

Women in England
Juliet Mitchell

Sixty-eight percent of the population of England is working-class. Accordingly, the same percentage of women are working-class; the majority of women are the wives and daughters of working-class men, and the majority of them are engaged in working-class work. . . . Although 50 per cent of men unionized, the figure is only 25 per cent for women. This is serious in a country in which until very recently, the working-class struggle (in so far as it has existed) has largely been through union activity. For many women — for instance domestic workers — no union exists. No one has calculated the number of women employed, at unbelievably exploitative rates, in home-based jobs; envelope addressing, typing, leafletting, knitting, 'finishing' from textile factories and so on. They are outside the computed work-force. The T.U.C. constantly urges the recruitment of new union members, but what about the creation of new (or more inclusive) unions to protect the ununionized? . . .

Over one third of the schools in England are single-sex schools. This is a considerably lower proportion than that of a decade ago, but expediency not policy has directed the change. The higher the academic standard of education, the more likely is it to be segregated. . . .

The effects of inter-sexual relations (private or public) of sexual segregation at school are hard to define precisely, but they are clearly of enormous importance. Easier to chart is the sexual discrimination within an educational system purporting to be equal. This discrimination, masked as 'differentiation,' pertains in mixed and segregated schools. It is a combination of attitudes that devalue a girl's achievement, and of a concrete lack of opportunities that determine it. For in following the trajectory of girls' education one thing, above all, emerges with crystal clarity. It is that there is no coincidence between the natural ability and intelligence of girls and the social devaluation they progressively undergo.

The vast majority of children change from junior school to secondary at eleven. The type of school they go to or the 'stream' or section within a school, is determined on ability — tested by examination or assessed by the teacher. The majority of children leave school at fifteen (with or without leaving examinations): those that stay on take first the Ordinary Level General Certificate of Education at sixteen, then the Advanced, at eighteen, and then leave possibly for higher education — University, Colleges of Education, Art, or Technology. At each point of measurement, eleven, sixteen and eighteen, girls perform marginally better than boys; but the direction of their achievement is different and, from the point of view of status and economic prestige, inferior. The range of subjects that girls take at 'Ordinary' level is narrower. More boys than girls stay on beyond the legally required leaving age, so that by eighteen, girls take only half as many 'Advanced' level papers as boys, and boys who are still at school outnumber the girls by two to one. By the time they get to university, women are only a quarter of the student body. Fewer apply for entrance, but also fewer succeed. With the exception of one or two of the newest universities none has a policy of sexual parity. Furthermore, the ratios of men and women will vary greatly according to the type of university. The decline in the percentage of women becomes sharper as the prestige of the university is higher. At the small civic university women are roughly 35 per cent of the students; at the larger civic university 25 per cent. But at Oxford and Cambridge they are only 12½ per cent. Post-graduate work sees the final step in the narrowing process between the sexes — 22 per cent of post-graduates are women, but if we exclude those who are qualifying for teaching with Diplomas of Education, the figure is only 14 per cent. . . .

For most women, whether working in the home or outside it, housework is an arduous job, taking between seventy and one hundred hours a week. The labour-saving gadgets of the feminine mystique are elusive: the usual home washing-machine in Britain does not do the washing for you (only the most expensive models do this), the average refrigerator is still so small as virtually to necessitate daily shopping for a family, the vacuum cleaner is heavy, and a great many households do not have even these gadgets. The prevalent nineteenth-century house is more staircase than rooms, central heating is rare, coal fires still common, canned, frozen and pre-packed food, two to six times as expensive as the root vegetables that need scrubbing or peeling. Twenty-two per cent of households have totally inadequate supplies of hot and cold water; over 18 per cent neither indoor toilet or fixed washbasins; 40 per cent have no refrigerator. And this is a welfare state with a low poverty rating . . . a 'consumer society'. The House of Pride is indeed built on sands of poverty: it is women who stand with their feet in the sand struggling to make the appearance of the home something to be proud of.

That the British working class should have been paralysed politically, and excluded from the Enlightenment and then from Marxism — all this, whether they knew it or not, was part of the good fortune of every bourgeois ruling class from 1848 onwards.

The Fateful Meridian
Tom Nairn

'The history of a party', wrote Antonio Gramsci, 'cannot fail to be the history of a given social class . . . writing the history of a party really means nothing but writing the history of a country from a particular, monographic point of view, throwing one aspect of it into relief.'[1] If this was true of the kind

---

"The Fateful Meridian," by Tom Nairn, *New Left Review*, March-April, 1970, Copyright ©1970 and reprinted by permission of *New Left Review*.

of party Gramsci was thinking of, parties fortified by a combative and internationalist ideology of class struggle, then how much truer must it be of the British Labour Party, which has always turned proudly aside from such ideas and consciously chosen an insular and national 'road to socialism'. 'British Socialism' was in essence the conviction that British realities offered a peculiar and privileged environment for socialist development, an environment not enjoyed by Kipling's 'lesser breeds without the law'. In moving to examine this conviction, perhaps the first question one should ask is in precisely *what* sense the history of British Socialism and the Labour Party can be said to coincide with the history of the British working class. The usual easy assumption (as common on the left as on the right) that Labour is 'the party *of* the working class' hides a morass of problems.

There is no fixed sociological essence, for instance, which such a party can be said to express in the 'of' of this dictum. If it expresses anything, it can only be the underlying historical *situation* of a class, in relationship to the rest of society, including its consciousness (true or false) of that situation. Such situations vary, from one society to another, and from one time to another, as both cause and effect of general social development; the element of consciousness in them fluctuates, perhaps, even more so. The question is then one of finding the factors of constancy in the situation.

So which constant elements of which historical situation are expressed in the 50-year old spirit and structure of the Labour Party? What social reality is actually mirrored in the ideas and sentiments of British Socialism?

In this regard, the most important feature of British Socialism — consonant with the whole British way of life — is that it always reflected a *past situation*. The modern Labour Party was constituted in 1918, and has preserved almost the same form up to the present. But this is not the past in question, this mere half-century of changeless tradition and ritual. The point is, rather, that this new-born party of 1918 itself reflected the spirit and situation of the working class and the intelligentsia as these had existed half-a-century before that: that is, it expressed their situation within the triumphant social machinery of British imperialism during the mid-Victorian decades after 1850.

By 1918, of course, this machinery was not working so well. The old imperial order had been under attack from without, and in crisis internally, for many years; it was already launched on the long, stubborn retreat which has lasted to the present day. The Labour Party was indeed a product of this crisis. The long revolutionary ferment of the years before 1914, decades of socialist agitation, a monumental increase in trade unionism, the visable and profound fissures within the ruling class, the great social shock and transformation of the First World War — all these had contributed to its formation. In it, the British working class sought for a new organization capable of meeting such great challenges in a new way. But from the outset its initiative was stultified. For the new body was cast in old attitudes, old ideas, in the assumptions which both workers and intellectuals had acquired during the previous century. From the beginning the tradition of all the dead generations had a quite decisive weight in Labour's outlook — and indeed, in the very structure and intimate functioning of the new party. Thus, the Labour Party looked backwards at its birth. It was ancient while still in the cradle. It arose, forced from the day of its first consciousness to confront an epoch of imperialist decline, an epoch marked by endless crisis, stagnation, frustration and futility — and it confronted them with a philosophy and an organization rooted in the preceding era of imperial confidence and stability. What past was this, which acquired such a magic new lease of life in 1918?

The Watershed of Defeat

British bourgeois ideology is in essence a containment and rejection of the class-struggle. It has traditionally taken the form of a conservative hegemony which, class-ridden, class-obsessed, class-prejudiced, affirmed social class in every respect in order to deny that it was a *struggle,* and that this struggle was the lever of social change.

In fact of course, a certain pattern of class-struggle in Britain was originally the very condition of the existence and perpetuation of this ideological system. It goes without saying that since the Industrial Revolution, the class-struggle has been fought primarily between the industrial working class and industrial and commercial property-owners. It has been marked by *three great phases of rebellion* on the part of the workers. The first — and most revolutionary — coincided with the long process of industrialzation itself, from the closing decades of the eighteenth century until nearly the middle of the nineteenth. The second phase occured some time after the high-point of British imperialist success, when the empire had begun to alter in character and decline in the face of competition from Germany, France and America: that is, from the close of the 19th century and through the First World War, until the General Strike of 1926. The third is occurring now, and accompanies the degeneration and crisis of the whole system.

Between the first and the second of these periods of active struggle there lay an era of defeat. This time of collapse and frustration from the 1840's until the 1880's, was decisive for the whole later pattern of the class struggle. During it, British conservatism finally crystallized into a durable social order still perfectly recognizable today (thanks to its later parasite, 'British

Socialism'). This mid-Victorian era, which it was once fashionable to despise and is now fashionable to admire, established a powerful consensus in the wake of an unprecedented victory in the class war.

The reason for the extraordinarily formative influence of this period is that in it *the exhausted quiescence of the class struggle coincided with the maximum florescence of British society in the world outside.* While at home the workers had been defeated and anaesthetized, and the bourgeoisie had settled into its heritage, abroad the power of Britain's economic system penetrated into every corner of the globe. Benefiting from its early start in the Industrial Revolution, British capitalism extended into a natural empire — the original, the true form of British 'imperialism' — which was not yet seriously threatened by rivals. In this unique conjuncture, the British economic revolution was carried outwards successfully while a social counter-revolution triumphed at its head and heart. The latter provided a stable basis for the former; the former gave the necessary external conditions for the latter, the prosperity and security that the conservative hegemony demanded.

In studying this hegemony, it will be necessary to look at (i) the *social structure* of Britain in the first half of the nineteenth century; (ii) the *cultural systems* and *political institutions* which assured ruling-class domination of it; (iii) the corresponding ideologies and institutions which the working-class created in its early, tragic resistance to this domination; and finally (iv) the *economic basis* of mid-century imperialism which founded and rendered possible the historical totality of the Victorian meridian.

Class Structure and Relations

What was the distinctive class structure which provided the key to this success and permanence of conservative English capitalism? It was the continued acceptance of rule by aristocracy, by the British landowning élite which (thanks to the 17th-century earthquake) was already well adapted to market-dominated society. It now became the ruling order of an industrial society as well. By the Great Reform Bill of 1832 and the Repeal of the Corn Laws in 1846, the bourgeoisie limited aristocratic rule the better to enjoy it. This paradoxical love-hate rapport between the dominant classes was the heart of the larger social consensus built upon it. It was a minor, tolerable contradiction which served to both mask and falsify the major one — that between these classes and the labouring proletariat. 'In no other country', wrote Marx, 'have the intermediate stations between the millionaire commanding whole industrial armies and the wage-slave living only from hand to mouth, so gradually been swept away from the soil. There exists no longer, as in continental countries, large classes of peasants and artisans. . . . In no other country, therefore, has the war between the two classes that constitute modern society assumed so colossal dimensions and features so distinct and palpable.'[2]

It has often been objected that this is an over-simplified picture: there were still huge numbers of people neither millionaires nor mere wage-slaves in Victorian Britain. However, the political and ideological weight of these numbers, the influence of the petty bourgeoisie as a distinct factor in the British social spectrum, did undoubtedly dwindle almost to vanishing-point. In part, this was due to the decimation of the peasantry. In part it was due to the suppression of British forms of Jacobinism, the extreme bourgeois radicalism which sometimes lent coherence to the stratum elsewhere. In part also, it was due to the peculiar susceptibility of the 'lower middle class' to the kinds of social and ideal mystification so prevalent in the British 19th century. Such political absence, such complete subordination of intermediate strata to ruling-class hegemony, was in fact a necessary condition of the British Constitution's two-part system, and a vital aspect of Victorian stability.

A more significant objection to Marx's view concerns the 'distinct and palpable features' of class struggle. No one could deny that distinctions of class were gross and extremely visible in Victorian Britain; they still are today. They were absurdly palpable, and absurdly felt, objectified in various styles of living, in clothes, in modes of speech, in grotesque forms of mock-feudal deference and snobbery, and so forth. The conservative counter-revolution turned Britain into a society of livid and obsessive class-consciousness. But it did not follow that such consciousness was symptomatic of 'war' or the wish for it. On the contrary; it was and to some extent still is a highly effective defence against class war, a passive reification of consciousness that corresponds to the inner rationale of conservatism.

The English renunciation of bourgeois Reason was also the renunciation of Equality, in that vital positive sense which had inspired all middle-class revolts against *ancien régimes* of privilege. Burke's 'natural subordination' demanded that social inequalities be retained, and reinforced. It demanded that — far from being hypocritically concealed, deprecated or wished away — they be boosted, force-fed, swollen into an immutable and omnipresent conscious reality, that they be the very mode of social existence for most people. Having chosen a pseudo-feudal mould, the British bourgeoisie was forced to then press everything and everyone into it. In this way, it gave rise to that oddity, a capitalist society where everyone 'knew his place' within a fetishized social hierarchy. If the fetish contradicted the rationality of the factory and the market-place, then (again) so much the worse for logic. British capitalism could do without logic. It had an empire.[3]

Although odd — by reference to most continental capitalism or the United

States — this British phenomenon was by no means unique. The development of capitalist society in Japan, for instance, has followed a pattern in certain repects similar. German capitalism up to 1945 offers another parallel, closer both geographically and in historical meaning, since it too reposed upon a certain social and intellectual rejection of the Enlightenment. In both these cases, however, the persistence of aristocratic rule or influence in a bourgeois society was much more closely identified with militarism than in Britain. The British landed élite was essentially a civil one, functioning through parliamentary politics, the church, and State administration, as well as through the army and navy. Its power was greater originally, because more broadly based, but also more diffuse and more adulterated by its social functions.

Although the link between bourgeoisie and aristocracy was the vital initial relationship of the class structure, its central and overall function was naturally the subordination of the working class. It was designed to project a fetishized class-consciousness downwards upon the masses. The model for the process came from the land, where the agrarian revolution which both preceded and accompanied the Industrial Revolution had ousted the peasantry and replaced it by an agricultural proletariat of wage-labourers. These new conditions had not done away with the quasi-feudal bonds of deference and hierarchy there, quite the contrary. For the general design of British conservatism was to extend the influence of such bonds as far as possible: it aimed, as it were, at the formation of an 'urban peasantry', at an urban working class with at least some of the characteristics of a quasi-feudal stratum.

Repression and defeat, notes Edward Thompson, had driven the British proletariat into a kind of social 'apartheid' during the earlier stages of industrialization. Such 'apartheid' was the necessary pre-condition of the conservative class-hierarchy. It was only the systematic fostering of this sense of irremediable and inherited difference, of social exclusion felt (even if not intellectually assented to) as a fact of nature. This was one of the most powerful weapons any conservative regime has ever had in its hands, worth any number of policemen. A conservative totality, and the broad distribution of property and power it represents, is bound to be safe as long as the various subordinate sectors of it have a consciousness of themselves *as* different and separate, as mere 'sectors' in the social space allotted to them. Such a sectional or corporate self-consciousness is the essence of social conservatism. It matters relatively little that it should be accompanied by a sense of grievance or injustice, by demands that wrongs be righted or demands for a 'square deal'. What counts is that the wrongs and rights are apprehended as those *of* the class, as opposed to the moments in history where a class desires to escape altogether from its 'apartheid' and identifies its rights with those of society as a whole. For workers, the reflex of class hiearchy was the aggressive consciousness of themselves as an 'estate', almost a separate 'nation' on its own. The very success of the conservative formula made it necessary to turn one's back on all that did not concern one. Yet in this way, the working class could not help protecting and conserving intact an essential 'social instinct'. The massive congealment of the Victorian social equilibrium compelled it to keep instinct wholly to itself; but in compensation, it could express it inwardly, in a network of distinctively proletarian bodies, sports, ideas and dialects. Hence the great strength of the British working class was later to be in the organizations which echoed and confirmed its corporate, separate existence — the trade unions. But, as the history of its political movements has shown so clearly, wider ambitions would be betrayed with a fatal ease in the context of conservative domination.

The Ideology of the 'Family Settlement'

What were the *ideological forms* of capitalist hegemony in Britain during the early 19th century? The British middle classes saw the French Revolution as an enemy because they had attained economic emancipation, even under their oligarchic government, and did not welcome a possibly more efficient rival to their mercantile empire. However, to fight against the Revolution meant to fight against most of what it stood for; and this was of course a good deal more than the ascendancy of the French bourgeois class. It was also the Enlightenment ideology which that class had made its own, to which it had given a logical and coherent form, and then practical expression in the institutions of the Revolution — the abstract, universalizing faith in reason, in the potency of ideas and of a liberated human nature.

Hence, at this vital stage of its evolution, the British bourgeoisie was forced to reject certain aspects of this great bourgeois philosophy. In the real situation of the times it could do this only by, in a sense, rejecting 'philosophy' as such. The colossal social change of its own Industrial Revolution was safer blinded. It had less to gain, and much more to lose, by a philosophically-based 'Jacobin' alliance with the propertyless against the British aristocracy and monarchy. It chose 'non-philosophy' therefore; but like all great and lasting ruling orders it needed some kind of ideology or informing principle to rule with, a mental world of its own.

The leading formulator of this ideology was Edmund Burke. Burke was the most articulate and influential opponent of the French Revolution, and also the most brilliant architect of the British conservative social fabric destined to endure for nearly two centuries after him. This theorist of bourgeois hegemony saw that it was necessary at all costs to save the traditionalism of the British *ancien régime* from being swept away by the Industrial Revolution and its effects. British capitalism may have 'logically' demanded a radical overhaul of institutions, ideas, and social habits similar to that going on in France — but, as a most penetrating recent commentator on his thought has said, 'so much the worse for logic'. 'Burke' — continues the same writer — 'grasped, however obscurely, that history sometimes transcends logic; that those were times when English society, to enter fully into its heritage, needed capitalism, and that capitalist society could not operate unless traditional morality was maintained and reinforced.'[4] Hence, far from being reformed, the old class distinctions, the old quasi-feudal institutions and observances should be reinforced and — in their essence — rendered permanent and dominant. It was to help, not to obstruct, the accumulation of capital that mystification should be stepped up, that 'the body of the people must not find the principles of natural subordination by art rooted out of their minds'.[5]

Here was the very central 'illogic' of the modern British way, the source of all its anachronisms. Here was the conservative genius of modern Britain, which turned away from Enlightenment logic and theoretical egalitarianism to foster social inequality and cultivate an insular pragmatism. 'Instead of casting away all our old prejudices', declared Burke, 'we cherish them to a very considerable degree and . . . we cherish them because they are prejudices; and the longer they have lasted, and the more generally they have prevailed, the more we cherish them.' Then everything — including capitalism — will stay 'locked fast as in a sort of family settlement; grasped as in a kind of mortmain forever'.[6] This paradox was what constituted the immense superiority of Burkeian conservatism to the merely bourgeois theory and ideology of classical British economics. Adam Smith, the father of the latter, said of Burke that he was 'the only man who thinks on economic subjects exactly as I do, without any previous communication having passed between us'.[7] Burke was indeed a perfect apologist for the new capitalist world of Smith and Ricardo, accepting the law of the market as an indispensable element in his 'family settlement'. But he could also see beyond capitalism, to its real social and world context; and it was the other inconsistent elements in the settlement which marked him out as a far superior ideologist to Smith or the later Utilitarian vulgarizers of classical economics. Through the direction he indicated, an anti-Enlightenment hegemony could be formed and sustained, acquire ideal and institutional form, and become the lasting framework of social evolution.

Before the emergence of a new conservative intelligentsia, there had been a marked tendency for the English bourgeoisie to recruit intellectuals from

Scotland. There, 18th-century society had stood in quite a different relationship to the Enlightenment. Enlightenment ideas, a certain tradition of abstract thought derived from Calvinism, and (above all) the extraordinary internal contrasts of Scottish society itself (where pre-feudal, feudal, and capitalist forms co-existed), had produced the Scottish 'historical school' of social thought. David Hume, the original and greatest exponent of British philosophical empiricism, Adam Smith, the founder of classical economic theory, and James Mill, the foremost vulgarizer of Utilitarianism, were all Scots. The greatest popularizer of romantic conservatism was also Scottish: Sir Walter Scott, who (in the reverent words of a contemporary American conservative) 'made the conservatism of Burke a living and a tender thing' in his novels.[8] It is worth remembering in this connection that Burke himself was also an outsider, an Irishman who never quite fitted in. When Dr Johnson's friend Mrs Thrale paid a visit to Burke and his sisters, she wrote afterwards: 'Irish Roman Catholics are always like the Foreigners somehow: dirty and dressy, with their clothes hanging as if on a peg.' It is interesting that at this period England relied to such an extent upon her poorer neighbours for intellectuals, much as — in Gramsci's analysis — bourgeois Italy relied upon certain social classes of the poorer Italian south.

Later, however, as these neighbours (especially the Scots) were more assimilated to the pattern of English conservatism, the British ruling class had to generate its own intellectual strata. It required an intelligentsia approximating to Coleridge's conception of a 'clerisy': A permanent, nationalized, learned order, a national clerisy or church (is) . . . an essential element of a rightly constituted nation, without which it wants the best security alike for its permanence and its progression; and for which neither tract-societies nor conventicles . . . nor mechanics' institutions nor lecture-bazaars under the absurd name of universities, nor all these collectively, can be a substitute. For they are all marked with the same asterisk of spuriousness, show the same distemper-spot on the front, that they are empirical specifics for morbid *symptoms* that help to feed and continue the disease.'[9]

To this historically-minded apologist of romantic conservatism (influenced by German Idealism) it was plain that the intelligentsia's function was vital. Without it, no 'organic' social order could hang together. The ruling class had renounced 'ideas'; it could not therefore renounce control of men's minds. But the only forms of control offered by the lumpen-bourgeois, crackpot empiricist philosophy of Utilitarianism were, precisely, the tract-society for the diffusion of 'useful knowledge' and the mechanics' institute. Hence, just as it gave birth to a paradoxical system of education whose object was not knowing but *being,* British conservatism generated an

intellectual class whose formative principle was less intellectual than a matter
of social function. But the function in question was the 'higher' one of ruling-
class hegemony, as distinct from the lower one catered for by the lecture-
bazaars and religious conventicles. This was a society which officially
distrusted and even despised the 'intellectual' (as bearer of abstract concepts
out of phase with the social fabric) and yet necessarily relied upon its higher
intelligentsia more than most others — that is, upon its own 'non-intellectual'
intellectual organically related to society, and entirely 'wedded to gradual
reform of accepted institutions and able to move between the worlds of
speculation and government'.[10]

This vital social group — writes N.C. Annan — 'began to form at the
beginning of the 19th century. A particular type of middle-class family then
started to intermarry and produced children who became scholars and
teachers. They joined those who at . . . Oxford and Cambridge were setting
new standards; they led the movement for academic reform within the
universities and sent representatives to the new civic academies; and their
achievements as headmasters at Shrewsbury or Harrow or Rugby (Public
Schools) were watched by the professional classes eager to educate their sons
well at schools where they mixed with those of the lesser aristocracy and
gentry.'[11] Firmly rooted in the educational world, these remarkably
influential and inter-related families 'gradually spread over the length and
breadth of English intellectual life, criticizing the assumption of the ruling
class above them and forming the opinions of the upper middle class to which
they belonged.' Far from rejecting family ties and social responsibilities, this
clerisy gloried in them, and helped to cultivate and diffuse a spirit of public
service and moral and religious dedication towards the fundaments of the
existing social order. They understood very well how essential it was to tackle
the 'disease' of the bourgeois society directly, by the formation and constant
improvement of a non-utilitarian elite, in an enclave designed for the
purpose. Here, mind, feeling and personality were moulded under conditions
different from those prevailing outside, nurtured more organically for the
paternal role awaiting them. In this way, by these custodians of the academic
enclave, was formed the modern British intelligentsia — 'The paradox of an
intelligentsia which appears to conform rather than rebel against the rest of
society . . . Here is an aristocracy, secure, established . . . like the rest of
English society.'[12] Here was an intelligentsia 'integrated', and yet not merely
subservient to the crude interests of one or another ruling group — its
'integration' was the occupation of a decisive, semi-independent function
where it worked actively to develop and change society, as an agent of certain
criticisms and mutations. This is perhaps the sense in which it can be said to
be a 'liberal' intelligentsia. Yet this term is greatly over-used in British self-

reflection. There were quite different kinds of 'liberalism' in the 19th century society, and the purpose of this one was clearly (and still is) the reinforcement of a conservative status quo.

At its best, the sensibility and outlook of this intelligentsia was perhaps represented by the educational reformer and essayist Matthew Arnold (his father was a major Public School reformer), or by the novelist George Eliot, with her — in her own words — 'conservative-reforming intellect' and her conviction that 'we may measure true moral and intellectual culture by the comprehension and veneration given to all forms of thought and feeling which influenced large masses of mankind.'[13] In her novel *Middlemarch* she wrote: 'There is no general doctrine which is not capable of eating out our morality if unchecked by the deep-seated habit of direct fellow-feeling with individual fellow-men.' The undoubted truth in the remark is nevertheless linked to a British distrust of 'doctrine', to the constant conservative preference for 'deep-seated habit' which was only possible in those conditions of British stability.[14] Progress, the intellectual drive towards betterment — 'the grand characteristic that distinguishes man from the brute' — is counterbalanced (sometimes more than balanced) by her deep feeling for 'the loves and sanctities of our life', with their 'deep immovable roots in memory'. Her dominant instinct, writes a commentator, was 'to cling to the old while accepting the new, to retain the core of traditions while mentally criticizing their forms.'[15]

Like any other intellectual class, this main corpus of the British intelligentsia produced a number of highly individual off-shoots who reacted against the dominant ethos. But it was not easy to react far. Intellectuals (by definition) subsist through some kind of dialogue with others, and the dialogue has to go on in a language mainly established by the majority and impregnated with its distinctive values and view of life. In this case the language was an authoritative one. It embodied 'the union of the intellectuals with the Civil Service, the Church, the Houses of Parliament, the Press, and the leadership of the political parties, through the ancient universities primarily, but also through kinship and through the social and convivial life of London upper-class society, (and) constituted a bond from which few could escape and which no country could then or has since matched'.[16]

The most prominent of these more individualistic voices (these 'intellectuals' in the more familiar sense implying abstract disgruntlement) were distinguished by their penetrating and direct critique of the economic realities of capitalism, and by their fierce hostility to its Utilitarian apologists. From the 'romantic revolt' at the beginning of the century through to its close, there was a continuous and coherent stream of such social criticism, standing in marked contrast to the general posture of the conformist intelligentsia. William Morris wrote that most had been 'coerced into silence by the measureless power of Whiggery'. But there had also been 'a few who were in open rebellion against the said Whiggery — a few, say two, Carlyle and Ruskin. The latter, before my day of practical socialism, was my master towards the ideal aforesaid . . . It was through him that I learnt to give form to my discontent . . . Apart from the desire to produce beautiful things, the leading passion of my life has been and is hatred of modern civilization.'[17] Morris, converted to communism at the end of his life, represented a transition from this tradition to the revolutionary movement of the 20th century (though, unfortunately, for other reasons a largely ineffectual one).

The limitations of even this 'open rebellion', however — and of the ways Morris had learned to give form to his discontent — were shown clearly in the *political* weakness accompanying it. This weakness had the same ultimate source as the defects that were to cripple the great working-class movement of the 1830's and 40's, but here it was being refracted through the thought and feeling of intellectuals. They were until Morris quite unable to feel any faith in the creative or revolutionary potential of the masses. Whereas in France there had persisted (and still persists) a kind of populist sympathy among intellectuals, deriving from historical experience of revolution, the long British counter-revolution had inculcated the profoundest fear and distrust of the 'swinish multitude', a fear upon which the whole conservative hegemony was really built up.

Hence, no sense of real democratic possibility accompanied their spiritual rebellion. Carlyle's denunciations of capitalist industrialism led him only to berserk visions of an aristocratic tyranny, or rule by 'strong men': he stood for 'fascist ideas fifty years before their advent', and 'advocated rule by the hero, by the man of action who must not hesitate to use force'.[18] Ruskin followed him, observed J.A. Hobson, in thinking that slavery is 'an *inherent, natural, and eternal inheritance* of a large portion of the human race — to whom the more you give them of their own free will, the more slaves they will make themselves.'[19] 'It is not merely a disbelief in the efficacy of representative institutions, but a deeper distrust of the ability of the people to safeguard or advance their own interests. Even those forms of organised self-help which have won the approval of many of our most conservative minds, the co-operative movement and trade unionism, evoke in him a doubtful and imperfect sympathy. Order, reverence, authority, obedience — these words are always on his lips, these ideas always present in his mind. Radical and revolutionary doctrine and movements, as he interprets them, imply the rejection and overthrow of these principles, and are denounced accordingly.'[20]

Such disbelief and distrust, however, merely assumed pathological form in

Carlyle, Ruskin and others. For the pathology was related to a normal state of the British intelligentsia. Fearful distrust of the masses was precisely what they shared with Bentham, the Steam Intellect Society, James and John Stuart Mill, Matthew Arnold, J.F. Stephen, Sidney and Beatrice Webb, and nearly everyone else. On this level, intellectual groups were indeed tied together by assumptions which reflected quite directly the origins and basis of conservative hegemony in Britain.

The British Constitution

If this was the nature of the ideological complex that governed British society, what was the main *institutional mechanism* of bourgeois class domination in Britain? In one sense, it is obvious that it was lodged inside the British Constitution. But the true nature of this habitation and name seems to have systematically eluded most of its commentators.

The British Constitution was once the unwritten code of political conduct evolved by the landowning class. In Burke's design for a new conservatism, it was stretched to accommodate the interest of the industrial middle class. The 'sanctity' of the parliamentary arena signified the need for society's ruling groups to sublimate their differences and conflicts there, rather than in open social struggles which might spread to the masses and threaten social stability. Clearly, if the new bourgeoisie of the Industrial Revolution was not to be 'logical', if it was to establish a ruling *entente* with the aristocracy instead of setting up its own institutions, then such a system was necessary. Equally clear, its purpose was conservative: it was for the maintenance of a more effective and lasting common front against the masses, Burke's 'swinish multitude'.

British conservatism was an inconsistent relationship between the new economic 'structure' of industrial capitalism and the inherited complex of old 'superstructures', in which the latter both disguised and cushioned the former, or — looked at in different perspective — the former used the latter to maintain social stability and create a consensus. Burke's primary political wisdom insisted that British capitalism should not merely carry the past on its back, or arrive at an unwilling compromise with it: the aim (and the achievement) was an enduring social fusion with certain elements of the past, after which capitalism lodged in a complete conservative universe of its own. The 'British Constitution' was simply the political form of this process.

For the complex British ruling group of the 19th century, such a form was eminently right. Through it, the interests of the bourgeoisie and the landowning class were mediated by two parties, the Tory or Conservative Party and the Whig or Liberal Party. Although the former leaned on the whole towards the landowners and the latter towards the industrial 'middle class', both parties were sociologically similar and numbered aristocrats and bourgeois among their ranks. It was easy, and quite common, for politicians to move from one to the other.

In his classical analysis of the Constitution, Walter Bagehot saw its conservative fusion of disparate elements as a contrast between (bourgeois) reality and (aristocratic) appearance: 'The English people yield a deference to something else than to their (real) rulers. They defer to what we call the *theatrical show* of society . . . The apparent rulers of the English nation are like the most imposing personages of a splendid procession; it is by them that the mob are influenced; it is they whom the spectators cheer. The real rulers are secreted in second-class carriages.'[21] Hence, conservative Britain was like 'a disguised republic' where beneath the traditional and aristocratic facade — 'sovereignty has passed to the . . . business-like board of management —- the Cabinet — to run the nation's affairs'.

However, he conceded that the 'facade' (or 'dignified parts' of the Constitution) was itself of great importance as an instrument of rule over the 'mob'. The monarchy, for instance: 'A *family* on the throne is an interesting idea also. It brings down the pride of sovereignty to the level of petty life . . . The women — one half of the human race at least — care 50 times more for marriage than a ministry . . . A princely marriage is the brilliant edition of a universal fact, and, as such, it rivets mankind . . . A royal family sweetens politics by the seasonable addition of nice and pretty events . . . It introduces irrelevant facts into the business of government, but they are facts which speak to men's bosoms and employ their thoughts'.[22] He also points out how naturally such a symbolic family can be the 'head of the nation's morality'.

But the 'theatrical show' was much more important than even Bagehot indicates. This was only the political part of a much wider apparatus of Burkeian 'natural subordination', and the bourgeoisie did not rule behind it so much as *through* it. Had this not been so, had not the facade of traditionalism been only a part of the larger fortress of conservative rule, then there would have been no reason for the Conservative Party to emerge finally as *the* party of the ruling elite. Yet this is what happened after 1900, in the face of the rising demand for independent working-class representation in parliament. Nor did it ever seem likely that the opposite would happen, in spite of the fact that the Liberal Party had for most of the 19th century been apparently closer to the spirit of the 'men in second-class carriages' and the 'business-like board of management', in spite of the fact that it (not the Tories) had been the natural home for the more purely 'bourgeois' elements of the British middle classes, for the Utilitarian-minded manufacturer and the Nonconformist professional man. Reality and appearance had (and have) quite a different real function from their apparent one, in the totality of

British conservatism.

Within the British Constitution a ruling class had settled its internal questions at the expense of the masses outside. The aim of the settlement was the maintenance of a certain kind of authority over these masses. It is the nature of this authority which marked out British from the other forms of bourgeois society. It was not mere coercive authority, nor yet the intellectually-based authority of bourgeois reason (as in American or French republicanism); it was rather, a paternalist authority resting upon deeply implanted customs of acceptance, upon social habits which had been given the power of taboo (of 'natural' inevitability which was of course really magical, or cultural, in origin). 'Separate the common sort of men from their proper chieftains . . . and they are a disbanded race of deserters and vagabonds,' Burke had said. The essential thing was that the common sort should themselves feel this would be true, that to break the custom would imply not liberation but chaos: this was the essence of 'natural subordination'.

That such a hegemony was successfully installed in the most advanced capitalist social order of the age is a truly remarkable historical phenomenon. It has never received anything like the attention it merits. It was only possible near the meridian of European conquest, within the society which led the offensive and had reaped the greatest rewards from it.

Once installed, however, the 'family settlement' has proved tenacious enough to resist the ensuing retreat. Indeed, its most important domestic triumph was to come. Since its mainspring was domination of the 'mob', it had to adapt to the slow progress of voting democracy, which placed some political power in the mob's hand by instalments throughout the 19th century. In part, this was done by retaining popular political allegiance to the traditional governing parities, and such allegiance has always been of significance. A considerable section of the British working class had always voted for the Conservative Party, rather than for the Liberals or even for 'their own' Labour Party.

But this was not enough. The British Constitution had to evolve a new organ to cope with such massive sociological change. How could this be done? The former 'two-party' system had worked by *not* being simply a mechanical expression of the two powerful political classes, the bourgeoisie and the aristocracy — by transcending their differences *against* the common enemy, in a common underlying conservatism. It was scarcely possible to re-form the two-party system so as to include the working class: the 'two parties' of the proletariat and the ruling class could not effect an identical rapport, because there was no other common enemy underneath to unite against. The working-class party, therefore, could not avoid being and remaining basically that: an irreducible entity.

Hence the vital thing was to prevent this entity from acting on the Constitution from outside. It is worth remembering here that this had nothing to do with 'socialism' in particular. As the Chartists knew only too well, any *radical* assault on the British Thing was intolerable to it, even if it remained within Jacobin or bourgeois-democratic limits: the point was, that it represented mass self-action from below, the popular initiative and creativity which really contradicted the family settlement. In the 20th century, of course, the peril could only be conjured away by more complex techniques than those employed against Chartism; but on the other hand, the era of Victorian 'stability' and imperial success had left such techniques to hand.

The answer was found in a popular political organization which *reproduced* the British Constitution within itself. Clearly it was necessary for the proletariat to hold itself enchained — to be its own paternalist regime, as it were — since it could not merge politically with the middle class in a contradiction-in-unity as the older parties had done. Hence it had to establish the contradiction-in-unity itself. It could only be a *simulacrum* of the whole: the entire British Thing in microcosm, Constitution, chieftains, customs, rites, sentiments, smugness, conservatism, mystified orderliness, religiosity, moral protest, intellectual bankruptcy.

Labour Party 'Socialism' was the extension of British-Constitutional one-partyism to the workers. The principle of Labour's constitutionalism is that the working class must be reasonably, moderately 'socialist' in outlook and aspiration, in the same way as the British bourgeoisie was reasonably, moderately 'democratic' or 'egalitarian' in outlook. In Burke's inimitable language (still ringing utterly true in the British atmosphere, after two centuries) the workers must feel instinctively that 'A spirit of innovation is generally the result of a selfish temper and confined views.' But the entire *real* sense of the bourgeoisie's 'moderation' (i.e. half-heartedness) lay in its need to dominate the lower classes: it sacrificed its own 'nature' for the sake of the stable enjoyment of its privileges which the conservative hegemony afforded. It 'gave up' its radicalism at a certain stage, when it was satisifed with the social universe it had half-inherited and half-created. The logic of the system demands, therefore, that the working class should pursue *its* 'interest' moderately for a certain season, and leave off when *it* is satisfied (when as much 'socialism' as it needs is attained). Satisfied *with what?* Safely dominating *whom?* In possession of *which* social universe?

The answer is: satisfied with a moderate slavery, safely dominating themselves, in possession of the universe of their own exploitation.

Owenism and the Enlightenment

The peculiar character of the mid-Victorian watershed can only be understood once the turbulent pre-history which it closed and concealed is itself remembered. The fact is, of course, that Britain was often haunted — and sometimes paralysed — by fear of revolution until the key period of mid-Victorian imperialist consolidation. Only in that period could the myth put down roots and project its false consciousness both forwards and backwards: a timelessly reasonable Britain where compromise is always king. Though long prepared by circumstances, the final advent of timelessness was quick. 'Sir Robert Peel had his country house fortified against possible attack in 1844', points out one historian, 'but if Palmerston or Derby had done the same in 1855 or 1858 they would have been the butt of every club in London'.[23] Confidence did not become the smugness of the British Ideology until after the defeat of Chartism.

It is now possible to consider the *ideologies* and *institutions* produced by the English working class, which both resisted and yet also objectively reflected the dominion of Burke's Mortmain and Bagehot's Constitution. It has been seen that British conservatism's essential impulse was to reject all the revolutionary aspects of the bourgeois Enlightment, to create an insular mode of domination from its own materials. However, it also absorbed certain other aspects of Enlightenment thought and held them inside the conservative hegemony, as subordinate forms more directly expressive of 'middle class' or bourgeois aspiration. There was, indeed, nowhere else such forms could come from. Hence, in the form of Benthamite Utilitarianism and its successors (notably Fabian 'Socialism'), the British bourgeoisie underwent its own comic, dehydrated version of Enlightment radicalism, a shrivelled and hollow caricature of the original. 'These continental writings that have set the rest of the world in a blaze, have never been widely popular with us,' remarked Bulwer-Lytton; 'Voltaire, Rousseau, Diderot, have been received with suspicion, and dismissed without examination: they were known to be innovators, and that was enough to revolt our sober certainty of waking bliss . . . A political speculator presents nothing interesting to us, unless we behead him.'[24]

It is thus particularly salutary to recall that the British working-class movement honoured the Enlightenment at the same time as the bourgeoisie was degrading it. While Malthus and Bentham were taking permanent possession of the middle-class mind (or rather, those few corners of it left vacant by lordolatry, Christian biogotry, and Constitution-worship) workers were engaged in a struggle to realize precisely those aspects of 18th-century rationalism which — but only when they had been defeated — Britain was to turn its back on.

The original situation of the British working class was necessarily as unique as the Industrial Revolution itself. It was the first modern proletariat. It had therefore very little to turn to, no philosophy or theory or organizational forms adapted to its novel conditions or existence. The older English Revolution of the 17th century was lost to sight; it had bequeathed only the dissenting Protestant sects, arthritic descendants of a once revolutionary puritanism. Marxist socialism lay decades ahead, in the middle and later years of the century. The great political lesson of recent history had been the French Revolution in its radical Jacobin phase; but the whole might of British nationalism and the British State had been devoted to destroying this model and all who would imitate it. Hence the task that faced British workers was very like creation out of nothing.

On the whole — in spite of inevitable weakness, and the inevitable defeat — it is the grandeur of this creation which still impresses. In 1827 Robert Owen told a working-class audience that, during the recent wars against the French, 'You passed a boundary never before reached in the history of man: you passed the regions of poverty arising from necessity and entered those of permanent abundance.'[25] The revolutionary socialist movement of the 1820's and 30s fought to realize Owen's ideas, the co-operative millenium which would take the Industrial Revolution out of entrepreneurial hands and 'establish for the productive classes a complete dominion over the fruits of their own industry ... An entire change in society — a change amounting to a complete subversion of the existing social order of the world.'[26] In its bold universalism and faith in human nature, Owenism was very characteristic of Enlightenment rationalism: it was another version of the great conviction that 'the Age of Reason hath at last revolv'd'.

Working-class politics and trade unionism began together inside the Owenite movement. (Later, they were completely divorced by the conditions of the Victorian consensus and, in spite of the syndicalist campaign of 1910-14, would never find again a comparable unity. Instead, they were to be stuck together and jointly subordinated to British conservatism, within the treacherous 'unity' of the Labour Party — where speeches about proletarian solidarity have always justified servitude, much as discourses on free trade and civilization justified imperialism). A kind of socialism was to be brought about by a 'General Union of the Productive Classes', which would simply expropriate the capitalist class. In a speech of 1833 reprinted in the Owenite paper *Crisis,* Owen said: 'I will now give you ... a short outline of the great changes which are in contemplation, and which shall come suddenly upon society like a thief in the night ... It is intended that national arrangements shall be formed to include all the working classes in the great organization, and that each department shall become acquainted with what is going on in other departments; that all individual competition is to cease; that all manufactures are to be carried on by National Companies . . .'

The dizzying ambition of this revolutionary unionism has led to its being severely judged by later commentators. It is more frequently dismissed under the heading of 'Utopianism', with reference to Engels' celebrated definition: '(a phenomenon) typical of the time when the working class is just separating itself from the propertyless masses as the nucleus of a new class, as yet quite incapable of independent action, and appears as an oppressed, suffering estate of society, to which . . . help could be brought at most from outside, from above.'[27] But in Britain it was hardly a case of Owen, the ex-manufacturer and philanthropist, handing down dreams to helpless masses. Owenite socialism was in fact picked up and carried along — somewhat incongruously — on the back of the first great working-class attempt at autonomous organization. When he returned in 1829 from establishing his 'Utopian' co-operative communities in America, Owen found to his amazement that his ideas had acquired quite new backing and interest among workers: 'The enthusiastic reception of his views in working-class circles and the rapid growth of working-class institutions opened up new possibilities, and suggested that perhaps here was the agency by which the change to the new moral world might be affected. In its attempt to capture the working-class movement Owenism developed along new lines.'[28] It was working-class action which turned Owenism into a significant force, in much the same way as, later, it made the inferior social doctrines of Fabianism into a force. Until then Owen's hopes, like those of the Webbs 'had been centred on "the most experienced and intelligent" men of the age', and he (like them) 'studiously avoided connecting himself with any sect or class or party'.

The Webbs themselves pronounced a characteristic judgement on Owenism, in their *History of Trade Unionism:* 'It is impossible not to regret that the first introduction of the English Trade Unionist to Socialism should have been effected by a foredoomed scheme which violated every economic principle of Collectivism.'[29] Miserably ignorant of the 'law of economic rent', that cornerstone of sensible Socialism, the Trade Unionists of the time wasted their energies dreaming of their own commonwealth, where they would work co-operatively for themselves and dispense for good with owners, parliamentary politics, all-knowing elites, and masterful bureaucracies. Thus, the 'foredoomed scheme' was rightly interred as a form of youthful and irresponsible romanticism. Up to a point this conception coincides with Engels' much more sympathetic and comprehensive judgement of Utopianism. The latter's main contention was that early socialism was premature because the 'new economic conditions' which alone could make it 'a historical necessity' were not there yet.[30] Owen's decisive 'boundary never before reached' had not, in fact, been reached when he believed; Engels thought that in 1892 it had, that at last 'this possibility is now for the first time here, but *it is here*'. The Webbs tended to identify the new conditions of a possible socialism with themselves, rather than with the march of economic history, but agreed in relegating previous forms to the museum.

But the 'museum' in such cases is partly in ourselves. Each generation has to see history afresh in terms of its own needs, and the present one is no exception. Engels and the Webbs lived in the great epoch of capitalist expansion, when the bourgeoisie had inherited the earth and there seemed few limits to power: naturally earlier attempts to stay or alter this colossal force seemed hopeless and premature. The new generation lives at a time when the inheritance, and the power, have dwindled both externally and within, when new conflicts and reverses appear on every side; and (without theoretical demonstration) it knows within itself that the possibility is indeed here. Naturally, therefore, 'Utopian' socialism has come off the museum shelf somewhat. In an age of 'Utopian Communism', it appears more as precursor than as a buried hope. It is a fact that even the more bizarre and fantastic features of Owen and Fourier now arouse interest, and appeal to people as being (at least) much more than grotesque diversions. While as regards the main outlines of their visions, which it was never too difficult to distinguish from the eccentricities, these appear quite remarkably untarnished when compared to the dismal souvenirs of Fabianism and British Socialism. 'King of passion', wrote Andre Breton of Fourier—

> 'An optical error is not enough to besmirch the clarity or reduce the scope of your gaze
> The calendar on your wall has taken on all the colours of the spectrum
> I know how without reserve you would love all that is new
> In the water
> That flows under the bridge.'[31]

For Owenism, the 'optical error' which really mattered was a political one. It derived from the reaction to the French Revolution, and made possible the fatally naive conviction that the existing State and political structure would somehow melt away once the 'thief in the night' had arrived. Who could oppose such a massive and persuasive presentation of thoroughly enlightened Reason? When the opposition did come, from a bourgeoisie more firmly in the saddle after the 1832 Refom Bill, the movement found itself politically unprepared and helpless, and so collapsed completely.

The general situation which led to this catastrophe is clearer by comparison with that of the French working class. In France, the Revolution and its heritage led in effect to a consistent over-politicization of response.

'The more developed and universal is the *political* thought of a people', wrote Marx, 'the more the *proletariat* — at least at the beginning of the movement — wastes its forces on foolish and futile uprisings which are drowned in blood. Because the proletariat thinks politically it sees the source of bad social conditions in *will*, and all the means of improvement in *force* and the *overthrow* of a particular form of State ... The workers of Lyons (in the 1834 insurrection) believed that they were pursuring only political aims, that they were only soldiers of the Republic when in reality they were the soldiers of socialism. In this way their political understanding obscured from them the roots of their social misery, it distorted their insight into their real aims and eclipsed their *social instinct.*'[32]

By contrast, the British proletariat was 'under-politicized'. Its social instinct as expressed in the socialist doctrines of Owenism was much clearer; but it had little idea how to realize this instinct. It was not following a political mirage, as the French workers did again in 1848 and 1870; but it did not possess the truth behind the mirage, either. Its lack of revolutionary experience and modes of thought placed it in the position of having to discover for itself (again in Marx's words) that 'revolution in general ... is a *political act* ... It demands this political act as it needs ... the dissolution of existing social relationships.'

The Parabola of Chartism

The discovery was made all right, after the collapse of Owenism in 1834, as the New Poor Law (that typical product of Benthamism) was put into force, and it became clear that only the bourgeoisie had benefited from the reforms of 1832. But it was made too late. Chartism altered and narrowed the focus of the movement to political aims, to the attainment of working-class power by the political reforms contained in the People's Charter. Only now, with every year that passed the ascendancy of capitalism increased, the repressive authority of its chosen conservative mode of domination was strengthened, and it became steadily more difficult for the proletariat to find the necessary allies in this struggle. The Chartist leader Harney saw the means of improvement in force well enough: 'I still believe it is physical force, or the fear of it, to which in the end we shall be compelled to resort — with me it is a question of time only.' Only in this way could what had become 'a war of class against class' be settled.[33] But by now the divisions within the ruling class had been reconciled sufficiently for its position to be unassailable, and it was still further reinforced by the Repeal of the Corn Laws in 1846 (when, again, working-class energies were mobilized behind a reform campaign with essentially middle-class objectives).

On April 10th, 1848, the year of continent-wide revolution, a huge Chartist demonstration assembled in south London with the intention of marching on parliament and forcing it to accept the Charter. The march was banned, the Thames bridges blocked by police and soldiers to prevent the demonstrators crossing to Westminster; and, after a time, the great meeting dispersed peacefully while a few leaders carried the petition to the Houses of Parliament in a cab. The Prime Minister of the day wrote to Queen Victoria: 'Lord John Russell presents his humble duty to the Queen, and has the honour to state that the Kennington Common meeting has been a complete failure.' Next day, *The Times* enjoyed a day of historic gloating: 'The April 10th, 1848, will long be remembered as a great field day of the British Constitution. The signal of unconstitutional menace, of violence, of insurrection, of revolution, was yesterday given in our streets, and happily despised by a peaceful, prudent, and loyal metropolis. That is the triumph we claim . . . This settles the question. In common fairness it ought to be regarded as a settled question for years to come . . . It is perhaps a fortunate circumstance that so momentous a question as the *free action of the British Legislature* should be settled thus decisively.'[34]

Under British conditions, the working class had not been able to find the revolutionary 'political act' needed, nor to evolve the universal 'political thought' that should have corresponded to its 'social instinct'. That Owenite socialism was a 'Utopian' conception mattered, in one sense, scarcely at all. It was a mass movement which, if it had found a valid political form and organization, would have eliminated its more eccentric aspects speedily enough. It would not have mattered if the working-class movement of the 1830's and 40's had achieved (in the first place) much less than even the demands of the Charter. What mattered was that the new class should achieve something in its own interests, and — above all else — *by its own efforts*. What mattered was that it should *make* history, by inflecting the mainstream of development directly (however slightly), and so acquire the political sense and self-consciousness of its own immense power. It was really against such a 'political act' that the British Constitution and the whole apparatus of conservatism was (and still is) mobilized. This is not to deny for a moment that the working class has had great influence or *effect* upon British history; but the difference between producing effects or changes mediated and controlled through the regnant system, and direct political action from below (even to obtain the same changes!) is all-important. It is absolutely crucial for a total system of paternalist domination like British conservatism to magically *appropriate* all central social and political initiative, in such a way that it can emerge or re-emerge from the top downwards, from the centre outwards, and be transformed *en route* into something safer ('compromise'). Outside the centre, on the other hand (where initiative does not touch the central ganglia) it is positively valuable to encourage self-activity, as both compensation and safety-valve: the multitude of independent associations, clubs and societies for this or that social and ethical purpose which proliferate in British life and give the appearance of a democracy.

If the immense historical energy of British conservatism later appeared as inert possession of the field, as almost a state of nature (practically absent from most political thought except as myth), this is the simple measure of its success: it is the underlying ruse of reason, in another form. For the great power and historical cunning of conservatism was also more than the expression of the task which it had to accomplish: it had, in the British working class of the industrial Revolution, by far the greatest and most formidable of social opponents. It took generations of every sort to subjugate this opponent; and it could not possibly have done it, had the opponent not been the historical first-born of his kind, and had not the possession of the world's largest empire buttressed all these efforts. A power is only overcome by a greater counter-power. The massive and theatrical dimensions of Britain's imperialism (both domestic and foreign) are not more than an adequate reflection of the potential power they were employed to repress.

Nor should it be forgotten that this victory was of world-wide significance. It was not a victory for the British ruling class or for British imperialism alone. That the first, and (for long) the largest working class in Europe was in this way imprisoned in the strongest and the best-equipped conservative regime of modern times, at the heart of a growing network of world exploitation, was a quite decisive success for the whole capitalist order. That the British working class should have been paralysed politically, and excluded from the Enlightenment and then from Marxism — all this, whether they knew it or not, was part of the good fortune of every bourgeois ruling class from 1848 onwards. Had it not happened, the class-struggle would have been different everywhere, not only in Britain (starting probably in 1848 itself). Had it not happened, capitalism's fate might have been radically different, in both the 19th and the 20th centuries. Marx and Engels looked forward to a revolutionary future, in their *Communist Manifesto* of 1848: they did not know to what a critical extent that future had already been betrayed and compromised even before the *Manifesto* appeared, in the heartland of capitalism.

The Material Basis: British Imperialism

'Poor old men', wrote a contemporary observer of some old radicals in 1856, 'The time for the fulfillment of their prophecy has arrived and departed ... Dispersed are the golden visions, the castles in the air, which formed their only heritage.'[35] At the mid-century equinox, conservatism had won the day. Burke's design for a bourgeois society held together by non-bourgeois ties, and Coleridge's vision of an 'organic' social order, were now realized or in course of realization. The most dynamic society in history had accomplished the miraculous feat of subduing its own violent social energies within a stable, traditional social consensus.

This miracle is the truly distinctive feature of modern British history, and quickly became the keynote of British self-awareness. This is the real reason why Britain is 'different', why British moral and political behaviour is (in its own estimation) so much better than the unreason prevalent elsewhere. The characteristic narcissism of later British imperialism from the 1880's onwards was founded upon it — upon the secure contemplation of what (by then) seemed inherent national virtues.

What was the *material basis* of this miraculous and fatal feat of the British ruling class? There can be no doubt that it lay in the favourable conditions created by British imperialism. By the time of the vital mid-Victorian conjuncture, the British empire was the largest, the oldest, and the most continually successful in the western world. Britain's whole economic evolution since the 17th century had been tied to overseas trade, plunder, and colonization. The Industrial Revolution itself was a product of Britain's earlier success as a mercantile empire: its 'motor' industry, the Lancashire cotton business, arose out of the slave trade, West Indian and American plantations, and the export of cotton products to the Orient. The conservative war of ideology against the French Revolution was also the last (and decisive) battle in the older commercial-maritime war with royal France. The downfall of Napoleon in 1815 made British economic domination of the globe certain, and the Industrial Revolution made it overwhelming. By mid-century, this network of exploitation stretched into almost every corner of the world, in the shape of territorial possessions large and small, enclaves, posts and trading-stations, free-trade treaties and 'spheres of influence': the facts and figures of British imperial power are well known.

The social and political interpretation of the facts is more disputed, however. Traditional interpretations of imperialism were influenced by its later development — by the features of 'New Imperialism', or the epoch of general territorial expansion and rivalry which marked the end of the 19th century and the start of the 20th. 'The orthodox view of 19th-century imperial history remains that laid down from the standpoint of the racial and legalistic concept which inspired the Imperial Federation movement', comment two modern authors.[36] But this concept was part of that movement's political and territorial mania, and reflected the wave of conscious imperialism which swept over Britain after the 1880's. Yet this self-conscious politico-military imperialism (jingoism) was to prove a transitory and somewhat unreal phenomenon in British history. It was the Britain's unsuccessful attempt at a response to the new challenges of the general imperialist era, when her already existing empire was under attack from France, Germany, and the other would-be imperial powers. But the empire which she had to defend was not primarily a 'territorial' one at all, and did not depend only on the formal annexation and subjugation of foreign countries and peoples. It was a 'free-trade' empire founded on British economic supremacy. 'The most common political technique of British expansion was the treaty of free trade and friendship made with or imposed upon a weaker state (e.g. Persia, Turkey, Japan, Zanzibar, Siam, Morocco, etc.),' continue the same authors, who go on to summarize the outlook of free-trade imperialism as 'trade with informal control if possible; trade with rule when necessary'. Occupation, war, and political rule had been used as instruments occasionally necessary to protect or extend the great British trading network.

Whereas the orthodox conception of empire saw the high-point of British power in 1921 (when Britain controlled more territory than ever before), a more realistic view locates it in the middle decades of the 19th century: 'The mid-Victorian years were the decisive stage in the history of British expansion overseas, in that the combination of commercial penetration and political influence allowed the United Kingdom to command those economies which could be made to fit best into her own.'[37] This was the real empire which long preceded the frenzy of 'imperialism' around 1900. For Britain, in fact, the late-Victorian years of territorial aggrandisement and combative 'colonialism' represented a *decline*. This decline was masked by the territorial growth, and by the formation of an imperialist ideology (whose influence still inclines one to identify the British Empire with the purple parade of Edwardian times); but it was perfectly sensible by 1900, and formed a main subject of political and social debate — already in 1900, as in 1970, the great problem was what had gone *wrong* with Britain, and what should be done to stop the rot, to make Britain 'competitive' and 'efficient' again.

The main territorial bulk of empire in mid-Victorian times consisted of the largely empty regions of the world which had been peopled by British emigrants: Canada, Australia, New Zealand. But these were not imperial 'possessions' in the sense which later became fashionable: the disastrous attempt to retain such control over the American colonies in the 18th century had convinced later British governments of the futility of direct political domination. The economic empire which was at its strongest in the Victorian 'golden age' demanded astonishingly little military force. Naturally, innumerable small wars punctuated the history of Britain's growth overseas; but they were never beyond the very limited capabilities of the country's antiquated and comically inefficient army. No serious attempt was made to reform the army until the 1890's, when the ageing Duke of Cambridge (a cousin of Queen Victoria's) was finally persuaded to resign as Commander-in-Chief, after 40 years' stout resistance to all forms of change. British imperialism depended upon the navy rather than the army. But naval power has much less effect upon a society than the maintenance of any army: it is absent most of the time, dispersed (in Britain's case) widely round the world, and much more of a separate social order divorced from the concerns of civil society. A permanent military caste and a large conscription-based army permanently installed within civil society is another thing altogether, as France, Germany, and Japan know to their cost (and as America is currently discovering). Imperialism is in fact normally militaristic, and society has usually to adapt itself to this in its ideas, its priorities, its very structure.

British imperialism, though the most successful economically, almost entirely escaped this fate. *It is this unique circumstance which explains the underlying link between a foreign imperialism and a domestic conservatism between a world-wide predominance and a relatively static and relaxed metropolitan society.* The British middle classes could afford their settled conservatism, their routines of complacency, precisely because empire cost them so little social effort even at its peak. After 1815, society was never mobilized in pursuit or defence of empire: imperial power was taken for granted, while the attention and efforts of the ruling class were concentrated on domestic problems (that is, essentially, on the problem of containing the working class). The lack of militarism was accompanied by an equal lack of 'imperialist' ideology. Sir John Seeley observed that before the 1880's — 'We did not allow Empire to affect our imaginations or in any degree to change our ways of thinking... We constantly betray by our modes of speech that we do not reckon our colonies as really belonging to us.' It was he who coined the celebrated phrase 'absence of mind', to describe British imperialism: 'We seem, as it were, to have conquered and peopled half the world in a fit of absence of mind.'[38]

Such an 'unconscious' imperialism was only possible once. It was granted only to the first great Western economic power which encircled the globe, only to the country whose Industrial Revolution had for a period set it so far in advance of others that no competition was possible. We see, therefore, that the peculiar contours of modern British society are due to more than the coincidence already noticed above — between the quiescence of class-struggle at home and imperial florescence abroad. They are also affected by the *peculiar character* of that florescence — by its relative ease, the relatively tiny political and military effort it involved, by the 'naturalness' with which huge economic gains were won and sustained. This provided the necessary environment for mid-Victorian 'equilibrium' — that is, for the refined, immensely self-confident conservative regime which seemed for a time to have solved all its basic problems. If the whole of British life remains haunted by such success today, this is not surprising. It would perhaps have been surprising if Britain had *not* over-adapted to such a unique and fortunate conjuncture.

The regime consolidated its success by attempting to integrate the subjugated working class more totally inside the conservative hegemony. Most accounts of this process focus upon its economic aspect. That is, upon the way in which a vital part of the proletariat was somehow 'bought off' by the system in the shape of the higher wages and better conditions which imperialism made possible. Thus, Engels wrote in 1881 of the British trade unions — 'which allow themselves to be led by men sold to, or at least paid by the middle class'.[39] Or again, in a letter to Kautsky of the following year: 'There is no workers' party here . . . the workers gaily share the feast of England's monopoly of the world market and the colonies.'[40] Lenin followed this line of explanation in his general study of imperialism, saying that the effects of imperialism in Britain were — '1) a part of the British proletariat becomes increasingly bourgeois; 2) a part of it allows itself to be led by men bought or at least paid by the bourgeoisie'.[41] This 'part of the proletariat' was the higher stratum of skilled workers who first organized themselves into trade unions, the 'labour aristocracy' which shared to some degree in the imperial 'feast' and in this way separated itself from the mass of workers. Thus, these workers were drawn towards integration with bourgeois society, into an 'assured position in society immediately below the employers, a position which merged with that of the shop-keepers, small masters, foremen, and the like', instead of becoming leaders of the masses underneath them.[42]

There is no question of the significance of this economic factor: it was certainly a necessary condition of 'integration'. But it must also be pointed out that it could only work in the way it did because of a number of wider social factors. After all, higher wages and improved material conditions in themselves do not necessarily imply a trend towards conservatism or satisfaction with the status quo. If such improvement brings those benefiting from it into conflict with traditional social barriers, for example (as has commonly happened in pre-revolutionary situations), then it produces frustration rather than acceptance. To be an instrument of social conservatism, material betterment must not engender conscious expectations society is then incapable of fulfilling.

In Britain, these economic changes took place under the most favourable circumstances for the status quo. The labour aristocracy flourished in the aftermath of class defeat, when the working class could only look back at a series of debacles and it seemed that all other alternatives were futile. For, even more important than this negative outlook, the society which had won the class war now possessed the most formidable battery of cultural weapons with which to follow up its victory. It was singularly well equipped to *form* the 'expectations' of the new stratum in a way convenient to itself. The labour aristocracy was a natural victim. Its whole tendency was to distinguish itself sharply from the 'unskilled' mass, but not so sharply from the lower middle-class strata above it. 'The boundaries of the labour aristocracy were fluid on one side of its territory (i.e. the middle-class side), but they were precise on another. An "artisan" or "craftsman" was not under any circumstances to be confused with a "labourer"!'[43] Across such fluid boundaries, the apparatus of British conservatism could of course work freely: the ideology of bourgeois 'self-help', the dogmas of free-trade liberalism enshrined in the Liberal Party, the various brands of respectability offered by the dissenting Christian sects, the temperance movement, the prevailing respect for hierarchy and 'knowing one's place' (especially if it was not quite the lowest), and so on. It was even possible to accede to the ultimate accolade, the condition of being a 'gentleman'. In an address on *The Future of the Working Classes,* the doyen of orthodox economic theory Alfred Marshall declared that 'Artisans . . . who are paid chiefly for their skill and the work of their brains, are as conscious of the superiority of their lot over that of their poorer brethren as is the highest nobleman in the land. And they are right: for their lot does just offer them the opportunity of being gentlemen in spirit and in truth; and to the great honour of the age be it said, many of them are steadily becoming gentlemen. . . .'[44]

The point is, surely, that the ambient conditions of British conservatism were such that it never *had* to rely simply upon the crude (and highly uncertain) technique of 'buying' or 'bribing' part of the working class. These economic metaphors conjure up an image of an elite of Judases betraying their class for a few pieces of silver; and as such, they represent a gross underestimation of the positive power of British conservatism. When Disraeli argued that the franchise could be extended to the working class because a considerable part of it would now vote conservative, he did not think this vote had been 'bought': the 'angels in marble', the new supporters of order waiting to be released, had been *won over* to conservatism. What was more, the victory was permanent: parliamentary politics since then are inexplicable except on the assumption of a consistent working-class conservative vote. Yet the capacity of the British capitalist order to 'buy off' its workers has (to say the least of it) fluctuated notably in the course of the last century.

Look at the problem from another point of view: there are indeed historical examples of class strategy involving 'buying off' the proletariat, in a much less metaphorical sense. The Giolitti regime in Italy before the First World War, for instance, which undoubtedly pursued a policy of 'appeasing' the northern 'labour aristocracy' and the trade unions, in order to avoid trouble and ensure the social stability which the growth of large-scale Italian industry demanded. For a time this policy had some success. Yet how limited and transitory such success proved, in Italian conditions! It appears historically as a short-lived tactic, scarcely comparable to the profound, organic, durable changes which the conservative regime in Britain managed to effect. So one is forced back again to the very different ambient social conditions in the two cases. Nor is it a matter of such conditions and their influence being 'vague' or indefinable. On the contrary, the striking feature of the Victorian conservative environment was (as we have seen) its concreteness, its positive plenitude, its total self-confidence. Naturally, such things are not measurable in figures: but this means only that they are historical reality, which the measurable elements should help us understand.

Thus, class defeat and imperialist triumph had led to the successful absorption of part of the working class into conservatism. This, in turn, delayed the political development of the workers for decades more: it ensured an effective hiatus in mass political consciousness for nearly 30 years, between the collapse of Chartism and the revival of socialist agitation in the 1880's.

British socialism was thus late, of course, in relationship to other countries. Her major socialist movement, the Labour Party did not exist effectively until after 1900, remained a minor party with very limited ambitions and power until 1914, and received its present form and constitution only in 1918 — that is, some decades after the social-democratic parties of the continent. It was late too, in the sense that in Britain it followed the rise of trade-unionism rather than preceding or accompanying it — hence, it was inevitably deeply affected (and indeed lastingly conditioned) by their economism and conservatism of outlook. British 'democratic socialism' was forced to grow in the shadow of the trade unions, dependent on their finances, overawed by their prestige, its room for political manoeuvre and theoretical development constricted at every turn by their caution and traditionalism.

But there is a third, even more important, sense in which the advent of British socialism was 'late'. It was tragically late *in relationship to the whole evolution of British society,* in relationship to the whole underlying imperial-conservative nexus. For by 1900, the long secular decline of this system was already under way; already, the gravest contradictions and difficulities were emerging remorselessly and threatening the basis of the great Victorian consensus. By 1914, the rot had deepened to the point of rupture and open conflict, from which Britain was saved only by the outbreak of war. By 1918, although war had to some extent restored the system's fortune, the stage was set for a further decline — for a prolonged process of involution and social paralysis, for an epoch of petrifaction which was destined to continue through various phases for half a century. This long and grim rearguard action was to constitute the universe of the Labour Party. It inherited a darkening world. The society into which it was born had reached a splendid zenith before it was even conceived, and could only slide downwards, in fits and starts, towards the present twilight era, gradually exhausting the great economic and cultural resources which it previously accumulated. The official ideology of 'British Socialism' has always been convinced that Britain provided ideal conditions for gradual, democratic progress towards socialism — thinking primarily of parliamentarism and the avoidance of conflict which marks British public life. In fact, the British social-democratic movement has never from the day of its birth known a society in expansion, a capitalism in vigorous growth looking confidently forward to unclouded skies — and, incidentally, generating the surpluses which a truly successful social-democracy demands. Instead, it has confronted an era of grudging retreat, of penny-pinching and postponement, of nostalgia and half-heartedness, of slow disintegration and sad frustration, where today is invariably sacrificed so that tomorrow can be a little more like yesterday. The Labour Party set out to build a new world in the crumbling mansion of British conservative-imperial hegemony. It has ended up as chief caretaker of the ruins.

There is no Parliamentary road to socialism
where that road is seen as an alternative
to the mass mobilization of the working class
to break the dominance of the industrial and
financial bourgeoisie.

The Failure
of the Socialist Promise
David Coates

There is no doubt that the major blockage on the ability of the Labour
Party to reform capitalism into socialism by the Parliamentary process, or
even to sustain major programmes of social reform, comes from the
institutions and representatives of corporate capital — both financial and
industrial. The immediate needs which these institutions have of the State set
the terms of reference within which the Labour Party in power has to act,
since they determine the conditions on which Labour policies of economic
growth can be achieved and co-operation with business ensured. These terms
of reference have been variously described. Corporate business certainly
requires of the State 'a "reasonable" attitude to key industrial and financial
interests; a willingness . . . to preach to the trade unions the virtues of
moderation in wage demands; a "sensible" attitude to tax reform; and a
sympathetic appreciation of the general requirements of an economy geared
to the profit motive'.[1] Financial institutions, and the Bank of England in
particular, have shown a persistent preference for fixed exchange rates, and
for the free movement of international currencies, and have argued strongly
for both Conservative and Labour Governments alike. And these general
requirements may well extend (at least as far as the multi-national
corporations are concerned), as Michael Barratt Brown has argued, to a list
of needs that seriously undermine the sovereignty and freedom of manoeuvre
of all Governments, including those of Labour. As he put it,

A favourable environment for the development of the multi-national
company will include at least the following elements:

1. legal protection for subsidiaries and joint companies operating inside

each national state, as favourable as that granted to indigenous companies;

2. taxation rates and concessions for subsidiaries and joint ventures as favourable as those granted to indigenous companies;

3. equal rights with indigenous companies to raise funds in national capital markets;

4. national prices and incomes policies that make possible long term advanced cost control in each subsidiary;

5. national education and training arrangements that provide reserves of skilled and qualified labour at all levels;

6. national industrial relations systems that ensure a dependable labour force at all times;

7. national policies designed to ensure steady growth of consumption and investment expenditure;

8. at the same time, freedom to move goods and capital funds between one country and another with minimal tariff, quota and exchange restrictions.[2]

But let us be clear on what is being argued, and what is not. By arguing that the Labour Party in power has to operate within the terms of reference set by the general requirements of an economy geared to the profit motive, this is not to deny that the Labour Government has its own power-resources, which it can use, and which give it leverage against individual firms and industries. On the contrary: many firms and industries, especially those selling large parts of their product to Government agencies, and those in need of investment grants and capital loans, will experience the Labour Government as a senior partner, able to shape their own patterns of profitability and growth directly. Moreover it is clear that the general set of relationships between a Labour Government and industry are affected, if only at the margin, by the degree of unity within the Labour Party, by the size of its Parliamentary majority, by the length of time it has been in office, and by its chances of defeat at the next general election. And all Governments, including Labour ones, possess a wide range of controls that directly affect firms, industries and even multi-national concerns.

But the danger of stopping the analysis at this point, which is precisely where most Labour M.P.s stop when talking of what 'they' will do to business and finance when in power, is in sliding from the recognition that all Governments have some power to the assumption that that power is unlimited. It is also to forget that the Labour Party, in its more radical periods at least, is promising not simply to *manage* the economic and social system, but to *change* it. As a result, if its own experience between 1945 and 1951 is any guide, a Labour Government is likely to meet opposition 'at every point at which power interests, rather than property interests'[3] are threatened. As Rogow put it, in a classic understatement of the power reality faced by every reformist Labour Government, in such a situation, 'the continued co-operation of vested power groups in measures of social change designed to reduce their power and influence can no longer be taken for granted'.[4]

Moreover, even if that opposition were miraculously to be absent, any Labour Government would still inevitably experience a tension between its reforming aspirations and its related search for co-operation with senior managerial personnel in a common drive for sustained economic output. For there are *real* limits to what a Labour Government can do, and to the type of policies it can actually pursue, limits that are rooted in the general requirements of capitalist private enterprise as a system, and these limits eat away at precisely those aspects of Labour policy that the Party periodically has offered to the electorate as a way of transforming capitalism gradually into a more socialist system. It cannot equalise incomes and wealth without destroying the basis of private profit and corporate endeavour. It cannot take over vast areas of profitable private industry without alienating future private investments and therefore economic growth. It cannot introduce major changes in the distribution of control *within* industry without inviting major ideological counter-attacks from the organs of private capital, and without driving major sources of future plant, machinery and output away to 'safer' political climates. It cannot even sustain exchange controls for any substantial period without provoking a hostile response from international financial agencies and without running the risk that the big multi-national corporations will be driven to redirect their internal resources towards its competitor economies. And as the Labour Party found in the 1960s, with dwindling international competitiveness of British industry, it cannot avoid taking an interest in cost-effectiveness within industry and in general wage rates and earning levels in the economy as a whole. That is, it cannot avoid playing a role in the control of the working class at the point of production.

For if the Labour Party is to achieve a sustained rate of economic growth from which to pay for greater social welfare programmes, educational expansion and the like, it has to provide when in office that economic and social environment in which private corporate profits can flourish, and in which the class prerogatives of senior managerial personnel can remain unchallenged. This shuts off the Parliamentary road to the socialist commonwealth; for as Raymond Williams has said

> The very institutions that would be forced to give up their private interests
> to the will of an elected government were the only institutions through

which the economy could be managed; unless, of course, socialist institutions were created to replace them. And it was just this option of the creation of socialist institutions which the Labour leadership had given up in advance. What was intended as a working compromise became first a constraint and finally a capitulation. The elected government could direct and manage everyone and everything else, but not capital.[5]

It is in this sense that the freedom of manoeuvre of the Labour Party in power is constrained by the 'health' of the economy in capitalist terms: by its cost-competitiveness, its overall profit rate, its productivity and its degree of re-investment. And here, as the politics of 'Catch-22' for the Labour Party, the paradox occurs: that the maintenance of such 'health' invariably strengthens the very capitalist class the Labour Government was supposed to control, and brings the Party in power into conflict with its own industrial wing and its own working class electorate, who then appear as a secondary blockage on the Party's freedom of manoeuvre.

For at the heart of the capitalist system lies the tension between the political economy of Capital and that of Labour, a tension which throws into fundamental doubt the Labour Party's traditional commitments to social unity, a national interest, and the gradual change of class society by consensus. That tension takes many forms: of wages against profits, of managerial prerogatives against working class job control, of capitalist exploitation against alienated labour, of the rich against the poor in a society divided by the class allocation of wealth, income, life chances and power. With a Labour Party experiencing and demonstrating the real limits on its freedom of manoeuvre imposed by corporate capital, it is hardly surprising that the working class and its trade unions have come (albeit slowly in its official voice, more rapidly in sections of its rank and file) to act as a secondary limit on the freedom of the Labour Party in power, by being reluctant to surrender easily any of its hard-won industrial control and living standards in a new Labour Government-inspired social contract.

The Labour Governments between the wars were not so constrained by working class trade union activity, since the industrial power of the class was effectively destroyed by the Depression. And even since the war, the labour movement has only been a secondary blockage, after capital, Labour Governments — more visible perhaps to the general newspaper reader, but in practice only making its resistance felt spasmodically, in isolated struggles — and at least until the late 1960s, doing so with a degree of reluctance that reflected the ideological ties between the Party and the class that were inherited from the 1930s. For the working class has less day-to-day leverage in the critical decision-making of capitalist enterprise, and therefore less immediate economic power against the State. It is true that its ultimate weapon — the strike — is as potent an instrument of pressure as any in the camp of capital, but it is one which is difficult to use, difficult to sustain, and open to immense ideological, legal and material counter-pressures from the State, the employers and the media. When that counter-pressure has been resisted the industrial power of the working class has been a major blockage on Labour Governments, but to deduce from its occasional use that the working class and capital balance in political terms 'is to treat as an accomplished fact' a working class industrial power that is in fact only 'an unrealised potentiality, whose realisation is beset with immense difficulties'.[6]

Even so, the industrial wing of the labour movement emerged from the war strengthened by full employment, and in the two decades that followed achieved a degree of industrial strength at the point of production in the critical growth and export sectors (over earnings, over job conditions, and over job security) that gave it something to defend against State encroachments. And the Labour Party, always inheriting in office severe international payments difficulties, found itself repeatedly having to initiate such encroachments. So that when in the late 1940s and throughout the 1964-70 administration the Labour Party in power found itself under heavy pressure from industrial and financial capital to curb the industrial power of its working class electorate, it found that electorate — in its industrial setting — a very reluctant ally in the 1940s, and by the late 1960s an almost totally unco-operative force.

For those very instabilities in Western capitalism (which were most evident in the particular weakness of its British section) that were forcing the Labour Party on such a path of confrontation with its working class electorate were also making themselves felt down in the factories and homes of the labour force. They were felt in the 1960s as increasingly State-induced: at best as inflation, and at worst as the intensification of work routines, short-time working and the threat (and reality) of redundancy. These very dislocations made sections of the rank and file of the trade union movement (and eventually even sections of its leadership) reluctant to surrender to the State any of its procedural controls of its substantive agreements, since these embodied the degree of control achieved by the working class over its living standards and its work routines. Or, if such a surrender was contemplated by the trade union leadership, it was increasingly as part of a package of changes that were anathema to corporate capital (including as they invariably did profit control, food subsidies and increased welfare payments). And so it was that the Labour Party in power repeatedly found that the area of consensus between competing social classes on which it predicated the whole of its politics was being narrowed to the point of extinction by the exigencies of capitalist instability. As Raymond Williams said, 'The middle ground of British politics always depended on the viability of British capital in a competitive world. As soon as this viability came into question, the sharp alternatives of cuts at the expense of one side of industry or the other had to be faced.'[7]

The consequences of this for the internal stability of the labour movement have been enormous. For the very failure of the Labour Party to deliver its more radical promises has eaten away at the relationship between itself and its working class base. That relationship has never been very strong. Organisationally the Party structure has never made any direct connection with the worker at the point of production. Socially, its leaders have increasingly shed (or never had) any working class experience or roots. And ideologically, the long-standing separation of industrial activity from political activity in the Labourist tradition has sustained a central ambiguity in the relationship between the two wings of the labour movement. But even so, by 1945 the connection between the working class and the Party was close indeed. Yet the failure thereafter of the Labour Governments to shift substantial degrees of power and resources away from corporate capital has left its working class electorate still subject to capitalist instability, still dependent on its own industrial efforts to achieve that degree of affluence, job security and job control that the Labour Party could not guarantee, and still subject to marked inequalities of power and wealth. And as such the working class electorate is left increasingly as, at best, a reluctant ally of a Labour Party whose response to repeated pressure from international and national industrial financial capital has been to adopt a 'managerial' attitude to the trade union movement and its activities that bodes ill for the continuing close relationship between the two wings of the labour movement. . . .

We need to note first that the instabilities of Western capitalism set real limits on the freedom of manoeuvre of any Labour Government, be it seeking total social transformation or merely substantial social reforms. Those limits are set both directly, via the Labour Government's relationship with corporate capital, and also indirectly, via the resistance to Government initiatives that those instabilities generate in the rank and file of the trade union movement. And that moreover, in such a situation it is hardly surprising that a Labour Party seeking a close and co-operative relationship with organised capital has tended to see the trade union movement as a blockage on its freedom of action, and has shown a propensity to turn against the militant sections of that movement with a ferocity that might not be expected from a party created 'to represent the labour interest in Parliament'. For this is but one important consequence of the Labour Party's general experience in power that there exist real and potent limits on its capacity to legislate successfully against the imperatives of the existing social order — real limits, that is, on the possibility of peacefully transforming capitalism into a 'new social order', or even of obliging a capitalist system and its ruling strata to accept major programmes of social reform. It is this repeated experience of the limits of the possible for the State in a capitalist system that has been one major factor pulling the Labour Party leadership away from radical programmes, and one major reason for that leadership's unimpressive performance when in office.

Before probing the consequences of this for the Labour Party's own development, we should note how it is reinforced by a secondary and related feature of Labour Party politics, namely by the Party's relationship with its electorate. For the utter dependence of the Labour Party in power on the voluntary co-operation of senior managerial personnel in private industry reflects the absence of any alternative power base within the labour movement itself to which the Party, in any confrontation with Capital, could and would be willing to turn. It reflects the absence, that is, of a radicalised proletariat able and willing to buttress Labour Party policy initiatives by industrial action at the point of production, and of trade union movement prepared to take on that role. There have been moments, certainly, when events external to the Party have produced signs of mass political radicalism in the British working class; and it has been at these points, and only at these points, that the Labour Party has found a radical programme both electorally vital and politically viable. But it is hardly too much to say that the 'reformism' of the Labour Party before 1970 was a temporary consequence of two wars and a prolonged depression, rather than something endemic to its whole mode of politics. For the Labour Party has never set out to create such a radicalised proletariat. On the contrary, such a radicalised proletariat has always been anathema to the Labourist tradition.

Instead the Labour Party has been committed to a theory of party-class relationships which gives the Party an educating role (between the wars, for example, as a socialist propagandist) but which restricts the Party programme at any stage to a point commensurate with existing levels of political consciousness in the Labour electorate at large. Indeed, its whole mode of politics, Parliamentarianism, has made this essential, as we shall see. And in its preoccupation with Parliamentarianism, the Labour Party has not even used Parliament, as many revolutionaries have used equivalent institutions elsewhere, primarily as a stage upon which to make agitational and propagandist statements that could connect with, generalise, and intensify the growing conflict between the classes at the point of production. On the contrary, Labour Party pronouncements on even industrial disputes have been uniformly hostile to mass radicalism, and have sought always to emasculate the class struggle by restricting it to constitutionally sanctioned channels. This is as true of its hostility to the General Strike of 1926 as it is of its reaction to working class industrial opposition to the 1971 Industrial Relations Act: that the working class should not challenge the legal powers of the State by extra-constitutional industrial means, even if those legal powers were visibly class-biased and even if the alternative is to surrender and wait for the next Labour Government. To the extent that the Labour Party has had any impact at all on patterns of consciousness in its working class electorate, it has been to constantly reinforce the illusion of the untrammelled sovereignty of the democratically elected Parliamentary State.

But in fact the Labour Party has had far less impact on the general level and type of consciousness in its working class electorate than have its political opponents. There are a number of reasons for this. In part, it reflects the control which private capitalists have retained over the mass media, and their willingness to use that control to defend their class privileges by sustained propaganda against Labour radicalism. The campaign against the nationalisation of steel, sugar, and chemicals at the end of the Attlee Government is a case in point. Much more importantly, it also reflects the fact that the gap between Labour promises and Labour performance in office always provides such propagandists with an enormous stick with which to beat the Party. This was particularly important in the 1950s, when the very failure of the Attlee Government to transform capitalism into socialism via public ownership, state planning and welfare provision left even Labour voters sceptical of the Party's pre-occupation with the further creation of public corporations. For the Party had promised working class emancipation and a qualitative change in human existence. It had created instead a bureaucratised public sector and a strengthened capitalist class. Here the limits of State power under a 'reformist' Government left, as an *electoral legacy* to the next generation of the Party, a generalised antipathy to nationalised industries and State planning, and a concomitant faith in a private enterprise system which had been strengthened by the Attlee Government's nationalisation policies. It left, that is, a 'conservative renaissance'[8] to which the Party leadership increasingly succumbed, and against which its counter-propaganda was increasingly defeatist and hesitant.

Yet the Labour Party could ill afford such listlessness in its propagandising, for the scales of history were, and remain, against it. It inherited a predominantly conservative electorate, with a popular culture rooted in a liberal-imperialist past. Admittedly, two world wars and the inter-war experience of capitalist instability had moved that electorate towards political radicalism, but still with a culture that contained within it the anti-socialist notions and aspirations of Victorian imperialism. It inherited also a class structure riddled with internal, subsidiary status divisions between occupational groups, and one which since 1945 has witnessed a substantial shift out of manual employment into white collar occupations that were traditionally less closely identified with 'the working class' and the Labour Party. It would have taken — and still requires — a massive ideological effort on the part of the Labour Party to have shifted that legacy. But, in the event, this was an effort which the Labour Party undertook only sporadically and with limited effect. All too often, the Party surrendered to existing levels of prejudice in an undignified search for votes on any terms, so reinforcing tendencies in popular culture that were inimical to radical social change on socialist lines. This has weakened the Party profoundly, as Anderson has observed:

> The real criticism to be made of them . . . that they *cannot* gain power as long as they sacrifice principle for the sake of winning elections. They may well win, but under these conditions 'power' is simply permission to operate the status quo. It has no purchase whatever on the statute of the society. There is no 'mandate' for changing this. Social-democracy is thus trapped in the closed circle of electoralism. It restricts its own freedom to win a partial power which is then further curtailed by its initial restriction. The result is a profound impotence and demoralisation.[9]

The precise manifestations and consequences of this varied over time. Between the wars, when the Labour Party faced an electorate shaped by political forces stronger than itself, it encouraged the Party to tone down the radicalism of its 1918 programme, until the severity of the Depression and the rigours of war presented to it an electorate demanding radical change. In the specific conditions of capitalist prosperity in the 1950s, the repeated evidence of electoral scepticism and hostility towards public ownership that the half-heartedness of the Attlee Government had itself created, was a major force pulling the Party leadership away not simply from its old 'reformist' trilogy of nationalisation, planning and welfare, but from any 'reformist' aspirations at all. And even in the changed conditions of the 1970s, when capitalist instability has undoubtedly created again a more generalised dissatisfaction within the Labour Party's potential electorate, the Party leadership are still under 'electoral' pressures to moderate their promises.

Of course, this attempt to moderate the Party's image partly reflects the leadership's realisation of how little they can actually do in power (though Labour politicians in the past have tended to forget this all too easily as the years of Opposition have lengthened). What the Party leaders cannot forget are the electoral pressures for moderation in their programme. For the Party's Parliamentarianism effectively isolates it from the points of working class struggle, and militates against effective propaganda work by the Party there. And yet this same Parliamentarianism makes the Party totally dependent upon an electorate (whose support it *must* win to be able to do anything in Parliamentary terms at all) — an electorate subject to waves of ideological pressure from the Party's political opponents. Indeed, the Labour Party's passivity and impotence before the electorate is even greater than this, for it is dependent if it is to 'win' State power, not simply on the generalised support of the electorate, but on the support of critical smaller electorates in a series of marginal constituencies. It *must* win these, and by definition these are the very constituencies in which party radicalism runs the greatest risk of voter-alienation and consequent electoral defeat. The massive Labour vote of Ebbw Vale would doubtless tolerate radicalism from the Party. Indeed the Labour Party's problem now is that its traditional vote in places like the Welsh valleys is being eroded by the Party's conservatism in office. But it dare not be more radical, lest its critical marginal vote be lost. Of course, there are those in the Party who argue that it should gamble, and educate its electorate in a radical alternative.[10] But even they have to concede that it *is* a gamble, and they have invariably gone along with a toning down of party programmes at election times that is commensurate with the political sympathies of the marginal seats. Even in power, as between 1964 and 1970, it was this sensitivity to the electoral proclivities of marginal seats and marginal voters which reinforced the tendency of the Party leadership to conservatism and moderation.

This twin experience, of the limits of State power and the logic of electoral politics under capitalism, is the source of the growing conservatism of the Labour Party's chosen agency of social change, the Parliamentary Party and its leadership. Together, they had effectively destroyed that Parliamentary Party by 1970 as agency of anything but its own desperate search for government office. This twin experience had whittled away the radicalism of earlier party programmes, and in the process had transformed the Parliamentary Party into a mechanism for mediating the immediate needs of the capitalist system to the working class, rather than one that could lead the class to transform capitalism, or even one that could effectively impose upon the capitalist system social reforms of sufficient scale to make a qualitative difference to the life experience of its electorate. And it had done this by educating the Parliamentary leadership into a definition of the 'realistic' in politics that was coterminous with the maintenance of the existing distribution of social power, and had in the process generated a set of leaders whose hypersensitivity to the imperatives of that realism left them as only pale reflections of their more radical younger selves. As a result, we are left, as Tom Nairn has observed, with a situation in which

> realism turns, in Labour leaders, into mere cowardice, a kind of timid hypnosis in the face of events; practicality turns into wilful short-sightedness, a ritual pragmatism wielded to exorcise the sort of theoretical thinking socialism requires; [in which] dignified reverence for the past becomes a depraved fetish-worship of idols which seem to change into dust at the very touch of such falsity.[11]

Now when faced with such a set of Parliamentarians, it is conveniently easy to restrict the explanation of Labour Party conservatism and failure in office to an analysis of the personalities that make up the leadership. The 'sell-out' thesis, . . . has a long pedigree in Labour Party polemic and analysis. So the Labour Party is explained and excused because some of its leaders found personal advantages in sucking up to the rich (the theory of the 'aristocratic embrace'). Or it is criticised because its constituency Parties have proved too fond of selecting M.P.s from middle class occupations (the theory of leadership 'embourgeoisification'). Or it is excused because some of its leaders, isolated from the rank and file, found solace in excessive sensitivity to Parliamentary procedures (the theory of 'parliamentary socialisation'). Or the Party is condemned because a good number of its leaders, overworked and overawed, fell victim to the dictates of their civil servants, (the theory of 'poor quality Ministers'). Clearly Labour Party history is rich in examples of all these, and no explanation of Labour Party politics can ignore them. J.H. Thomas was undoubtedly under the domination of his Permanent Secretary, Sir Horace Wilson, whom he knew affectionately as 'Orace'.[12] Herbert Morrison was clearly passionately committed to Parliamentary procedures and norms. Ramsay MacDonald clearly accentuated the trend to conservatism by his personal foibles and growing empathy with aristocratic ladies. But the trend existed in any case, and it is no accident that the Parliamentary leaders of the Labour Party have succumbed to these tendencies. For the logic of their conservatism is rooted in the general character of Labour Party politics.

For what characterises that politics is that it generates sets of leaders who, in office, experience particular problems, and particular possibilities of success and failure. To achieve power at all, as we have seen, they require the support of marginal voters. Then, when in power, they need the co-operation of the hierarchies of private capitalism that surround them. They both daily experience the potential offered to them when that co-operation is forthcoming, and the frustration and impotence that follows its withdrawal. And in both cases, their daily experience of office, and their observation of it from afar when in Opposition, underline how essential it is for the Labour

Party leadership to establish their 'respectability' in the eyes of the power-groupings that they face. So the desperate search for 'respectability' and the repeated attempts to 'prove their fitness to rule' which characterise the speeches and policies of Labour Ministers are no accident of Ministerial personality (though they may be accentuated by that). They are rather rooted in the Labour Party's need for co-operation. They are the visible admission by the Party's leaders of the limits of State power. And given the Labour Party's pretensions to be a party of social reform, this 'respectability' is always in doubt. Business co-operation is something on which the Party's leadership can never automatically rely, since it is something which the Party's radical rhetoric in Opposition has invariably done much to put in jeopardy. And so paradoxically, the stronger the Labour Party politically, the more radical its programme, and the louder its left wing, the less secure will organised capital feel, and the more that it will demand of the Labour leadership as 'proof' of that Party's 'soundness' and suitability for co-operation. Only the peculiar situation of post-war mass radicalism eased this corporate pressure in 1945, and even then it was fully back in evidence as early as 1948. Edmund Dell has described the daily reality of this lack of confidence in Labour Governments felt by business leaders:

It would be wrong to imagine that when government talks to industry it is a conversation between institutions. It is in fact a conversation between individuals. Possibilities of misunderstanding and resentment are therefore greater when there is a Labour government. As individuals and as members of the Labour Party, Labour ministers have political presumptions and ideals which are not shared by the great majority of the leaders of industry. However enthusiastic Labour ministers may be at encouraging the development of the private sector, however much they may consult, however slow they may be in extending the public sector, there is a residuum of doubt and distrust in the minds of industrial leaders. As an unknown Junior Minister I was once taken for a civil servant by the host of a lunch party of businessmen and received condolences on having the task of serving Labour ministers. Even where Labour ministers show themselves understanding of the problems of industry there remains the question of taxation of personal income to act as an irritant in these relationships. As individuals industrial leaders objected to the level of taxation. If they were owners they objected to the close company provisions. If they were senior executives in large firms perhaps with little private capital of their own, they objected furiously to the disallowance of interest on bank borrowings. I remember one industrialist, who had been more friendly and co-operative than most, exploding about the effect of that measure on his standard of living. There was not much that a Labour government could do for industry in general or for his company in particular which would compensate him for the personal consequences of that decision.[13]

This is the paradox at the heart of Labourism — that Michael Foot has called 'the fundamental and fatal contradiction of the Labour Party'. It was a dilemma clear to Aneurin Bevan as early as 1931, that:

> In opposition, the Labour Party is compelled, by the nature of the class struggle, to take up an alignment which hamstrings it when in office. A Party climbing to power by articulating the demands of the dispossessed must always wear a predatory visage to the property-owning class . . . although all the time its heart is tender with the promise of peaceful gradualism. It knows that the limited vision of the workers will behold only its outward appearance, but it hopes that the gods of private enterprise will look upon its heart. In either case, one must be deceived. To satisfy the workers the Labour Party must fulfill the threat of its face, and so destroy the political conditions necessary to economic gradualism. To calm the fears of private enterprise it must betray its promise to the workers, and so lose their support.[14]

When in power, the pressures on the Labour Party leadership to take that second option, 'to betray its promise to the workers', are enormous . . . . Senior managerial personnel in the major private industrial and financial agencies possess a number of potent sanctions against a recalcitrant Government which in the past they have been prepared to use. So even in the Labour Party's modest history, its leaders have known strikes by senior managerial personnel, ideological offensives against certain of its policies, flights of capital out of the country, and dictation of domestic and foreign policy terms by those in control of international lending agencies. Indeed, the very international competitive weakness of British capitalism and the legacy of an Imperial past have left every post-war British Government particularly dependent on these last mentioned financial agencies. This has given British finance capital a particular leverage on the Labour Party in power, precisely because its co-operation has been vital to stem the short-term net export of funds that would otherwise send the economy into a payments deficit with the usual crippling effects on domestic interest rates, economic growth and manufacturing investment.

Yet it is significant that the Labour Party in power has only rarely experienced these breakdowns of co-operation between its leadership and the well-organised representative of industrial and financial capital. Instead and more normally, as we have seen, the relationship between the State and the capitalist sector has been strengthened under Labour. For the threat that a radical Labour Party poses to the existing distribution of class power has been neutralised over the years far less by class coercion and lack of co-

operation, far more by the *incorporation* of the Labour Party leadership into
the command structures and world view of the ruling groups that the Party
once existed to bring down. It was this process of incorporation that Labour
Party militants of the 1930s, in their anticipation of open class confrontation
when the Party took office, failed to envisage; and which the later apologists
for State power under Labour, reacting as they were to the confrontationist
expectations of Cripps, failed to see.

Two sets of relationships experienced by Labour politicians are
particularly significant here. Their experience of Parliamentary procedures
and atmosphere is clearly one force incorporating many M.P.s into less
radical ways. As Bevan said, the radical M.P. must really be on his guard:

> To preserve the keen edge of his critical judgment he will find that he must
> adopt an attitude of scepticism amounting almost to cynicism, for
> Parliamentary procedure neglects nothing which might soften the
> acerbities of his class feelings. In one sense the House of Commons is the
> most unrepresentative of representative assemblies. It is an elaborate
> conspiracy to prevent the real clash of opinion which exists outside from
> finding an appropriate echo within its walls. It is a social shock absorber
> placed between privilege and the pressure of popular discontent.[15]

This certainly was the experience which Fenner Brockway observed in the
1930s, that in particular the 'social life associated with Parliament blunts the
sense of identity with the working class in their struggle'. All too often, he
recorded, 'one saw Labour M.P.s falling to the glamour of the social life of
the other side, steadily leaving their own class behind them and becoming
conditioned by the amenities and atmosphere of the class which exploited the
very men and women whom they had been sent to the House of Commons to
represent'.[16] Even Nye Bevan himself, though he was a radical on the Left of
the Party for virtually his entire Parliamentary career, fell under the spell. As
his biographer and colleague, Michael Foot, put it, the impotence of
Parliament in the 1930s and his own struggle with the Party leadership might
easily have induced in Bevan

> a hostility to Parliament itself, reinforcing the old semi-syndicalist
> theories of industrial action which he had brought with him to
> Westminster in 1929. But curiously the effect was the opposite . . . even
> while the institution was failing so pitifully to mirror the turmoil outside,
> he acquired a deep respect, almost a love, for the House of Commons. He
> saw it as a place where, given a proper use of its possibilities, poverty
> could win the battle against property without bloodshed. Not that he
> enjoyed, as a substitute for political action, the cosy conventions of the
> Parliamentary game. He never shut his ears to the storms outside. . . . Yet
> gradually and imperceptibly — and the fact was of considerable
> importance for his own future and the Labour Party — he came to regard

Parliament as the most precious potential instrument in the hands of the people. Doubtless his own powers in the arena influenced his views. It would be harsh to blame a great matador for upholding the virtues of bullfighting.[17]

Yet Parliamentary socialisation can be, and has been, resisted — at least by those few M.P.s for whom the Commons was never more than an arena in which to make propaganda for the class struggle going on outside. Far more insidious, and ultimately more crucial, is a second set of relationships of incorporation between Labour Ministers on the one side and their senior advisers in the Ministries on the other. This seems to have been, and to remain, the major and most potent mechanism by which Labour Party politicians are absorbed into the ruling ideas of the day. It is the ability of private capitalism to dominate the definitions and policy options perceived by a Labour Government which holds the key to the absence of more frequent and more open withdrawals of co-operation by various sections of the British ruling class whenever the Labour Party is in power.

For the Labour Party in office is enveloped in the 'conventional wisdoms' of the day, operating in a 'reality' defined for it by the civil servants of the public *and private* bureaucracies and that it faces (in the Treasury, the C.B.I., the Bank of England and so on).* Because the Labour Party coming into power inherits a situation in which there is a close inter-penetration of personnel, institutions and attitudes between the State bureaucracy and the private bureaucracies of industry and finance, so it inherits a government machine which offers it only a limited range of policy options, and which tells it repeatedly that only a limited range of 'solutions' are possible to 'problems' that are themselves defined by civil servants operating within a world view and set of class interests shared with the senior echelons of private capitalism. At its most extreme, no Treasury Minister has presumably faced a brief in which the policy options before him stretch from devaluation and deflation on the one side, to workers' control at the point of production at the other. On the contrary, the choice of policy options is structured and restricted: such that,

Only a small band of the full range of alternative policies is effectively ventilated and disputed. Indeed, on some issues the band may be so narrow

---

*Even the first Labour Government met this problem. As Ramsay MacDonald said in 1924, 'until you have been in office, until you have seen those files warning Cabinet Ministers of the dangers of legislation, or that sort of thing, you have not had the experience of trying to carry out what seems to be a simple thing, but which becomes a complex, an exceedingly difficult, and a laborious and almost heartbreaking thing when you come to be a member of a Cabinet in a responsible Government.' (Quoted in Lyman, *The First Labour Government 1924*, p. 138).

that decisions seem not to be 'made' at all — they just flow automatically from the 'climate of opinion'.[18]

This is very clear in the kind of information coming to Labour Ministers from the Bank of England. Readers might compare the marked similarities between the 'doom warning' given to (and believed by) Philip Snowden in 1931[19] and Harold Wilson's description of life with the Governor of the Bank of England. A typical example from Wilson's memoirs runs as follows:

> The Governor was in his gloomiest mood and clearly felt that the financial end of the world was near. More speculation, more trouble for the pound could only mean the collapse of the world monetary system. The dollar would be engulfed: it might even go first . . . He pressed the point further and I said that if the issue was as bad as he thought, then I would be ready to fly to America for talks with the President and the Federal Reserve Authorities.[20]

Contrary to the Governor's prophecy, of course, the financial world is still intact, but Ministers getting that on a daily basis must surely be forgiven slightly for losing touch with reality. As at least one of the 1964-70 Ministerial team has said, this kind of relationship was a crucial factor in what he termed 'the drift to the right' of the last Labour Government. It is not simply the Governor of the Bank of England. It is also that Labour Ministers

> are constantly in contact with the 'establishment' . . . higher civil servants, leaders of industry and commerce and leaders of the various pressure groups who have access to Ministers' offices. Most of them are very good people and they do not, of course, all think alike. But they tend to transmit the conventional wisdom of the upper-middle classes of the South East of England.[21]

To this enmeshing of the Labour Ministers in the ruling ideas of the day, the Labour Party makes its own contribution, by repeatedly failing to generate *alternative* definitions, detailed policies, *and* the social forces on which to break through the material and ideological domination of this class of men at the top of the industrial, financial and public bureaucracies. As a result, so all pervasive are these orthodoxies, so united are these bureaucracies in their definition of 'important problems', 'policy alternatives' and 'desirable solutions' that the Labour Party in power faces a body of ideas that appears not as the embodiment of the interests of the ruling class alone but as the embodiment of the interests of the society as a whole. The Labour Party in power, that is, faces a truly 'hegemonic' power structure, before which Labour Party politicians find themselves helpless, lacking as they do a counter-definition of reality of the same force and any alternative power base on which to put that counter-definition into practice. And so their very impotence without the co-operation of this hegemonic power structure only persuades them, on a day to day basis, that they really do face only the set of policy alternatives that they are offered by their civil service.

The situation has been well summed up by John Saville, an argument that is worth reproducing in full.

When a Labour administration takes over the Government they inherit a large bureaucratic apparatus that is continuing to administer the affairs of the country. The first thing a Labour Government does is to carry on, using the accepted and traditional practices and procedures. Its ministers slip into the seats just vacated by their Tory predecessors, and are served by the same Civil Servants whose social background is attuned to Conservative traditions. Socialists even of a moderate kind are rare in the higher reaches of the Civil Service: left wing socialists entirely absent. Labour Ministers are for the most part men who have spent many years already in Westminster: Parliamentary practices and procedures are accepted as right and proper and fundamentally unalterable, including the fiction of the neutrality of the Civil Service. Assuming that the Government has some reforming intentions, the complicated processes begin of drafting new legislation and then getting it accepted: first from within the Civil Service and then by Parliament. The pressures on a Minister from his Civil Servants, from outside vested interests, from the Tory opposition in Parliament are intense and continuous; and the more radical the measure the greater the weight of opinion and interest with which the Minister responsible will have to contend. In the case of legislation that is genuinely reforming in intention the pressures to narrow its scope and limit its application will be unceasing and unrelenting; and the reform when it finally appears as an Act of Parliament will be a good deal more orthodox and limited than when it began its passage as a draft measure . . . It is the density and tenacity of conservative institutions in Britain that defeats the genuine reformer and when reform is finally granted, often after years of weary struggle, its significance is usually exaggerated.[22]

In such a situation, it is no accident that the 'class' content of the Labour leadership's aspirations should drain over time, not least because it is the manifestations of working class aspirations which create problems for them in their dealings with the City and with organised business. As politicians in power they depend for their success on their ability to find the common ground between opposing class forces; or, failing that, on their ability to ally with the stronger class. For the alternative for them as Parliamentarians is total ineffectiveness and likely electoral defeat. So, out of their daily experience, the Labour Party leadership are driven to a view of 'reality' which defines as 'the problem' those working class forces which make more difficult the establishment of close working relationships with the senior managerial strata of private industrial and financial capital. Out of the logic of their own politics Labour leaders are drawn away from their class perspectives and their class roots, and emerge highly sensitive to the requirements of the capitalist structure that they face, increasingly socialised in the norms of Parliamentary gradualism, increasingly prone to define reality from a managerial standpoint, increasingly reluctant to mobilise or radicalise their own working class base, and increasingly willing to use State power (at times of class crisis) directly against the material interests of the working class that they claim to represent.

Nor is it an accident that the Labour Government in 1931, in 1948, and in 1964-70 seriously weakened itself defending the parity of the pound sterling that the Conservatives calmly abandoned immediately on taking office. For the hyper-sensitivity of international financiers to Labour plans, and the capacity of flights of money abroad to cripple production at home, leaves the Labour Party leadership *necessarily* sensitive to the City's demands. For the financial institutions of the City actually possess a series of material sanctions whose short-term impact on Labour Government policies is considerably greater and more immediate than anything that industrial capital or the organised working class can muster. Indeed these moments of capitalist crisis demonstrate the bankruptcy of the Labour tradition, as the leaders of the Party are driven to turn the power of the State machine against their own plans and against the living standards and industrial power of their own working class electorate. For in a very real sense the Labour Party leaders have *no choice,* if they are to win the co-operation of organised capital, if they are to create the economic conditions in which organised capital can afford to co-operate, and if they are to 'prove' that they can be trusted to rule. Or rather, precisely because they failed to mobilise any alternative source of political power in their own working class electorate, they have no choice. It is from the logic of their own politics that they find themselves isolated from their own rank and file, under the intense personal pressures of office, and with ideological defences that are inadequate to repel conservative orthodoxies. And so ultimately Labour Party leaders find themselves in this ludicrous situation: formally socialist M.P.s, but in reality dependent for their definition of the 'national interest' on the specifications of the central institution of British finance capital. The bankruptcy of Labourism could nowhere be more clearly demonstrated than in this. . . .

There is either no road to a socialist Britain left to this generation, or there is a new one, to be made against and in spite of the Labour Party and its politics. For with hindsight it is clear that the Labour tradition as a vehicle for socialism contained at its outset the seeds of its own failure. At the heart of the recurrent emergence of conservatism in the history of the Labour Party stands the impossibility of the Parliamentary road to socialism. For as the international history of the working class, from the rise of Hitler to the bloody overthrow of Salvador Allende all too bitterly demonstrates, the power of the Parliamentary State is apparently not open to those who seek fundamental social transformation of a socialist kind. It would be pleasant, easier, convenient and gratifying to think that this were not so — that there was a peaceful and constitutional route to a socialist society of free men and equal men; and it is easy to see why early Labour Party politicians thought that they had found it. For they had watched for so long Conservative and Liberal Governments in power, implementing policies by receiving the obedience of senior administrators and the loyal co-operation of powerfully placed groups in industry and finance. And if they could do it, why not Labour also? But these early Labour Party politicians failed to see that there is a fundamental incompatibility between the goal of socialism and the basis of power of the Parliamentary State. The power of the Parliamentary State depends precisely on this obedience of administrators and on this loyal co-operation of powerfully placed citizens. Yet socialism involves nothing less than a sustained assault on the powers and privileges of the very class of men who head the administration, and who control the private hierarchies of business and finance; and the one thing in which they will be neither loyal, obedient nor co-operative is their own social demise.

For the men who capture the Parliamentary State will not receive loyalty, obedience and co-operation from the private power-centres that surround them if the implementation of socialism is their goal. No ruling class in history has voluntarily surrendered its prerogatives and power. Rather such a class has (and invariably will) deploy the full range of its sanctions against any set of Parliamentarians bent on its destruction: sanctions rooted in its class position under capitalism, and stretching from administrative obstructionism through economic dislocation, financial movements, and ultimately to the use of force itself. If the extremities of these sanctions have not been seen in Britain, this is not because the ruling class here is more constitutionalist than sane. It is because the Labour Party has never seriously challenged its fundamental powers and prerogatives.

The Parliamentary State would offer a road to socialism only if the men entering government were able and were willing to turn to an alternative power base for co-operation and support — only, that is, if they were willing and able to 'walk on two legs' by using the industrial power of the working class at the point of production as a counterweight to the obstructionism and resistance of the privileged classes under challenge. But tragically, those who have subscribed to the Parliamentary road to socialism have made it *the* article of their political faith never to encourage, and always to oppose, the emergence of such a potentially radicalised proletariat. They have understood the Parliamentary road to socialism as precisely the *alternative* to this more violent confrontation of class with class, and have accepted a definition of constitutionality in politics which denied to the working class the right to use their industrial power to support their political ends — a right which industrial and financial capital exercise themselves daily in their dealings with the Parliamentary State. In consequence, the Parliamentary road to socialism, in seeking to avoid a confrontation of classes 'on the terrain of class' (in the factories and on the streets) has invariably, and must always, be abandoned in the face of ruling class opposition or maintained at the cost of socialism itself. Sadly, there is no Parliamentary road to socialism where that road is seen as an alternative to the mass mobilisation of the working class to break the dominance of the industrial and financial bourgeoisie. This is the unavoidable lesson of the Labour Party's repeated retreats from its socialist promise in the twentieth century.

**The wealth of Northern Ireland is concentrated
in the hands of a small number
of large British firms.**

---

*Ireland: The Role of
the British Army*
Chris Harman

One of the greatest propaganda myths of our time is that the British army went into Northern Ireland originally to protect the Catholics and stayed on to prevent a 'civil war' between Catholics and Protestants. . . .

The original conquest of Ireland by British armies 300 years ago had a simple purpose: to ensure that the wealth of Ireland was controlled by the British ruling class. The same considerations underlie the role the British army plays today. The basic fact ignored in all the propaganda of the British press is that the wealth of Northern Ireland is concentrated in the hands of a small number of large British firms.

From *The Struggle in Ireland* by Chris Harman, Socialist Workers and Printers Publishers Ltd. (London, 1974), and reprinted by permission from Sun Distribution International, 14131 Woodward Ave., Highland Park, MI 43203.

A complete list of British firms in Northern Ireland would be long enough to fill pages of this pamphlet. In the manufacturing field they range from GEC to Rolls-Royce in engineering, through Metal Box and Oneida Steel in light engineering, and subsidiaries of British American Tobacco and Rank in cigarettes and food, to Courtaulds and ICI in textile manufacture. There are subsidiaries of British subsidiaries operating — the engineering firm of A Kirkland is part of the Courtaulds group, as is Bairnswear.

In the distribution industry the picture is very similar — the shopping centre of Belfast is dominated by British Home Stores, C & A Modes, Marks and Spencer and Littlewoods. The older 'department stores' are also under the control of British interests — the Belfast city centre store, Robinson and Cleaver, is a subsidiary of Sir Charles Clore's Sears Holding.

With financial institutions the story is the same. After a long process of takeover and merger by the Midland and Westminster banks there has been no independent Northern Ireland bank since 1965. So although it is difficult to obtain precise figures, it is possible to state that almost all the finance capital, the bulk of distributive capital and perhaps as much as 75 per cent of manufacturing capital in Northern Ireland is directly under the control of British capitalism. Such a stake, needless to say, gives British capitalism almost total control over the Northern Ireland economy.

British capitalism's interest in Ireland is not confined to the North. By March 1972 there were no fewer than 986 British subsidiaries in the south and 65 per cent of manufacturing industry was controlled by foreign, mostly British, capital. Of all the new industrial projects undertaken during 1960-1970, 70 per cent were accounted for by non-Irish firms. In the same period 74 per cent of the total investment in new enterprises was made by these companies.

British companies themselves accounted for 44 per cent of new projects, American for 25 per cent, German for 18 per cent and other countries, notably Japan, for 13 per cent. To get some idea of the scale involved, the total of US investment over the period — £42 million — was the same as that of all Irish-owned firms.

The most frequently given explanation for these extremely high levels of foreign investments is that the governments, north and south of the border, have offered various incentives to attract foreign capital. Grants up to 45 per cent of the cost of new plant and equipment are made.

But there is a second 'attraction' which is less frequently publicised — the low level of wages in both Northern and southern Ireland. In March 1972 the director of the Industrial Development Authority boasted that labour costs were more favourable (to the capitalist class) in southern Ireland than in the rest of Europe. Figures produced by the Department of Employment in 1970 showed that in every industrial group, wages in Northern Ireland were lower than in the rest of the UK. Taking the average across all manufacturing industry, wages in Northern Ireland (hourly rates) were only 78 per cent of those in the rest of the UK.

The combination of tax-free profits, substantial capital grants and low wage levels means, of course, that investment in any part of Ireland can be a very profitable exercise. It is practically impossible to get figures for the North, but they are not likely to be very different from those for the south which show that the rate of profit on industrial capital shows a rise from 11.5 per cent in 1959 to 15.6 per cent in 1964. It remained at that high rate until 1966 when it began to rise again. These rises took place while the rate of profit in Britain was falling.

However, British capitalism's interest in Ireland is not limited to the actual capital stake it has here. Ireland is also Britain's third largest export market — more than 55 per cent of Irish imports come from Britain, and more than 65 per cent of total Irish exports go to Britain. Almost 75 per cent of Northern Irish imports come from the rest of the UK. So the combination of a large and highly profitable capital stake and a large and subservient market makes the whole of the Irish economy an area which the British capitalist class will want to keep at almost any price.

The British press continually tried to portray the British army in Northern Ireland as a gallant bunch of heroes, preserving law and order at enormous danger to themselves. Many socialists and trade unionists in Britain fall for this line. After all, most of the rank and file soldiers are working class lads who join the army because of unemployment or to get out of humdrum dead-end jobs. It seems rough on them to be shot at and attacked by rioters.

But the soldiers do not determine the job they do. They have to obey the orders of their officers. Failure to do so means serious criminal charges. And these orders are based on the continuing need of British capitalism to protect its wealth in Ireland, North and south.

The task the soldiers are made to do is not the protection of the lives of the majority. Their task is to prop up the form of government the rulers of Britain have decided to impose in Northern Ireland. Until 1972, that meant propping up the totally sectarian Orange state. Since then, it has been to prop up a form of British rule which makes a few concessions to the Catholic middle class, but which offers no solution to the problems facing workers, Protestant or Catholic. The army's orders are quite simply, to crack down with massive force against those who oppose this form of rule, and to crack down hardest against those who oppose it most.

The army has been used in the crudest way to attack viciously those sections of the Catholic population who oppose British rule completely and who back the Republican ideal. It has also been used, but in a less consistently vicious manner, to intimidate those sections of the Protestant population who support the idea of British rule, but not in its present form with the concessions to the Catholic middle class. . . .

If troops raided the working-class areas of the big industrial cities of Britain, arresting people by the thousand for no cause, pouring teargas into family homes, beating up those who protested, tearing up floor boards and breaking up furniture, shooting rubber bullets at point blank range into the faces of housewives, there would be deep anger among all sections of organised workers. Trade unionists and socialists would have no hesitation in giving their full support to those who fought back against the troops, even if we might criticise the methods they used.

Yet such is the situation in Northern Ireland today. It is up to socialists in Britain to cut through the barrage of propaganda created by the press, the TV and the radio, to point the finger at those really to blame for the violence and sectarianism and to show the same solidarity with the Republicans fighting repression as we would with workers fighting attacks by the army and police in England, Scotland or Wales.

We have to say quite clearly that the people of Ireland have every right to try to control their own country by driving out the British troops — and if British soldiers are killed in the process, that is the fault of British governments for sending them there. Our slogan has to be 'British troops out of Ireland'.

What the Left does not have, economically and especially politically, is any convincing alternative program.

Britain Needs a New Left
Raymond Williams

"Are the English quite sane?" The question has often been asked with resigned good humor. It is now sometimes asked seriously, with impatience and even with anger. American friends seem to get off the plane expecting anything from straw in the hair to blood in the streets. The usual slow, kindly muddle may for a time reassure them. Whatever may be wrong it is not of that order. But you don't have to look around long, as a visitor or native, to know

---

"The Impossible Society: Britain Needs a New Left," by Raymond Williams, *The Nation,* June 28, 1975 and reprinted by permission of the publisher.

that it is now in the strict sense, an impossible society; or, to put it more scientifically, that it is undergoing strains, tensions, divisions, that are unlikely to
be bearable in their present forms. Back in the early 1950s, when nothing
seemed to be moving, I got into the habit of saying that the one thing certain
about an impossible situation is that it will last. I don't say that now. Almost
everything is moving, and the scientific thing to say would be that Britain is in
a period of radical and deeply contested transition. But that's only half a
statement since it makes no sense unless we say transition to what.

If I had been writing a month ago I would have written mainly about the
rate of inflation, now climbing above 20 per cent. In the months ahead, it will
remain the central topic. But of course all economic problems are fought
politically, and the strangeness of the present situation is that this central
political struggle has been cut across by a major political campaign of
another kind: the referendum on continued membership in the Common
Market. This is not just a temporary complication; its result seems certain to
affect the balance of forces in the central struggle. That is why it is important
to see what has happened in what is really, in this form, a residual issue.

After the economic crises of the early and mid-1960s, which showed the
chronic relative weakness of the British economy, exacerbated by its
dependence on imports for half its food and by its overextended and specially
exposed position in the international monetary system, a crucial decision —
to join the Common Market — was taken by the large industrial and finance
capital institutions, and by the leadership of both main political parties. A
necessary part of this strategy was that the trade unions should be brought
under tighter controls, and this again was attempted by the leadership of
both parties. All the key economic and financial decisions of the past ten
years have been in line with this strategy. The consequent alignment of the
economy is, within capitalist terms, irreversible. Nothing is easier than to go
back to some selected date — 1946, 1966 — and prove than an alternative
policy was then possible. This becomes more plausible the further you go
back, but it is in any case irrelevant: the key dispositions, in investments and
markets, have been made. The fact that joining the Market was delayed by
the French added to the political difficulties, but the main trend of economic
alignment continued in any case.

The final formal negotiations, and the present Labour government's so-
called renegotiations, found some marginal flexibility but were mainly a
ratification of key decisions that had already been made. But the strategy still
depended on controlling the unions. Otherwise an already weak British
capitalism would prove, in the new situation, even less competitive. Wilson
with one kind of legislation, Heath with another, and both with every
conceivable device for controlling wages, attempted this necessary part of the

strategy. Each in turn failed. The most spectacular defeat of what, taken as a whole, was a rational capitalist strategy, came with the victory of the miners' strike and the fall of the Heath government in March 1974. This coincided with a major worsening of the general economic situation and with the effect of increased oil prices which were to shake even very much stronger economies. From that point on, given the lines of the strategy being followed, things were out of control.

The truth is that, added to the general factors of inflation, which affected all capitalist economies, there was a special factor of a quite open class struggle which the capitalists and the alternative political leaderships were steadily and visibly losing. Many Left commentators put it the other way around, denying that wage increases contribute significantly to inflation, and presenting wage struggle as essentially defensive. In local terms that is often true, but it is an extraordinary underestimate of the real situation. Over the past seven years, and especially over the past two, the organized working class has acquired and exercised an effective power of veto over any capitalist strategy. When inflation rose to 20 per cent, earnings rose 30 per cent. From that 30 per cent you must deduct taxes, but it is still true that the most powerful unions had vetoed, in practice, the attempts to reduce consumption significantly, and to increase profitability and investment, on which the whole strategy depended.

It has more recently been part of the strategy to increase unemployment, that being the classical way to reduce wage pressure. But, though employment has been falling, as one capitalist institution after the other, including some of the very largest, has moved into severe financial crisis, the veto, on the whole, has been exercised there also. Massive state investment and emergency loans have been mobilized, from taxation and borrowing, not simply to re-equip British industry, which is the accepted capitalist strategy and the policy of the political leaderships but also, on quite different criteria, to save jobs. Britain consequently shows up very badly in comparative figures for inflation, but very well in comparative figures for unemployment. Meanwhile the real pressure is being felt, not only by less organized groups but conspicuously in social expenditure. Every kind of public institution is under extreme pressure, and the quality of life to which they so evidently contribute is deteriorating day by day. It is this overall situation that leads to descriptions of the society as "ungovernable"; a phrase started by the Right, passed on to American and other foreign journalists and then reimported as objective description. What it means is that the society is, for the time being at least, ungovernable according to any rational capitalist economic and political strategy.

So are we "slipping," as is also reported, "into a social revolution"? I have to say that I wish I could see any signs of it. This is the scare talk of the Right, designed to mobilize foreign and domestic opinion for a new attempt to break the unions. And this, as I see it, is the real danger. For what the unions have had, so far, is a veto, a decisive or effective negative. What the Left does not have, economically and especially politically, is any convincing alternative positive program. That is where the effects of the referendum campaign may be especially damaging.

Back in the 1960s, the Left correctly identified the general capitalist strategy and its connection with the Common Market. It became axiomatic, on the Left, to oppose it. By the 1970s, even after formal accession, the opposition was still strong enough to force Wilson into double-talk about renegotiation, to keep the Labour Party together. The Left's strategy was then clear: to prevent capitalist solutions within Britain, to defeat the Common Market alternative, and then on a broadly popular basis to move steadily toward Socialist solutions. The essential political ingredient of this strategy was popular majority against the Market. For two or three crucial years, until 1974, they had it, and the strategy held together. The twists and turns of the Labour Party leadership, which went through the motions of renegotiation and then announced its support for the Market, were of course predictable and predicted. But this promised a bonus. After defeat in the referendum by a popular anti-Market majority, the Right would be driven out of the leadership or even the party, and the full opening to the Left would be there.

Well, it didn't happen that way. And it could never have happened that way. It was an intoxicating prospect, but it was based on illusions characteristic of the old Left. The temporary popular majority against the Market was really a vote against rising prices, of the kind which had been cast in turn against both Labour and Conservatives. The Socialist case against the Market is the same case that Socialists have to make against Britain's capitalist state. Yet to preserve the anti-Market popular majority this had to be displaced, in the end, by fantasies about British independence. Solid anti-Market opinion was composed almost equally of Socialists who opposed international capitalism and of the far Right and nationalists who wished to preserve an old-style Britain. Hence the extraordinary alliance of the anti-Market campaign — the old Left and the Powellite Right. Some Socialists keep their own case clear, but the thrust of the campaign was toward British independence, and at the end of a period of repeated economic failures it was never likely that this would be widely enough believed. When a positive alternative policy was looked for, it had to be either to go on as we once did (choosing the "open sea," as the Anti campaign kept quoting from Sir Winston Churchill) or (but to keep the potential majority together this had to be underplayed) to move rapidly to Socialist controls on trade and capital, in an effective siege economy. The first alternative had become incredible; the second, for which an economic case can be made, had so small a political base (remaining small because it could not be openly campaigned for, though if the campaign had been explicit it is doubtful, in present circumstances, if it could have been significantly increased) that the old Left was actually risking the kind of crisis which would make rigid controls inevitable, and in which the most likely political outcome would be the rigid controls which the Right has been repeatedly trying, thus far unsuccessfully, to impose.

So gross a political miscalculation throws light on the ideological condition of the old Left. And that they were joined, if rather cynically, in the name of unity by most of the Marxist Left, is equally revealing. The old Left (and I know this because I grew up in it) has always linked a social-democratic ideology with affirmation of the uniqueness of British society and its traditions. In a crisis like the present, it can speak of international capitalism as if British capitalists were not part of it, and of British freedoms as if we did not live in what is at best a capitalist democracy, with manipulative electoral politics and with substantial integration into an American political and military hegemony. As they tried to cover these contradictions, they became more and more incredible.

Meanwhile most of the Marxist Left, still weak and peripheral, had failed (as who has not?) to develop a contemporary theory and strategy against advanced international capitalism. Much of its rhetoric and its *elan* comes from revolutions undertaken in quite different circumstances, and these are made to compensate for its failures to defeat the enemy at home. Only one tiny group, Communists for Europe, and a few independents like myself took a different line, arguing that we had to fight international capitalism beyond the limits of the nation-state, and that the strength of the Left in Western Europe, in conditions of contradiction between European and American capitalism, was a realistic basis for a quite different political strategy.

Two final points. The old Left went into this campaign in the same negative spirit as the trade unions exercise of the economic veto. Each now risks a similar kind of defeat, in the changed conditions of the referendum result. It is only by raising the stakes that either can survive: politically by moving very fast into the Common Market institutions, where the Right and Center are already firmly established, and where the struggle for an elected and legislative Parliament will be crucial; economically, by moving on from the veto to positive and selective programs for controls on investment and employment — an attempt to command resources, rather than to react sullenly to their present distribution. It will be hard either way, but if the effort is not made there will be a rapid move to the Right: not fascism but a capitalist authoritarianism backed by an explicit or implicit political coalition stretching from the Labour Center to all but the Powellite Right. That coalition was forming during the referendum campaign, and it will now be very much harder to fight because the case against it has been so negative, so residual and so deeply unrealistic.

Then a brief note on the actual voting. What is most significant is that the old Left, the old Labourism, didn't hold even the organized working class. On the evidence we have so far, the "yes" vote, for staying in the Common Market, had majorities in every social class, in both sexes and in all major parties. This will be explained away as the result of manipulation by the parties and the media, and there was certainly plenty of that. But the majority among trade unionists cannot be explained away. In this, as in other matters, there is more realism, at least of a short term kind, among actual working people than among their official representatives. Indeed it is just that which the Right can now exploit, and which the old Left, by its unrealism, has left open to exploitation. It is then indeed time, as has been theoretically clear for twenty years, to build a new Left which can speak to our changed and changing condition.

2. France

In this section on France, Claude Bourdet, correspondent in Paris for *The Nation,* reviews current French politics with a special focus on the Presidential elections of 1974. Bourdet points up some of the major problems facing the Left and the Right in the immediate future and provides an excellent introduction to the more lengthy selections that follow. Charles Posner provides a brief overview of modern France including the controversial role of planning.

Andrew Feenberg follows these introductory pieces with an examination of The Events of May, 1968. During this brief period French monopoly capitalism was shaken to its foundations by a movement for "Socialist Revolution" led by students and factory workers. The May crisis revealed the fragility of the modern capitalist state and will not soon be forgotten by the French bourgeoisie. Owing to a lack of carefully integrated alternatives to the status quo, an absence of political direction, and certain opportunistic tactics employed by the French Communist Party, the movement floundered and failed. Feenberg's analysis of the Events offers a number of useful insights into France while providing an essential perspective for grasping more recent developments. In reading #9, the same author assesses the common electoral platform of the French Communist and Socialist parties, agreed upon in 1972. Critiques of this "peaceful road to socialism" emanating from radical leftists in France bring to mind those offered by Coates on reformism in Britain, as well as the fate of Allende's Popular Unity coalition in Chile. It is imperative to consider whether Leftist electoral success would signal a socialist transformation of French society or simply new management for capitalist society.

In an excerpt from his influential book *The State in Capitalist Society,* Ralph Miliband records the sorry history of previous attempts by the French Left to use the capitalist state machinery on behalf of real social and economic change. Too often this has only served to divert legitimate unrest into sterile electoral politics that bring no redress for the victims of monopoly capital. Additional difficulties with the *Programme Commun* are taken up by George Weisz who also discusses various aspects of France's recent capitalist crisis. Weisz, as did Feenberg, raises the specter of fascism as a possible avenue for a desperate ruling class.

Finally, Rand Smith, a political scientist from the University of Michigan, investigates the issue of workers control in France. The thrust of this piece might be contrasted with most traditional political science studies of France which claim that people do not want to participate in governing. Here the reader is encouraged to reevaluate the origins of and conventional views on participation and government categories that invariably exclude one's job. However, as another student of self-management contends

> What one is at work is the major part of what one is in life. Yet it is commonly felt that what happens in these collectivities of human activity is the responsibility of 'the management,' 'the authority' in charge, etc., etc. To accept this attitude is altogether to deny a socialist attitude to life. This is true in a number of senses. First of all, it is a denial of social responsibility. Secondly, it is a rejection of one's most potent source of social power. Thirdly, it means foregoing any part in making the decisions which most crucially concern the enjoyment of one's own life, the meaning of what one does in life, the effect of what one does on other people. Fourthly, it surrenders to an indeterminate 'they' 'the people in charge' concern for the development of the productive forces on which more than anything else the richness and scope of social life depends and from which, if abused, the worst horrors and disasters for humanity can result.[1]

Smith probes the obstacles facing the French Democratic Confederation of Labor (CFDT) in obtaining self-management. His study is based on research conducted in the city of Grenoble during 1973.

[1]Stephen Bodington in Ken Coates (Ed.), *Can the Workers Run Industry?* (Nottingham: Bertrand Russell Foundation 1968), p. 105.

Half of France voted for Mitterand in
order to have a real, deep change. And
Giscard had to assert, over all the media,
with all the huge financial means at his
command, that he "too was in favor of
change." Will words now be enough to
satisfy everybody?

The End of Gaullism
Claude Bourdet

That was the closest shave in the history of French elections. Valery
Giscard d'Estaing [was] elected as the third President of the Fifth Republic
by something like 350,000 votes out of a voting population of some 30
million. He got a little more than 50 per cent, Mitterrand a little more than 49
per cent of the total: it was really one-half of France against the other. But the
two halves are not at all similar. Opinion polls and studies by political experts
have shown that a majority of men voted for Mitterrand, a majority of
women for Giscard; most of the younger generation also voted Mitterrand;
and of course, the overwhelming majority of wage earners did the same.
Moreover, it has been noticed that between the first ballot on May 5, and the
second on May 19, a noticeable percentage of people who had voted for
Giscard and the other candidates of the Establishment transferred their votes
to Mitterrand, while the reverse seldom happened. Not only did the
advantage of Giscard and the right wing shrink between the two polls, but
experts agree that his very marginal victory is due in large part to the
extremely low rate of abstention (12.5 per cent). Those who stay away from
the polls in France as in most countries, are the "nonpolitical" members of
the population, people who just don't care, and are interested only in having
"business as usual." The right wing alone can get such people to participate
— if, that is, it can create a real panic. That is exactly what happened: the
"Red scare," especially on the second round, brought to the booths large
numbers of tottering old ladies and the usual type of small-town Babbitts
who normally say, "Politics? I don't care, it's all corrupt."

All this indicates that Giscard d'Estaing is essentially the President of the
business world, big, medium and small; of landowners, big and medium, of
the backward part of the feminine electorate, generally manipulated by the

"The End of Gaullism," by Claude Bourdet, *The Nation*, June 8, 1974 and reprinted
by permission of the publisher.

more reactionary elements of the Catholic Chruch (in many rural areas the parish priest has as much voting influence, especially on women, as he did seventy years ago) and, finally, of the older people. That doesn't mean, of course, that everyone voted to type. In France, as in America, a proportion of manual laborers and of young people vote for the Right, and there were prominent businessmen who called for a vote for the Left. But the general trend is what counts, and it is unmistakable: this was a class vote, more so than in any other French election for a long time.

Of course, American readers will say to themselves that this 50-50 balance between two major parties or coalitions, one of them substantially representing the wealthier elements in society, the other one the less privileged, has become a more or less common phenomenon in most Western countries, and does not prevent a government from operating normally. However, there is a big difference in this respect between France and countries like the United States, Britain or Western Germany. In France, we have a Presidential system like that of the United States, but the constitution concocted in 1958 by General de Gaulle for his own use gives the President definitely more power than any President of the United States has ever enjoyed. Moreover, the voting system that de Gaulle also introduced for parliamentary elections has been rigged to make gains there easier for the Right, more difficult for the Left. That is why the present French Parliament, elected in 1973, has an overwhelming right-wing majority, with the Left, which polled nearly as many votes then as it did last month, grossly underrepresented. This Parliament will sit for four more years, unless Mr. Giscard should find it an inconvenience to him. But why should he?

This distortion of the electoral balance is what makes the situation in France so different from what it is in the United States, Britain and Germany. In those latter countries, and many others, the party or coalition that is beaten in a general election still has a substantial representation in the legislature. The opposition is not powerless, and the government must take care not to outrage a strong minority opinion.

The curious thing is that exactly that would have happened if Mitterrand had been elected. He would have faced a right-wing Parliament and, if it had proved unmanageable and he had been forced to call for a parliamentary election, the new Parliament, even if it had swung somewhat to the left (especially if elected under a new, more honest voting system) would still have retained a strong Right opposition which Mitterrand, for all his Presidential powers, could not have ignored. Giscard d'Estaing, on the contrary enjoys today the delightful position of having both these Presidential powers and a ready-made Parliament, which will do as it is told for the next four years.

That is why the Presidential election was so important for all the French underprivileged classes, for organized labor, for progressives and liberals generally: it was the one opportunity to challenge and to balance in the near future the power of the French Establishment, which has been managing the country as a family business for the last sixteen years. The opportunity has now been lost; plutocracy is back in the saddle, powerful as ever, and the Left has no effective parliamentary recourse, no way to resist politically the business world and entrenched wealth, for whom Valery Giscard d'Estaing is one of the shrewdest and most energetic champions. During the past six years as Minister of Finance he has, with his tax policy, his policy of agricultural and industrial prices, his building policy (fine homes for the well-to-do; few houses for those who really need them) and his general income policy, served those interests in the most ruthless fashion. The result, as stated by that practiced economist, Pierre Mendes-France, has been to distribute the growth of the French economy in such a way that the richer part of the population has received by far the larger slice of the cake. After the recent victory, Giscard will, of course, continue on these same lines.

It is therefore not astonishing that the Left, and especially organized labor, is considering another way to fight the tremendous power of the Establishment. This alternative was mentioned during the election by leaders of the Left and by union leaders, but it is much more an inevitable development of political dynamics than a matter of decisions by organizations and their leaders. Half of the country, and much more than half of its active forces (youth, working class, et al.) is going to be, at least for the next four years, in a state of political underprivilege — sadly underrepresented in Parliament and not represented at all by the President. It must find another way to express its needs and make its power felt, but the only course that lies open is industrial action — wage demands, strikes, demonstrations, etc. Moreover, it is quite probable that these weapons will be taken up not only in the industrial world but among farmers and small shopkeepers, who have already reacted violently against the present trend toward monopolistic shopping centers and large agricultural concentration.

Apart from these developments in the possession and application of power, the French Presidential election has uncovered several interesting political phenomena. One of them — notwithstanding what was said above — is the noticeably reduced effectiveness of the "Red scare." Giscard certainly owes his success to the manipulation by the right wing of a large part of the electorate, which was subjected to a "Red scare" so reckless that it verged on the absurd (one minister said on the radio that if Mitterrand were elected, the Red Army would soon be in Paris). But although the mass press, the radio and television overflowed with many frightening suggestions, almost half the country nevertheless voted for Mitterrand. And since the percentage of actual Communist votes in the country is not above 20, more than half of Mitterrand's supporters were non-Communists who refused to be scared. This is definitely a new state of mind, and it is bound to become even more apparent in the months and years ahead. This time, although the Right spent millions on Giscard's campaign, in which the Communist peril played a noticeable part, the scare tactics were far less effective than in 1969, when Pompidou was elected, or at the 1973 parliamentary election.

Indeed, the time seems to be coming when the Communists will have to be accepted in the normal political life of the West, as they are already in Finland and Iceland, and as has just happened in de Spinola's Portugal. This has come about in part because the Western Communist Parties (even the French party, one of the most monolithic and bureaucratic) have taken their distance from Soviet policy. During the campaign, the Soviet ambassador paid a visit to Mr. Giscard d'Estaing, Finance Minister but also Presidential candidate. This courtesy could have hurt the Left (even if it was not meant to do so) by showing Giscard as a "man of peace," but it was astutely seized upon by the French C.P. The party paper, *L'Humanite,* published a stern protest against a Soviet intrusion into French internal politics.

And in part the change has come in the wake of the Russo-American detente. World capitalism can't have its cake and eat it — it can't both cozy up to the USSR and keep the "Red scare" alive. But the main factor for the Communist comeback in democratic politics is the fact that many people have gradually realized what Francois Mitterrand realized a long time ago and made the backbone of his position — that if the Socialists reject the Communist alliance, they must perforce fall back on an alliance with the Center and the Right. That is a platitude, but it has far reaching consequences. For more than ten years after 1947, as a result both of American pressure and Stalinist policies in the USSR, the Socialists *did* repudiate the Communist alliance, and associated themselves with groups on their Right. Thus, they were pushed into reactionary policies, both in the colonies and in France, lost membership and votes, and were thinned down to a point where they ceased to be of any use to their more powerful conservative allies, who abruptly dropped them. That experience similarly opened the minds of even die-hard anti-Communists like former party Secretary General Mollet and Mayor Defferre of Marseilles (who was to be Mitterrand's prime minister) to the advantages of renewing the pre-1947 Socialist-Communist alliance.

It has been clear for some time, not only to Mitterrand but to a growing sector of French opinion, that it is misleading to compare situations in France with those in Eastern Europe, as has been the custom of those anti-Communists who go about muttering "remember Prague." In 1948, the

Czech Socialists were forced into union with the Communists and then eliminated from power. But Czechoslovakia was under the threat of the Red Army, whereas France is in the American zone of influence. It has been there ever since Yalta, and the more so today after the super-Yalta concluded between present American and Soviet leaders. The Red Army is going to stage no "summer maneuvers" in France, and even if they were not as shrewd and sensible as they are, the Communists would know that their only chance of coming back into French politics is to be loyal and relatively unobtrusive partners in a Popular Front. *They* have no recourse other than an alliance with the Socialists, whereas if the Communists had not behaved well, Mitterrand could at any time have got rid of them and formed another majority from forces more to the right, as the Socialists did after 1947. At that time, the change was made not because the Communists misbehaved but because their elimination was a condition of Marshall aid, and also because they opposed the war in Indochina.

Another new phenomenon is the virtual disappearance of traditional or orthodox Gaullism. Jacques Chaban-Delmas, former prime minister under Pompidou, wartime Resistance leader and staunch Gaullist, was the Gaullist candidate during the first round. Many people expected him to lead the field, but he polled only 15 per cent, as compared to Giscard's 32 per cent, and had to retire ingloriously after asking his followers to vote for Giscard. There are a number of reasons for this poor performance. Pompidou, and Giscard himself, laid the train for Chaban's embarrassment a long time ago, when Pompidou dismissed him as prime minister, calling Messmer in his place, and Giscard let "leak" from his finance ministry to the left-wing press information that Chaban-Delmas had used some elaborate oddities in the taxation regulations to reduce his income tax to a pittance. Giscard was already preparing his Presidential future and Pompidou was eliminating orthodox Gaullism, with which he had been (if not openly) on the worst possible terms since he and Giscard got rid of the General himself in 1969.

But behind these palace quarrels lies a broader consideration. Gaullism was an artificial phenomenon, a myth created around a single man. De Gaulle was used by the Establishment, but was relatively independent of it, in the 1960s as in the 1940s. He was able, therefore, on the one hand to bring into the Gaullist camp a lot of working-class and *petit-bourgeois* votes and support, and on the other hand he could force the ruling class to accept a relatively neutralist and anti-colonialist policy that ran squarely counter to the feelings of the French business world. Even his internal policy, which stressed "participation" — that is, cooperation between capital and labor and some management power for the workers — offended French capitalism, but had to be put up with as long as he lived. After his death, Pompidou toned down Gaullist policy in both foreign and internal affairs, but could not do away with it entirely. Now, with Pompidou dead, things are returning to their natural order. Most of the Gaullist politicians and statesmen are right wingers, and were supporting Giscard openly or secretly, even during the first round. Chaban-Delmas tried to create a middle-of-the road image, "between the extremes," but the simplifying effect of a Presidential election does not tolerate such subtleties. Giscard appeared as the sharper and stronger Establishment candidate, Mitterrand as the only working-class candidate, and that was that. There was no room for Chaban's Gaullist "third way."

It is now doubtful that Gaullism can even survive. Chaban has lost all credibility, and most of the other leaders are already Giscard's men. Some prominent Gaullists of truly progressive convictions, like former Ministers Jeanneney and Pisani, and former deputies Vallon and Rousset, called upon their followers to vote for Mitterrand, and it was apparent from the election figures that quite a number of them responded. This is General de Gaulle's second death.

However, there are areas in which even such a conservative statesman as Giscard d'Estaing can hardly go back on de Gaulle's legacies. One, of course, is the colonies. De Gaulle's policies were ambiguous for a long time; he was largely instrumental in developing and maintaining French colonialist attitudes from 1945 to 1958 by threatening to denounce the leaders of the Fourth Republic as defeatists and traitors if they gave up the smallest chip of France's Empire. But after 1958, coming to power on an ultra-colonialist wave, he reversed his policies and did precisely what he had blackmailed his predecessors into not doing. Giscard d'Estaing, even if he wanted to (which he doesn't), cannot go back on decolonization.

He might like to reverse de Gaulle's policy of independence from the United States, which was followed up to a point by Pompidou and his foreign minister, Jobert. But here also de Gaulle left a situation that will not be easily changed. He proved (what Tito, Nehru and others had proved before him) that in a world where power is balanced between the United States and Russia, no country is required to become a satellite if it is not militarily occupied by one of the giants. It can *choose* to join with one or the other, but it does not have to do so. This was amply demonstrated by France in the years of Gaullist rule, and it is therefore impossible to assert that France, being part of the West, *must* obey American orders — the assumption that was official policy during the Fourth Republic. It is probable that Giscard's policies will be to a degree warmer toward America, but there is a limit beyond which be cannot step without creating hesitations and antagonism among his followers.

Moreover, the policy of relative independence has created certain business links with the USSR and the other Socialist countries, with China, with Algeria, with the Arab countries in the Middle East; these are important not only to France's balance of payments and oil supplies, but to the turnover and profits of many powerful industrial and financial firms. The ties will curb any disposition that Giscard might have to comply with Dr. Kissinger's urgings that France return to the traditional American nursery of obedient infant-states.

He may indulge in some European developments to please both the men in Washington and his new ally, Jean Lecanuet, the leader of the non-Gaullist Center. Mr. Lecanuet is an extreme pro-American politician and a European supernationalist. He thinks that his party, a remnant of the old Christian Democratic party of 1945, might regain some strength if it could participate in a united Western Europe, with a European capital and a European Parliament; recent achievements by the Christian Democrats in Germany and Italy encourage Lecanuet in these views.

But there are also limits to the "appeasement" of European supernationalism. Neither Britain or Italy, not even Germany, seems ready for such a development. "Europe" will be mainly a catchword for political homilies for many years to come. So, if I am right, not many changes are to be expected from Giscard d'Estaing's Presidency; it will, I think, be "business as usual" for the next period. But that, precisely, may be the hitch. Half of France voted for Mitterrand in order to have a real, deep change. And Giscard had to assert, over all the media, with all the huge financial means at his command, that he *too was in favor of change."* Will words now be enough to satisfy everybody?

It is necessary to clear up some widely held misconceptions about modern France.

Modern France
Charles Posner

It is necessary to clear up some widely held misconceptions about modern France. French society has recently been taken as an example of a modern and efficient consumer society. Writers have stressed her rapid development, her ability to change, the advances made by French management, the

From the "Introduction" to *Reflections on the Revolution in France: 1968* by Charles Posner (Editor). Copyright © 1970 by Penguin Books Ltd. and reprinted by permission of the author and Penguin Books Ltd.

efficiency of the French work force and French administration. These statements are only partially true. France is both highly developed and also very much underdeveloped. France is clearly one of the most industrially advanced countries in Europe, having made use of the most up-to-date industrial and managerial innovations. But these innovations have not been widely adopted. They have never penetrated beyond a few leading firms. Not only is France still one of the least urbanized countries in Western Europe but she has yet to develop the large enterprises and financial markets characteristic of an intensive economy. Merging small enterprises has been strenuously resisted by the CNPF (the French Confederation of Industries) largely dominated by relatively small provincial interests. The attempt to turn Paris into a banking centre to rival the City of London has met with no more than the suspicion of a French bourgeoisie which prefers hoarding gold bars and investing in property to buying shares and bonds. In recent years, France has built some of the most modern urban industrial complexes in the Paris region, in Rennes, Grenoble, etc., whilst also maintaining a large backward rural and small-town population with a surprisingly large political influence. France has pioneered the most successful administrative and planning system in Europe, the *Commissariat au Plan,* a range of associated and subsidiary agencies for development and research, an extremely efficient informal network between private industry and the Government, and State financial and advisory services which to many foreign industrialists and social scientists are the hallmark of the modern industrial state; whilst alongside one finds a weakened but still vigorous political system, out of touch with modern developments and requirements, still living in the nineteenth century. France has some of the most proficient technological institutions in the world in the *grandes ecoles* preparing administrators, civil servants, managers and technologists alongside one of the most archaic university systems, churning out increasing numbers of disillusioned graduates whose qualifications are irrelevant to social needs. In the eyes of many European industrialists and planners from Franz-Josef Strauss in Germany to Barbara Castle in Britain, France is the country which has most nearly perfected the ideal administrative system. Since coming to power in 1958, the Gaullist regime has streamlined the administration, removed parliamentary blocks to efficiency and clearly delineated responsibility. Yet this supposedly efficient system depended on the acquiescence of a large traditional middle class more interested in small immediate profits and speculation than in planning for the future and long-term industrial expansion. . . .

France has changed enormously since the War. In 1945 France was still a rural country with over 35 per cent of her population directly employed on the land. Her industrial sector was small and concentrated in a very few areas. She was largely dominated by a small-town bourgeoisie. Yet from 1945 to 1966 the percentage of people employed in agriculture declined from 35 per cent to under 15 per cent, a drop greater than any recorded in a comparable period of any Western country in the throes of industrialization. France became an industrial country almost overnight and was changed beyond recognition. She has also undergone a political revolution, the Gaullist *coup d'etat* of 1958, the purpose of which was to solidify the great economic gains made during the 1950s for the middle class and to give France the kind of efficient political system that went along with her new aims.

These aims themselves have been fostered by something the French have called rational or indicative planning. Planning became the official ideology of her industrial expansion. Economic planning was supposed to be the definitive solution to all the political problems which hounded France in the past. The general view was that France had been politically unstable because not enough care was taken in making decisions. Planning would expand the economy, make available a greater number of consumers' goods and thereby lessen tension. If the economy were planned, the heads of the *Commuisariat au Plan* emphasized time and time again to allay the fears of the small businessmen, politics would cease to be contentious and violent. Hence planning assumed that political stability, social satisfaction *and* the modern industrial state's crying need for stable markets and a pliant labour force could be married successfully. In practice things never worked out this way.

Planning is less than useful as a means to decide what is good for a society as a whole. Planning can no more than indicate 'how to' once 'what one wants to do' has been decided. But 'what one wants to do' is the essence of politics. In France, the planners glossed over this problem with the assumption that value and social utility were determined by some inexorable, indeed metaphysical, laws of natural progress. That is, they stated that people do not and cannot decide what they want; only the 'market' can. In the cold light of day, planning required not only the effective neutralization of the trade unions, but was controlled by a meritocracy from which trade unionists were excluded. Under the planning system, the State occupied a role closely aligned to the new industrialists. Amongst its many duties, it had to guarantee and guide investment, which the private sector could no longer do, provide those services and social measures to maintain, equip and train a modern labour force, assure the means of enforcing these policies as well as a network of educational and cultural facilities required by the modern industrial society. The State readily made use of its immense financial powers and of the large nationalized sector to secure expansion, stability, keep down wages and buttress the private sector. But the Fourth Republic did this badly.

It was open to too much influence from those opposed to these changes. For the industrialists and the new generation of managers and planners, the old Gaullist theory, enunciated as early as 1944, of an association between capital and labour was not only a useful slogan to describe their aims but Gaullism was a movement in which they could actively take part. By stressing the need to rejuvenate the 'outmoded and stultified political institutions' of the Fourth Republic, Gaullism paraphrased their ideas about bringing the administrators to power. General de Gaulle's ambiguous rhetoric not only complemented the day-to-day work of the new technocrats labouring behind the scenes like Jacques Chirac and Jacques Foccart but also appealed to the traditional middle class brought up on the profit motive, notions of strict economy and the patriarchal State. This strange combination of the old and the new brought de Gaulle to power in 1958 and his ability to manoeuvre between these camps kept him in power.

Economically and *socially,* the post-1958 Gaullist governments have depended upon the close cooperation between the new industrial sector and government administrators. But *institutionally* and *politically,* Gaullism has depended upon the traditional French middle class. By appealing to continuity, order and tradition, Gaullism secured the support of the traditional middle class and by window-dressing its major decisions with a mask of rhetoric, and in periods of crisis, like the Algerian War, pointing out that the alternative to Gaullism was chaos or the 'totalitarian danger' from the Left, the Gaullists put the seal to an alliance of mutual convenience between two very different groups with very different ambitions.

Gaullism's attraction and power have been based upon a shot-gun marriage. What was the rule of the expert to one group was the rule of tradition and stability to the other. To maintain its alliance, Gaullism tried to make every social and political institution respond to each partner. These institutions were designed to smother the gaping contradiction between the integrated economy sought by the planners and the liberal economics and liberal State espoused by the traditional middle class.

The university was the hothouse of these contradictions. On the one hand, the planners envisaged a revamped university as the training centre for a new generation of scientific managers and demanded it be equipped with modern curriculum and research facilities. People like Marc Zamansky, the Dean of the Science Faculty in Paris, and Rector Capelle called for a technologically based university system. On the other hand, the traditional middle class saw the university as a kind of 'finishing school' where it was not vital to spend vast sums of money on equipment or on revising the classical liberal arts education given by university faculties.

After much pressure from the planners, the secondary-school system was made more vocational. As part of the reform the *baccalaureat* (combination of leaving certificate and entrance examination to university) was slightly changed. But because funds were earmarked for the French nuclear deterrent, to satisfy the vanity of the traditional middle class, there was no provision for financing the reforms and by 1968, the lycee system was in a state of disorganization.

In the eyes of the planners, the traditional notion of representative democracy was outmoded and inefficient and called for changes either through the direct representation of interest groups or by strengthening the hand of the executive and administration. But in the eyes of the traditional middle class Parliament guaranteed a tried and tested system of compromise and bargaining. The Gaullist compromise was to maintain the parliamentary system but with greatly reduced powers.

In its prime the Gaullist State succeeded in discrediting the parliamentary democracy of the Fourth Republic and, more importantly, converted the Communist and Socialist opposition from an opposition that challenged the legitimacy of a capitalist society into a 'loyal and official opposition.' These parties never challenged the basic assumptions of the planners. They merely demanded that the benefits of the consumer society be more widely distributed. They never questioned what was meant by a higher rate of growth and increased productivity. Their trade unions bargained for wages and never considered the question of increasing their role in running their factories and workshops. Because they gave up the idea of changing society, they were geared to assuring peaceful bargaining over wages and conditions in the factory. Whether intentionally or not, the result was that power was kept out of the hands of the rank-and-file unionists to an extent greater than in most other European countries. It is little wonder that trade-union membership has declined since the war, that trade unions have found it difficult to enroll young workers and that France has one of the lowest rates of trade-union membership in Europe (only 20 per cent against 48 per cent in Britain and 35 per cent in Germany). But so long as Gaullism maintained a tolerably high rate of growth, the trade-union leaders were reasonably satisfied and the ordinary worker seemingly apathetic. . . . The traditional opposition ceased to oppose the values of the established political system. It worked within the system and accepted the reforms initiated by the Gaullist regime.

One should not lose sight of the fact that the Gaullist state clearly failed to satisfy the immediate bread-and-butter demands of the great majority of manual workers. Except in the great strikes of 1947 they have not been able to coordinate their actions and in the private sector have been little problem to management. . . . The idea of Revolution was raised only during the early years of the movement's growth and was only resurrected in time of political or structural collapse.

In France the vast majority of the working class fit into this category. Their trade unions are the CGT, closely affiliated to the Communist party and the CGT-FO, a much smaller federation traditionally close to the Socialist movement. Although they never departed from the ideology mentioned above they have acted somewhat differently. Because they have remained small, because the manual working class never accounted for more than 30 per cent of the population, they were never able to obtain the rights and recognition of British trade unionism. Even though their claims were no more than quantitative claims the spirit of revolt was kept alive because they had never been able to secure the most minimal demands. Surrounded by enemies on all sides, French trade unionism never accepted middle-class norms to the extent they were accepted in Britain. It formed its own cultural values and remained stubbornly independent, critical and totally undeferential. . . . In normal times the political organizations representing the manual working class were reformist. Indeed, the PCF was satisfied with an advisory role in the Popular Front Government of 1936 and a minor role in the 1945 Government. When it came to a choice between supporting striking workers and remaining in the Government, the party tried to maintain its ministerial positions. In both 1936 and 1947 the party attempted to stifle the strike movements. Its rationale was that one could not be aggressive to the extent that one endangered the party. But the problem they never solved, and indeed, never spelled out, was that if one did not risk the party organization then one did not fundamentally challenge the capitalist regime. In opposition the PCF plays an unconstructive negative role. Not only does it not draw up a strategy comprised of revolutionary demands, it stifles these demands, for the reason that demands like those for democratic planning proposed by the CGT in the 1950s would upset the balance of power between the party and the trade union, or those like workers' control would mean reorganizing the party.

The PCF is governed by a number of conflicting purposes. It is supposed to be a revolutionary party, the representative of the manual working class. But the manual working class, as we have seen, is not revolutionary in a permanent sense. It is supposed to put forward their immediate demands and has organized itself in a hierarchical and ponderously bureaucratic fashion to do this efficiently. Yet this form of organization defies its revolutionary vocation. . . . Every offensive action of the working class from the sit-in occupations of 1936 to the strikes of 1947, 1966 and 1968 occurred outside and despite the PCF.

But the groups the party represented were potentially revolutionary. If the way were opened for them, if the perspective were made clear, if a spark came from outside, and if they were thrust into a position where they were forced to act, the native receptivity of a genuinely revolutionary working-class culture was there.

The first step toward revolution was taken: everyone ceased to obey, to conform to their social and economic roles. The society was as though liquified, the rigid forms of its institutional structure melted down into their human basis.

The May Events
Andrew Feenberg

Paris: May, 1968 — a revolution which failed. The "Events," as the French called them, are now almost forgotten. French communism prefers to forget a student-led revolt, its own panic, and a humiliating defeat in the elections which followed. Gaullism has buried many of the reforms which grew out of May. It has no desire to cast a backward glance on its own past crisis. Reporting on May in the United States was so inadequate that there is not much to forget here. In any case, the theoreticians of the New Left were uncomfortable with the similarity of May to classical proletarian revolution, no longer supposed to be possible in advanced capitalist society. The rest of the country may remember images of burning autos, heaps of odd little Deux Chevaux, Peugeots, Renaults.

Five years later the student movement is in worldwide decline. It is now obvious that May was the culmination of the rising tide of student activism in the sixties. There were a few later high points: the "Hot Autumn" in Italy in 1969; the reaction to the Cambodian invasion in the United States in 1970. But there has been nothing on the scale of May since, and the sort of radical student movements which emerged in the sixties seem unlikely to go so far again.

For a brief moment May was a symbol, with repercussions in such places as Italy and Mexico. It seemed possible to universalize the model, to initiate offensives from a student base, which would bring strong governments to

---

their knees. Now that is past. May appears simply as an historical event and can be treated as such. One can ask: why did the student movement peak in France in 1968? Some particular characteristics of the French nation at that time must explain it.

The weakest link

According to Lenin, the international political and economic system is like a chain, the strength of the whole depending on the strength of its weakest link. There at the weakest link in the chain, where the system is least able to adapt and keep pace, social and political conflicts may brim over, leading to a violent revolutionary explosion.

Lenin's theory contrasts with that of Marx. In a century when England and France were by far the most advanced countries in the world, Marx asserted that they showed their poorer neighbors the image of their own future. Marx believed that communism had the best chances of success in the most developed countries where the strongest capitalist economies confronted the best organized working classes. The Marxian theory may someday be validated, but in the meantime it is Lenin's metaphor which, since October 1917, has been most useful in understanding revolutionary history.

The analysis of the most advanced country remains extremely important for evaluating the "normal" development of the others, for extrapolating from their present situation their probable future. But at the same time, it should not be forgotten that the Russian Revolution demonstrated that the contradiction between the more advanced countries and their most disadvantaged competitor may be more significant for the latter than all established precedents of development.

In the less advanced countries, lacking the flexibility of wealth and the resiliency of a strong economy, the pressure of competition and responsibilities imposed by a richer neighbor may cause the system to crack. A poorer country which escapes revolution may continue to follow the lead of the most advanced country, but where an accumulation of problems creates a revolutionary situation, it may go under before it can follow the path laid out for it.

All these considerations apply to the case of France in 1968. France was then the weakest link in the *advanced* capitalist chain, the country in which all the strongest pressures and heaviest responsibilities weighed on one of the most outmoded social systems in the West. Slow to make the transition to "consumer" society, with an economy far less modern and efficient than that of Germany, not to mention the United States, France was still the unavowed, but unchallenged, political leader of Europe. The attempt at "Americanizing" France, at creating a streamlined technocracy, was frustrated by a rigid, hierarchical bureaucracy in business and government, and the ever-present threat of a powerful communist opposition justified every conservative resistance to change.

Though France had nuclear weapons, more than half the apartments in its capital lacked hot water. It aspired to the integration of all classes in a prosperous economic life, but its workers had the longest hours and the lowest wages in democratic Europe. Its youth seemed increasingly stultified by the new popular culture, at least to a casual observer, and yet the mystique of "old" Left militancy survived among it. France sponsored a peace negotiation in which an insignificant state was expected to impose recognition of its national independence on the United States, while the French government customarily refused to negotiate with the unions which represented its own citizens.

All this said, it is clear that the weakest link in the chain in 1968 was a great deal stronger than was Russia in 1917. The Gaullist regime survived by sacrificing de Gaulle. France today has surrendered the international role which was so difficult to sustain in the years preceding 1968. Its economy has expanded rapidly since then, while recessions in Germany and the United States have strengthened its relative position. The moment of crisis was not so long nor its cause so deep as one might have supposed at the time. But before the moment passed, the French demonstrated the possibility of revolution in the "affluent" society.

The economic problems of France were due in part to the persistent survival of a huge peasanty and petty bourgeoisie. These classes are neither efficient producers nor distributors. In the context of modern monopoly capitalism, they are dysfunctional groups, doing poorly with limited means, tasks which would be better performed by employees of large corporations. In terms of its class content, monopolistic rationalization and modernization means the liquidation of these survivals of competitive capitalist society. But independent producers and distributors are willing to make tremendous efforts and financial sacrifices to preserve their independence. They can be wiped out rapidly only where the government openly favors their larger competitors through tax laws and subsidies. This the French government, unlike that of the United States or Germany, has never been able to do.

The reasons for the delay in the rationalization of the French economy are quite complex. Small peasant property was a widespread phenomenon in the eighteenth century already, and it increased rather than decreased in the nineteenth. By the time the Third Republic was founded, this huge mass of radical, anti-socialist voters was already strong enough to protect itself politically. Later it was to become the main bulwark of French capitalism in the struggle against the working class. At no point was it possible for the sort of objective alliance of labor and big business which characterized the New Deal to further capitalist rationalization against the will of these groups. Gaullism inherited this same voting base with all its limitations. No more than previous bourgeois governments was it able to mount an aggressive attack on small business and farming. Indeed, after May 1968, de Gaulle seems to have intended just that, with the result that his electoral majority dissolved and an apparently more conciliatory candidate replaced him.

Before the May Events, the Gaullist response to the relative backwardness of the economy was to mobilize the entire force of the state in the fight to hold down workers' wages. The fall of the last trade barriers in the Common Market, projected for the summer of 1968, hung like the Sword of Damocles over the French economy. Huge investment programs were initiated to prepare for this eventuality at the expense of the working class. Workers suffered indirectly too, as housing, road construction, and other public service projects were slighted for subsidies to heavy industry in the race against time and the Germans.

But competition with other Common Market nations was only a part of the problem. Competition with the United States, with its crushing economic superiority, was still more intolerable for the French. American business controlled numerous patents essential to production in the advanced sectors of the economy. The very symbols of French economic prestige, such as the Mirage jet and the SECAM color television system are tributary of American patents. In some cases, American foresight and a more risk-oriented business mentality enabled American corporations to obtain important patents from Europeans and then to license applications in Europe itself. The brain drain, which was still an important fact of life in 1968, also gave the United States an advantage in this area. As the richest capitalist nation and the center of research and development for all of them, the United States gained immense advantages. Many European writers, notably Jean Jacques Servan Schreiber, proclaimed that the "technological gap" between their countries combined and ours alone would never be erased.

Furthermore, American corporations could buy European ones easily, with over-valued dollars or with money raised in Europe and put at the disposal of American enterprise. Thus American business rapidly penetrated every Western European nation, bringing whole sectors of production, such as computers, into its orbit. The export of profits from these European subsidiaries of American corporations hurt, but worse yet, combined with American technological superiority, it promised a sort of neo-colonial exploitation of Europe by America. It is not so easy to remember now, since the dollar crisis, the sense of inferiority and defeat of nations like France only a few years ago, confronted with the economic might of the United States.

Journalists and historians like to find the source of de Gaulle's anti-Americanism in his unhappy relations with Roosevelt. This no doubt influenced de Gaulle's personal feelings, but for those feelings to be translated into policies and acts of state more was required than a thirty-year-old private feud. The economic situation of Europe in fact justified and rendered politically rational the personal feelings of the man, de Gaulle. All Europe suffered the humiliation of American economic domination, and all Europe agreed tacitly with de Gaulle that the solution lay in more trade with Russia, Eastern Europe, China, and the Third World, trade based on a political stance independent of the United States. Thus while de Gaulle made the speeches, the Italians and the West Germans multiplied business deals with new partners on an unprecedented scale.

Yet it was only in France that the speeches could be made. It is obvious that no German or Italian leader could make anti-American statements without appearing to be ungrateful for post-war help, without, indeed, appearing to wave the Nazi or the fascist banner. Britain remained tied to the Commonwealth and therefore to the only military power capable of protecting it — the United States. France alone could assume the role of spokesman for a new, independent Europe and this it did in the person of de Gaulle. His rhetoric, anti-colonial and nationalistic, was like that of the chief of state of some under-developed country. But de Gaulle was nationalistic not just for France but for all nations, nationalistic not from some nostalgia for days gone by but from a sense of the future, of the polic-entric world coming into being. So he was cheered in Poland, Quebec, the Arab world, and Latin America for identifying his cause with that of all peoples dominated by stronger powers.

All this is not to make a hero of de Gaulle. He combined a relatively progressive foreign policy with a reactionary domestic policy, in an amalgam which corresponded precisely with the interests of French capitalism. And it was the French people who paid the price of his *politique de grandeur*. Atom bombs, foreign aid, and political turnabouts cost money which might have been used to improve public services, education, and medical care. Universities were overcrowded, civil servants and workers underpaid, social security benefits and national health insurance reduced. All this seemed too high a price to pay for a dubious greatness.

The State against the society

Every system of domination permits a certain limited autonomy to those under its sway, beyond which initiative is transgression and the violence of the dominators the ultimate argument for submission. Systems of domination are by nature "over-extended." They all push their boundaries well beyond the safe limit within which the united opposition of the dominated would prove insufficient to overthrow them.

In all such systems social time and space are discontinuous and fragmented, while that of the state is continuous and unified. The empire is united and its conquest divided, and thus the homogeneous dominating group gets the better of heterogeneous and mutually isolated peoples whose individual rebellions cannot stand up to imperial power one-by-one, one after another. Between each revolt there is no connection except that established in defeat through the intermediary of the state which confronts them both. Thus the unity of the empire is the guarantee of the essential continuity of domination and power that underlies the discontinuity of protest and rebellion. Even though united action by the dominated would represent an unconquerable force, the genius of the empire is able to keep them under control precisely by preventing their union. Only a solidarity transcending the space and time of domination could shake the empire. The constant concern of those in power is therefore to maintain the conditions of their control by shattering all solidarity among the oppressed, reducing their challenge to manageable components, subject to instrumental manipulation.

This basic image of imperial power serves just as well to explain the operation of the state, in conflict with the society it rules, as it does more obvious forms of international domination such as colonialism. In the case of the Gaullist state, no better image could be found, as is clear when the technocratic mask falls and the raw opposition of social forces brings out the true nature of French society. Indeed, so true is this that after May, de Gaulle, already famous for having decolonized France's African empire, was said to be preparing a corresponding "domestic decolonization." But no such benevolent intentions were manifested before the Events. The French lived under a system based on the maxim "divide and conquer," applied within rather than without and masked by a technocratic ideology.

It should be said that de Gaulle's republican authoritarianism was nothing new for France. France has a heritage of geographical concentration of power and wealth in Paris, and Paris itself has for centuries been a social pyramid leading up to the intoxicating position of Monarch, Emperor, Premier or President, depending upon the prevailing constitution. The Fourth Republic had been a brief interlude of government with a weak executive branch and a correspondingly increased parliamentary and public participation in political life. De Gaulle's Fifth Republic consisted chiefly in de Gaulle. All others were clients, courtiers or impotent enemies of the regime.

The pyramid of power rose to a single individual who not only claimed to be the right man for the job, but the only qualified one. Opposition in the parliament was dismissed as mere remnants of the old "system of parties," and opposition in the press and the population was taken as disloyal nay-saying. De Gaulle, in his own eyes, was no ordinary leader but the nation personified. From this point of view no legitimate disagreement with de Gaulle could possibly arise.

Although the advantages of such a system for a ruler are obvious, the disadvantages may well outweigh them. Responsible for all decisions, de Gaulle was responsible for all failures and errors. Irreplaceable by the normal democratic process because of the absence of a real alternative within it, de Gaulle could only be replaced outside it. Contemptuous of dissent, de Gaulle could not compromise with it. The pyramid was stable so long as it stood on its base, but turned over it teetered and nearly toppled.

De Gaulle had a political style as Chief of State which exaggerated the worst features of French bureaucracy while expanding its dominion. The corporate bureaucracy was centralized rapidly under his rule, as state-supported business mergers concentrated French industry to keep pace with the great German and American giants. The university hierarchy received a technocratic face-lift (the "Fouchet Reform") which left it essentially as it had been when Napoleon first created it. The government bureaucracy increasingly centralized all political power, channelling it up to the cabinet, itself responsible to de Gaulle. The nationalized radio-television was supervised by a special committee of cabinet ministers, which paid particular attention to the content of news broadcasts. ("They have the press, we have the televison," de Gaulle is said to have remarked.) And just before May, the powers of local governments, already small, were reduced still further.

In a difficult economic situation, caused in part by inefficient bureaucracy, the government responded with bureaucratic solutions. To compensate for their competitive disadvantage and the relatively small scale of many of their corporations, the French introduced a modicum of central economic planning. Le Plan was a set of predictions and directives worked out by economists in consultation with business, some union, and government leaders. It was designed to chart the course of the economy over a five-year period. Its strictures were never obligatory, but they were influential. In any case, they corresponded to a whole mentality, which made the operation of the economy a matter of public policy and the state an obvious and unblushing ally of big business.

Already at the top of the hierarchy of government, education, and mass communications, de Gaulle also seemed to assume direct responsibility for the economy through the plan. Economic life was politicized and the pattern of economic development of the nation as a whole open to political criticism. Thus where le Plan predicted 500,000 unemployed, the unemployed knew who to blame for their plight; not just their former boss, but de Gaulle as well.

The state was strong under de Gaulle, stronger than it had been in France since Louis Napoleon. Its autonomy and power had been a necessary condition for de Gaulle's accomplishments: the termination of the ruinous colonial crises and the creation of economic and political stability for the middle class. But the extremely authoritarian, bureaucratic form of the state was just as important as its acts. The refusal of social spontaneity and even of the collegiality of liberal management theory corresponded with the opposition of de Gaulle's goals and those of the population as a whole. Bureaucratic control from above was just the other side of implicit and anticipated opposition from below. De Gaulle, as the embodiment of the national interest was also first among French bureaucrats, a dominating power experienced by the mass of the population, even by many of those who voted for him as a ruler and not as a representative.

Of course de Gaulle was elected, but for various reasons many Frenchmen felt that they had no alternative to him: at the time of the Liberation, he ruled as the head of the Free French; in 1958 he was the only alternative to fascism; in 1965 the opposition candidate, Francois Mitterrand, represented an electoral alliance of socialists and communists who had not even worked out a common program. De Gaulle was fully aware of these facts and did not hesitate to bring them forth in his defense, daring the French to do without him.

It was on this basis that de Gaulle refused to recognize the legitimacy of the opposition. His government was confident that no coherent alternative to its policies could be defined. The Communist Party and working class revolution appeared as the only basis for a consistent opposition policy. But there were comforting signs of a "pacification" of the class struggle. The workers seemed to be settling down. The unions had not been able to unite against the government or the corporations to make their strikes really hurt in many years. The power of the state had become so great that no one dared offer it a serious challenge outside the parliament which it controlled.

Gaullism was also confident of victory over the communists on the electoral terrain. Before May, if the Left could hope to win the next elections, it had nevertheless become increasingly difficult to convincingly propose the socialist solution to the problems of the nation. The Left still drew many votes but nowhere near so much enthusiasm as in the past. Communist militancy, both rhetorical and real, was steadily declining. The Gaullists congratulated themselves on these signs of ideological decadence and decreasing combativity of the working class and its party. They must have felt they had a fairly clear field, even if some hard fights remained to be won in the next few years.

In fact no common ideological front against Gaullism could be constructed. The opposition of the population was thus condemned to remain in the form of particular protests in behalf of particular interests. No new concept of the national interest, based on mutual agreement between opposition groups, could be opposed to that of de Gaulle. This is not to say that Frenchmen failed to fight for their interests against de Gaulle. On the contrary. But each group presented itself alone and isolated. Also, without a general program of change, they were more often than not compelled to retreat before the government's plans. It was also easy for the state to discourage solidarity between the different interests by showing up each one to the others as an egoistic particularism. The Strong State did not retreat before opposition, which in its eyes was little more than treason to the nation. Instead, the government judged the measured progress of every sector of national life and, to use the French term, "parachuted" in reforms and wage increases wherever they fit into the plan. Moreover, where particular interests persisted in asserting themselves, the ultimate argument of the Strong State, the police, was always ready to intervene to re-establish "order."

Thus the Gaulist state gradually became a sort of legal dictatorship based on: the division of its enemies, the fear inspired by its communist opposition, its political and economic successes, and finally its police. The government seems to have believed that the increasing prosperity and prestige of the nation could be relied on to slowly quiet those clamoring for change without understanding its "laws," eventually leading the population to passive submission to a successful and benevolent paternalism. Meanwhile, the Strong State played its hand, gambling on the future wealth and prestige it was preparing by present sacrifices, on nationalistic pride, the division of its enemies, and the passivity of the people.

Perhaps this system would have been accepted by the population had it had a more active political role in determining the policies it was supposed to obey. No doubt these conditions which were tied to an enormous progress over the immediate post-war period, would not have inspired violent reactions in a country without revolutionary traditions. And of course, a society which was not saturated with the idea and the aspiration of prosperity might well have been content with a relative amelioration of its economic situation. But the propaganda of affluence and consumer society creates tensions among large groups excluded from the feast of plenty. Moreover, the French did resent their exclusion from the great decisions of their nation, and have a revolutionary tradition which is, as the month of May proved, still quite alive.

Communists and students

Until May 1968, it seemed quite impossible to imagine any great movement for fundamental change in France without the communists at its head. Foes of Gaullism from the beginning, party of the working class, state within a state, the communists seemed destined to be the core of all opposition so long as they were not in power. But the French Communist Party has a long and checkered history of cycles of great failures and surprising comebacks, which always fall short of success. The terror of the bourgeoisie for more than a generation, they never committed an unequivocally revolutionary act against it. Aware that a revolution which fails is as horrible for the proletariat as is a revolution which succeeds for the bourgeoisie, they have been cautious, biding their time till their forces were strong and united and the situation ripe. The auspicious moment has been long in coming.

The nearest thing to it before May was the general strike of 1936. This period of turbulence promised revolutionary changes in France. But the Party did not have a parliamentary majority and refused to encourage the workers to seize power by more direct means. Instead, the communists aided the moderate socialist Leon Blum, whose Popular Front government they shored up in the Chamber of Deputies. This government facilitated the return to normal and granted many union demands.

The great crisis passed without a revolution. Maurice Thorez justified the decision to let the opportunity pass in the following words:

> We do not have the entirety of the population in the countryside behind us, ready as we are to go all the way. We would even risk alienating the sympathy of some sectors of the petty bourgeoisie and the peasants of France in certain cases. So? . . . So, we must learn to end a strike as soon as we have obtained satisfaction. We must even learn to accept a compromise if all our demands have not yet been accepted, once we have obtained victory on the most essential demands.

A vast popular movement followed this advice and permitted its energies to be dissipated in negotiations.

Perhaps nothing more could have been accomplished in the context of that time. Certainly the Popular Front movement was a great and heroic one, which cannot be belittled. Yet the performance of the communists in 1936 reflected all the ambiguities of their style of politics. They constantly made references to revolution and appealed to extra-parliamentary forces, at least until recently, but were not really willing to push for a total confrontation. They ended up with the disadvantages inherent in being an electoral party and a revolutionary organization at the same time, instead of getting the most out of both strategic positions.

In the last decade this ambiguity has been steadily disappearing. The communists have developed a new approach, based on complete commitment to a peaceful and democratic take-over, without revolutionary afterthoughts. Communist Party theoreticians were convinced that monopolistic modernization would generate increasingly intense conflict between small proprietors and large ones. This tendency promised a sharp turn to the Left by groups such as the petty bourgeoisie and peasants which had traditionally looked to the Center and the Right for leadership. The electoral base for a new popular front was coming into being, and moderate socialist parties could expect to swell with new voters, enlarging them to the point where a communist-socialist alliance would embrace a majority of the population.

In response to this analysis, the Communist Party revamped its image, playing up its past respect for the democratic process, and loudly announcing its willingness to continue this policy in the future. The communists attempted to broaden their appeal by proposing moderate and democratic reforms of many social institutions, designed to improve the economic situation of the poor and the not-so rich. Meanwhile, their socialist allies went off to battle with an even more moderate image and worked to unify themselves in a single party capable of holding its own in a popular front government.

Together the two partners came within a few percent of a majority in the elections of 1967, the Communists with a healthy 22.5 percent of the total vote. But the appearance of unity masked very real, unresolved differences. The communists still called for much more extensive nationalizations than the socialists; the socialists still had a mildly pro-American, anti-Soviet foreign policy. No common program could be worked out under these conditions. In fact, neither partner to the alliance was convinced of the sincerity of the other, the communists doubting the commitment of the socialists to a popular front, the socialists doubting the commitment of the communists to democracy.

The communists' abandonment of revolutionary rhetoric and the general lack of enthusiasm for a moderate program had the apparently minor disadvantage of encouraging the formation of extreme-Left groups on the radical fringe of the new popular front. Trotskyism revived and a new deviation, Maoism was added to the list. The Communist Party and its union federation, the CGT (Confédération générale du travail), resisted the inroads of these left-wing vigilantes, excluding them from political meetings and driving them away from the factory gates. This was, of course, necessary, if the communists were successfully to maneuver toward their right without losing their hold on the workers to their left.

By May 1968 the struggle against "leftism" was in full swing. Thrown back on themselves, the extreme Left groups (dubbed *"groupuscules"* by their opponents) had developed a characteristic mentality, as anti-communist as anti-capitalist, as opposed to one another as to the Gaullist regime, as violent in words as impotent in action. With perhaps several thousand militants to their credit, they were doomed to fail in the task they had set for themselves: winning the workers' confidence and leading a revolution. Their agitation excited only indifference in the mass of the population, thoroughly committed to traditional democracy, or uninterested in the bombastic verbalism of powerless mini-vanguards.

What eventually gave these groups an importance was their close relationship to the student milieu from which they sprang. For they were products, of a peculiar variety to be sure, of the same conditions and problems which during May radicalized the mass of French students. It was, then, not so much the *groupuscules* which led the student movement, but the student movement which, during May, gave small vanguard sects an historical task and with it a new lease on life.

For many years the French student movement had been aware of the inevitability of some sort of crisis in the university. One tendency of this movement explained the crisis as a part of the larger class struggle. For these theorists, students were rapidly being transformed from a privileged elite into a cultural proletariat, turned out on the diploma assembly line, threatened by unemployment, deprived of all voice in the management of their place of work. On the Left of the Communist Party, there were some who sympathized with this position. But during the years immediately preceding the May Events, the consolidation of Gaullist technocracy seemed to discredit their views. The students were more and more thought to be interested only in their own personal advancement, in fashions, and in rock-and-roll. The student unions themselves very active in national politics in the past began to decline, and in some cases to tie themselves to narrow corporatist programs of reform.

But this was only a temporary situation. The university had eventually to be adapted to its changed function in the society, and this adaptation finally revealed to the students themselves what only a few theorists had known a few years before. The "Fouchet Reform" played this eminently pedagogical role. It was supposed to adapt French higher education, along American lines, to the needs of the society, harmonizing the "production" of the university with the prevailing economic demand for competence. A new method of selection was to be introduced to eliminate the current "over-production" of the universities, particularly in the humanities, where unemployment already plagued recent graduates. The reform, in spite of pretensions to liberalism, in no way improved the quality of student life. The often denounced "mandarin" system, for example, in which a few top professors dominate their subordinates while avoiding all contact with the students, was maintained intact. The Fouchet Reform was not only contested and refused from the beginning by the politically active students and their union, but it was so incompetently applied that dissatisfaction quickly spread to the mass of students.

This attempt at imposing increased regimentation and diploma-line speed-up, combined with the prospect of future unemployment, showed French students that they lay somewhere closer to the bottom than to the top of the social hierarchy. But to the extent that the conservative political and economic system of France seemed solidly in place, a desire for change frustrated at home was translated, first into an enthusiastic solidarity with those fighting beyond the borders, and second, into a desire to imitate their violent methods of struggle. Movements and demonstrations in support of the Vietnamese, Che Guevara, and German student revolutionaries sprouted up, and the intense struggle of the underdogs for power in the Third World encouraged the students themselves to pass to action in defense of their interests. Needless to say, the turn to the Right of the French Communist Party did not appear to these new Leftists as a positive factor, but more as a confirmation of their suspicion that no really revolutionary movement was possible in France.

In sum, the students found that no adequate expression for their unease and no adequate defense of their interests existed anywhere in the society. An enormous tension was built up which had no outlet, as the government's reforms led to a worsening situation and the sphere of direct, potentially revolutionary action against the society was foreclosed by the communists. And with no buffers of authority standing between de Gaulle and his Minister of Education, on the one hand, and the victimized students, on the other hand, the issues in the university quickly took on a political character. Soon the university was ripe for rebellion. And once this link in the social chain had broken, the others followed, one by one, until the whole society was rocked from top to bottom.

The revolution in the revolution

France is not the only country with a Communist Party committed to a legal, electoral strategy. In fact, in this respect the French Party follows the line adopted by many pro-Soviet parties throughout the world. The Chinese and the Cubans argued actively in the sixties for an alternative strategy of armed struggle, and this alternative was defended in the West by the rising

Left movements which appeared outside the communist parties in this period. In 1968 the debate over Maoist and Guevarist violent revolutionary strategies was very lively. The "peaceful way to socialism" was under constant attack everywhere.

It was Regis Debray's contribution to this debate which had, in the context of the May Events, the broadest impact and the greatest relevance. In *Revolution in the Revolution* Debray argued for the Cuban strategy of immediate armed struggle in Latin America. For him, the principal lesson of the Cuban Revolution is the proof that the official communist parties are not necessarily the revolutionary vanguard of their societies. The argument does not sound particularly impressive in the United States today, but in countries with strong communist parties implanted in the working class, it is difficult to reject the heritage of past revolutionary struggles and start afresh. To do so goes against a deep instinct of revolutionaries, who live in a world where unity in struggle is so vital that it deserves to be preserved even at the cost of many compromises.

Cuba was actually the first place in which the position for which Debray argued paid off. There a communist revolution was led by a group without party affiliation, over the head of the official Communist Party. Castro concluded from this experience: "Who will make the revolution in Latin America? Who? The people, the revolutionaries, with or without the Party." Debray comments,

> Fidel Castro simply says that there is no revolution without a vanguard: that this vanguard is not necessarily the Marxist-Leninist Party, and that those who wish to make the Revolution have the right and the duty to constitute themselves as a vanguard, independently of these parties.[1]

This is the "revolution in the revolution," and it came to France in May.

It all began in Nanterre, a new university in the suburbs of Paris. Tired of talking for nothing year after year, several *groupuscules* at Nanterre united on a common program of action. They agreed to disagree on the big theoretical questions and set to work on some concrete local problems. They named their organization the March 22nd Movement, after the date on which they had occupied the campus administration building. They then set about radicalizing the university in a way new to France. They interrupted classes to give speeches on Vietnam, agitated constantly among the dormitory students, and went out in force to the nearby factories and slums. They gradually created an atmosphere in which the university could not function "normally."

A series of weak-minded decisions by administration and government followed. Police were called on campus, classes cancelled, and an attempt made to stamp out the radicals. But the steady escalation of state violence

against the students only succeeded in moblizing them in ever-increasing and
more combative numbers. Soon the official student union and the professors'
union were forced to take a stand, and they supported the movement, further
isolating the authorities.

Throughout the first days of the crisis the Communist Party denounced
the activities of the March 22nd Movement as "adventurist provocations,"
which could only succeed in closing the university. The communists
evidenced a touching concern for the rights of the great majority of serious
students who desired to take their exams. The leaders of the Movement,
Dany Cohn-Bendit in particular, were pilloried daily in the communist press
in terms surprisingly similar to those of the Right. Cohn-Bendit was called a
"German anarchist" by the communists and a "Jewish troublemaker" by the
fascists. The communist paper *L'Humanite* joined a rising chorus of attacks
on the "small minority," the "dozen *enrages*" who were the cause of all the
trouble. What the communists could not understand was that their
traditional "adventurist" foes had become something more than a few
scattered obsessives of the revolutionary verb. They had become, in fact, the
vanguard of a mass student movement on an unprecedented scale. In this
context, the distinction which the communists, like the government, made
between the "good" students, who wanted university reform, and the few
"bad" ones, out for revolution, could not possibly impress anyone. As for the
communists' stated fear that the whole movement had been engineered by the
government or the C.I.A. in order to discredit the official Left, was simply
laughable in the existing situation.

The students, who were now demonstrating by the thousands and the tens
of thousands, felt they had a cause of their own, and not only resented being
accused of falling under evil influences, but even identified with and
supported these very influences. Thus, the students responded ironically to
the often repeated insults addressed to their leaders. They had become,
thousands strong, a giant *groupuscule,* a horde of "Left-wing adventurists,"
as the original few swelled with the youth of Paris. And so, they cried out as
they marched through the streets in mile-long columns. "We are a
groupuscule," "A dozen *enrages,*" "We are all German Jews."

The night of May 10 to 11, thousands of students and young workers who
had come to join them, built barricades in the Latin Quarter, fought against
all odds, and were brutally beaten by the police. This event caused a
shockwave of indignation throughout France. Suddenly, the divided society
was able to unite in anger at this intolerable treatment of its young. Acting
together for the first time in years, the various social groups of which the
society was composed broke through the barriers to unity and, out of
solidarity with the fighting students, threatened to demonstrate and strike for

an end to Gaullism.

The communists were finally forced to moderate their attacks to the Left for a time and offered some support for the more moderate student demands and for an end to police repression. They participated in mobilizing the enormous solidarity strike-demonstration on May 13, in which nearly a million people, many of them workers, marched together. To cut off the growing movement, the government offered concessions to the students, such as the re-opening of the Sorbonne. But public outrage could not be silenced so easily. It is very dangerous for the Strong State to retreat, for its retreat signals to all enemies the existence of an efficacious form of action, and gives them the courage to employ it. Compromise, offered too late by a regime which rarely employs it does not excuse its past errors and re-establish confidence, but demonstrates its vulnerability.

Thus, when the students trooped back into the Sorbonne on May 13, it was not with the intention of returning to their books and their exams. They did not feel that it had all been an unfortunate misunderstanding. "Socialist revolution" and not "University reform" was now the slogan which mobilized the masses of students and, surprisingly, they received an answering call from thousands of workers who began to strike and to occupy their factories all over France.

A general strike gradually paralyzed France, spreading through the factories, the bureaucracies, and the mass media. The society declared war on the state, as everyone simultaneously presented their own particular demands and vented their grievances. The first step toward revolution was taken; everyone ceased to obey, to conform to their social and economic roles. The society was as though liquified, the rigid forms of its institutional structure melted down into their human basis.

But for this crisis to become a successful revolution, the people in revolt had to be able to unite behind a real *political* alternative to Gaullism, an alternative which integrated the solutions to their specific problems in a new concept of the society as a whole. Furthermore, leaders representing such an alternative would have had to structure an attack by the movement on the existing government which, however weakened by social upheaval, stood as a permanent potential source of civil war and repression so long as it was not overthrown. It was precisely these elements which were lacking in May.

The students, knowing their own weakness all too well, did not propose their own revolutionary candidacy, but called for the workers to seize power. The workers turned to their party, the Communist Party, to press the movement forward to victory. But the Party responded by discouraging revolution. Fixated in an electoral strategy, without a real common program with the socialists, locked in a verbal struggle with the forces in the street, the communists were in no position to lead a revolution. Pursuing their analysis of French society, they persisted in believing that they could come to power by free and regular elections. A revolution in France in 1968 seemed like an absurdity to them, those who proposed it like hopeless romantics or even government agents. As far as they could see, the chances of profiting from the situation created by the students were slim, the risks of trying enormous. The "capital" of revolution had become too great to invest in such a risky venture.

Afraid that the striking workers would be isolated and crushed by the rest of the population, they attempted to terminate the crisis as quickly as possible, converting the political and social issues raised on the places of work into purely economic demands for higher wages and shorter hours. But de Gaulle could have asked no greater favor from his old enemies, the communists. The movement could only constitute itself as a revolutionary one by transcending the fragmentation of particular interests and struggling around social and political themes. The communist strategy, to the extent that it tended to shatter all such unity and reduce all the various struggles to particular operational components such as higher wages, recreated in the midst of a near-revolutionary crisis, the very conditions of Gaullist rule. Thus, when the Party forced through negotiations with the government and the bosses, and agreed to shift the terrain of struggle from the streets and the factories to the ballot box, it multiplied the faltering power of the state to the measure of the crisis. Under the impact of the combined pressure of the government and the communists, the revolutionary tide receded and soon "order" was restored.

In the end it is difficult not to sympathize with the skeptical students, convinced that the Party betrayed the revolution from opportunism and cowardliness. In fact, things were no doubt much more complicated. It is true that during the crisis certain important classes remained on the sidelines, or rallied around de Gaulle. The peasants failed to move decisively and the petty bourgeoisie was, on the whole, hostile to the movement. Furthermore, many workers were themselves unprepared for a revolution, a fact not independent of the electoralist position of the Party. The communists were also right to point out that the bourgeoisie was not so weak and divided as to be incapable of mobilizing a counter-attack against the Movement. To this extent, they were right to fear the isolation of the workers, particularly in the context of a classical insurrectionist strategy.

However, the Party drew astonishing conclusions from these elementary considerations: that the Movement should be fought ideologically every inch of the way, that the students had to be everywhere cut off from contact with the workers, that the force of the Movement should be spent and squandered on an inflationary wage settlement which would inevitably fail to raise the standard of living of the working class significantly, and that the only meaningful terrain of struggle prepared by the movement could be an electoral one. Conclusions such as these proceeded from an incredibly narrow and ultimately conservative vision of the class struggle, not simply from a wise prudence in the face of possible disaster.

It is true, of course, that the communists avoided the worst with their strategy: a white terror and the dismantling of all working class organizations. But since when does revolutionary prudence mean castrating revolutionary movements in order to preserve "revolutionary" parties? It was, of course, desirable to avoid a premature insurrection under unfavorable conditions, but the Movement could have been allowed to expand and to unfold its potentialities, generating new forms of struggle and new organizational links between different sectors of the population, preparing the ground for an active fight after the termination of the strike. It is difficult to believe that this was impossible, that only an objective alliance of the communists and the capitalist state could have avoided a civil war.

Examples of tactics that might have been employed are numerous. The May Events showed that under advanced capitalist conditions, students, educated employees, executives, engineers, skilled technicians, journalists, are potential allies of the working class. It simultaneously showed that the old reticence of small farmers and businessmen is still as strong as ever in the past. This was a new factor in the situation which the communists failed to comprehend. In effect, if the traditional reluctant allies of the proletariat are being replaced today by new and more enthusiastic ones, then the establishment of contacts between these latter and the working class, the development of unitary grass roots organizations and strategic conceptions should be a primary goal of a revolutionary party. The May Events opened the possibility of establishing new relations in struggle between mental and manual labor in France. The communists fought to create an atmosphere in which such contacts would be impossible.

Again: in a country where economic objectives are determined by a master plan set up by government experts, it would have been possible assuming the necessity of a negotiated settlement of the general strike to use the force of the Movement to impose important and coherent alterations in the economy. The struggle for a sort of "counter-plan" would have transformed working class solidarity in the strike from a sentiment into a consequence of a deeper socialist rationality, which could have been understood by the entire population as signifying the readiness of the working class to create a new and better society.

At another level, the Party's strategy, by its fearful refusal of confrontation, placed the Movement in a weak and impotent position. The *minimum* immediate *political* goal of the Movement should have been de Gaulle's departure, the election of a compromise Leftist candidate to the presidency, and the continuation under this new regime of the struggles begun in May on a long term basis. Had the Movement been more aggressive throughout, it might have been able to obtain this result.

Legislative elections, such as those which de Gaulle granted in July, corresponded to no possible goal of the Movement. Gerrymandering and the participation of irregularly elected representatives from the colonies make the Chamber of Deputies an instrument of the government. Presidential elections in France are the only ones in which the majority really rules. This is all the more true in a situation such as the crisis of May and June. For the French constitution is so set up that it would really be impossible to run the country if the President were not of the same party as the parliamentary majority. Furthermore, the President of the French Republic has the power to rule by decree in a crisis situation. Knowing all this, a people frightened by the prospect of revolution and civil war could not be expected to prolong and intensify the crisis by voting in a parliament which would paralyze the government and invite a state of martial law.

The mere fact that de Gaulle was able to hang on to power predetermined the results: it gave the Right a rallying point and left it in control of the levers of the state during the elections, while forcing the Left to terminate the movement and to battle feebly from outside the corridors of power for entry. The Left entered the elections divided and confused, discredited both by its refusal to seize power and by its half-way flirtation with revolution.

In the final analysis, the real "betrayal" of the French Communist Party lay in its total lack of trust in the unfolding Movement around it. Every trace of revolutionary spontaneity and combativity had to come from outside the Party and struggle against it. Every new organization at the factory or neighborhood level, every new crossing of social barriers in the formation of new links of solidarity between different strata of the population met its disapprobation. Rarely has a communist party taken the bitter and cynical tone of the French one to discuss a movement of this magnitude occurring at its own doorstep. Rarely has a communist party been so alien to revolutionary history in the making.

The lessons of May were learned: thousands of Communist Party members quit in disillusionment and dismay shortly after the Events. In the months that followed, thousands of others joined, their anti-capitalist but non-revolutionary consciousness finding an exact counterpart in the Communist Party. Similarly, after May, the *groupuscules* grew by leaps and bounds to perhaps ten times their original size. But the attempt to build a revolutionary party alongside the Communist Party has not been very successful. The combined repressive force of the communists and the state has frustrated it at every turn.

Since May the French bourgeoisie has run scared. It first attempted to co-opt as much of the reformist content of the Movement as it could, to use the Movement as a lever for the monopolistic rationalization of the society. The Gaullists announced that they were the "Imagination in Power" for which the students had called. The failure of this experiment led to de Gaulle's fall from power. . . .

The naive self-certainty of the hey-day of Gaullism is over, as is the equally naive self-certainty of an opposition which once appeared to be sincerely committed to the overthrow of capitalism. If the May Events have left a permanent mark on France, it is at the very least in this way: by eliminating all equivocation and ambiguity from the situation, by making common knowledge the insights of a few, by spreading a veritable plague of lucidity which must ultimately be subversive of both the government and the opposition.

Whether May was otherwise a dead-end, like the revolutions of 1848, or a precursor, like 1905 in Russia, that is another question which this essay does not pretend to answer.

Chile has not frightened them; the lesson they draw is to go slowly. One hears, "France is not Chile," as if that settled the matter once and for all.

Socialism in France?
The "Common Program" and
The Future of the French Left
Andrew Feenberg

Toward a Common Program

The Electoral Platform of the French left is contained in *The Common Program of Government of the Communist Party and the Socialist Party.* . . .[1]

From "Socialism in France? The Common Program and the Future of the French Left," by Andrew Feenberg, *Social Revolution,* January-March, 1974, copyright © 1974 and reprinted by permission of the publisher.

Signed on June 27, 1972, the Common Program was the outcome of a long struggle that more often opposed than united the two parties involved. . . .

What kind of life is promised by the Common Program? The program is not wholly socialist, but it does rest on the nationalization of the largest corporations. All banks, savings and loan associations, and insurance companies will be taken over by the state. All mineral resources, the armament industry, space and aeronautics industries, and nuclear and pharmaceutical industries will be nationalized. Most of the electronic and chemical companies will be taken over. In other sectors the state will buy stock, in some cases a majority of it, as in steel, oil, air and sea transport, water purification, telecommunications and privately owned highways. All this will enlarge a public sector that already includes railroads, the telephone, television and radio, a large part of the automobile industry, gas and electricity. Economic planning in the public sector will be democratized and decentralized to include the participation of local political representatives, workers, and consumers. In addition, strict exchange controls will be introduced to protect the franc, and capital movements of multi-national companies will be supervised carefully by the government.

These extensive nationalizations and controls would seriously weaken the power of the largest capitalist groups in France. With the economic might of the state so reinforced, broad changes in social life could be made.

In the economic sphere the Common Program calls for full employment and a rising standard of living. But what is perhaps more important, it proposes an end to wage discrimination based on age, sex, and nationality, and a minimum wage which will be increased more rapidly than higher wages. New laws will govern work pace, limit night shifts, and restrict the amount of time a worker can be assigned to the hardest and most dangerous work. Research on more humane technologies will begin. Workers employed at the most painful and boring jobs will benefit from a reduced work load at equal pay, and the time freed can be used for job training in more interesting work.

The rights of the petite bourgeoisie and the peasantry will be protected and extended in the context of general economic modernization. Small farmers will be favored at the expense of agri-business, and the government will encourage the formation of production and distribution cooperatives and the utilization of the best available technology. Similarly, small shopkeepers, craftsmen, and middle-sized business will be protected from capitalist concentration. The tax structure will be reformed to place more of the burden on larger corporations. The government will make generous loans to small businesses that want to modernize or band together in cooperatives. The spread of department stores and supermarkets controlled by the monopolies will be slowed, and small business owners will be helped to form large-scale cooperative centers of distribution.

Only big business and the very wealthy are attacked in the Common Program. These groups will have to pay higher taxes and contribute to the solution of the transportation and pollution problems that they have created.

The Common Program promises free and adequate medical care, while preserving the right of patients to choose their doctors and the freedom of doctors to continue as private practitioners. Sick pay will be increased to normal salaries. Elected councils will govern the social security system, which administers both pensions and medical insurance.

In other spheres, collective needs will be given a high priority. City planning will attempt to equalize the growth of the various urban centers and insure all of them adequate services. (At present Paris dominates and plunders the nation.) An effort will be made to insure that class segregation does not increasingly divide the population into homogeneous neighborhoods. The government will promote the construction of 700,000 dwellings a year, restore old quarters, and guarantee those displaced by urban renewal the right to resettle in the same area that they used to live in.

Tenant unions will be recognized and will hold a majority of the seats on the administrative councils of public housing projects. Tenant and local governmental representatives will join the boards of directors of private construction companies working on government contracts. Public transport will be financed by the state and by a progressive tax on companies situated in the region served. Where public transport already exists, employers will pay for its work-related use by their employees.

The schools will be used to struggle against existing cultural inequalities. All education will be nationalized and free, and students will receive a small salary based on need and, to a lesser extent, on achievement. Class size will be reduced and special tutoring will be developed. Religious education in the schools will be abolished. Civics courses will be made relevant by the consideration of the problems of economic and social life, international affairs, and the problems of imperialism.

The distinction between technical and academic high schools will be gradually eliminated, so that all young people can receive a broad education. New laws will remunerate workers who wish to return to school to improve their qualifications, and teachers will be encouraged to continue their education after graduation. Educational institutions will be democratized and freed of rigid state control. Students will be consulted at all levels in decision-making.

The government will favor the development of cultural activities by reducing the work week to increase leisure and by giving local communities the funds to establish cultural institutions and activities. "Thus leisure time will not be reduced to the reconstitution of labor power."[2] The government will cooperate with cultural producers in finding ways to break the financial control of capital over movies, theatre, books, records, television, and so forth. Nationalizations and government stock purchases will have this effect in some cases. The government will also commission more works of art.

The equality of women will be guaranteed in all spheres of life. Maternity leave will be extended to sixteen weeks, and one thousand new day-care centers will be opened. Special leaves will be available for parents caring for sick children. Sex education and birth control information will be promoted. Abortion will be legalized, although the Common Program remarks curiously that it "will not be considered as a means of birth control."[3]

Science and technology will be enlisted in the struggle against pollution and for the preservation of the environment. Businesses that damage the environment will have to pay for its repair. Polluting technologies will be replaced when alternatives are available or can be developed.

The Common Program also includes provisions for increasing individual freedoms, reforming the police, guaranteeing the rights of prisoners and the independence of lawyers, abolishing the French equivalents of the CIA and the special police forces, insuring the freedom from censorship of the news, and decentralizing and democratizing the government bureaucracy.

In international affairs the new government would abolish the French nuclear strike force, stop arms sales to colonial regimes, recognize the right to self-determination of the last French colonies, work for the dissolution of both the Warsaw Pact and NATO, and continue to cooperate with the Common Market.[4]

This then is a sketch of a program which, if implemented, would bring about a broad democratization of French social life and a great increase in the power of the people in the face of capital. How can you be against it? This is a question I have posed many times to friends on the radical left in France, most of whom are in fact very hostile to the Common Program. Their strongest objections are not to the content, described above. They all suspect that the leaders of the official left are afraid or incapable of actually implementing the provisions of the program. They note the ambiguity of many chapters and the lack of specifics in others, and they argue that the official left will push everything in the document in a conservative direction once it is in power. Some objected to the weakness of the comments on women's liberation and migrant workers. Others felt that this was simply no way to make a revolution.

Activists of the radical left are unanimous: the official left parties, especially the Communist Party, seem to them nothing but social-democratic reform organizations. At best they are good for rationalizing the capitalist system, and at worst they are likely to repress the extreme left and the working class even more vigorously than the Gaullists. Beneath the surface of these objections, one senses a terrible cynicism that is justified by the role of the official left in the May Events.

The most serious critics of the Common Program reject the idea of an electoral path to socialism. Radical leftists in the PSU and the CFDT, for example, are suspicious of electoral appeals to the middle strata because they think that the primary basis of unity between these groups and the working class should be the hegemony of the latter in the workplace and the community. They see the existing parliamentary institutions as essentially bourgeois and antagonistic to the new forms of government, based on councils, that they want to create.

For broad sectors of the population, the Common Program really does seem to represent their common opposition to the established society. And from the American vantage point, it is difficult to reject a program of this type that is backed by hundreds of thousands of activists and millions of voters. If only we were so far along the road! Still, there are serious problems with the Common Program and the alliance that supports it. There are problems with the model of socialist civilization that might emerge from a successful "transitional" regime. Worse still, there are doubts about the practicability of the whole concept of a transitional regime in light of the Chilean experience.

The Model of Civilization

Many radical leftists reject the Common Program because they claim it is committed to the perpetuation of the very sort of bureaucratic "consumer society" that prevails under capitalism. It is true that the program does not openly challenge the basic premises of this model of civilization: its hierarchical organization of the labor process, its inflated bureaucracies, its emphasis on private consumption and multiplication of false gratifications for false needs. To those who call themselves revolutionaries in France today, the program therefore appears to be an attempt to *conserve* the system intact, while softening its edges with reforms such as improved public transport and a formally more democratic organization of the government bureaucracy.

These criticisms reflect familiar themes from the May Events in which the thinking of the radical left is rooted. In May, the revolutionary students developed a new critique of advanced monopoly capitalism and of their own future role within it as members of the middle strata. As one tract put it:

Today the students are becoming conscious of what is being made of them:
the executives of the existing economic system, paid to make it function
better. Their fight concerns all the workers because it belongs to all of them:
they refuse to become professors serving a teaching system that selects the
sons of the bourgeoisie and eliminates the others; sociologists designing
slogans for the government's electoral campaigns; psychologists charged
with organizing "work teams" in the interests of the boss; executives
charged with applying to the workers a system that subjugates them as well.

Another self-explanatory tract by the students asks, "Why do they fight?"
and answers, "Because they refuse to become the watchdogs of the
bourgeoisie."

An important theoretical pamphlet from the May Events goes further. It
argues that the middle strata, as a sector built and inflated by capitalism
largely to control the labor force, poses, by its very existence, a serious threat
to the development of a free socialist society. As members of these strata, the
authors feel it particularly important to analyze this problem and to build a
revolutionary strategy that takes it into account. They claim that the middle
strata's control over the economy gives them the power to re-emerge after a
social transformation as

a new bourgeoisie, rebuilt on the basis of all the hierarchical advantages of
power and knowledge. This new bourgeoisie would lack juridical status, but
it would be a functional bourgeoisie nevertheless. That is why the doubts of
the students about the content of the tasks they will later perform, their
denunciation of the bourgeois University and their critique of repressive
roles, are so profoundly opposed to the entire electoralist strategy of the
French Communist Party.

This is however clearly vital today. What fundamental changes would be
brought about by a socialism in which the same workers would go every
morning, subjected to the same advertising, to the same factories where they
would find the same tasks and be under the orders of the same foremen?
They have emptied the idea of socialism.[5]

Such questions are still asked today on the radical left by those who oppose
an "anti-capitalist" strategy to the official "anti-monopoly" one.

The critique of capitalist models of consumption during May was more
diffuse. French socialists and communists were accused of wanting to
universalize consumer society rather than wanting to abolish it in favor of
new and liberating models of social consumption. This theme was closely
related to the critique of the official left's fixation on electoral power and the
existing state. Voting was denounced by parts of the radical left as the
supreme act of passive consumption and liberal authoritarianism. One tract
argued that "the instrument of capitalist power ... no longer resides so much
in this latter [the state] as in the submission of the workers to models of
consumer society and to all the differentiated forms of authority which
assure its functioning."

The official left regards these charges as utopian. It argues that the system cannot be transformed overnight, that a transitional regime under socialist leadership is needed as a prelude to bigger and better things. Parties that reject "consumer society" when workers are just beginning to be able to participate in it, or that challenge aspects of the hierarchical social organization from which large strata of potential socialist voters still profit, can never hope to build an electoral base for a transitional government.

This is why the Common Program takes for granted the persistence of so many regressive features of the established society. The CP and SP argue that they are attempting to build socialism with "men as they are, not as they should be." More radical demands would be objectively counterrevolutionary because they would confuse and divide the potential electoral base for socialism.

Indeed, how can one attack the automobile as a prime example of false gratification under capitalism when so many French workers have only begun to acquire this mixed blessing in the last decade? It is easier for prosperous revolutionaries living in desirable sections of Paris or in green suburbs to dispense with this questionable luxury than for those who live in dreary industrial slums. Similarly, an attack on the privileges, the status, and the incomes of the middle strata has an ultra-left content. Like "middle peasants" in the Chinese Revolution, these groups must support the left for it to succeed in France. It is difficult to see how support can be mobilized by criticism of their role in the capitalist hierarchy from which they profit in small ways.

These sorts of arguments are familiar to many American New Leftists, who are frequently criticized by liberals for their "counterproductive" methods. Yet the problem in France is perhaps more complicated than here. Some real struggles have dramatized the tension between the radical critique of advanced capitalism and the potential social base for its overthrow.

In May '68 many students felt betrayed by the working class, which transformed its general strike into a major wage offensive instead of mobilizing a direct assault on the state. Was this (as many students believed) a sign of the "integration" of the working class, of a definitive collapse of its socialist aspirations under the combined pressure of consumer society and the Communist Party? Or was it an illustration of Rosa Luxemburg's dictum: "Every great political mass action, after it has attained its political highest point, breaks up into a mass of economic strikes?"[6] If it was the latter, there would have been no betrayal, no defect in the will to socialism, but only a defect in the power to obtain it. Whatever the answer, it is certain that many workers were insulted by student criticism of their attempts to meet their economic needs, which are still mediated by the wage system and the market in consumer goods.

There was a later attempt by the CFDT union, under the influence of radical left activists, to promote "anti-hierarchical" wage struggles, designed to diminish the economic gap between different categories of employees. This offensive apparently met with strong resistance from better-paid workers and members of the middle strata. The majority of those groups felt threatened by movements that reduced their relative advantage, so that "anti-hierarchical" strikes split rather than united the workers. This result was particularly frustrating to the organizers, who had initiated the struggles precisely to overcome the effects of the wage differentials established by capitalism.

The communist-led CGT anticipated just this result and opposed such struggles from the beginning. It argued that capital could well afford to redistribute the same size wage bill more fairly among the labor force especially if as a result the better-paid workers were bound more tightly than ever to the system in the defense of their interests. The CFDT eventually abandoned anti-hierarchical struggles.

These conflicts and failures are ominous because the problems would be intensified in a transitional regime. If the radical left critique cannot be successfully embodied in practice today, when will it ever be? Once in power the socialist movement seems likely to grow even more committed to the mechanisms of social differentiation and control made available by capitalism. It may find these mechanisms essential to its continued power and gradually create not socialism but a state capitalist system based on the same depoliticized, gadget-crazed, bureaucratically repressed social base that capitalism is building today. Then the "transitional" regime would prove to be simply a more humane and efficient way of defusing social conflict and reproducing the established system.

Supporters of the Common Program might reply that they intend a major shift away from just such a state capitalism. What better start in the struggle against generalized and wasteful private consumption than reforms such as the proposed development of public transport and child care, the changes in city planning and public housing, the decentralized financing of culture and democratization of education? Taken together and developed to the limit such reforms promise a collective orientation toward a more liberating model of consumption.

What is more, the ecology chapter promises a radical transformation of the technological base of the system. After proposing that polluters pay environmental reparations, it says, "In the future, the solutions will be sought in the modification of production processes and products produced rather than in emission controls."[7] This modest sentence in fact implies a massive restructuring of industry and consumption.

The same sort of defense could be made on the issue of bureaucratic hierarchy. The spread of "democratic management," the election of representative governing bodies for major bureaucracies like social security, and the democratization of administrative practice can provide the basis for a realistic attack on hierarchy. Wage differences will be gradually narrowed by the proposed minimum wage policy. The Common Program also challenges the technological base of the disqualification of the labor force and the consequent multiplication of bureaucracies standing over it. The program says, "One of the criteria of industrial policy will be the production of machines and the perfection of technological processes aimed at improving the nature and interest of work."[8] This passage goes beyond mere job enrichment or enlargement in saying that a radical restructuring of technology is necessary to "requalify" the labor force and provide interesting work.

I have tried to construct the best defense I can for the Common Program, but I am not sure I believe it. The authors of the program may have in mind the sort of points raised here, but how many readers will come away from it with such notions? The program does not, in short, propagandize for a truly different model of civilization.

While theoretical discussion of some of these problems does go on, it is largely unconnected with practical work. I have noted the experiment of the CFDT with new types of wage struggles, but there is not much else to point to. As one supporter of the official left recently told me, there are two kinds of proposals in the Common Program, those that express an already existing public demand or political practice and those included to show that the left is open to new ideas. Unfortunately, the passages that promise the most change seem to belong to the latter category.

A wholly negative conclusion is not appropriate. The openness of a left that has often been described as "the stupidest left in the world" is amazing. This openness deserves to be tested. The fact that the radical left formulates its critique at all indicates that the test will probably take place.

The Lessons of Chile

As for the problems of a primarily electoral strategy, these do not seem to bother the official left very much. Chile has not frightened them; the lesson they draw is to go slowly. It diminishes rather than increases their revolutionary fervor. One hears, "France is not Chile," as if that settled the matter once and for all.

There can be no doubt that the alliance of the French Communist and

Socialist parties is not the Chilean Popular Unity. The coalition in Chile was far to the left of its counterpart in France. The difference shows up in the style of the programs. The orientation of the Common Program is summed up in the slogan: "To Live Better, To Change Life." The program of Chile's Popular Unity was Marxist social and economic analysis of the system. By the fourth paragraph the reader is confronted with the following:

> What has failed in Chile is a system that does not meet the necessities of our times. Chile is a capitalistic country dependent on imperialism, dominated by bourgeois sectors that are structurally linked to foreign capital, and cannot resolve the country's fundamental problems. These are the same problems that derive from class privileges and which will never be renounced voluntarily.[9]

In spite of the bold talk about moving France toward socialism, the actual ambitions of the Common Program are quite modest. A new government might carry out a few reforms and then accept its fall from power when the capitalist counter-attack convinces the mass of voters that socialists do not make good administrators of a capitalist system. Then the precedent of Chile would be irrelevant, and it would make more sense to refer for models to social-democrats like Harold Wilson and Willy Brandt.

If elected, the French left would be in a stronger position than was Allende. The electoral system guarantees that the left will not elect a president without an absolute majority of the voters, and if it can do that then it will be able to provide itself with a manageable parliament. Perhaps the greatest advantage of the French left is the immensely stronger position of France in the world political and economic system. France is a wealthy country with a per capita income nearly equal to that of the United States and a highly diversified economy. It is surrounded by countries governed for the moment by liberal regimes friendly with its own Socialist Party. An American blockade would be impossible to organize. All this is not to say that France is safe from American economic intervention, but the consequences would not be as devastating as they were in Chile.

Still, taking all this into account, the moderate and confident tone of the Common Program veils the economic troubles that would face a socialist government, and the fact that the CP and SP are to the right of the aspirations and struggles that could be mobilized during a transitional regime. The moderation of the program expresses the conditions for electoral success among groups outside the working class. Yet nothing guarantees that to this appeal there would correspond a willingness of the petite bourgeoisie and peasantry to support the regime even moderately.

The program contains some awareness of the explosive potentialities of a transitional situation. Anticipating capitalist resistance to a new government, the Common Program includes proposals for immediate exchange controls to protect the franc from an outflow of capital. In addition, the army will not be further professionalized. Draftees will continue to form its basis, and they will serve for six months. Regional reserves will be organized. All soldiers will have the right to receive the newspapers they prefer. There will be no social or political discrimination in the recruitment of officers. The chapter concludes,

> The government will count on the unflinching loyalism of the commissioned and non-commissioned officers. Outside the service they will benefit from all civil rights; their material and moral interests will be defended. Their eventual reintegration into civilian life will be guaranteed.[10]

Yet there is clearly either hypocrisy or self-delusion in the happy picture painted in the Common Program. It seems most unlikely that exchange controls, however sophisticated, could prevent an immediate economic crisis. The "unflinching loyalism" of the army is a bad joke. It is less than fifteen years since the last attempt by portions of the army to make a coup d'etat in France. Everyone knows that the small professional core of the French military is led by and largely composed of graduates of the colonial wars, schooled in disrespect for freedom and human life, trained in torture and political repression.

These modest defensive measures would be sufficient only if the left could confine the movement within a narrow social-democratic framework, a framework within which it might well be defeated in any case by a capitalist counter-offensive at the strictly economic and electoral levels. But if this reformist scenario is not intended by the signers of the Common Program then their proposals for the defense of the regime are dangerously misleading.

If the French have any advantage over the Chileans as far as policy toward the military is concerned, it is their extreme cynicism about the army. It would not take much argument to convince them that in a crisis the professional army would try to overthrow a socialist government. The main hope lies in the draftees, who are relatively unindoctrinated and lacking in military esprit de corps. They are no more mystified than the population at large by the ideology of neutral military professionalism which fooled so many in Chile.

But since the division and not the loyalty of the army is the ultimate support of republican legitimacy, it would seem necessary to move quickly and decisively from the beginning to demobilize and dismantle the professional military apparatus, substituting for it a less dangerous entity. The Common Program does not promise such an approach. The leaders of the French left seem to prefer to wait hat in hand on their own future executioners rather than to take the risks (much smaller than they would have been in Chile) of going on the offensive quickly, before economic difficulties eroded their political support.

The problem of the independent middle class is extremely complicated. If one assumes, as does the Common Program, a rising national income, then it seems reasonable to assume also that the petite bourgeoisie and the peasantry can be bought off with suitable reforms. But what justifies such optimism? The Common Program approaches this question as though it spoke for the Swedish Social Democratic Party, about to be re-elected for the umpteenth time.

The petite bourgeoisie and the peasantry are relatively conservative social groups in spite of their grumbling and they form a large part of the base of Gaullism. In difficult economic conditions they will be hard to please, and once mobilized against the government the situation would deteriorate rapidly, as it did in Chile. France is better off than Chile in this respect too, of course, but that is because these classes are smaller and less central to the economy, not because they are more likely to follow the leadership of the left.

The sort of lengthy, peaceful transition to socialism proposed by the French left requires economic and political stability to reward and reassure the petite bourgeoisie and the peasantry. Like the Popular Unity in Chile, the French left hopes that its reforms will release new productive forces to counter some of the effects of capitalist economic attacks. These gains are to provide the economic base for a broad class alliance.

But as the Chileans learned, such a strategy threatens to fly apart at both ends. The middle class is easily pushed to the right by economic difficulties. And French workers, sensing the weakness of the regime, as did their Chilean counterparts, may initiate powerful strikes and factory occupations in the private sector, shattering the moderate posture of the socialist movement.

How would a French socialist regime react? The first French socialist to enter a government, Alexandre Millerand, became infamous when the army was called to suppress a strike. This is one of several precedents that haunt all radical left reflections. Nevertheless, the Common Program does prepare a different option, which might be called "flight-forward" socialization. It declares, "The progress of nationalizations will be linked to economic development and to the demands of the masses, who must assume the broadest responsibilities. This is why when the workers express the will to see their enterprise enter the public or nationalized sector, the government can propose this to the Parliament."[11] If such a strategy were implemented in a crisis it might well be the way out of the bind into which the Chileans fell: restraining working-class militancy to placate a hostile middle class and losing on both sides.

These comments are not so much criticism of the Popular Unity in Chile, as arguments that the French left would have no excuse for being caught in the same traps, given both its strength and the possibility of learning from the Chilean experience. The electoral victory of the French left could be the start of a transition to socialism, but only if all of the ambiguities of the Common Program were rapidly resolved in favor of an aggressive strategy. However, it is likely that the Common Program, with all its present ambiguities, will continue to guide the actions of the CP and the SP for some time to come. Whatever the outcome of future electoral struggles, the extra-parliamentary forces will have the opportunity to play a crucial and perhaps decisive role; we can hope that they make the best of it.

Communist participation, far from notably 'radicalising' the government, helped on the contrary, to 'de-radicalise,' or at least to subdue the most militant part of the working-class movement. This was what de Gaulle had hoped for when he took Communists into his government.

The State in Capitalist Society
Ralph Miliband

The important question about social-democratic and other reforming governments has to do with the objective nature of their reforms and, more generally, with the net impact of their tenure of office upon the economic and social order and upon the configuration of privilege and power in their societies. In order to gauge this, it may be best to look at the concrete record of some governments which have been committed, within the context of the constitutional regimes of advanced capitalism, to substantial measures of economic and social reform.

The first such government to require consideration is the Popular Front government of Léon Blum, brought to office as a result of the elections of 26 April and 3 May 1936. After the second ballot on the latter date, the forces of the Popular Front had won some 376 seats, with 147 seats to the Socialist Party, 106 to the moderate and bourgeois Radical-Socialist Party, and 72 to the Communist Party, the rest being shared by smaller political formations of the Left. The new opposition, for its own part, had some 222 seats, dispersed over a number of more or less right-wing parties.[1] The victory of the Left was thus quite clear and unmistakable, and constituted without any doubt its biggest electoral success in the interwar years. It also constituted, or appeared to constitute, a spectacular demonstration of left-wing, radical and democratic strength against the threat of Fascism, both from inside France and from outside. Furthermore, the victory of the Popular Front was almost immediately given an entirely new dimension by the massive wave of strikes, with the occupation of enterprises by the strikers, which swept over the whole of France. It is scarcely an exaggeration to say that this 'revolution of 1936,' as it has been called, was a most dramatic working-class rebellion, albeit a mainly peaceful one, against managerial authority and domination, and an equally dramatic assertion of labour demands for improved conditions.

In this sudden and potentially dangerous confrontation with labour, capital could only, given the magnitude of the movement, expect relief from one source, namely the new government itself. This it obtained in full measure, though at a price.

The Popular Front government, under the prime ministership of Léon Blum, had come into being on 4 June, one long month after the elections, and was composed of Socialists and Radicals, the Communists having rejected ministerial participation even though they promised conditional support to the new administration.

There was at least one thing over which the government and its opponents, inside Parliament and outside, were wholly agreed: the strikes and the occupation of enterprises must be brought to an end. On the eve of his appointment, the new socialist minister of the interior to be, Roger Salengro, had said: 'Let those whose task it is to lead the trade union movement do their duty. Let them hasten to put an end to this unjustified agitation. For myself, my choice is made between order and anarchy. Against whosoever it may be, I shall maintain order.'[2]

On the other hand, circumstances were not such as to enable the government to do this by force; and to give it due credit, it did not contemplate any such action. What it did want was to bring the agitation to an end by peaceful means, and it achieved this, or at least created the conditions for such an outcome, by bringing capital and labour together and have them accept the famous Matignon agreements. These agreements endorsed the 40-hour week, a general increase in wages of the order of 7 to 15 per cent, and the acceptance by the employers of substantially enlarged trade union rights. In the course of the following few days and weeks, these agreements were given the force of law, together with statutory provision for an annual fortnight's holidays with pay, the extension of compulsory schooling to the age of fourteen, the dissolution of a number of Fascist-oriented organisations, the nationalisation of the production of war material, the reform of the Bank of France, and a variety of other measures of financial and agricultural reform.

These, and some subsequent measures of reform for which the Popular Front government was responsible,[3] are not to be dismissed as altogether negligible. Yet it has been observed, by a writer not noticeably on the Left that:

> . . .the economic and social measures of the Popular Front, which were thought at the time to be quite revolutionary, seem now extraordinarily timid when compared to what has been achieved since then in France and abroad, not only by governments of the left, but also by governments making no profession whatever of radicalism.[4]

This judgement, it may be argued, takes too little account of the change of perspective which the passage of thirty-odd years has brought about; and it may also be said that it underestimates the difficulties and the resistances which the Blum government faced.

But such arguments are only valid within the context of the government's whole orientation and purpose. *Given that orientation and purpose,* it is perfectly true that Léon Blum and his socialist colleagues (not to speak of his Radical ones) could not be expected to overcome the innumerable difficulties they faced, which were genuine enough, or to break down the resistances which stood in their path.[5] The original Popular Front programme had envisaged an even more modest series of reforms than were eventually carried out; and the main reason, it can hardly be doubted, why the government went somewhat beyond the programme is that it found itself, on coming to office, in the midst of a social crisis of vast dimensions which it could only hope to control by immediate and tangible concessions to the working classes. Furthermore it is in the highest degree unlikely that the government's initial programme of reforms would have encountered so little opposition in the Chamber of Deputies, in the Senate (where the government was in a minority), from employers and from all conservative forces in general, had there not prevailed a situation of acute crisis. In this sense, popular militancy was the government's truest, indeed its only ally, and the best hope which Blum and his socialist colleagues had, not only of forcing through further and more extensive reforms, but of carrying their wavering or hostile Radical partners with them.

It was only on the strength of that popular militancy that they could have hoped to do a great deal more with the power they had obtained than they had originally intended. Instead, they did their best, by minimal concession and massive objurgation, to discourage militancy, and thus deprived

themselves, *quite deliberately,* of their only real resource against a badly
frightened, disoriented but formidable opposition. Once relieved of its
immediate fears, that opposition regained its confidence and began, with
ever greater effectiveness, to fight back; while the government itself began a
process of retreat which was to end with its resignation in June 1937.
Whether it could have achieved more in the face of the political, financial and
international difficulties it confronted may be a matter for argument. What is
not is that it had no wish to try. Léon Blum had made it absolutely clear, after
the elections, that he intended to 'administer the bourgeois state' and to 'put
into effect the Popular Front programme, not to transform the social
system,'[6] and that he had no intention of transforming the *exercise* of power
into its *conquest.*[7] The narrowing of perspective which this choice imposed
upon him and his government ensured, quite apart from external
contingencies, that the impact of the Popular Front 'experiment' upon the
French social system would remain a very limited one and that it would not
fundamentally affect the distribution of economic and political power in
French society.

Mention must also be made . . . of France at the time of its liberation in
1944, when traditional elites, massively discredited by their wartime record
of collaboration with the enemy, were, for a brief moment which must have
seemed interminable, effectively bereft not only of any degree of political
influence over their own destiny and that of their country but also of the
protection of the state, since the state on which they could rely had ceased to
exist — and this at a time when a resurgent and armed Left seemed about to
come into its own.[8]

But here too the reality was very much less dramatic. There were two main
(and related) reasons why appearance so belied reality. The first was the fact
that de Gaulle had managed, during the war, to gain recognition from all
Resistance movements, including the Communists, as the leader of the
Resistance and therefore as the leader of the government that would rule
France once it was liberated. But de Gaulle's purpose throughout the war was
not simply to liberate France; it was also to prevent liberation from assuming
a revolutionary character and from providing the Left, particularly the
Communists, with an important, let alone predominant voice in the post-
liberation settlement.[9] In this, the general was extraordinarily successful.

But that success was made a great deal easier by a second factor in the
political situation of France at the time of the Liberation, namely that the
French Communist Party, though bent upon major economic and social
reforms, was in no sense committed to anything resembling a revolutionary
bid for power, and accepted, with little difficulty, a minor place in the
reconstructed Provisional Government which de Gaulle appointed on 9

September 1944. That government included two Communists, one as minister of air and the other of public health. It also included four members of the Socialist Party; but no suspicion of socialist leanings could possibly be attached to the rest of the government, some of whose members, for instance René Pléven and George Bidault, subsequently became leading conservative politicians in the Fourth Republic. In any case the government was dominated by the general himself, who could always be relied on to opt, in the economic and social fields, for orthodox rather than radical policies.

Nevertheless, even so essentially 'moderate' a government could not avoid, and had indeed no great wish to avoid, commitment to a substantial, if limited and unsystematic, programme of nationalisation, which encompassed the northern coalfields, the Renault works, gas, electricity, the Bank of France and the four major credit institutions. Even less than in the English case were these measures intended to serve as the first step in the wholesale transformation of the French social and economic order. Their purpose, in the eyes of most members of the Provisional Government, and certainly in those of de Gaulle, was to strengthen the role of the state in an economic situation which urgently required its intervention; and the same purpose was also to be served by the planning mechanisms which were then set in place. But intervention was intended to occur in the context of a predominantly private enterprise economy, whose continuing private and capitalist character was taken for granted both by de Gaulle and by most of his ministers. As the Socialist minister of production put it at the time, 'a wide free sector remains the fundamental condition of French activity and economic recovery.'[10]

Just over a year after the Liberation, on 21 October 1945, general elections gave the Communist and Socialist parties an absolute majority in the new Constituent Assembly, and also in the country. . . . The 'classical Right' had been utterly defeated at the polls. But a new, heterogeneous, Christian Democratic party, the Mouvement Republican Populaire, had polled some 4,780,000 votes and obtained 141 seats, against 148 for the Communists and 134 for the Socialists. There was much radicalism in the M.R.P., but that party soon, and inevitably, became a precious political substitute for explicitly conservative parties and served, *faute de mieux*, as a crucially important instrument of conservative purposes. Or rather, it was able to play that role because of the Socialist Party's determination not to participate in a government which would not include the M.R.P., who in turn wanted no one but de Gaulle as president of the new Provisional Government. The Communist Party, which would have preferred a Socialist-Communist government without de Gaulle, readily subdued its own demands for the sake of governmental participation; and its leaders also agreed to their exclusion by de Gaulle from any 'strategic' ministry, such as defence, interior, or foreign affairs.[11] Instead, they got four 'economic' ministries: economic affairs, industrial production, labour and armaments; and Maurice Thorez became one of four ministers of state, or super-ministers, who had, however, more rank than power.

In accepting so many rebuffs and compromises the Communist leaders were no doubt giving concrete expression to the 'national' image they were then ardently concerned to project; and they may well have believed that their participation in what was a clearly non-socialist and even anti-socialist government was a necessary stage in a process of advance which must ultimately lead to a socialist conquest of power, with their own party at the head of affairs.

If this is what they did believe, it turned out to be a very bad miscalculation. Communist participation, far from notably 'radicalising' the government, helped, on the contrary, to 'de-radicalise', or at least to subdue, the most militant part of the working-class movement. This was what de Gaulle had hoped for when he took Communists into his government: 'At least for a certain time,' he wrote later, 'their participation under my leadership would help to assure social peace, of which the country had such a great need.'[12]

The situation was not much transformed by de Gaulle's abrupt resignation on 20 January 1946. The ministry which was then formed by the Socialist Felix Gouin included an additional Communist, who became head of a department concerned with ex-servicemen and war victims; and Maurice Thorez became vice premier. The French Communist Party, penetrated as its leadership was by 'the spirit of Yalta,' proudly continued to call itself 'le Parti de la Reconstruction Francaise,' and it may well have deserved the appellation. But the 'reconstruction' in which it played so notable a part was that of a predominantly capitalist economy, and the renovation which occurred was that of a regime whose main beneficiaries were not the working classes but those capitalist and other traditional elites whose situation had at the time of liberation seemed so parlous. Here too, it is a matter for argument whether a different strategy would, in the circumstances of the time and from the point of view of the Communist Party and the working classes, have yielded better results. But it can at any rate hardly be doubted that the Communist presence in the government between 1944 and 1947, when the Communist ministers were forced out, entailed no threat to the French dominant class, and was in fact of quite considerable advantage to it.

The *Programme* seeks to organize "a union of
all the social groups that are the victims of
large-scale capital and its politics."

The French Left Closes Ranks
George Weisz

Until recently, France's economic future looked bright. Its 5.8 per cent
annual growth rate since 1960 has been the highest in Europe and the third
highest in the industrial world, behind Japan and the USSR. Certainly it has
been accompanied by a high rate of inflation, but this hardly seemed
alarming to economic analysts — at most, a price to be paid for industrial
development. A 1973 report by the Hudson Institute predicted that by 1985
France and Sweden would be the richest nations in Europe. All this optimism
has been challenged by recent world events.

The problem is deceptively simple. Oil imports will add more than $18
billion to the financial deficit, despite a 10 per cent curtailment of private fuel
consumption. Limiting industrial consumption means economic slowdown
and unemployment; continued large-scale consumption means even higher
inflation. In fact, government indecision is leading to the worst of both
worlds. For 1974, economists are predicting dramatic economic slowdown,
with the growth rate down to 3 or 3.5 per cent and inflation skyrocketing at
from 12 to 15 per cent. The public seems to share this view. In a poll
conducted last December, 66 per cent of those interviewed believed that
France was entering a period of economic crisis. A month later, the same poll
found that 89 per cent held this opinion. In a February poll 52 per cent of the
population expressed lack of confidence in the government's ability to
handle the economic situation. . . .

Inflation has already passed 4 per cent since the first of the year, and is
being felt in every sector of the economy. Short-term layoffs are becoming
standard in the automobile industry, and everyone is wondering what will
happen at the end of the school year when hundreds of thousands of young
people are let loose on the shrinking job market. The French working classes
are no more willing than their British counterparts to pay the costs of the
crisis. Labor unrest is slowly but surely becoming more serious, especially in
the public sector. Employees of the nationalized banks are striking, and were
joined briefly on March 21 by gas and electricity workers. Even the police

"Program for a Crisis: The French Left Closes Ranks," by George Weisz, *The
Nation,* April 20, 1974 and reprinted by permission of the publisher.

were highly visible in the massive demonstrations against high prices that took place that day. Railroad workers are on the verge of action, and strikes in the private sector have closed down Ford, Rateau, Grundig and numerous textile factories in the north. To make matters worse, a new education law has brought high school students back into the streets. So far their numbers have been relatively small, since the law does not take effect until 1978, but the press has been openly wondering if conditions are being created for a repetition of the labor-student street alliance that led to May 1968. . . .

And yet, while labor action is rapidly spreading and polls indicate massive dissatisfaction with the government, the Left has been behaving with a curious restraint and caution on the political front. This partly represents an effort to project an image of responsibility and moderation, as befits the leadership of a future government. But more is involved than that. Behind the air of quiet confidence that the Left is cultivating lies uncertainly and anxiety about the response of the ruling class to the threat of a unified and powerful Left. Equally important, traditional Marxist and reformist programs are being called into question in the wake of the economic crisis that threatens the Western world.

The flood of public opinion polls that have been released since November suggest that there is a good deal of mistrust among the middle classes for a Left that includes the Communist Party. Still, the real danger is seen as coming from another direction; it is summed up in a report by the CFDT as follows: "In this situation of crisis, three types of evolution appear possible in short or middle terms — a modernist, replastering, spreading fascism, the leftist alternative." Since no one on the Left believes that liberal modernism can succeed in France, fascism is seen as the only real alternative. Even the liberal *Express* has been voicing fears about the drift toward authoritarianism. The rhetoric of public order favored by the government, the widespread use of wiretapping and censorship and, most important, the consistent reliance on huge numbers of armed police to maintain order indicate that civil rights and individual freedom are not major concerns of the Gaullists. All that is really necessary for a hardening of the regime is to convince the middle classes, already terrified by the specter of depression, either that the militancy of the Left is responsible for their plight or that public order is a prerequisite to salvaging the economy. Hence, the Left is stepping gingerly.

More terrifying than a hardening of the present regime is the prospect of a military *Putsch* on the model of the Chilean counterrevolution. Unless one is actually living here, it is difficult to imagine the effects events in Chile have been having on the Left. Everyone, including François Mitterrand — the candidate of the united Left in the coming election — is writing articles or books on the lessons to be learned from the experience. The depth of feeling has been so great that one of the few times the PCF has compromised its image of respectability has been to support the occupation of the Chilean Embassy by a group of young leftists.

It may be an overreaction to assume that the counterrevolutionary tendencies of the Chilean generals is shared by the French military elite. But it is not exactly reassuring that General Beavaller, former Secretary General of the armed forces, recently advocated in an article for an armed forces journal a wider participation of the military in matters concerning "general security with regard to the different menaces which weigh on a nation."

It is equally disturbing that during the past two years the minister of the army has transformed the military police into an espionage network which rivals that of civilian Renseignements Généraux. The situation is common knowledge only because the civilian intelligence officials resent the competition and have been complaining publicly. It is widely feared that the army is collecting precise information on leftist groups in order to be able to step in, replacing the police, in the event of a leftist electoral victory.

If that were not enough, *Liberation* last month published leaked documents that described plans drawn up in May 1968 by the Marseilles security police to detain leading local leftists in a soccer stadium in the event of a serious threat to the regime. Parallels with Chile have been difficult to avoid.

Since 1972, three parties, the PCF, P.S. and Radicals de Gauches, have been united for electoral purposes under the banner of the *Programme Commun.* The document, inspired by several years of Communist initiative, deliberately ignores the most sensitive areas of disagreement among the partners: attitudes toward a united Europe, national defense and the Soviet Union. These omissions will in time come back to haunt the alliance, but for the moment they have permitted the formulation of a comprehensive and well-defined domestic policy that, until recently, seemed a promising rallying point for the entire French electoral Left.

The *Programme* seeks to organize "a union of all the social groups that are the victims of large-scale capital and its politics." Claiming that capitalist society is in the midst of a crisis it cannot resolve, the document advocates a reorganization of power directed toward decentralizing and democratizing the political process, and a broad program of social welfare. These structural reforms are to be paid by (a) nationalizing the banking and financial sectors; (b) completely nationalizing key industries such as pharmaceuticals, armaments and space and aeronautics, and selectively nationalizing important parts of others (the electro-chemical industries for example); (c) closely regulating the rest of the economy. These measures will permit funds to be channeled away from certain sectors, like defense, and toward social welfare. At the same time, the structural rationalization of industry will increase productivity and prevent the squandering of resources, thus further increasing the funds available for social welfare.

The unanimous response of the leadership of the alliance to the energy crisis has been to argue that it is an inevitable outgrowth of the contradictions within capitalism, and could have been largely avoided had the *Programme Commun* been in effect. Almost to a man, the Socialist, Communist and labor leadership has affirmed, in speech after speech, that the *Programme Commun* is the only way to resolve the economic crisis. It would establish the machinery necessary to regulate and rationalize the economy, and would direct it toward fulfilling national needs, rather than those of individual profit. Equally important, it would stimulate growth by increasing internal consumption. Here spokesmen for the alliance have managed to combine a defense for the immediate economic interests of their constituents in the face of the government's austerity strategy with the traditional economic orthodoxy that internal consumption is the dynamic force behind economic expansion. In the words of Georges Seguy, leader of the Communist-controlled CGT, "the priority of priorities remains in the defense of purchasing power and of employment," and, "the solution [to the economic crisis] does not lie in austerity but in the expansion of the internal market."

Recently, however, in response to increasing complaints from the rank and file that the *Programme Commun* is too vague and does not address itself sufficiently to the immediate issues of the crisis, and to polls indicating deep mistrust for the Left's economic policies, the party leadership has moved to adapt the *Programme* to the new political-economic conjuncture. Several commissions appointed for the purpose have already begun their deliberations, and very quickly a rift has begun to grow between the two major parties of the coalition. The Communist leaders appear to be closely attached to the actual formulations of the *Programme*. It represents years of campaigning on their part, as well as two years of complex and difficult negotiations. The Communists, therefore, are understandably opposed to substantive changes, which might threaten the consensus that has been established and weaken certain formulations they have fought hard to impose. They envisage only minor, technical changes in the *Programme*.

The Socialists, on the other hand, seem less tied to the precise formulation of the *Programme* and more concerned to establish an image of flexibility and competence. They are willing to make more serious revisions in response to the crisis; finding new ways to finance social measures, reconsidering the list of industries to be nationalized and dealing with immediate problems caused by the crisis, especially those of energy supplies and prices.

And yet this disagreement remains minimal when compared with the community of opinion that unites the parties. Both groups agree, first, that the French crisis results from the structural contradictions of world capitalism and that its worst effects stem from the weakness and blindness of the French Government. Second, they deny that any *fundamental* shortage of energy prevents the continued expansion of the French economy. Third, they agree that the expansion can be achieved by a program of nationalization and economic regulation, aimed at satisfying communal needs such as transport, housing, energy and social welfare, and by a redistribution of wealth aimed at increasing internal consumption. . . .

On a deeper level, the Left has been forced into a corner by the very nature of its reformist strategy. Trying to create an alliance of all the groups oppressed by monopoly capitalism, it has been forced to satisfy a wide range of differing interests. In addition to promising material benefits, it promises that everyone will enjoy a qualitatively better life. In addition to decisive and rational state control, it offers widespread localization and democratization of political power, and promises that employees will participate in the management of economic enterprises. It proposes to nationalize certain industries, but assures wage earners that nationalization will affect only about 2.5 million out of 15 million salaried employees. It promises small business that a large private sector will continue to exist, and that not even nationalization of banks and financial institutions will affect the savings of individuals or the capital of small enterprises. On occasion, this strategy has necessitated rather strange contradictions, which have prompted some to question the wisdom of a policy seeking to associate such diverse and disparate interests. Still, there seems little alternative if one is committed to bringing socialism about by democratic means.

Such a policy, however, contains certain inherent constraints and weakness. First of all, it imposes an extremely ambivalent attitude toward instances of economic crisis. A crisis is necessary to mobilize diverse and even competing groups against capitalist institutions. And yet the sense of crisis must be kept within bounds, lest it create anxiety rather than dissatisfaction and risk polarizing social groups. Panic breeds extremist positions in defense of narrow and immediate interests. Under such conditions a policy of reformist reconciliation is virtually impossible. Only this strategic necessity can fully explain the Left's refusal to abandon the rhetoric of optimism and of moderation for pessimism and militancy.

Second, the strategy ultimately rests on the persuasiveness of the offer to provide a good life for *all*. It depends on a willingness to believe that there is enough for everyone, if only it is distributed properly, and that those who have managed to accumulate some of the benefits of the consumer society will be able to retain them. The offer ultimately assumes that only the very rich and powerful have anything to lose under a Socialist system of government. The problem is not simply that in proclaiming a policy of redistribution within an economy of austerity and limited growth, one risks alienating the progressive middle classes. The working class and all the disadvantaged have been infected by the American consumer dream. Thus, long before the present debate took shape, George Marchais in his introduction to the *Programme Commun* was denouncing all forms of "Malthusiasmism" which denied the possibilities of progress and the "accumulation of social wealth."

This raises one final point. An important current behind the pessimistic analysis reflects not only economic necessities but a long-standing objection — on the part of environmentalists and of libertarian and romantic foes of centralization, bureaucracy and the blind pursuit of industrial civilization — to the historical course of the Socialist movement. These various groups declare that socialism is duplicating all the worst features of monopoly capitalism. For them, the energy crisis is less a tragedy of incalculable dimensions than a godsent opportunity to reverse a dangerous process of evolution. It requires that, once and for all, socialism present a qualitatively different social vision to the Western world. Michel Bosquet of *Le Nouvel Observateur,* for instance, suggests an image of the "frugal" society made necessary by an increased poverty of resources, but which is also designed to free man from a nightmare world of endless industrial growth and consumption. Basing his thesis on the ideas of Ivan Illich and the Dutch Socialist Sicco Mansholt, he offers the vision of a society in which the limitations of natural resources are respected, in which overproduction and planned obsolescence are replaced by the production of fewer and more lasting items, satisfying the real needs of all.

Gilles Martinet, of the P.S., replies that such dreams can be popular only among intellectuals who have achieved a degree of comfort that allows them to scorn consumer society. For the masses, the desire for "gadgets" is real and legitimate, since in the vast majority of cases they make life considerably easier. Nevertheless, he admits, there are natural limits to consumption, and to promise everyone the American dream is fundamentally dishonest. All that socialism can offer is a democratic control over the processes that decide what needs will be met by production. For the immediate future, the most that can be done is to revise the economic aspects of the *Programme Commun,* while stressing its "qualitative" aspects. But one should, he insists, be fully aware of the dangers implicit in a program of economic slowdown and austerity.

In the end, the French Left is faced with an almost impossibly difficult decision. If, as is probable, it maintains only slightly altered, an optimistic forecast and program, it risks losing all credibility. Even more alarming, should the Left come to power and be proved wrong, it will be forced to take highly unpopular measures, for which it and the public are unprepared. Massive dissatisfaction will then either bring in a Chilean-style counterrevolution, or oblige the Left to maintain itself by force. If, on the other hand, the Left offers the nation a different vision — one that appeals to intellectuals because it stresses equality, participation in decision making and a better quality of life — it risks losing the support of a public whose primary desire is to attain economic security at a level of material comfort. Whatever the outcome, it cannot fail to have international repercussions because similar decisions will have to be made throughout Europe.

Self-management, in the CFDT's view, aims ultimately at restoring the individual's sense of personal responsibility for collective affairs by transforming the basic structures of capitalism.

The Movement for Self-Management in France: The Case of the French Democratic Confederation of Labor[1]

Rand Smith

Workers' control of production, the great dream of nineteenth-century French Revolutionary Syndicalists, has reappeared on the agenda of French leftists in the 1970s. Beginning with the mass strikes of the May, 1968 "Revolt" — many of which aimed at increasing worker participation in industrial decision-making — advocates of worker self-management (*autogestion*) have increasingly demanded that basic decisions of production in the workplace be made by workers who carry out production. Unlike the earlier Revolutionary Syndicalist movement, however, which remained limited to a relatively small number of trade unionists, the present movement for self-management includes France's second largest trade union (with about 800,000 members),[2] the French Democratic Confederation of Labor or CFDT, as well as the "new" Socialist Party led by François Mitterrand.[3] The demand for workers' self-management is certainly not new; what does appear novel is the organizational following this demand has quickly attracted.

Unfortunately, analysis of the movement for self-management has not kept pace with the growth of the movement itself. *Autogestion,* as one French journalist recently remarked, may have become a "magic word" on the lips of French leftists;[4] however, its "magical" properties have not been subjected to critical scrutiny. The following discussion attempts such an analysis by examining the principal trade union component of the movement for self-management, the CFDT.[5] Understanding this trade union — the only *worker* organization that is advocating workers' self-management — should shed light on the possibilities and limits of the movement for self-management in France as a whole. I propose, then, two main tasks: (1) to describe the CFDT's program for self-management — what the CFDT and its members are seeking to achieve, and (2) to evaluate the CFDT's prospects for attaining its goal of self-management. The theme I shall develop may be summarized as follows: despite an ideology which stresses the goal of self-management and an orientation on the part of those CFDT members interviewed which favors worker control over production, the CFDT faces sizable obstacles in developing patterns of self-management in the workplace. Those obstacles arise at three principal levels: the level of worker consciousness and acceptance of self-management, the level of the individual plant, and the wider level of the municipality, region, and nation.

The research upon which this discussion is based was undertaken in the southeastern city of Grenoble in 1973. Grenoble is a modern industrial, research, and tourist city with a metropolitan population of about 300,000. It has an active political left, with strong Communist, Socialist, and Unified Socialist parties. Trade unions as well are highly active, organizing roughly the same proportion of the local workforce as they do nationally — about 20 percent. The CFDT in Grenoble is also represented in proportion to its national strength — about one-fourth of all organized workers, or about 5 percent of the "organizable" workforce. Thus Grenoble constitutes a rich yet manageable research site for analysis of French trade unionism. For a period of seven months I attended meetings of three CFDT *sections syndicales* (plant union branches, or simply "sections") in four large metallurgy plants. During this period I interviewed virtually all of the CFDT militants, or activists, in these sections, as well as a random sample of rank-and-file members in one of the sections — a total of fifty-nine members. I also carried out extensive discussions with CFDT officials at the city, department, and regional levels.[6]

The CFDT and Self-Management

For the CFDT, self-management represents a relatively new plank in its ideological platform, having been first used by the union during the May Revolt of 1968.[7] In a communique on May 16 which urged support for the strikes of students and workers, the CFDT stated:

> In declaring its solidarity with the student demonstrations, the CFDT has felt the deep motivations underlying them. The students' struggle for the democratization of the university is of the same nature as that of the workers for democracy in the factories.

The union declared as well that:

> In place of industrial and administrative monarchy, we must substitute democratic structures based on self-management.[8]

During the May Revolt, CFDT sections played a dynamic role, frequently pushing such demands as the extension of union rights in the plant, employment guarantees, and a voice for workers in plant management. By contrast, plant sections of France's largest trade union, the General Confederation of Labor or CGT, most often stressed demands such as wage increases and reduced hours, which could be more easily ceded by management.[9] In challenging the right of the *patron* to rule in his own plant, the CFDT claimed to be contesting the legitimacy of the capitalist order itself.

Since the May Revolt, the CFDT has continued to contest the legitimacy of capitalist society. At its 1970 convention the union affirmed its belief in the class struggle and sought to spell out more fully its image of democratic socialism based on three "pillars": self-management, social ownership of the means of production, and democratic planning.[10] While anti-capitalist, the CFDT program bears little resemblance to a conventional Marxist critique which usually stresses the exploitative economic aspects of capitalism. The union's program attacks, rather, capitalism's social and psychological effects, particularly the stress in modern society on unplanned, private consumption coupled with demeaning, meaningless work. Holding that contemporary capitalism does not fulfill collective needs, the CFDT claims that public goods and services are sacrificed for private consumption goods. At the same time, capitalism perpetuates the divisions and inequalities of a class system. Economic power remains in the hands of few individuals or corporations, leaving the great mass of people cut off from effective economic power and subordinated to a system which refuses them all opportunities of responsibility.

Self-management, in the CFDT's view, aims ultimately at restoring the individual's sense of personal responsibility for collective affairs by transforming the basic structures of capitalism. By socializing the means of production, self-management would place economic decision-making power in the hands of the mass of workers, not in those of a small class of owners and managers. To the extent possible economic power would be diffused and decentralized; however, not only workplace organization but long-range economic goals as well would come under collective control. Self-management, then, would also entail a process of democratic planning, whereby workers participate in setting general economic policy.

Self-management, according to the CFDT, refers not merely to a new way of running factories, but to a system of social organization. This view implies that as long as dominant political power is held by capitalist political forces self-management strictly within the plant will remain a fiction. In other words the transition to socialism based on self-management presupposes not a general strike or the spread of "islands" of self-management from factory to factory, but a political transformation. Given that self-management implies the "social appropriation of the means of production" — which by definition in capitalist society are largely in private hands — such social appropriation can only be carried out and enforced by a new political authority — a government of the Left.

For the CFDT the necessity for political change does not mean, however, that its role is merely to defend workers' immediate interests such as wages while waiting for the political parties to make the revolution. Whereas only revolutionary change, not piecemeal reform, will ultimately provide the possibility for self-management, certain kinds of intermediate reforms — reforms which challenge management's right to control production — can help develop a necessary understanding of self-management on the part of workers. The CFDT sees its role in bringing about revolutionary change as one of mobilizing workers around such workplace reforms.[11]

Despite the CFDT's bold critique of the present capitalist order, the union's vision of a new order based on self-management remains nebulous. How will a decentralized yet planned economy operate? How will the socialist system deal with clashing group interests; for example, between workers and consumers over the question of factory pollution? Even within the plant, how will workers decide what is to be produced and how it is to be produced? How will prices be set in an economy which is "socialized" yet not run by the state? Such questions meet the quite logical, yet unsettling response from CFDT leadership:

> The construction of a system of self-management will be done by the workers themselves. That is why the CFDT doesn't have in its pocket a perfect and definitive model to propose or impose.[12]

Not having a model "in its pocket" has meant, for many CFDT members, not having a handle on what self-management means. For a number of members and sympathetic critics, as well as non-affiliated workers, the term self-management has become a cliche which confuses more than clarifies.[13] Delegates attending the CFDT's 1973 convention in Nantes (which I attended) expressed this confusion, calling for less talk of a utopian system of self-management and more attention to the concrete concerns of workers. The prevalent sentiment of these delegates did not necessarily represent ideological opposition to self-management itself; more likely such dissatisfaction reflected the militants' frustrations with having to render comprehensible to dubious rank-and-file members and non-unionized workers a concept they themselves had only incompletely grasped.

Such confusion over the meaning of self-management surfaces clearly in interviews with Grenoble unionists; when asked what self-management connotes to them, twenty-eight percent could give no meaning. Most of those who did offer a reply sounded a similar general theme: "the possibility for workers to take charge of their own affairs"; "a system whereby people become truly responsible for themselves and for others"; "a new society in which workers and no longer capitalists control production." Only a handful of respondents linked self-management to other institutions such as the school or neighborhood association, or discussed how a plant might be self-managed. The inability to discuss self-management in any but the most general and vague terms is strong indication that the concept of self-management remains hazy for most CFDT members.

The inability to articulate a clear definition of self-management does not mean, however, that CFDT members consider self-management unimportant as a long-range aim, nor, more significantly, that they do not favor or fight for the kinds of workplace demands that would lead to increased worker control over production. In the first place, CFDT members in Grenoble do consider self-management to be an important union goal. When asked to evaluate the importance of self-management as a union demand, over three-fourths of the respondents rank it as either very or fairly important. Discussions with these members further reveal that most of those rating self-management of little or no importance as a *demand* support it as a long-range *goal;* these respondents simply feel that self-management does not represent a negotiable demand that one can place on the bargaining table.

CFDT members interviewed in Grenoble also express a strong orientation toward increased worker control over production. When asked whether they feel that the interests of workers and owners are generally opposed, over four-fifths of the sample responds affirmatively. These CFDT members are

Table 1.   Preferred Method of Plant Management

Preferred Method	Percentage
By a management of workers, elected by workers and responsible to them	71%
By a management composed of both worker and owner representatives (cogestion)	20
By the State	5
By all workers directly	2
As it is now	2
By the labor unions	0
%=	100%
N=	(59)

dissatisfied with the present system of plant management; in reply to the question of what form of plant management they prefer, they clearly indicate a desire for increased worker control, as Table 1 indicates. Only one person among those interviewed expresses preference for the present arrangement, while over 90 percent favor some form of worker participation in management. The clear preference of respondents is for management by worker representatives, elected by and responsible to workers in the plant.

Further evidence of these CFDT members' concern for questions of control emerges as one narrows the inquiry to specific problems of plant operation. Presenting each respondent with a list of various functions involved in plant operation, and basing my question on the supposition that workers in the coming years will increase their power in the plant, I asked each member to indicate in order of preference which three areas of plant operation should be considered priority targets for increased worker control. Plant functions listed range from the general areas of "organization of production" and investment and financial management to the determination of salary and work hours (see Table 2). My contention is that these various functions can be considered to form an approximate scale of scope of control, ranging from high to low. For example, priority given to such questions as organizations of production, investment and financial management, selection of direct supervisor, and organization of work posts would indicate a greater concern for control of the production process in its entirety than would priority given, for instance, to salary and work hour determination and internal discipline. Since the question posed is identical to one employed in a recent survey by Gérard Adam and colleagues, I am also in a position to compare by CFDT sample with a randomly selected, national sample of workers.

Table 2.   Enlargement of Workers' Power in the Plant:
           Most Important Concerns

Percentage

	1st Choice		Sum of 3 Choices[1]	
Function	*Grenoble sample*	*Adam[2] et al. sample*	*Grenoble sample*	*Adam et al. sample*
Organization of production	18%	9%	51%	18%
Investments, financial management	18	3	46	10
Selection of direct supervisor	10	2	17	7
Division of profits	10	11	33	38
Organization of work posts	9	6	43	23
Firing	9	6	26	17
Hiring	7	20	17	31
Work hours	7	8	24	48
Promotion	7	3	12	15
Internal discipline	3	4	9	16
Salary	2	28	23	67
%=	100%	100%	—	—
N=	(59)	(1116)	(59)	(1116)

[1] *Percentages do not total 100%, as multiple responses were possible.*
[2] *Source: Gérard Adam, et. al., L'Ouvrier francais en 1970 (Paris: A. Colin, 1970), p. 173.*

The findings indicate that Grenoble CFDT members generally favor enlargement of worker power over those aspects of management which require the greatest scope of control. Organization of production and investment and financial management — functions most often mentioned by respondents — necessitate control over the production process as a whole; the assumption of these functions by workers or their representative would entail a basic change in plant authority relations. Less emphasized by respondents are functions which require less general authority, that is, functions which could be accommodated more easily within present plant authority relations — internal discipline, salary, work hours, hiring, and firing.

The clarity of CFDT members orientation is further accentuated when compared with the national sample of workers. Data from this sample indicate that workers in general hold priorities strikingly different from the Grenoble group: most frequently chosen by these workers as questions of importance were such functions as salary and work hours determination and hiring — functions which would require comparatively little worker control over the production process as a whole. Certain of these functions, for example, have already been assumed by workers in general or by labor unions in several Western countries: "flexible hours" arrangements, union control over hiring and firing, and the like. In relation, then, to French workers in general, CFDT members interviewed in Grenoble appear much more concerned with questions of control over production.

In summary, based on this admittedly limited sample, the following conclusions may be drawn regarding the CFDT's program for self-management. The notion of self-management itself remains vague, even utopian, for most of these CFDT members. Yet despite the absence of a clear idea of how self-management would actually function, these members evidence a desire for increased worker control over production. In light of this finding, one might suggest that the tenuous connection, for CFDT members, between the long-range goal of self-management and concrete plant reforms may not really matter; and orientation toward increased worker control by CFDT members will certainly help the union *build toward* self-management at some future date. I would hold, however, that this lack of a link between long-range goal and present orientation underlines a more general problem for the CFDT: the difficulty of elaborating an overall strategy that is coherent, focussed, and, ultimately, realizable. I shall explore this evaluation in the following section.

Evaluation of Prospects: Obstacles to Self-Management

Desire, unfortunately, doesn't necessarily dictate reality. Although these members favor greater worker control of the workplace, the CFDT faces sizable barriers in its efforts to achieve that control. Michel Crozier's observation of nearly two decades ago remains generally valid:

> What is striking in the French case . . . is the extreme psychological importance of workers' control demands, and at the same time the very weak practical role of union organizations and of workers themselves in economic management at all levels.[14]

It is hardly startling to note that self-management remains a remote possibility for the CFDT; it is important, however, to understand the reasons why. For the CFDT obstacles to the development and achievement of self-management arise from three principal levels: (1) the level of worker acceptance or worker "consciousness" of self-management, (2) the level of the individual plant, and (3) the wider level of the municipality, region, and nation.

1. *Worker consciousness.* In the first place, understanding and acceptance of the idea of self-management by French workers remain highly problematic. In a few recent strikes, workers have indeed based their demands on issues of control over production. Unsurprisingly, in such strikes the local CFDT section has assumed the lead in pushing those demands.[15] While strikes aimed at workers' control are certainly on the upswing,[16] such strikes still remain the exception rather than the rule.[17] Whether they represent the wave of the future is, at the least, unclear. French workers have not necessarily renounced their revolutionary tradition and adopted the aspirations of the middle class, but neither have they demonstrated universal, sustained support for the issue of self-management. A principal problem for the CFDT is convincing French workers of its importance.

In trying to develop worker understanding of self-management, the CFDT has experienced two kinds of difficulties: (1) imprecision over the meaning of self-management, and (2) uncertainty over the role of the union in building worker consciousness. As I have already mentioned, on a strictly ideological level the CFDT suffers from an ill-defined long-range program, which may serve to widen the distance between non-unionized workers and the CFDT rather than to decrease it. As Daniel Mothé, an astute observer of French unionism (and CFDT militant), has remarked:

> . . . (T)he ideas of self-management have remained unabsorbed by the mass of workers because these ideas have not been translated into concrete demands and hence often remain abstract concepts, inseparable from the future socialist system itself.[18]

Translating those abstract concepts into concrete demands poses a second major difficulty for the CFDT in its attempts to develop worker consciousness of self-management — the organizational problem of defining the CFDT's role in engaging in workers' struggles. The problem may be phrased as follows: How can the CFDT heighten worker consciousness of self-management, while remaining at the same time an organization which practices *internal* "self-management" or democracy? The issue in brief, is one of a tension between two opposing organizational styles: populism versus elitism or, as some Marxists have defined it, "spontaneity" versus "vanguardism."[19] To what extent will the CFDT act either as "*porte-parole*" (or mouthpiece) or as "vanguard" with respect to the mass of workers?

The crucial question for the CFDT in seeking to develop worker consciousness of self-management is not that of strictly following either of these organizational models; that would clearly be impossible in either case. Rather, the central problem is that of following, in a consistent manner, a strategy which integrates elements of both models, elements of both "spontaneity" and "vanguardism," rank-and-file participation and leadership. The key organizational question, then, becomes: What role will spontaneous worker expression play in the development of union strategy, and what role will the "enlightened" leadership assume? As one French analyst phrases the problem:

> How to achieve a balance between indispensable leadership by militants and development of spontaneity by the rank-and-file? This spontaneity is necessary for worker enthusiasm, but on the other hand, is spontaneous development of strikes possible without the presence of organizers who can guide the action?[20]

Both the CFDT ideology and practice, however, remain ambiguous on this question. The CFDT defines its role with regard to rank-and-file workers — and hence its role in seeking to build worker understanding of self-management — as

> ... being capable of providing necessary information, of organizing and leading debates, of allowing workers to express themselves, to choose their objectives and their means of struggle, to fit their objectives and action into an overall strategy.[21]

This definition of the CFDT's strategy reveals an evident lack of clarity regarding the union's role in worker mobilization. What does it mean to be "capable of providing necessary information, of organizing and leading debates, of allowing workers to express themselves?" Further, whatever the organizational forms and practices employed to perform these tasks, how can the CFDT insure that these forms and practices lead to heightened worker understanding of self-management? Might not the CFDT "provide information, organize debates, and allow worker expression," only to find itself pushing, for example, only wage demands — and not demands for greater worker control over production? The principal difficulty for the CFDT in this regard is not that it places the "spontaneity" model above the "vanguard," or vice versa; rather, the problem is that the CFDT attempts to base its action on a program that does not provide clear prescriptions for its own role in collective actions. It is therefore often difficult for the CFDT to develop worker support for increased control of production because the CFDT itself has not clearly defined its own role in developing that support.

2. *Obstacles within the plant.* In addition to the problem of worker consciousness, the CFDT faces constraints to the development of self-management which arise within the enterprise. The plant represents a difficult arena for effective CFDT action for two principal, related reasons: (1) the lack of institutionalized union power in the plant, and (2) the structural weakness of many CFDT sections. First, until 1969 French unions lacked the right to organize and collect dues within the plant or to appoint

plant delegates with the power to sign collective agreements. At the same time, management had no obligation to permit union organizing or to deal with union representatives; in the main it refused to do either.[22] In the wake of the May 1968 Revolt, the National Assembly enacted a statute establishing the principle of plant union organization; however, circumscriptions on that principle still severely limit the ability of unions to organize freely. The 1968 statute, for example, applies only to enterprises with fifty or more employees, thus excluding one-third of industrial workers and three-fourths of those engaged in commerce; the statute also excludes all public enterprises. Further, the 1968 act does not effectively seek to block coercive employer practices to inhibit unionization. Employers still hamper union elections by restricting the posting of announcements, still shunt union leaders into undesirable or isolated jobs, still even fire "agitators" who try to organize.

Plant-level collective bargaining still remains rudimentary; the great bulk of union-management bargaining takes place at regional and national levels far removed from the plant.[23] Further, recognized union responsibilities within the plant — particularly, administering the plant committee and processing workers' grievances — do not translate easily into issues or demands that permit negotiation or collective action. Plant committee operation and grievance procedures are closely regulated by law; union control over these functions is either weak (as in plant committees) or closely prescribed (as in grievance questions). In both areas union latitude for negotiation with management remains constricted. And workers are not likely to mobilize over an individual worker's grievance or over a typical plant committee concern such as the location of the plant's vacation colony (an issue I heard discussed during a CFDT section meeting).

Plant responsibilities of French unions may appear relatively limited to American eyes: French employers, however, view the expansion of those responsibilities with something akin to horror. It has been only fairly recently that employers have shown a willingness to negotiate seriously with unions, and much of that "willingness" must be credited to governmental pressure. Employer hostility to union presence in the plant remains by and large a given of French industrial relations. Recent legislation such as the law of December 1968, coupled with governmental encouragement of improved "human relations" in the plant have encouraged increased bargaining between unions and employers; however, many observers still find employer intransigence a stumbling block to effective union recognition.[24]

The local union's role, then, is circumscribed by both legal-institutional limits and employer hostility. These two factors effectively the plant section's efforts to push demands in the plant and to contest management's prerogatives. To the extent that these restraints curtail the section's ability to mobilize workers around plant issues capable of resolution at that level, the section experiences difficulty in proposing intermediate reforms which build toward self-management.

Related closely to the section's lack of an institutionalized role within the plant is a second factor which hampers chances for effective CFDT action in developing self-management; the section's structural weakness. The CFDT section is often too small and too isolated to intervene effectively in plant action.[25] To work toward intermediate reforms compatible with the long-range goal of self-management requires not only a union orientation toward demands which challenge management's traditional rights; it also requires sufficient organizational strength to push those demands. While CFDT members in my sample clearly hold such an orientation, their union sections frequently lack the strength to give that orientation concrete expression. Often lacking a significant following among workers, facing competition from a larger and sometimes hostile union, meeting intransigence from management — CFDT sections possess restricted options. They can attempt to push demands by themselves, yet, as respondents admit, this strategy is rarely effective. But, according to these respondents, to act in concert with the CGT — which brings increased organizational leverage vis-a-vis management — usually entails a softening of claims, a shift away from "control" demands toward narrower demands such as wage increases.

These conclusions regarding the section's marginal institutional role and its structural weakness do not assume, however, that gaining a secure, recognized position in the plant and building organizational strength would necessarily clear the road to self-management. A long-range strategy of workers' control must, obviously, emphasize issues of union rights and recognition as a first step in gaining a foothold in the factory. The issue of union rights carries with it, however, certain risks. The most obvious of these is the risk of union co-optation by employers and the state. As American employers learned years ago, an effective means of controlling union militancy is cooperation with unions. Rather than oppose union organizations, American employers in the post-World War II period have generally sought a *quid pro quo* with unions: the assurance of rising wages (linked, of course, to rising productivity) in exchange for the guarantee of steady production and industrial peace.[26]

Though a similar pattern of business-labor collaboration appears unlikely to develop in the near future in France, it is by no means out of the question. The administration of President Giscard d'Estaing has, for example, recently proposed "enterprise reform," a plan for associating workers more closely with plant operation and mangement. The aim of the government is clear; a government spokesman admits that "what we are trying to do is to justify the market economy by giving labor an established role in the way management functions."[27]

A second risk attends a strategy aimed at enlarging the section's role in the plant: the possibility that the section's energies may remain focussed solely on the plant. In developing *plant* unionism the CFDT section runs the danger of becoming an organization whose sole sphere of interest is its own plant. Individual sections conceivably could develop considerable power within their plants; however, without an overall regional or national program for extending these gains, the drive for increased shop-floor union power could be channeled easily into a series of relatively harmless plant level struggles. Though strictly local, plant issues are no doubt important, the possibility exists that such issues, rather than encouraging mobilization across plants and industrial sectors, may in fact serve to limit it.

3. *Obstacles outside the plant.* This risk of section "corporatism" comprises one aspect of a third set of obstacles to the development of self-management, namely the problem of linking plant-level issues to general organizational strategy for building self-management.[28] Of course left political groups everywhere face the task of joining local issues with broader regional or national questions; such a task offers no easy solution. How to connect, for example, the demand for greater worker say over production in a single plant with the goal of a national economy based on self-management? Without a coordinated approach to plant-level questions across, at a minimum, plants in the same industrial sector within a given region, union plant activity will likely remain isolated, unconnected, and easily contained by employers.

The problem of linking plant-level issues to general strategy for change suggests an important source of tension regarding internal union operation; a tension between centralization and decentralization of union decision-making. Any complex organization in its internal authority relations exhibits a greater or lesser degree of centralization. A given degree of centralization offers both advantages and drawbacks; for example, strong centralization facilitates coordination and control throughout different organizational levels, while it may inhibit flexibility and responsiveness in the face of changed conditions on any particular level. On the other hand, decentralization generally facilitates responsiveness of individual sub-units, but may hinder coordination among those sub-units. While no particular degree of centralized or decentralized control is *a priori* "best" (that would depend on organizational goals and a host of other factors), one may reasonably suggest that for an organization such as a labor union seeking radical social change, both coordination among sub-units, or plant sections, *and* responsiveness of those sub-units to the immediate environment are equally desirable. To develop systematically one of these attributes at the expense of the other leads either to rigid control from the top or to individualistic, unsystematic action at the base. I hold that the CFDT's tendency to give priority to responsiveness of individual sub-units — often at the expense of coordination among those sub-units — hampers to some extent the union's prospects for achieving self-management.

I have argued elsewhere that strong *decentralization* characterizes authority relations in the CFDT, with local units — departmental unions, city federations, and plant sections — exercising varying but generally wide latitude for autonomous action relative to each other as well as higher units. Such local-level autonomy, while allowing flexibility and responsiveness to immediate constituents, frequently leads to a kind of organizational "every-man-for-himself" orientation on the part of plant sections. Coordination of action, exchange of information, and mutual support among CFDT sections are often not maximized. Left to fend for themselves, individual plant sections fight insufficiently armed on difficult terrain.

Implications for the building of a coherent organizational strategy necessary for achieving self-management are evident. Rather than merely point out weaknesses, however, one may suggest some concrete steps the CFDT could take in trying to obtain, not greater centralization at top levels, but greater coordination among local and regional units. First, there is a need for increased attention to "inter-professional" action, that is, action coordinated among all workers in a given locale. In Grenoble the *Union Interprofessionnelle de Base* (U.I.B.), a structure whose purpose is precisely to develop such tasks, meets sporadically if at all and commands little attention from local militants. Given adequate staffing and interest by section activists, the U.I.B. could serve as an effective focus for increasing common perspectives on local and regional problems among militants in different industrial sectors, and for developing common collective demands across those sectors.

Second, within individual industrial sectors (metallurgy, chemicals, construction, and so on), much could be done to develop greater coordination among plant sections in a given locale. The city federation, for example, functions chiefly as an information exchange, not as an effective planning and coordinating body in its own right. Developing and carrying out medium-range campaigns for increased worker control over production in a particular industrial sector is well within the range of the city federations.

Third, at the national level development of both "inter-" and "intra-" professional action, across and within industrial sectors, is needed. The implicit theme of the 1973 convention — "less ideological rhetoric, more concrete action" — may well presage greater national-level concern with such questions; certainly there is room for such concern. Particularly within the individual federations, national leaders could begin pushing coordinated efforts to increase workers' voice in decision-making at the industry level. Given the centralization of collective bargaining in general, such efforts might promise impressive payoffs. While not promising self-management tomorrow, modest steps such as the three I have mentioned — by focussing energies on the linkage between plant-level problems and broader strategic questions — might aid the CFDT in attaining greater coordination of action across various units while maintaining a basically decentralized, hence responsive organizational structure.

Conclusion

While strongly backing demands for increased worker control within the plant, the CFDT confronts considerable obstacles both within and outside the workplace. First, the problem of building worker understanding of issues of self-management remains a significant long-range challenge to CFDT members. In addition, concerted efforts to widen access to decision-making centers in the plant must rank high on the union's agenda. Such efforts must focus as intensively on developing solid union structures as on increasing formal union voice in plant policy decisions. Finally, the CFDT faces the difficulty of integrating plant-level issues and struggles into an overarching, coordinated program for economic and political change. It is clear that success in any one of these three areas will not suffice to construct an effective organizational force for self-management; all three must be develop simultaneously.

Recent research, as well as the May 1968 Revolt, suggest a growing awareness of and desire for "industrial democracy" in France.[30] But the translation of that desire into concrete political reality requires more than expanding consciousness and even massive rebellion. It requires construction of a broad but focussed movement of political and labor groups capable of giving that consciousness an organizational form. That the CFDT now plays, and will play, a major role in the building of that movement is unquestionable. What remains problematic, however, is the success the CFDT will meet, given the considerable obstacles confronting it.

3. The Federal Republic of Germany

Alexander von Brunneck begins this section by tracing the evolution of social forces in West Germany since 1945, focusing on the crucial early period. He maintains that the opposition of United States occupation authorities to any socialist alternatives for the Western Zone was the major influence shaping West Germany's political and economic reconstruction. Support among the working class for an anti-capitalist "new order," and the existence of widespread plant-level control by workers' councils sympathetic to socialist objectives had encouraged many leftists to assume the impending demise of German capitalism and thus an inevitable transition to economic democracy. In short order, however, the representatives of German monopolies were provided with the Marshall Plan capital they needed to regain dominance. Almost concurrently West Germany was integrated into America's international policy of anti-communism, allowing for massive German rearmament and military expenditures — a further boost for big capitalists.

The manipulation of the working class after 1945 is carefully examined by Frank Deppe, who believes that an absence of revolutionary leadership was critically important in permitting a successful capitalist restoration. For example, after capitulating to capitalist economic principles, the trade unions had no alternative but to help German industrialists produce at low cost (low wages) in order to guarantee high profits for the creation of more jobs. Working class moderation allowed German businessmen to obtain a solid position in the world market. Politically, the workers' movement was effectively neutralized by making representation in Parliament an end in itself. Without recounting the history and significance of representative institutions under capitalism, it can be recalled that "the principle of representation was conceived, desired and stabilized as a constitutional norm of the bourgeoisie with a particular function of repression against the masses and in order to keep them *peacefully* and efficiently away from the centres of state power."[1] In Germany, Parliament has functioned as a safety valve for the dominant forces by ideologically reconciling class antagonisms. This is the context in which the post-war direction and substance of West German politics must be studied.

More currently, John Holloway takes up the issue of 'private sector' concentrations of wealth and power in the Federal Republic, a subject of intense, albeit severely circumscribed debated in recent years. Holloway tends to doubt whether the negative consequences of existing property relations can be substantially altered by reformist schemes. He maintains that attempts to further integrate the workers into Germany's advanced capitalist society through codetermination (*Mitbestimmung*) only serve "to blur the fundamental conflict between the interests of labour and those of capital." As Ken Coates and Tony Topham have concluded elsewhere, under the German system "workers' representatives at the local level have become absorbed in the routines of management and now constitute a privileged and isolated grouping, quite alienated from their constituents. The workers' leaders are in this way incorporated into a structure which remains no less hostile than ever to the interests of the work force as a whole."[2] At the same time it must be noted that the established trade unions themselves have long been a stabilizing force in the system as they provide vital services to the ruling groups. Through their examination of the function of immigrant workers in the FRG, Stephan Castles and Godula Kosack raise further questions about the commitment of German trade unions to working class interests.

Finally, Wolfgang Nitsch uses the resignation of Chancellor Willy Brandt on May 6, 1974, as a vehicle for commenting on recent

political history in the Federal Republic. The dismal record of the
German Social Democratic Party (SPD) in promoting the welfare of
working people is detailed. After many years of Christian
Democratic (CDU) rule the SPD became a viable government
alternative precisely because it no longer offered any real threat to
social and economic oligarchies. An early step in the direction was
the SPD's repudiation of socialism in the Bad Godesberg
Programme of 1959. In other words, SPD began to participate as one
of two or three parties within a closed circle where real political
change was no longer an option. In the eyes of the masses the
'openness' of Germany's parliamentary system appears to be upheld
if the major working class party periodically wins an election — and
this provides a very concrete function for big capitalists concerned
with 'stability' and 'social peace.'

[1]Giovanni Agnoli, "Political Parties and Parliament in West Germany,"
International Socialist Journal (July, 1966), p. 258.
  [2]Ken Coates and Tony Topham, "Participation or Control?" in Ken Coates (ed.),
Can the Workers Run Industry? (Nottingham: Bertrand Russell Foundation, 1968),
p. 232.

**The United States successfully prevented,
sometimes with threat of direct violence, all
attempts to transform the capitalist conditions
in the direction of socialism.**

Twenty-fifth Year of
The Federal Republic:
Basic Structure of its History
Alexander von Brunneck

The Influence of the Occupation Forces after 1945

With the close of the Second World War, Germany and all Germans lost their political sovereignty. The occupation forces became the sole authority over the political development of Germany

Although the three major powers — the United States, England, and the Soviet Union — had pledged in the Potsdam Agreement to treat Germany as a single unit, they in fact soon took steps which divided the country. The Soviet Union alone determined the political and social development in the Soviet Zone, in accordance with its interpretation of the Potsdam Agreement. The United States became the determining power in the three western occupation zones.[1] England was so economically dependent on the United States that for all practical purposes she had to turn over all her sovereign rights in Germany to the Americans.[2] France had the smallest occupation zone, and for the totality of Germany this territory played a very insignificant part. Although at first France was able to prevent the development of centralized German institutions in the Western zones,[3] in the final analysis it was unable to oppose the intentions of the United States.

The long-range goal of the United States in the war had been essentially to break through its economic isolation of the twenties and thirties and to create as large a market for its goods and capital exports as possible in Europe and the Third World. After 1945, a considerably higher export rate became highly desirable for the United States in view of the danger of economic depression following the end of the armaments boom.[4] As a result, all capitalist countries, but especially Germany and Japan, were to be coerced to

---

"Twenty-fifth Year of The Federal Republic: Basic Structure of its History," by Alexander v. Brunneck, SOAK, Wunstorf, Federal Republic of Germany, 1974, and reprinted by permission of the publisher.

give up their aspirations for economic self-sufficiency. Furthermore, the large trade blocks of the European colonial powers were to be dissolved, the Sterling Block in particular. The American goals began to be realized with the Security Agreement of Bretton Woods in 1944, with the GATT Agreement of 1947, and with other, in part bilateral agreements, especially with relation to the former leading trade power prior to 1939, England.[5]

The United States' plan for "One World" which would stand open to unlimited American exports was endangered, however, by the growing strength of the Soviet Union and the various socialist movements in the Western European countries, which were oriented to the Soviet Union only to a certain degree. The Soviet Union opposed an unchecked access to its markets for American commodities and capital, because the extension of American private capital would have endangered her socialistic form of production relations. The socialist movement in the western countries, which had gained momentum in the struggle against Fascism, aimed towards non-capitalist forms of organization after 1945. Broad measures of nationalization were carried out in England and France. The western socialists were not interested in the unimpeded importation of American commodities and American capital because they saw in this a threat to their concepts of partial socialistic transformation of the national economic system.

The United States attempted to realize its interests in Europe on two levels:[6] First, it attempted the "containment" of the political influence of the Soviet Union in Europe after 1945 and later the "roll-back" of Soviet socialism. Secondly, it subsidized the capitalist forces within Europe in such a manner that socialist movements began to lose their effectiveness. The massive economic support of the Marshall Plan was designed to insure that European economic reconstruction would remain within capitalist forms.

The policies of the United States in Europe took shape in three ways in the occupation zones:[7]

1.   The United States successfully prevented, sometimes with the threat of direct violence, all attempts to transform the capitalistic conditions in the direction of socialism.[8] Thus, for example, the American occupation forces in Hessia outlawed the socialization of mining industries, which had been voted for in a plebiscite.

2.   The United States strengthened in various ways private property and entrepreneurial initiatives. By giving support to the private rather than the public sphere in making the necessary investments following the wartime devastation, the United States made sure, particularly in the ERP (European Recovery Program),[9] that the laws of capitalist production were reinstated. Gradually a certain level of prosperity was possible also for the common

people. Because of the relatively low consumption in the Soviet Zone, which continued for some time, a large percentage of the people mistook the contrast between East and West as proof of the superiority of capitalist economics, a misconception which led to the general weakening of all socialist positions.

3. The United States attempted to prevent the Soviet Union from exerting any influence on the West, even though the Potsdam Agreement had provided for Soviet participation in matters affecting its own interests. The right to codetermination by the Soviet Union of policies in the western zones was based in the provision that Germany was to be treated as one economic and political entity after the separation of the areas East of the Oder/Neisse line. The economic structure was not supposed to be changed immediately, according to the Potsdam Agreement, although the great concentrations of economic power were to be abolished in order to prevent a revival of National Socialism and rearmament in Germany. The Potsdam Agreement also guaranteed reparations to the Soviet Union, which in effect were also to be provided from the western occupation zones. For reasons of national security, the Soviet Union had an interest in the policy of reducing large industry, and it needed the reparations for the reconstruction of those parts of the Soviet Union laid waste by the Germans.

But the United States avoided allowing the Soviet Union any influence in practical postwar policies in the western zones, especially in the plan for international supervision of the Ruhr Valley. In May 1946 the United States discontinued the delivery of reparations materials from its zone.[10] At the Moscow Conference of Foreign Ministers from March through April 1947, the western powers under the leadership of the United States were no longer willing to make concessions to the Soviet Union with regard to Germany, but instead demanded the practically unconditional acceptance of the American program.[11]

The Soviet Union could not give up the implementation of its security and reparations interests in Germany. In accordance with its own interpretation of the Potsdam Agreement, it carried out in its own zone the measures that seemed necessary, though such measures were understood at first as only temporary. The Soviet Union introduced broad expropriations and extracted high reparations from Germany's factories and their daily production.

On the other hand, the United States shaped the western zones exclusively according to its own interests. The United States preferred total supervision of half of Germany to partial supervision of the whole. The unavoidable outcome was the economic and political division of Germany.

The Socialist Alternatives

Following the unconditional surrender of national socialist Germany, there began, at first hesitantly, a discussion in all political circles about the causes of the defeat, which was regarded as a catastrophe, and the principles to be followed in establishing a new Germany. Two schools of thought developed: one side oriented itself to the past and to humanistic and Christian ideals; the other side rediscovered socialist ideas. Both forms of reorientation were at first very much intertwined, and at the outset they were not felt to be contradictory. As the question of reconstruction became more and more practical, however, more openly expressed conflicts of interest developed. Eventually the humanistic and Christian ideas became superficially associated with the reconstruction of capitalism and became the official ideology of the state under the alliance of the Christian Democratic Union and the Christian Socialist Union. The socialist alternatives that had played an important role in the general public consciousness following 1945 came to lose their political relevance.[12]

It was not a foregone conclusion that the realization of socialist alternatives was impossible. In the years following 1945 there was broad recognition that the capitalist economic system had been decisively involved in the rise of National Socialism. There was general skepticism that the difficult task of economic reconstruction could be accomplished under the old social conditions. Wolfgang Abendroth describes the "surprising, quick, broad and profound renaissance[13] in response to the problems" of socialist thought: "In the younger generation of the German intelligentsia of that day, socialist ideas were taken up purposefully as almost a matter of course. This younger generation rejected the dogmatism and the bureaucratic apparatus that the workers' movement had necessarily developed in response to its needs prior to 1933 (thereby making socialist theory unfruitful). Now it began to suspect a revival of this dogmatism and bureaucratism in the Communist and Socialist Parties, and started to search for ways to develop further a theory with the vitality once exhibited by the dialectical method of Marx and Engels."[14] The broad spectrum of socialist discussion was given theoretical expression in the two leading intellectual journals of that time: *Der Ruf* and the *Frankfurter Heften.*[15]

Socialistic demands met with broad acceptance in the populace in the early years after World War II. That is revealed, for example, in the plebescite on the Hessian constitution of December 1, 1946. The constitution was accepted in its entirety by 76.8% of the eligible voters. In accordance with the ordinance of the American military government, a special plebiscite was held on Article 41 of the constitution, which provided for the nationalization of the assembly and energy industries and state control of large banks and insurance companies, among other things. This provision had already been passed in the state congress by the Social Democratic Party, the Communist Party, and the Christian Democratic Union; only the LPD (Liberal Democratic Party) had opposed it. In the required plebiscite 72% of the eligible voters were in favor of Article 41. Only due to the intervention of the military government was the decision prevented from being put into effect.

In 1946 and 1947 there were large strikes and demonstrations for the socialization of the mining industry. Two different parliamentary sessions passed laws for the socialization of the coal industry (on January 25, 1947 and on August 6, 1948). Both laws were suspended by the British military government.[17]

The bourgeois parties also advocated initial steps towards socialist positions in the first years following 1946. Although the FDP/LPD usually opposed such steps, it was a relatively small party. The CDU was the most important bourgeois party, and it supported common economic ownership and economic planning oriented towards common welfare while maintaining a fundamental recognition of private property.[18] "The capitalist economic system is not adequate for fulfilling the vital interests of the state and of the social life of the German people," the CDU commented in its Ahlener Economic Program for North Rhein Westfalia of February 3, 1947.[19] From the beginning, however, the economic and political program drafts of the CDU were contradictory and half-hearted.[20] The CDU/CSU resolved these contradictions in favor of uncompromising involvement in neo-liberalism in the form of "social free enterprise" in a practical way with the currency reform and in a theoretical way with the Dusseldorfer Guiding Principles of July 15, 1949.

The behaviour of the SPD was clearer.[21] Kurt Schumacher declared at the first postwar party congress of the SPD in 1946 in Hannover[22] that socialism was the "order of the day."[23] The concluding resolution of this congress stated: "Present-day Germany is no longer in a position to maintain the entrepreneurial economics of private capitalism and to pay speculative profits, capital dividends and land rents."[24] In its socialist conceptions the SPD made a sharp break with the authoritarian and bureaucratic aspects of Stalinism.[25] It summarized its ideas in the concept of "democratic socialism".[26] Democratic socialism took as its basic premise the idea that individual freedom and social justice would be possible only with a consciously planned, but at the same time democratically controlled organization of the economy. The SPD therefore promoted extensive nationalization together with broad mechanisms for participation and supervision by the individual citizen, measures which were supposed to guarantee a democratic economy.

The SPD tried to implement its concept of democratic socialism in the provinces by means of nationalization and the introduction of citizen participation; it failed, however, largely due to the opposition of the occupation forces.[27] In the agencies of the "Bizone", the predecessor of the Federal Republic, the SPD was reduced to taking the role of the opposition party.[28] In the Parliament, it attempted to keep the constitution open for democratic socialism, which was to be introduced after winning a majority in the first federal elections.[29] But the SPD received only 29.2% of the votes in the elections held on August 14, 1949. Thus, it took the role of the opposition party in parliament as well as in economics. Its program of democratic socialism remained, however, the most important alternative to the "social free enterprise" of the CDU for some time.

After a long period of internal disputes, the trade unions arrived at a position which essentially corresponded to that of the SPD. In the "Economic and Political Principles of the German Federation of Trade Unions" of October 1949,[30] extensive nationalization and the introduction of elements of economic democracy were proposed. The implementation of these goals was stopped primarily by the opposition of the occupation forces and later by the CDU/CSU governments. The only permanent success the trade unions could hope to achieve, then, was equal representation in the coal, iron and steel industries. It became clear that the efforts of the unions for a new organization of the economy had failed when the laws of 1952 were abolished.[31]

Among the groups advocating a socialist alternative, the KPD (Communist Party of Germany) took a unique position.[32] It too proposed the socialization of the central areas of the economy, but it did not regard socialism as the "order of the day." First of all, it demanded full realization of a bourgeois democracy, in order to prevent the re-emergence of Fascism.[33] Despite this, the KPD was regarded as a radical party because of its identification with the Soviet Union, its support of the changes taking place in the Soviet Occupation Zone (GDR), and its activity in the factories and trade unions.[34] Since the politics of the Soviet Union with regard to postwar Germany and the political development of the Soviet Zone were regarded by the masses as negative and threatening, the KPD easily became the main focus of anti-socialist criticism, which, however, was directed at the trade unions and the SPD as well. The KPD's offer to work jointly with other parties in tasks of reconstruction was soon rejected. The SPD backed down because of the identification of the KPD with Stalinism. The bourgeois parties feared that the KPD would be a threat to capitalist restoration. With the intensification of the East-West conflict, and the successes of "social free enterprise", the KPD lost influence. In the federal elections of 1949 it received only 5.3% of the vote; in 1953 it was even less successful with a total of only 2.2%.

Economic and Political Reconstruction

The opportunities for realizing socialist alternatives declined with each year after 1947. The United States had already guided the West German half-state down the path to capitalist restoration and the establishment of a parliamentary and constitutional democracy. These goals were soon accepted by the bourgeois groups in West Germany and were followed by the bourgeois parties, who ruled alone in the economic council after 1947 and in the Federal Republic after 1949. The new economic and political organization finally received such general acceptance that the SPD gave up its socialistic alternatives in the Godesberger Program of 1959, and the Trade Federation did likewise in the Dusseldorfer Program Principles of 1963. By the beginning of the sixties the relatively broad socialist movement of the forties had been reduced again to some small politically insignificant circles.[35]

The Economic Reconstruction

The American occupation forces had done everything in their power to preserve the traditional economic organization of private capital in a neo-liberal form. They had prevented nationalization and had argued that the German government could decide on this question once elected. All the time, of course, they hoped that this nationalization would never take place, a hope which proved justified. The Americans had carried out a currency reform in the western zones which had made the previous form of monetary regulation superfluous and thus cut West Germany off from the Soviet Zone economically. By means of generous aid — especially through the European Recovery Program and the Marshall Plan — private capital received the necessary resources for investment. And even after the founding of the Federal Republic, the occupation forces retained broad rights in the economic structure, which gave them the opportunity to prevent all potential socialistic alternatives.[36]

It was hardly necessary to make use of these rights. The CDU/CSU was quite consistent in implementing its program of "social free enterprise". On one hand, it provided private property with guarantees of the means of production; it dispensed with measures taken by the allies to dissolve or limit large concerns; it passed very weak cartel laws and attempted to promote the middle classes as much as possible.[37] On the other hand, the CDU/CSU took steps to insure that a portion of the new prosperity was shared with the masses, in order to give proof of the legitimacy of the new economic system.

The general economic conditions improved visibly from year to year after the currency reform, as did the situation of the individual. This process appeared to many as an "economic miracle" after the deprivations during and following the war. In actuality the apparent upward development from "nothing" was little more than the reasserted momentum that follows from the economic laws of normal capitalist accumulation, which had for a time been ineffectual during the war. The economic upswing of West Germany in the fifties was no miracle, but the reestablishment of the long-range "trend towards economic development" which had been interrupted by the events of the war.[38] The above average rates of growth were a result of several interrelated factors: the industrial facilities in West Germany were already extensive, but had not been completely utilized prior to 1948. The potential work force was highly competent in the use of these facilities. And the work forces, particularly those who had fled from the Soviet Zone/GDR, were compelled by the high rate of unemployment to work for low wages. Because of these factors, profits during the early years were relatively high, permitting ample resources for new investments and reinvestments. Finally, the traditional industrial structure of West Germany provided for fulfilling the export needs of the new system of world markets then forming. This series of favorable factors led in the beginning of the fifties to a rapid compensation for the setbacks to economic development incurred during the war. The gross social product in the first half of 1950 surpassed that of the last "normal" pre-war year, 1936, measured according to 1936 prices.[30] The pre-1936 level of private consumption was not surpassed until the second half of 1951, measured in 1936 prices.[40] The Federal Republic quickly caught up with the international technological development. This in turn was expressed since 1951[41] in the secure position in the world market and in the favorable balance of trade.[42]

In the general public consciousness, the economic recovery of West Germany was not, of course, viewed as the reassertion of capitalist laws of accumulation and therefore as a phenomenon vulnerable to crises and limitations, but rather as the success of the system of "social free enterprise" in contrast to the socialist alternatives. Because the reconstruction of the economic system had taken place under the auspices of "social free enterprise", it seemed to prove the conclusion that all other possible forms of economic organization would have been less successful. The defenders of the "social free enterprise" system constantly claimed that it alone was capable of providing an economic advance, and that only it could guarantee that this advance would continue. Since the capitalist relations of production were being maintained and the United States retained its overwhelming influence, this was probably true in certain ways. But these factors were not emphasized; instead, the level of economic development in the German Democratic Republic, which lagged markedly behind that of West Germany, was offered as proof of the superiority of "social free enterprise". The poor economic situation in the GDR was explained with a simple reference to the fact that communism instead of "social free enterprise" ruled there, and time and again the reference to the inadequate supplies in the GDR was used to lend legitimacy to "social free enterprise" in the eyes of the masses. That the relative economic backwardness of the GDR could only in part be attributed to the inadequacies of its planned economy and that certain historical conditions played an important rule in the development of the GDR was not mentioned. The various forms of reparations to the Soviet Union weakened the GDR considerably, and the GDR received no such subsidies as were provided for West Germany in the Marshall Plan. The GDR possesses less raw material than West Germany. Also, emigration to West Germany up to 1961 caused serious losses.

The Political Reconstruction

The West German restoration on the political level took a course similar to that at the economic level. The course set by the occupation forces under the leadership of the USA was eventually accepted by broad segments of the population.

The three occupation powers strove to establish for their zones a separate, single West German state with a democratic and constitutional federative government. This desire of the Western powers became clear when the "Frankfurt Documents", which contained the order to draft a legal code, were handed over to the West German interim presidents on July 1, 1948. None of the parties permitted to participate in the government at that time contested the necessity of founding such a state. Only the German Communist Party opposed the founding of the Federal Republic with the argument that such a move would prevent the unification of Germany. In view of the unstable political situation in the years 1948 and 1949 and the importance of the national question in the consciousness of the masses, the danger arose that this rejection of the new state would find supporters, especially if it should really prove to be the case that the new state would not promote unification. In actuality, it became clear within a short time that the legitimacy of the new state was generally accepted.

The establishment of the new state was facilitated by more factors than the simple economic reconstruction associated with it. The parliamentary and democratic constitutional form of the Federal Republic seemed to draw the correct lessons from the National Socialist past and at the same time seemed to be the only alternative to the state organization of the GDR, which was felt by many to be threatening. Above all, the parliamentary and constitutional form of the Federal Republic was accepted because it offered real advantages in the area of civil rights, which were felt to be lacking under National Socialism and in the GDR. A few examples: The possibility of free emigration (as well as free tourism with the unregulated possession of the necessary cash), a press free of censorship by the authorities, judicial protection against arbitrary political persecution, and the unhindered importation of those cultural and commercial artifacts the public might consider attractive, from the Boogie Woogie to the petticoat.

The political system of the Federal Republic was soon more deeply anchored in the public consciousness than that of the Weimar Republic. In view of the fact that the Germans had obeyed National Socialism practically to the point of capitulation, this was by no means a predictable development. But the acceptance of the new political system was based only to a slight degree on a rational understanding of the experience of National Socialism. The feelings of impotence and the misery of the early postwar years were much more decisive. Compared to Germany's immediate postwar position, any new form of political organization was bound to appear as progress. The new state won sympathy primarily through the economic and political advantages associated with it. The parliamentary and constitutional components of the new state were legitimized above all by the existence of another German state with an entirely different structural framework. Thus the establishment of bourgeois democracy had less to do with the experience of Nazi terrors than with the immediate and permanent alternative of a socialist state.

The Foreign Policies of the Federal Republic

The new state had to pursue a strictly pro-American, anti-Communist line in its foreign policies. This was not merely a result of the supreme authority of the Western occupation forces, which was directly in effect until 1955, and of the alliances with the West thereafter. Integration with the West was unavoidable, particularly for economic reasons. Due to the Second World War, West German industry had lost its traditional markets in Eastern and Southeastern Europe. For German industry, integration with the international division of labor, which had intensified after 1945, could be guaranteed only through close economic and political cooperation with the West, since the Soviet Union was relatively weak. Economic integration of the Federal Republic with the West also coincided with the immediate interests of the western European countries and the United States. This economic integration was concretized when the Federal Republic entered the European Coal and Steel Community in 1951 and the European Common Market in 1957.

On the other side, the new state had to establish a consistent demarcation from the GDR and its patron the Soviet Union. Despite its economic and political weaknesses, the GDR represented a two-fold threat for the Federal Republic. First, it presented a concrete alternative to the "social free enterprise" system. If the reconstruction under the system of "social free enterprise" should fail, involvement of the masses on behalf of an economic system like that of the GDR was a possibility. Secondly, the mere existence of the GDR was a challenge to the national legitimacy of the Federal Republic. As long as the national question was felt to be a burning and unresolved issue, there was always the danger that essential structural aspects of the Federal Republic might be sacrificed for the sake of reunification. Such structural changes in a reunited Germany would have resulted from certain demands on the part of the victorious powers, especially the Soviet Union; and, in addition, these changes would probably have come into effect, for the SPD and the KPD would have played a decisive role in a united Germany, due to the different traditional voting patterns in various parts of the GDR. Such possible developments for a united Germany were portrayed by the CDU/CSU administrations as the "abandonment of Germany to Bolshevism." In order to prevent these developments, the CDU/CSU administrations steered a maximal course regarding the question of unification. It aimed at the unconditional military, economic and political abandonment of the GDR by the Soviet Union to the West. The Soviet Union could not agree to this, for it would then be guilty of conceding the Americans an increase in their sphere of influence. The Soviet Union did not, however, demand that a unified Germany be integrated into its sphere of influence, as was constantly asserted by proponents of reunification in the Federal Republic. The broadest concessions by the Soviet Union in the question of reunification were made in its note of March 10, 1952. There the USSR offered to conclude a peace treaty providing for a freely elected German government with the goal of a unified democratic Germany. Economic structural changes were not provided for directly. The single decisive provision was to be the permanent military neutrality of Germany.[43]

The SPD and the KPD in the Federal Republic supported a testing of this offer in negotiations with the Soviet Union. The Federal Government of Germany and the western powers demanded, however, that a reunited Germany had to be free to enter into a treaty with the West. This was an unacceptable condition for the Soviet Union. Serious negotiations on the unification of Germany thus never took place.

Instead, the federal government took up the Western "politics of strength" with regard to the GDR and the Soviet Union. Continuous economic and military fortification of the West was supposed to force the Soviet Union in some undefined way to agree at some future time to the conditions for reunification set by the West. Shortly after the Paris Accords of May 1955, however, it was revealed that unification would never be reached in this manner.[45]

From the present-day viewpoint, the biggest problem concerning such politics is the question why these German policies, which were based to such a large degree in "deception and and self-deception",[46] were not perceived as such, but on the contrary met with a broad consensus in the Federal Republic. A decisive factor in this was probably the fact that the GDR and the Soviet Union could be stylized as the aggressive enemy of all that was being accomplished in the Federal Republic. The structure of the Stalinist system of government, the comparatively poor living conditions of the GDR and the behavior of the Soviet Union towards Germany and the Eastern European countries after 1945 lent credence to such an image. There were objective reasons that the representatives of the reunification politics of the Federal Republic could use at that time to present the Soviet Union and the GDR as an absolute enemy with whom one could not negotiate and to whom not even the slightest concession could be made: the separation of the Oder/Neisse territory, the demand for reparations, the Berlin blockade, June 17, 1953, the holding of prisoners of war until 1955, the suppression of the uprisings in Hungary and Poland by Soviet troops in 1956 and the endless conflicts over Berlin. Since the Soviet Union had managed to realize its political, economic and military interests in Eastern and Central Europe, it seemed obvious that it would attempt the same in Western Europe. Under these circumstances the conviction spread that it was better to cultivate a part of Germany as a "bulwark against communism" than to make even the slightest concession to the Soviet Union for the sake of a reunified Germany.

The notion of a Soviet threat eventually became so widespread that the provisions for a new German army could be put through. At the beginning of the Fifties there was still a widespread protest movement against rearmament, reflecting the experiences of the Second World War.[47] The movement lost momentum with each passing year, even though no one could prove that the Soviet Union would attack Western Europe. It is doubtful whether the Soviet Union ever had such an intention. She could not fail to see the risk of retaliation by America's vastly superior atomic weapons of the Fifties. The high military expenditures of the Soviet Union are explained by the fear of military intervention by the West under the "roll back" strategy; and secondly by the necessity of widely distributed troop contingents to provide discipline in the dependent Eastern European states.

Under these conditions the greatest advantages gained by the participation of the Federal Republic in defense matters was in the area of ideology and politics. It provided a catalyst for demonstrating to all citizens that the Federal Republic would not be a partner in negotiations, but rather an enemy of communists, and that the Federal Republic stood unconditionally in the Western camp. Rearmament, entrance into NATO and the achievement of sovereignty in 1955 was a package deal reflecting the pressure situation of the Federal Republic's foreign policies. West Germany was granted self-determination only when it agreed to join the western, capitalist camp under United States leadership.

The State under the CDU

It was in this context that a political and social system developed that later came to be called the "CDU-State." In 1949, the question as to which party would guide the government in the new state was still open. The election results in 1949 were close. The CDU/CSU and the SPD received almost an equal number of votes (31% for the CDU/CSU, and 29.2% for the SPD). Adenauer was elected as the first president of the Republic with a single vote majority by the representatives of the bourgeois parties. The policies of the government under the CDU/CSU leadership met with considerable opposition. Only after the elections of 1953 did the CDU/CSU make a breakthrough. The party made about a 14% gain in votes, taken mostly from other bourgeois parties. Its coalition thus gained a broad and secure majority in the parliament. In contrast, the SPD had suffered a slight decline in votes to 28.8%. The visibly successful economic reconstruction, which was claimed as the accomplishment of "social free enterprise," was a decisive factor in the election victory of the government coalition of 1953. The trend towards the CDU/CSU continued in 1957 when it reached a full majority with 50.2% of the eligible votes. The elections of 1961 and 1965 established the CDU/CSU coalition despite some losses in votes.

In the course of its long rule in the Federal Republic, the CDU/CSU managed to achieve all of its concrete goals in internal and external affairs. In addition, it was able to gain general recognition and almost unopposed acceptance of its social and political values. It's conceptualizations determined not only daily politics, but also the whole structure of the political system. In the latter the CDU/CSU resorted to certain humanistic and Christian value judgments, usually in very abbreviated form, expressing an extremely undifferentiated anticommunism, widespread political and intellectual conformism and strongly authoritarian traits in many social spheres. The political significance of this ideology of the "CDU-State" lay primarily in legitimizing the basic structures of the "social free enterprise" system.

The economic successes guaranteed apparently by the CDU/CSU gained such momentum that the spectrum of possible political alternatives were drawn ever further to the right. Independent socialist groups practically ceased to exist. In 1956 the KPD was outlawed and its members persecuted. The SPD and the trade unions had to give up essential parts of previous socialist programs. In day to day politics they even took up the ideas of the federal government. In 1960, for example, the SPD adopted the foreign policy of the federal government.[48]

The churches had a relatively important impact in the reconstruction period. The church was obviously the only institution that had shown resistence to both National Socialism and communism. Furthermore, it seemed to offer an ideology and ethic formulated well enough to be suitable for the restoration of capitalism.

There was little call for critical thinking under these conditions during the reconstruction phase. Instead, recourse was taken to the humanistic intellectual traditions of the bourgeoisie, fortified with some modern imports from western countries, such as Existentialism. National Socialist content in the materials of schools and colleges were superficially purged. The substitution of democratic content remained often formal, however, and not very convincing.

Corresponding to political and intellectual conformism were widespread authoritarian traits in society and politics. The masses attempted to overcome the insecurities which resulted from the war and postwar experiences by identifying with the strongest power in the world, the United States, and with its alliance, NATO. Imitation of the rich western countries seemed to them to be the quickest way to achieve economic progress. Critical opinion was reserved for administrative disputes, not for the substance of problems, which was shunted off by recourse to formalities, or, when necessary and possible within the framework of the constitutional state, repressed by judicial means. An expression of the authoritarian traits of the period can be seen in the fact that the first Chancellor of the Federal Republic, Adenauer, was regarded as an imposing father figure. He personified not only the whole success of the Federal Republic, but he also visibly held the confidence of the powerful figures in this (and, as it seemed, also in the other) world. Adenauer's autocratic style of leadership and his advanced age only added to his charisma under such conditions.

The masses adjusted to the new state as well as they could. Strikes and oppositional actions became rare. While the question of rearmament had mobilized large numbers at the beginning of the Fifties, the "fight against nuclear death" was only a last failing attempt to arouse a larger political movement against the "CDU-State."[49]

Conformism and submission to authority can indeed be traced to traditions of authoritarianism in former German states and to fascism. But the most important basis for conformism can be found in the conditions of the reconstruction period itself. Following the misery of the war years and the postwar years, security in the lives of the individuals became more important than political actions. The pressure of a competitive market economy with a relatively high unemployment rate was felt also at the beginning of the Federal Republic. It forced wage earners to accept the conditions of the system. In view of the increasing success of the Federal Republic, there eventually appeared to be no chance of achieving relevant structural changes. The course of economic reconstruction in the Federal Republic required the exploitation of available, but unutilized production capacities. Under these conditions a unified and energetic initiative seemed more important than long discussions about a course that obviously could not be changed anyway. The "factual necessity" of reconstruction had lamed political imagination.

The new system seemed to have established itself for good. Continuous economic growth, increasing world-wide recognition and internal stability made a long rule by the CDU/CSU seem likely. In 1959 even an objective observer like Kurt Pritzkoleit answered "certainly not"[50] to the question whether or not the SPD would have a chance to take over from the CDU/CSU.

The New Liberality after the End of Reconstruction

The decline of the "CDU-State" began in the early Sixties. In 1959 the CDU/CSU entered its first crisis when Adenauer announced his candidacy for the office of president, but then decided not to run.[51] When the Berlin wall was built in 1961 the whole impotency of Adenauer's German policy was revealed. No possibility for a reaction had been provided. In the federal elections somewhat later in 1961, the CDU/CSU lost votes, the number declining to the 1953 level. With the "Spiegel affair" the "CDU-State" reached a turning point in its development. At this point the federal government took such dictatorial administrative and judicial measures that a large liberal counter movement was stimulated.[52] It was in the "Spiegel affair" that the new forms of democratic involvement became visible which later emerged in the telephone tapping affair, the issue of "state of emergency laws" and in the student movement. In many respects the "Spiegel affair" represents a turning point also in the history of the Federal Republic.

The economic and political conditions of the Federal Republic had changed so much by the beginning of the Sixties that it seems justified to describe the subsequent time as a second major phase in the history of the Federal Republic.

The second phase is characterized by a new liberality corresponding to the end of the reconstruction period and the beginning of a new political system.

The new economic situation in the Federal Republic can be described as follows: The setbacks suffered in the war and postwar period had been fully compensated for. Production had reached the highest level possible with the available work force. With the building of the Berlin wall the supply of new skilled labor from the GDR was cut off. To increase production, additional automation and new technology was required. Therefore it became necessary to increase substantially investment in training the work force and in research and development in order to meet the new requirements of production techniques. More and more foreign workers were brought in to fulfill the need for unskilled labor.

During the first half of the Sixties it gradually became clear that the whole sphere of research and education had to be modernized.[53] Since it was no longer sufficient to simply draw upon available reserve resources, but rather to expand technological and economic potentials, it became necessary to give more room to experiment and cooperation. This emerged first in the educational sphere, where liberal models of reform gradually displaced the authoritarian patterns of the Fifties.

The need to change the basic economic structures became quite clear with the collapse of Erhard's economic policies in the recession of 1966/1967.[54] As long as the problem was limited to utilizing unused resources such as facilities, know-how and labor reserves during the reconstruction period, the economic policies of the state required comparatively minor corrections of the general economic course. But when the reconstruction phase ended, not only did new political structures emerge, but more important, the normal cycle of capitalist crises again took effect. With this the systematic prevention of crises and the control of competition by Keynesian economic policies became necessary.

Along with changes in the economic structure, the changed situation required new foreign policies for the Federal Republic. The national question had ceased to be a serious threat to the internal structure of the Federal Republic since the beginning of the Sixties. The form of reunification thought to be most desirable by large segments of the population was no longer possible. The Soviet Union and the GDR had repeatedly stated from 1955 on that reunification according to earlier proposals had become out of the question. The failure of East-West conferences in the last half of the Fifties confirm that a reunification had become more and more remote. The Berlin wall seemed to completely cement the political status quo in Germany. After the extreme danger of the Cuban crisis in 1962, the United States and the Soviet Union established unqualified recognition of each other's spheres of influence. The Moscow nuclear test ban of 1963 was the first clear expression of this new relationship of the two world powers.

In the Sixties the "CDU-State" began gradually to lose its footing under these conditions. An unsuccessful financial policy and helplessness in the face of the recession led in 1960 to the "Great Coalition" with the SPD and to the end of years of cooperation with the FDP. Only a broad alliance between the CDU/CSU and the SPD could meet the challenges of the new situation. Actually, due to its minister for economic affairs Karl Schiller, the SPD alone was capable of developing an economic policy for managing the new situation. . . .

The social-liberal coalition has thus far not altered the economic and political foundation of the Federal Republic. The grand socio-political alternative advocated by the SPD as late as the Fifties has disappeared from the program. The new SPD-state appears to be the executor of the old "CDU-State" in nearly all areas. A close look almost always reveals that the policy of the SPD/FDP government is a continuation of old policy in an historically up-to-date form.

Given this continuity, there is one difference. Within the SPD and, to some extent within the FDP as well, the old political tendency to strive for middle and long term social change in structure still survives, as does even the hope of realizing socialist alternatives. Because the SPD does not simply repress the expression of social contradictions, but rather permits some degree of movement and action in some areas, it can hold open the possibilities of fostering a new and third phase in the history of the Federal Republic of Germany, a phase to follow the present one.

Translated by Charles Spencer and James Elliott.

After the so-called collapse of 1945,
the German industrialists still possessed the
most powerful industrial empire in Europe.
Therefore the power of the economic
elite was not in any sense destroyed.

Workers and Trade Unions
in Post-war Germany
Frank Deppe

In 1945 Germany was in a state of chaos and total destruction. But a careful examination of the situation shows that housing and communications had suffered much more than industrial equipment and plants. Though they may have been covered with rubble, machines and other equipment of vital importance were still intact and could easily be salvaged and repaired. Heavy industry, the life-blood of German imperialism, had suffered very little. According to Pietre's calculations, the percentage of unsalvageable equipment in the various industries was the following: mining 10%, steel 10%, tool machinery 15-20%, textiles 20%, chemicals 10-15%, automobiles 40%.[1] Balfour concluded from this:

> "In Germany, the popular partrimony suffered more than anything else. The unrepairable damage done to industrial equipment was then not so heavy, even though the disorganization and the collapse of communications following the defeat made things look worse initially."[2]

After the so-called collapse of 1945, the German industrialists still possessed the most powerful industrial empire in Europe. Therefore the power of the economic *elite* was not in any sense destroyed. Since its foundations were intact, although they could not be immediately put to use, it is closer to the truth to say that this *elite* only had been temporarily put on ice, or, in a sense, sterilized. Production was blocked by the destruction of infra-structures, by difficulties in securing supplies and naturally by the limitations imposed by the Allies. But, just as soon as the Marshall Plan and the measures for monetary stabilization went into effect, the resources of German industry, which the initiative of the workers had actually increased, could be exploited to the fullest. . . .

"Workers and Trade Unions in Post-War Germany," by Frank Deppe, *International Socialist Journal,* February, 1967, copyright © 1967 and reprinted by permission of the editor and publisher.

The economic *elite* was not the only one to survive the "collapse". Those persons and groups holding important posts in the State administration, in the military, in the Church, the judicial system and in education — and who in these positions had represented the interests and ideology of the ruling class — proved to have been equally resilient, and in some cases to have even increased their power. According to a study by Edinger,[3] in 1952, all of the Generals in the Federal Army had served Hitler's Wehrmacht. One out of every two high state officials had held a similar position during the Nazi period. Only among the Ministers, parliamentarians and political leaders was the percentage of *cidevant* very low.

In other words, the basic structures of capitalist rule remained intact in post-fascist society. The substitution of the Nazi political *elite* undoubtedly brought a new element into the situation, and it is this element that characterizes the development of post-War capitalism: the compromise of the ruling class with parliamentary democracy, a compromise made easier by the favorable disposition of the workers and reinforced by the ideology of anticommunism. Moreover, this compromise was founded on a certainty that the executive power was solidly in the hands of conservative elements and protected by the coalition with the United States and the Western world. Nevertheless, in order to protect its traditional strongholds, German capital had to prevent the pressure of the working class from transforming the liberal State into a social State. Jean Marie Vincent has written:

> "In fact the problem of the German bourgeoisie was much less to reconstruct its industrial plants, as to shield them from the activities of the working class movement, and to put them back into operation in conditions which would assure the continuation of profits"[4]

But what was the condition, the conscience, the organization and strength of the working class after 1945? This class had been the hardest hit by the war and was reduced to a state of absolute misery. In 1948, real wages had barely reached 67.5% of the 1938 level,[5] and in 1951, this level was still a thing of the future. Unemployment varied between one and two million workers from 1949 to 1951. These figures by themselves give only the vaguest idea of the real drama but, are enough to point out the central problem for the elaboration of a socialist line in German society immediately following the War: what was the effect of these conditions of misery, unemployment and hunger on the political conscience and capacity for action of the working class?

That sort of economic determinism that holds that class consciousness matures when the contradictions of the capitalist system becomes sharper is not borne out by the facts. Until the time of the monetary reform, in spite of modern productive apparatus, there no longer existed a capitalist market, in the true sense of the word. Money had lost its value as a means of exchange. According to a United Nations survey on the period *money had been substituted by barter, by the payment of wages in goods and by other primitive forms of economic exchange.*[6]

To this we must add the demographic and social consequences of the war and the collapse. The demographic structure of West Germany was completely disrupted. In 1949, it was calculated that in the territory of the Federal Republic alone, there had been a population loss of somewhere around two million people and this was excluding prisoners of war and disabled.[7] These losses were offset by the influx of refugees, calculated in 1950 as 9.4 million persons. The final result was thus an excess in population.[8]

Poverty, insufficient housing and employment, the break down of the structure of the family and social and cultural behavior only added to the collapse of all community spirit. "One of the characteristics which first strike the observer is the self-centeredness of the average German."[9] This theory of the "reference to the Ego," advanced by more than one sociological study of post-War German society,[10] can only be explained by the economic conditions of survival. The individual had been forced to become socially self-sufficient and his ability to understand the relationships of cause and effect of economic and social domination and oppression had been correspondingly lessened. And this meant a decrease in the formation of his political conscience.

The clash between limited self-centered interests also weakened the traditional means of the working class struggle — as, for example, the strike — by destroying those bonds of proletarian solidarity on which their effectiveness as a class action are founded. In an every-man-for-himself situation, the political categories of the class struggle lose their meaning, even though the objective condition of the proletariat is far from being overcome, and, as in the case of post-War Germany, may even have been extended to society as a whole in an incredible process of pauperization. In Germany, the individual could no longer conceive of a political struggle between groups, each characterized by particular class interests. Not only had the struggle degenerated into a mass of potential and immediate competition between individuals, the social hierarchy had been disrupted by the sudden rise of various kinds of black marketeers and speculators.

Furthermore, large numbers of workers in the factories had been given a voice in fixing their wages, which were often set by their own leaders and particularly by the Shop Councils. This also contributed to deadening their political conscience. In reality, the necessity of easing the misery and hunger of the population represented the most urgent task and overshadowed all other demands.[11] In their anxiety to better their immediate lot, the workers tended to lose sight of the importance of national and international decisions and of capitalist restoration.

The workers and their unions had objectively become the protagonists of the first attempts at reconstruction, and as such they bore a part of the responsibility. But this practice role did not find any counterpart in the field of political and economic decisions, either because of actual discrimination or because of their excessive faith in the support of the Western powers. Cut off from the centers of political decision-making, they also found themselves excluded from the political struggle. This points up another aspect of post-fascist German society, which is that the general social and economic crisis had no effect on the political organization of society. The collapse had swept away the Nazi hierarchy, only to replace it with the unlimited executive power of the occupation authorities. The problem of State power — guaranteed "by the bayonettes of the Western occupation powers,"[12] as well as by the Soviet bayonettes — had been removed from the political struggle as a practical objective. Thus the decisive aim of the class struggle disappeared — not only because of the structure of political power, but also because the party and trade union leaders of the working class greeted the orders of the occupation powers with enthusiasm or resignation.[13]

An examination of the possibilities and difficulties of a socialist policy between 1945 and 1949 must go beyond the consequences of the collapse of Nazism, the economic crisis, the social upsets and the immediate power relationship among the classes. Lukacs has written that the concept of post-fascist society implies the inevitable effects of the Nazi regime, that continue even after its collapse. These effects are to be found in an inherited legislation, in traces of Nazi ideology, and in the absence of what had been the opposition *elite,* now absorbed in daily administrative tasks.

Twelve years of ideological "tuning" had formed an antidemocratic and anti-socialist mentality that could not be eliminated overnight. The effects of this mentality remained, either in the form of apparently a-political resistance or in the form of an authoritarian attitude in economic and social policy. The only concrete possibility of combatting this situation was a vast program of education, including the exercise of democratic responsibility in the economic and social field. But despite some initial good intentions, the occupation authorities never exploited the possibilities of organizing such a program, and thus the "elimination of Nazism and militarism in all its forms" met the same end as the "re-education" programs for the German population. On the contrary, this authoritarian mentality, together with the restoration of West German imperialism, became an essential element for the role assigned to the new German State in the anticommunist "crusade".

The few existing studies on the political conscience of the German population in the early post-War period substantiate these statements. As early as 1945, a survey carried out among German prisoners of war showed that their identification with the Nazi war had been deep rooted, and their faith in a "final victory" totally irrational.[14] Another survey done in the American zone in 1948, revealed that 55.5% of the persons interviewed held that Nazism had been "a good thing in itself, but simply badly handled."[15] This conviction was particularly strong among veterans and prisoners of war, who seemed to have no idea that they had been used and even less of the nature of the system that had exploited them. On the contrary, alongside the disappointment for the collapse of the Third Reich and its powerful position in Europe, there had developed a sort of retrospective psychological mechanism that created "legends of past splendors."[16]

Aside from the vast study conducted by the Institute of Social Studies of Frankfurt in 1950-51 — which revealed the low frequency of expressions indicating a positive attitude toward democracy and everything that democracy implies[17] — the Allenschach Institute of Demoscopy investigated the aftermath of Nazism in 1949. This study, which had the merit of containing some very precise political questions, also confirmed the lasting positive identification with Nazism:

> "The majority of this people has never been able to see the spiritual criminality of a system that elevated opportunism to the level of an ideology. Despite everything that has been written to point out the truth, the facade of the *social State,* which hid the most complete exploitation, has lost none of its attraction. It would be mistaken to draw the conclusion that the Germans have remained firmly tied to Nazism. They cannot understand — as this study clearly reveals — what they should see in Nazism, if not a comfortable, peaceful life. The few years of apparent well-being under the Third Reich are not understood as a change that prepared a tragic future, but rather as a masterpiece of political leadership."[18]

The de-nazification campaign itself — launched with the aim of punishing the guilty and educating the deluded — reveals the weakness of the occupation policy. The measures taken had a purely administrative character and were not accompanied by a parallel process of democratic education and improvement of material living conditions. As such, if anything, they contributed to maintaining and consolidating anti-democratic attitudes. If the de-nazification program ended up in this sort of bureaucratic formalism, the reason is to be found in a mistaken evaluation of Nazism on the part of the Americans, who held that the pro-Nazi mentality and the political responsibilities involved could be judged and overcome on the basis of formal judicial measures alone.

The SPD in the Nordrhein-Westphalen Parliament expressed a much more realistic evaluation in 1948: "A real de-nazification, which also does away with Nazism and militarism at the same time, is only possible if the social structure of capitalism is overcome."[19] Here is the central reason for the failure of de-nazification. Every action that hindered a thorough-going social revolution — the only thing that could have destroyed the roots of fascism — worked to the advantage of the reactionary forces. And although at the moment these forces were facing de-nazification courts, the approaching cold war soon proved this to be the case beyond any doubt.

All this without counting that the punishment handed down by the allies tended to hit the "deluded" — who had often suffered greatly from the war — just as often as it did the representatives of the regime, and this provoked a growing hostility among the population. Those socialist and communist trade union officials who had initially considered de-nazification an essential element in the social revolution and had therefore supported it wholeheartedly were discredited. Alfred Grosser has pointed out this reversal in the objective effect of the de-nazification policy:

> "By dangling the threat of punishment over the heads of millions and millions of Germans, they (the Allied, ed.) prevented the mass of the population from forming a common front with the victorious powers against the authors of their misfortunes. On the contrary, they permitted the formation of a sort of feeling of solidarity among the Germans incriminated, no matter what their degree of guilt, directed against the Allies."[20]

The "social-defeatism" (expressed in the "without me" attitude)[21] as well as the disinterest in politics that characterized the first years after the war are undoubtedly connected with the de-nazification and re-education campaign of the occupation powers. However, this thesis cannot be extended to all the social classes, in the same degree. If we examine the mass of persons punished during the campaign, we discover that de-nazification dealt a severe blow to the middle and upper social strata; but, at the same time, it was these strata that formed the social base of the bourgeois parties in the coalition that formed the first West German government.

This contradiction can only be understood in the framework of an anticommunism that became the official ideology of the restoration. It must be added, however, that this anticommunism — "this defense mechanism against self-incrimination"[22] — already had solid roots, since millions of persons were implicated in the network of guilt surrounding the Nazi extermination campaigns. By this, I do not mean to say that the pro-Nazi diehards managed to move into the formal democracy of the new State on the coat-tails of anticommunism; but what did survive was the identification with the aims and means of the fascist war. Admiral Doenitz superbly expressed this sentiment in his last speech: "Hitler's struggle against the

Bolschevik tide was a good thing for Europe and for the world."[23]

Those theories that seek to explain this defeatism and political alienation as a typical phase in "technical, scientific and bureaucratic minded society" overlook the historical continuity and political function of a conscience characterized by the need for economic security and by militant anticommunism. During the post-war period, these two elements in the authoritarian mentality were no more overcome than were the basic structures of capitalism. On the contrary, their reinsertion into the normal pattern of thought was one of the conditions for the restoration process. . . .

The political experiences of the working class, those experiences that historically develop its class consciousness as the capacity to understand that revolutionary transformations are necessary, had been brutally interrupted twelve years before. However, and this is important from the point of view of the formation of a socialist consciousness, people still remembered that

> "twelve years before, all of the parties that rejected socialism and supported the capitalist order, by approving the laws that turned power over to Hitler by acclamation, had given their consent to the involution toward barbarity, and that in the first years after 1933, only the socialists, among all the political movements, had denounced this involution that led to rearmament, war, and catastrophy, in their tenacious . . . clandestine propaganda."[24]

In the first years after the war, socialism was therefore the spontaneous, but not politically reasoned and assimilated, answer to the immediate needs for peace and well-being of the popular classes. For their part, the programs of the socialist forces embodied these popular aspirations: improvement of the food situation, a halt in the dismantling of industrial plants, increased housing construction, assimilation of the refugees and others damaged or ruined by the war, a fair distribution of the tax burden, etc. Thus the identification of the trade unions was — as Pirker has observed — essentially a-political.

> "The employed in general held that it was necessary to get the factories, production, and the economy running again, before worrying about political and party questions. They felt that the socialism of the united trade union was free of party coloration and as such expressed a general orientation and will."[25]

And here we must deal with a decisive aspect — perhaps the fundamental point — of the socialist policy in post-fascist German society. Between the immediate needs of the working class and it class consciousness; between its identification with the every day socialist slogans and the socialist program for the transformation of society, there was a sort of "vacuum". For this reason, the situation was open to either a socialist solution or to a capitalist restoration. It also very clearly points out the historic tasks of the political leadership of the working class.

The real measurement of the success of this leadership could only be its ability to bridge over this "vacuum" with a class consciousness, in the course of the political struggle. Being content with rallying the masses on the basis of their immediate needs alone meant shutting the door on the future. Capitalism, once it got back on its feet, would solve the problem and end the game in its own favor.

As early as 1947, in the last issue of the socialist journal *Der Ruf,* then shut down by the American military government, H.B. Richter put his finger on the real reason for the working class defeat — the same as in 1933 — namely the absence of a truly revolutionary leadership. This weakness had left the field open to the counter-revolution in historically favorable conditions:

> "This is the real 'historical' situation of the present moment. It is a situation that foreshadows a European socialist revolution, which could easily turn into a defeat, even before it gets under way, just as in the past many revolutionary situations have turned into victories of reaction. The reason has never been in the objective situation, but only and always in the subjective factor, which is the incapacity of the proletarian leadership."[26]

But the "vacuum" of conscience at the level of the masses also existed at the leadership level, and this explains many errors and weaknesses. This "vacuum" had been created not only by twelve years of manipulation of the conscience of the masses, but also by the severe losses in political cadres, particularly among the Communists and the Social Democrats. This meant that the leadership of the German trade unions was left mostly in the hands of reformist elements, whose preparation dated back to the bureaucratic trade union apparatus of the Weimar Republic and who bore, at least in part, the responsibility for what had happened later.

The trade union leaders of this sort entrusted all questions of the economic and social order to the good faith of the Western powers and to the expected electoral success of the SPD.

> "They were not able to overcome their underestimation of the question of power and of the extra-parliamentary struggle, their parliamentarian illusions; they showed a faith that bordered on credulity in the promises of the Western powers, as well as a lack of confidence in the strength of the working class and in its ability to re-build on its own. They tended to increasingly restrict the role and the duties of the trade unions and further developed the old line of pure, 'a-political' trade unionism."[27]

To this must be added their theoretical inability to grasp the real terms of the restoration process, a thing which lay at the bottom of their parliamentarian illusions. According to these illusions, there was no possibility of capitalism taking hold and thriving in West Germany again; all attempts at restoration would rapidly degenerate into economic chaos and thus quicken the electoral victory of the Social Democrats.

The 1953 elections, which gave an absolute majority to the CDU, banished these illusions, but the damage was already done. The indifference to politics, the apathy of the members, the patronage, and the weakness of the trade union position today are not, as the bourgeois theorists would have it, the result of a disappearance of ideologies in the face of the social leveling of highly industrialized society. They are the result of a trade union policy that, at the decisive moment, was afraid of the class struggle.

Not that the unions did not see the developments of the restoration in their true light, on the contrary they often saw them quite well, but after noisy protests and pseudo-revolutionary threats, they accepted them and soon began to offer their collaboration. On a few occasions, the working class rebelled against this line, but the program the DGB approved in Munich in 1949, was more a list of real and potential defeats for the movement, than a line of action.

At that time, the trade union leaders were still not aware that they were headed for a general and definitive defeat. They still saw the DGB as an organization with aims that went far beyond a simple wage policy. They were still threatening and shaking the strength and combative spirit of the organized workers under the noses of the enemy. Today it is pathetic to listen to the words of Kummernus, the then President of the OTV:

> "The German trade unions are not just machines for keeping wages on the move; they are fighting organizations, ready to do battle for democracy and freedom, whether a part of the employers and a part of the Federal Government like it or not."[28]

The following years saw the trade union movement enter into conflict with a capitalism on the road to stabilization and expansion, with the first capitalist governments and with Parliament of the Republic. In these years it was decided just how far the chain of trade union defeats would be allowed to go. At the same time, in the contradiction between the demands of economic democracy and the restoration of imperialistic capital, the future role of the German working class was being prepared.

Despite the cartel laws and despite the
SPD's pledge to achieve a greater measure of
economic democracy, the period since the
war has seen the formation of ever larger
units of economic power.

Decentralisation of Power in the Federal Republic of Germany

John Holloway

Economic Deconcentration

The issues which are at the centre of political discussion in Germany today
are concerned with attempts to control or democratise the social power of the
'private sphere'. These issues are, principally: competition policy, capital
formation and codetermination.

The pre-war German economy had been heavily concentrated with the
market dominated by a small number of enormous cartels. Many of the
cartels were associated with the rise of the Nazis to power and the latter had,
after 1933, sought to 'rationalise' the economy by giving cartels a compulsory
and quasi-official character.

Consequently, decentralisation of the economy by the Allies, as provided
for in the Potsdam Agreement, was seen as an attempt to democratise the
economy. Although much discussion was devoted to the problem of
breaking up the monopolies and cartels, the effects were very limited. In the
coal and steel industries, measures taken by the Allies were quickly overtaken
by the industry's own reorganisation of itself into larger units again. The
Allies' attempt to break up the Big Three banks (the Dresdner Bank, the
Commerzbank and the Deutsche Bank) in Western Germany into thirty
smaller banks was an even greater failure: by 1950 the three banks had all
emerged again with their former power. The greatest effect of the policy was
in the chemical industry, where the giant IG Farben was broken up into the
three smaller giants, Farbwerke Hoechst, Badische Anilin und Soda Fabrik
(BASF) and Bayer. The general failure of the policy may be attributed to a

number of causes: the organisation of industrialists to protect their own interests, the disagreement among the Allies as to the desirable degree of deconcentration, the general lack of enthusiasm on the part of the Allies for the policy and, above all, the need to make the German economy viable in a world market. If German firms were to withstand international competition, they should not be too small: in this sense liberalism was, from the start, an illusion.

Despite the liberal, free market, antimonopoly ideology of the Christian Democrats, their economic policy, especially during the 1950's, encouraged concentration, principally by means of granting tax advantages to large concerns. The very favourable amortisation provisions under the law on income tax helped self-financing and were of particular advantage to already existing firms, with the result that many of the old names were able to maintain their position. Of the fifteen largest firms in the late 1950s, eleven had already belonged to this group before the war. Measures which contributed even more directly to industrial concentration were the exoneration of non-distributed profits and the exemption from turnover tax of transactions between legally autonomous companies which were closely affiliated. For 1965 alone, it has been calculated that this later concession cost the government 600 million DM, and that one company, the August-Thyssen Foundry, saved 40 Million DM. This provision naturally encouraged large firms to buy up clients, suppliers, etc.

The inevitable price of the 'economic miracle', of boosting profits in order to stimulate private investment and of making German industry internationally competitive, was to create large inequalities of wealth and a great concentration of economic power. An inquiry ordered by the government in 1960 and published in 1964 showed that concentration had increased considerably since 1954. In that period, the share of the fifty largest industrial enterprises in the total industrial turnover had increased from 17.7 per cent to 22.8 per cent. The influence of banks in the control of industry is enormous: although the banks themselves held at the time of the report only 4.9 per cent of the capital of companies quoted on the stock exchange this masks their true power, for they are allowed by German law to represent clients in general meetings of the companies of which they are shareholders. The report revealed that 75 per cent of the capital of 427 companies (representing three quarters of the capital of companies quoted on the stock exchange) was controlled by the banks in 1960; of this, the share of the Big Three banks was 70 per cent. There is nothing to suggest that the process of concentration has slowed down. On the contrary, all the available data suggest that the process of concentration is continuing, even accelerating. [Table 1] shows how the concentration developed in some of the leading

Table 1 Development of the Degree of Concentration in leading branches of industry in the FRG (in percentages)

Concerns per branch	Share of turnover		Share of the number of people employed in the branch	
	1961	1969	1961	1969
3 concerns of the chemical industry*	38	49	41	46
8 concerns of the electrical industry**	60	68	62	68
4 concerns of the steel industry***	61	65	66	60
5 concerns of the car industry****	76	92	61	76

* Farbenfabriken Bayer AG, Farbwerke Hoechst AG, Badische Anilin-und Soda Fabrik AG.
** Siemens AG, AEG Telefunken, Robert Bosch GmbH, Grundigwerke GmbH, IBM Deutschland Internationale Buromaschinen GmbH, Brown Boveri & Cie, AG, Standard Elektrik Lorenz AG, Felten Guilleaume Carlswerke AG.
*** Thyssen, Mannesmann, Hoesch, Krupp.
**** Volkswagen Werk AG, Dainler-Benz AG, Adam Opel AG, Ford Werke AG, Bayerische Motoren Werke AG.[1]

branches of German industry.

In 1969, although there were 71,842 registered companies with a nominal capital of 91,040 million DM, 304 (or 0.42 per cent) of these companies had at their disposal 58.5 per cent of this capital.[2] A similar process of concentration is, of course, common to all capitalist countries, but concern with economic power or 'economic democracy' is a particularly important issue in German politics.

The measures taken by the government to meet the dissatisfaction caused by this concentration of economic power are of two kinds. Cartel laws seek to prevent the formation of such large units and to check abuses of their power. Other measures purportedly aim, not at breaking up these units, but at democratising them from within. The most important of these measures are those concerning codetermination (*Mitbestimmung*) in industry and the formation of capital in the hands of the workers (*Vermogensbildung in Arbeitnehmerhand*).

The first project for a Cartel Law to control and promote competition in the Federal Republic was presented by the Federal Economics Ministry as early as 1949. The original draft reflected the ideas of the Freiburg School which held cartels and monopolistic concentrations to be dangerous and incompatible with a market economy, and proposed that cartels should be prohibited. This also reflected the wishes of the Allies (who had already prohibited cartels by a law of 1947) and no doubt the interest of American firms eager to capture the European market.[3] The German employers' associations, however, opposed this plan, arguing that concentrations and cartels are not bad in themselves, but, on the contrary indispensable to economic rationalisation and progress, and that consequently only abuses should be controlled. Negotiations between the government and the employers continued for more than seven years — the 'seven years war' it has been called — and the outcome, the Cartel Law (*Gesetz gegen Wettbewerbsbeschrankungen*) of 1957, has been hailed as a victory by the employers.[4] The 1957 Law does not prohibit fusions or other forms of concentration, but merely requires that the most important mergers should be notified to the Federal Cartel Office established by the Law, which is empowered only to require a public explanation of the conduct of the parties concerned. Unlike the position in the United States and in Britain, the federal authorities have no power under the 1957 law to prohibit a merger judged detrimental to the public interest. Restrictive agreements between firms or groups are forbidden, but there are many exceptions provided to this rule and there is only a limited restriction of price-fixing.

The Cartel Law has been applied with moderation. In the first ten years of the Law's operation, 4,546 proceedings were initiated concerning suspected infringements of the Law. Of these 3,842 were abandoned, 1,482 because there was a change in the conduct under investigation, 2,421 'for other reasons'. In only five of the cases was a fine actually enforced. As we have seen, concentration has continued unabated. The attitude of the authorities — of the Cartel Office and particularly of the Bonn government — towards competition has changed since the mid-1950s. The model of perfect competition has now been replaced as the ideal by that of 'oligopolistic competition'. The trend towards concentration has come to be regarded as inevitable and indeed, in view of increased international competition, especially since the formation of the EEC, as beneficial. The state has come to encourage, and even to subsidise, the creation of larger units in some branches of industry. Some indication of the rate at which concentration is proceeding is given by the fact that the number of mergers notified to the Federal Cartel Office (and only the biggest mergers have to be so notified) rose from 15 in 1958, to 38 in 1962, 50 in 1965, 65 in 1968, 168 in 1969 and 305 in 1970.[5]

It is unlikely that the new Cartel Law, enacted in June 1973, will have any great effect on this trend. This law prohibits price-fixing, but does nothing to hinder price recommendation by producers, which has grown greatly in importance in the past year, and has an effect similar to that of price-fixing. A limited control of mergers is also introduced for the first time: mergers between firms with an annual turnover of 500 million DM or more must in future be notified to the Cartel Office. The Cartel Office will then examine whether the fusion will give the new firm a dominant position on the market and thus limit competition. If this is the case, then the Cartel Office has power to forbid the merger or break up the new firm, or to impose conditions on the merging firms. It remains to be seen what the policy of the Cartel Office will be in deciding whether to make use of its power. Both present trends and the fact that the Law was supported by all the parties in the Federal Parliament suggest that the Law will do no more to halt concentration than did its predecessor.

The reason why the effect of any Cartel Law of this type must be extremely limited is surely that it is essential for the economy of any country that the industry based in that country should be able to withstand international competition; any government which seriously strikes at the power of its industry will damage the economic prosperity of the country and so undermine its own popularity.

The policy of diffusing property, or encouraging the formation of capital in the hands of the workers, is the other keystone of the liberal policy to combat the increasing concentration of property. According to Ropke, one of the leaders of the Freiburg school, it was not enough to dismantle the monopolies and so reduce the size of economic units, it was necessary also to create a 'people's capitalism' by diffusing the property in these units throughout all layers of society. This was adopted as the policy of CDU about 1949, as a concession given to the workers' wing of the party in return for their abandoning demands of nationalisation. The model held up as a goal and opposed to monopoly capitalism, was that of a 'people's capitalism', in which the workers would also be property-owners and, as such, have a share in the wealth, independence and responsibility which property brings with it. This idea has played an important part in German social policy since the founding of the Federal Republic, not only under CDU-dominated, but also, with a different emphasis, under SPD-dominated governments.

Among the measures taken under this policy there has been a series of laws, the so-called '312DM' and '624DM' laws, designed to promote the distribution of companies' shares among their employees. These laws encourage companies, by means of fiscal and parafiscal advantages, to pay their employees a premium of up to 624 DM a year, a sum which must be saved in some way, either by investment in the shares of the company or otherwise. Although two-thirds of all employees have 'benefited' from these provisions, the average amount per worker involved has been rather small and the laws have made little impact on the economic structure of the companies affected.

The other major series of measures taken to make the dream of a 'people's capitalism' come true aimed not at the workers of a particular company but at the population as a whole. This was the series of denationalisations or 'privatisations' undertaken between 1959 and 1965. The CDU/CSU government had inherited from its predecessors a large amount of state-controlled industry. Partly as an expression of liberal faith, partly to meet growing disquiet caused by the increasing concentration of economic power and partly to protect the people against the temptations of communism,[6] it was decided to denationalise, at least in part, three state-owned firms, Volkswagen, Preussag and the Vereinigte Elektrizitats and Bergwerke A.G. (VEBA). Since the aim was to promote a wide distribution of property, the shares of the companies could be bought only by those with annual incomes below a fairly modest limit (8000 DM for single people, 1600 DM for a couple), and only in a very limited quantity. To prevent the shares being bought up subsequently by someone interested in gaining control of the company, it was decided that nobody could dispose, in a general meeting, of a number of votes greater than one thousandth of the subscribed capital. The sale of the three companies was a limited success, in that it increased several-fold the number of shareholders in the Federal Republic: thus Volkswagen, the largest company in Germany, is now owned by about one and a half million shareholders.

But, although these various measures may have increased the number of shareholders, they have not brought about any significant change in the structure of economic power. The fact that a person holds a small number of shares in a company does not give him any say in the running of the company. The main effect is rather to place his capital at the disposal of the big shareholders or managers who control the company. This is true whether the small shareholders are employees of the company (as under the 312DM and 624DM laws) or not. The powerlessness of small shareholders is illustrated by the first general meeting of Volkswagen, in which six thousand shareholders took part:[7] after various proposals from those present had been rejected, the proposals put forward by the management were accepted by massive majorities.

That the impact of measures taken in this field has been little more than ideological is demonstrated by a study published in 1971.[8] This showed that in 1960, 1.7 per cent of the households of the Federal Republic possessed 70 per cent of the productive property. In 1966, after the denationalisation of

Volkswagen and VEBA had intervened and the first two '312DM' laws had been passed, the same proportion of households possessed 74 per cent of the productive property of the country.

The new 'capital formation' plan put forward by the SPD and accepted by a large majority at the party conference at Hanover in April 1973, recognises the futility of earlier plans. According to this plan, all enterprises with a taxable profit of 400,000 DM or more would have to contribute each year a certain (not yet fixed) percentage of their profits into a central fund, in the form of shares. In the first year, the income of this fund would be 5,000 million DM. All workers in the country with an annual income of less than 36,000 DM (48,000 DM for married workers) would receive a certificate each year giving them drawing rights on the Fund to the value of 200 DM; these certificates could be cashed only after seven years. The capital of the Fund would be used to grant loans to finance social investment.

The plan abandons the liberalism of earlier plans in that it aims not so much at increasing the power of wealth of the individual worker as at increasing collective power over the economy. The plan would indeed do little for the individual worker: 200 DM is little more than half the average weekly wage, and it is quite likely that the amount gained in this manner would be compensated for by lower wages. But it would give considerable power to the controllers of the central fund. It is calculated that after ten years the Fund would own about 25 per cent of the capital of all the larger companies in Germany, and that in thirty to forty years' time, the Fund would own virtually all German industry. Two-thirds of the board administering the Fund would be elected by the 20 million workers with certificate rights: each member would, according to the plan, represent about 50,000 certificate holders. The other third of the board would be representatives of the public interest. In practice, it is expected that the Fund would be controlled by the trade unions.

The fact that this plan has been accepted by the party conference of the principal government party does not mean that it will be put into effect. The SPDs coalition partner, the FDP, has its own capital-formation plan. This is somewhat similar in form, but it would benefit not only employed persons, but all residents in the Federal Republic. What is more important, there is no attempt to create a new central power in the economy; the funds created would be decentralised and administered not by the trade unions, but principally by the banks. Although both government parties are thus pledged to bring in a major reform in this area, they have so far been unable to reach a compromise.

These plans pose many interesting questions, but their full implications are best appreciated when related to the current discussion on codetermination

(*Mitbestimmung*). Like capital-formation plans, plans for codetermination[9] aim at democratising economic enterprises from within. But unlike the other two policies already outlined, the policy of codetermination did not spring directly from post-war liberal ideology. Rather, its adoption by the Federal government was originally a concession granted to the trade unions by the CDU. In view of the delicate state of the economy at the end of the 1940s, Adenauer agreed with the leader of the trade union federation (DGB), Boeckler, that if the unions were moderate in their wage demands and cooperative in their general approach, he, Adenauer, would see that a law was passed granting their demands for codetermination. In fact, the unions' wishes were met only in relation to the coal and steel industries; the codetermination they demanded was implemented in this area by a law of 1951, the *Montanmitbestimmungsgesetz* (MBG). By the time the law relating to the rest of the economy (the *Betriebsverfassungsgesetz*) was passed in October 1952, the position of the unions was no longer so strong and they were forced to accept a compromise.

The 1951 law, which applies to coal and steel firms with more than 1000 employees (orginally about a hundred in number, now about sixty), provides for equal representation of workers and shareholders on the 'supervisory board' (*Aufsichtsrat*) of these companies. Of the eleven members who normally sit on the board, five are chosen by the shareholders and five represent the employees of the company; a 'neutral' eleventh man is then chosen by the other ten. Of the five workers' delegates, three are chosen directly by the unions and two, who may of course be also members of the union, by the workers themselves. The equal representation of shareholders and workers applies only to the supervisory board, and not to the board of management (*Vorstand*) which is responsible for the day-to-day running of the firm. With regard to this board, the law provides only that one of its members, the work director (*Arbeitsdirektor*) may be appointed by the supervisory board only with the agreement of the workers' delegates. Nor are the workers represented at the general meetings of the shareholders of the company, which retain the ultimate power of decision.

The later law applies to all companies employing more than 500 people, but the representation of the workers on the supervisory board is limited to one-third, and there is no equivalent to the work director of the MBG. This general law has not worked well: many companies have taken steps to reduce the powers of the supervisory board, and the unions, dissatisfied with their representation, have done little to make the law work effectively.

Since their congress in Dusseldorf in 1963, the trade unions, after a period of disenchantment with the whole notion of codetermination, have been demanding the extension to all large companies (between 400 and 600 in all) of a model similar to that which now applies to coal and steel enterprises. A modified version of the DGB plan was adopted by the SPD in 1968. Although the present Government has promised to legislate on this issue during the current session of Parliament, the same difficulty has arisen as in the case of property formation. The coalition partners, the SPD and the FDP have so far been unable to reach any agreement. The FDP has put forward two plans of its own, one of which maintains majority representation for shareholders, while the other accepts parity for shareholders and workers, but insists that, in addition, a special position should be given to representatives of the senior salaried staff (*leitende Angestellte*).[10] The SPD and the unions object to this on the grounds that such representatives would tend to support the interests of the shareholders.

Given the influence of the FDP within the coalition, and given the fact that the SPD appear to be losing popularity to the FDP and to the CDU/CSU opposition, it is clear that the SPD plans on codetermination and property formation will have to be significantly modified if legislation is to be passed in this session. If, as a result of the strength of the unions and the left wing within the SPD, no compromise is reached before the next elections, then all one can say is that the present leadership of the SPD is unlikely to try to win an absolute majority in Parliament by basing its electoral campaign on a radical call for economic democracy.[11]

Nevertheless, the reforms planned by the SPD raise many interesting questions. Even if they became law without being modified, would they radically alter the structure of socioeconomic power? If both plans came into force, it would mean that within a few years, trade unionists and other representatives of the workers would form a majority on the supervisory boards of all large public companies, for, in addition to the seats which they would acquire under the codetermination law, they would soon be entitled to representation as shareholders under the capital formation law.

In so far as these measures would allow the representatives of the workers to participate in the wielding of economic power, they would indeed represent a step towards the goal of 'economic democracy'. That such a step would be very limited and that it would make very little difference to the way in which this power is used, is suggested by the experience with the MBG in the coal and steel industries.

Experience in this sector has shown that workers' representatives on supervisory boards have acted very much like any other members of those boards. The system has generally worked to the satisfaction of the shareholders in the enterprises effected. Thus, Herman J. Abs, the banker, was able to say at the CDU Party Conference in 1954:

'On the basis of the experience with it [codetermination] so far, I see it as a real success. It will, I believe stay with us in the future, so long as the social partners continue to strive for loyal cooperation and each is ready to give the other his due'[12]

The experience is even seen as making a positive contribution to management in so far as it promotes better industrial relations within the firm. Indeed one of the arguments on which the DGB has based its demand for an extension of codetermination is that it is in the interests of economic efficiency. As a leading industrialist put it:

'The trust between management and workers is made stronger and firmer, and that mutual mistrust which, under the slogan of the class struggle, has for so long burdened and, in part, poisoned the relations between the social partners, shall once and for all be overcome in an honest partnership between management, workers and shareholders'.[13]

The 'improvement of industrial relations' is perhaps the principal effect which the MBG has had. There has been no effect on the rate of concentration in the coal and steel industries. There has been no effect on the large number of pit closures in the coal industry, nor on the number of redundancies: at most one can say that the process of redundancy has been carried out more 'humanely'. There has been no effect on wage policies, nor on authoritarian and hierarchical structures within factories.

It may be argued that all this is due to the particular shortcomings of the MBG. Thus, the workers' representatives on the supervisory board are not protected against dismissal. Nor is there any possibility of making these representatives accountable to the workers, for they are obliged not to divulge confidential information disclosed in the meetings of the supervisory board. Most important of all, s.6 of the MBG obliges all members of the supervisory board, including the representatives of the workers, to work for the 'good of the enterprise'. But to place too great an emphasis on these provisions,[14] important though they are, is perhaps misleading. In a competitive market economy, it is not the law, but the necessity to survive which compels directors and managers, whoever they may be, to act in the interests of the enterprise, to compete for profits, to withhold information from their competitors and therefore from their workers, to hold down wages and to 'rationalise' their production and make men redundant when it is necessary. The achievement of codetermination or indeed of 'workers' control' will not make very much difference to this unless it is accompanied by other, more far-reaching measures.

The creation of a central fund controlled by the trade unions is unlikely to be any more effective in bringing about radical change. The effect of such a fund would depend on how the fund was managed. If the fund were invested in the most profitable manner, the social effect would be no greater than that of the creation of a large unit trust. If, on the other hand, the investment of the fund were inspired by social objectives, then the scheme would be less profitable to the individual worker and the general effect would be similar to that of a state subsidy in the area concerned.[15] There would also be considerable problems in the coordination of the social activity of the fund with that of the state. It may be argued that the long-term implication — the acquisition by the fund of almost all German industry in about forty years time — is revolutionary. This may be so, but it is clear that such a long-term socialisation of German industry could not take place without provoking considerable opposition, and it is hard now to say how the governments in the intervening period would react to such opposition.

This is not to dismiss the reforms proposed by the SPD as meaningless. Clearly, they do mark a reaction to dissatisfaction caused by the existing property relationships and they would mark a real shift in power to the trade unions. But it is only if such reforms were seen as being steps towards a much more fundamental change that this power could be wielded in a manner which would transcend the constraints imposed by competition in a market economy. It is much more likely, however, that such reforms would have the effect of further integrating the unions into the capitalist system and hinder them in their task of representing the interests of the workers. Whether the workers are made small shareholders, as under CDU plans, or the trade unions gain control of large amounts of capital, as under the SPD plan, the effect is the same: to blur the fundamental conflict between the interests of labour and those of capital.

Despite the cartel laws and despite the SPD's pledge to achieve a greater measure of economic democracy, the period since the War has seen the formation of ever larger units of economic power. Although the proposed reforms aim at democratising these units from within, such a reform, if it does come about, would make little difference to the fact that the power of these large units is wielded in the pursuit of private interests, in the pursuit of profits.

* * *

The trend towards the concentration of economic and political power is inevitable in an advanced capitalist society, and the West German experience provides but one illustration of the forces at work in all such societies. The same process of economic concentration is common to all advanced capitalist countries (and takes place, of course, not only within those countries but at an international level). This is inevitable in a competitive economy. The competition is most likely to be won by those enterprises which are the most highly and efficiently mechanised and which possess the largest funds for technological research and for marketing their products. Thus, 'the average size of enterprises increases uninterruptedly; a large number of small enterprises are beaten in the competitive struggle by a small number of big enterprises which command an increasing share of capital, labour, funds and production in entire branches of industry'.[16] In no country has this process been halted by antitrust legislation. Competition is increasingly international and, even leaving aside the direct influence of big business on government, no government is likely to take action which would damage the competitiveness of its industry.

The growth in the size of enterprises, or, more specifically, the increase in the scale of the investments undertaken by these enterprises, has contributed to that other phenomenon of modern capitalism, the growth of economic planning by the state and of state intervention in the economy. The scale of these private investments, and the risk involved as a result of the high rate of technological innovation, compels large enterprises to plan their production, marketing, research, etc. on a long-term basis. This in turn leads to pressure on the state to stabilise those conditions (labour costs, consumption, etc.) which play an essential part in the internal planning of the large enterprises, in other words to plan itself and to take action to avoid the conjunctural fluctuations of the economy. This, together with other social and economic pressures,[17] has led to attempts by all Western governments systematically to 'manage the economy'. . . .

The unions have not led a real struggle
for change. Above all, they have never used
their main weapon, the strike, to force
the bosses to improve
immigrant workers' conditions.

Immigrant Workers and Trade Unions in the German Federal Republic

Stephen Castles and Godula Kosack

Since the middle of the sixties, West German capitalism has been running
into increasing difficulties, which has reduced willingness to make economic
concessions to the working class. The result has been a gradual move away
from the apathy characteristic of many workers during the period of the
"economic miracle" (1949-65), and an increase in class conflict. A peak in this
development was the unofficial strike movement in 1973. A new factor in this
movement was the leading role played by immigrant workers in many strikes.
In some cases they led the strikes or even struck alone, in others they acted
as a catalyst in factories where German workers were also militant.

The militancy of the immigrant workers creates fresh and pressing
problems for the trade union leadership. In order to understand these and the
measures which result from them, two questions must first be answered:

1. What function does the employment of immigrant workers have for
West German capitalism and what changes have there been in this function
over the last fifteen years?

2. What is the general function of the trade unions in West German
capitalism and what is their specific function in regard to the immigrant
section of the proletariat?

After this we will describe the actual policy of the unions since the
beginning of the recruitment of the foreign labor.

The Function of Immigrant Labor
In West German Capitalism

The employment and super-exploitation of underprivileged groups in

From "Immigrant Workers and Trade Unions in the German Federal Republic," by
Stephan Castles and Godula Kosack, *Race and Class,* copyright ©1974, and reprinted
by permission of the authors and *Race and Class.*

most capitalist countries — for example, the blacks in the U.S.A. and South
Africa, the rural-urban migrants in Italy and Japan, and the immigrant
workers in almost all Western European countries — has two main
functions:

1.   The unemployed masses form an industrial reserve army which puts
pressure on wages, thus helping to keep the profit rate high.

2.   The working class is split according to race, nationality or area of
origin.[1]

The underprivileged position of one section of the working class is
complemented by the somewhat better position of another section. Like the
whites in the U.S.A. and South Africa, the indigenous workers in Western
Europe tend to have certain privileges, better working conditions and higher
pay. The mass media, the official propaganda apparatus and the educational
system deepen the split in the working class by spreading nationalism and
racism in order to gain the collaboration of the privileged section of the
working class in oppressing the other. The result is the creation of a "labor
aristocracy" prepared to defend its apparent economic and social security by
betraying its real class interests. This weakens the labor movement.
Discriminatory legislation (in Germany the Auslandergesetz — Foreigners
Law — of 1965; in Britain the 1971 Immigration Act) denies vital civil and
political rights to the already underprivileged section of the working class,
which deepens the split.

The use of an external or foreign reserve army became necessary for the
capitalists in West Germany later than in other countries. Up until 1961 three
other labor sources were available to put pressure on wages, keeping up
profits and allowing the long-lasting export-led boom known as the
"economic miracle." These were: the large numbers of unemployed created
by the collapse of the Nazi war economy in 1945, the seven million expellees
in the territories lost to Poland, the Soviet Union and Czechoslovakia at the
end of the war, and three million refugees from the German Democratic
Republic. The first labor shortages appeared in building and agriculture in
the mid-fifties, and the bilateral labor recruitment agreement with Italy —
the first of its kind — was made at this time.

The employment of immigrant workers was initially regarded by
employers, unions and government as a temporary measure. But by the
beginning of the sixties the existing domestic labor reserves had been
absorbed, the stream of refugees from East Germany had stopped, and it had
become apparent that further internal reserves (rural-urban migrants, not-
yet-employed women), could not be mobilized to an appreciable extent.
Nationalization and the replacement of relatively labor-intensive methods of
increasing production by capital-intensive methods were not in themselves

sufficient to maintain the growth and competitiveness of West German industry. Capitalists began to recruit (through an efficient state recruitment system) large numbers of workers from the undeveloped parts of Southern Europe and from Turkey. In this way they were able to prevent rapid wage growth in the unskilled and semi-skilled categories.

By the mid-sixties the employment of immigrant workers had become an essential part of West German economic structure. By 1966 there were 1.3 million immigrant workers (not counting dependents). But the government continued to emphasize that immigration was not a permanent factor for Germany, in order to avoid making the social expenditure — on housing, schools, health facilities — which was already necessary. The employers regarded the immigrant workers as a "mobile labor potential," as Ulrich Freiherr von Gienanth, an official of the German Employers' Association, put it. They could be got rid of quickly in case of economic difficulties. "It would be dangerous to limit this mobility through a large-scale settlement policy," wrote Gienanth in support of the government policy.[2]

The advantages (for the bosses) but also the limitations of this labor market policy became apparent in the 1966-67 recession. The causes of the recession were, on the one hand, the increase in wage levels in the years immediately preceding, on the other, the rising level of international competition. The recruitment of immigrant workers could not hold back wage growth to the same extent as had formerly been the case with the internal labor reserves and the refugees from East Germany. The immigrants were mainly without industrial training and experience, lacked general education, and most could not speak German. Their competition could not hold down the wages of skilled and non-manual workers, who together make up more than half the labor force. The braking effect on the wages of unskilled and semi-skilled workers was not sufficient to prevent considerable growth in the general average wage level at this time. The employers used a recession to control wage-growth and restore "labor discipline." A further advantage for the bosses was that they were able to export a substantial part of the social costs of unemployment. For although the number of immigrant workers sank by 400,000 in only a few months, the number of immigrants receiving unemployment benefits was never more than 29,000. In addition a large-scale propaganda campaign against the immigrants by the bosses and their mass-media led to a considerable increase in hostility towards immigrants at this time. The immigrant workers were used as scapegoats to divert attention from the real causes of the recession.[3]

On the other hand the limitations of the "mobile labor potential" policy also became evident. The number of immigrant workers did not fall below 900,000 although large numbers of Germans became unemployed. It became obvious that immigrants could not always be easily replaced by German workers, because they were concentrated in certain industries (building, engineering, chemicals) and above all in certain socio-economic groups (unskilled and semi-skilled manual). Qualified German personnel were often unwilling to take such jobs. In addition, the employers frequently sacked older German workers rather than young immigrants who, due to their lack of industrial experience and their need to earn a lot quickly, could often be conned into working their guts out on piece-rates. Moreover, even then a large number of immigrant workers had already brought over their families and become firmly established in a specific area. All in all, it proved impossible to make the immigrant workers bear the full burden of unemployment in the recession.

After the recession the number of immigrants employed rose steeply once again, reaching a peak figure of 2.4 million in 1973. Including dependents, there must be close to four million immigrants in West Germany. Eleven per cent of all employed persons are immigrants, and the quota is far higher among manual workers in industry — 20 to 25 per cent. In addition to its political function for the ruling class (division of the workers), immigrant labor has today a double economic function: one section of the immigrant labor force remains a "mobile labor potential" which can be moved from branch to branch or sent home as the interests of capital dictate; another section provides most of the labor in certain industries and occupational categories (those with the worst pay and poorest working conditions). This second group cannot be dismissed easily, as there are not enough German workers willing and able to replace them.

The legal and administrative measures of the German authorities reflect the role assigned to immigrant labor. Immigrants' political rights are severely restricted by the Foreigners Law and by new regulations issued since. A special department of the Verfassungsschutz, the German equivalent of the F.B.I., watches over immigrants, and it is known that the authorities tolerate the activities of Spanish, Greek, Persian and other secret police and even cooperate with them. Any immigrant who steps out of line is likely to be expelled immediately. A system of varying types of residence permits conferring different rights helps to divide the immigrants among themselves: hard-working, "politically reliable" immigrants get privileges compared with the others. On the other hand, efforts are made to keep part of the immigrant labor mobile, in order to save the social costs which cannot be avoided in the long run in case of permanent settlement. The state government of Bavaria went so far as to introduce a "rotation policy," according to which no immigrant should be allowed to stay more than five years. Such measures are in part a reaction to the growing unwillingness of immigrants to accept the worst social conditions, which has been shown in a wave of rent strikes and squatting in the last few years. A further measure has been the recent increase in the recruitment fee of the state recruitment service: an employer must now pay DM. 1000 (over $350) per worker, instead of DM. 300. This has had little effect, however, since many employers (illegally) pressure the workers into paying the fee back to them.

The Function of the Trade Unions with Regard to Immigrant Workers

The trade unions of the German Federal Republic have long since become a stabilizing factor in the capitalist system. With its Dusseldorf Program of 1963 the D.G.B. (German Trade Union Federation) accepted the capitalist form of economic growth and made this its own goal. This means that the unions — like the employers — must have an interest in guaranteeing capital accumulation through high profit rates, which means relatively low wages. The unions are therefore compelled to restrain their members from wage demands and industrial action which might endanger the high profit rates.

On the other hand, the unions cannot openly oppose the day-to-day interests of their members. This would lead to a weakening of the union's basis through loss of membership, so that it would no longer be capable of carrying out collective bargaining or industrial action. Such weak unions do not even serve the interests of the bosses: the ideology of "social partnership" requires unions at least strong enough to canalize and restrict the demands of the workers.[4] If the unions become too weak the probable result is spontaneous mass movements outside their control, which may eventually lead to revolutionary forms of organization. Thus even unions which support the capitalist system cannot afford to entirely ignore the demands of their members.

The unions therefore work in the following way: they represent the interests and demands of the members to a limited extent. In case of disputes they take over the leadership and then take the steam out of the movement through long-drawn-out negotiations and formalized procedures which eventually only get out of the bosses what these can afford to pay without endangering profits.[5] The increasing difficulties of West German capitalism in recent years make this double task of the unions more and more arduous. The capitalists attempt increasingly to move away from a free labor market in order to allow long-term planning of wage costs. Incomes policy in Germany takes the guise of voluntary "concerted action" and "stability policy" in which the unions participate. This makes it increasingly difficult for the unions to even appear to represent their members. The result is an increasing tendency towards spontaneous movements — notably the waves

of unofficial strikes in 1969 and 1973 — which question the policies and
structures of the unions.

What does this dual function of the unions mean for their policy towards
immigrant workers? In so far as the recruitment of immigrant workers serves
capitalist growth, it is supported by the unions. However, as the presence of
immigrant workers tends to harm the interests of German workers by
keeping down wages, the unions must try to alleviate these effects. They do
this by demanding equal pay for immigrant workers and by calling for
measures to aid social integration from the government. Integration and
control of the immigrant workers also fits in with the interests of the union
leadership, who fear that immigrants may become more militant than
German workers. Through measures like the setting up of advisory services
and the publication of information in foreign languages, it is hoped to get the
immigrants into the unions and to reduce their potential for independent
unofficial action.[6]

The unions face a dilemma: on the one hand, they must try to prevent
immigrants being used to put pressure on wages, on the other hand labor
immigration is profitable for capital just because it keeps wages down and
splits the working class. If the unions carry out their system-stabilizing task
of limiting wage demands, then they must act against the demands of the
members, who want this downward pressure on wages eliminated. The
unions try to solve this contradiction by trying to convince the German and
immigrant workers with resounding phrases that their interests are being
looked after, while at the same time pursuing a policy of disciplining the
immigrant workers. The dialectical repressive function of the unions is
shown in their policy towards immigrant workers yet again: the unions can
only support the capitalist system if they are able to appear not as oppressors
but as mediators, on the one hand between labor and capital, on the other
between German and immigrant workers. The unions tend to lose their
function to the extent that the workers come to understand it. But if the
unions are no longer capable of fulfilling their integrative mediation
function, then the workers are compelled to fight — either spontaneously or
in new organizations — against the now evident power of capital.

Union Policies Towards Immigrant Workers

The contradictory aims of the unions are justified in the following way by
the Federal Executive Committee of the D.G.B.:

> In order to surmount existing labor market bottlenecks, the D.G.B. and its
> member unions agreed in principle in 1955 to the employment of foreign
> employees. They saw in this a necessary contribution to safeguarding full
> employment in an expanding economy and at the same time a practical step

of social and trade union solidarity. In order to prevent foreign employees being used as wagecutters, the D.G.B. demanded right from the outset that recruitment abroad should not be carried out directly by the employers but rather in the framework of definite labor market policy through the Federal Labor Office. The Federal Government agreed to this. In every case the principle of equality with German employees in wages, labor and social rights is to be applied.

In fact, the legal recruitment monopoly of the Federal Labor Office does not prevent illegal recruitment by so-called "slave dealers," nor does formal equality prevent de facto discrimination against immigrants at work. Even real wage equality would not prevent the foreign reserve army from putting pressure on wages, as the expended labor in itself tends to keep wages down. As to the working and living conditions of immigrants, it is therefore not so much what the unions have achieved in terms of formal guarantees that counts, but rather that they have to fight actual discrimination and to achieve concrete improvements.

The unions have protested against the more spectacular examples of "slave-dealing." They have demanded better working conditions and safety regulations, they have complained about the bad housing conditions and restricted educational opportunities of the immigrants, they have demanded reforms in the Foreigners Law to ease family reunification and to give "well-behaved" immigrants the right to settle in West Germany. But all these campaigns have taken the form of verbal demands and appeals to the humanity of the exploiters. The unions have not led a real struggle for change. Above all, they have never used their main weapon, the strike, to force the bosses to improve immigrant workers' conditions. They have done little more for the immigrant worker than to play the role of a social fire brigade, which appears where the system shows its worst aspects. They act like a charitable organization which alleviates the worst effects of the capitalist market economy and in doing so helps to safeguard the system as a whole.

The analogy to a charitable organization is not coincidental. In West Germany social work with immigrants has been delegated by the government to voluntary organizations, mainly religious ones. Like these, the unions have set up advisory offices, which are partly financed by the government. Here immigrants can get advice on problems concerning work, family, housing, law and so on. The unions treat the other social services as competitors, as the following quotation from a report of the Metal Workers Union (I.G.M.) shows:

> Where these social services detect a weakness in the work of the trade union organization, where there are no shop stewards for the foreign colleagues or where the stewards remain passive or do not receive adequate support,

particularly where the works council does not take action in the case of complaints from foreign employees, there the social services take special satisfaction in outdoing the union in its very own field — particularly in the eyes of the public and the foreign employees.[8]

In examining the relationship of the unions to the immigrant workers, one cannot limit oneself to describing special union social services for them. Much more important is the participation of the immigrant workers in the normal life of the union, as shown by membership and the holding of union offices. At the beginning of 1971 the six main immigrant nationalities (Yugoslavs, Turks, Italians, Greeks, Spaniards, Portuguese) had an average membership rate of 22.4 per cent. The Turks and Spaniards had the highest membership rate (27 per cent), followed by the Italians (23 per cent), the Greeks (22 per cent), the Yugoslavs (17 per cent) and the Portuguese (15 per cent). The membership rate varies considerably from industry to industry. The Chemical Workers Union (I.G. Chemie) has organized 43 per cent of all immigrants working in its sector.[9] Nearly one third of all immigrant workers in the metal industry are members of the Metal Workers Union (I.G. Metall), indicating a membership rate only slightly below that of German workers. This is all the more astonishing when one takes into account that most immigrants are of rural origin and that trade union membership may lead to repressive measures by the reactionary governments in the countries of origin upon return.

But immigrant workers are considerably unrepresented among trade union office holders. In 1973 only 5,633 foreign workers were elected as shop stewards of the Metal Workers Union — 4.7 per cent of all stewards elected.[10] This is an improvement compared with 1970, when only 2.4 per cent of all stewards were immigrant workers, but is still low when one considers that about 10 per cent of the union's members are immigrants. On average there is one foreign shop steward for about every forty foreign union members in the metal industry, compared with one German steward for every fifteen German union members.[11] Under-representation is still greater with regards to works councils.[12] Since 1972 foreigners have had equal rights to be elected as works councillors, but they still have to overcome greater difficulties than German colleagues when they wish to represent their compatriots. The Metal Workers Union only puts immigrants with a good knowledge of German on its candidates lists, which excludes many able and militant immigrants. Unions often give the best places on the lists (which is decisive due to the system of proportional representation) to workers who have been in the factory longest. This practice is disadvantageous to immigrants, and was one factor in the conflict between immigrant workers and the works council at Ford of Cologne during the strike in August 1973 (which will be described below). A Turkish union member standing for election in the 1972 works council elections was assigned, despite his popularity, a very low place on the candidates list. When the local union leadership refused to give him a better place he stood for election on an independent list and was elected with a very large number of votes. Against this, the works council majority refused to apply for him to be released from work to carry out his works council duties, accusing him of anti-union behavior.[13]

Altogether, 1,445 immigrants were elected as works councillors in the metal industry in 1972; that makes 2.2 per cent of the total elected. This compares with an immigrant share in the labor force in the factories concerned of 14.2 per cent.[14] It seems likely that immigrant workers are even more under-represented in other industries, with the possible exception of chemicals. The degree of under-representation varies from nationality to nationality and is probably greatest for the Turks, the largest and on average most recently arrived group of immigrants. The Greeks, Italians and Spaniards are somewhat better represented, though still much worse than Germans.

If the unions seriously want strong immigrant participation, then they need to take measures to improve the representation of immigrants in trade union offices and works councils. The Ford strike showed how great the gulf between the unions and the works council on the one hand and immigrant workers on the other has become in some cases: here the Turkish workers refused to negotiate with the employers if the works council took part in the meetings. They regarded the works council as a tool of the bosses which had sold them out. The under-representation of immigrants in union representative functions leads to the supposition that the union leadership wants only the passive membership of the immigrants, but is basically concerned above all with the interests of the German workers.

The most important criterion for the policy of the unions towards immigrant workers is their behavior in actual industrial conflicts in which immigrants are involved. Here it is only possible to mention a few cases, which however may be regarded as fairly typical for the behavior of the unions.[15] There are three basic types of conflicts, which require varying responses from the unions.

Firstly, there are general conflicts between labor and capital, which are not necessarily carried out within the factory. The most important case was the anti-immigrant campaign between 1964 and 1966.[16] This was a large-scale propaganda campaign of the bosses, who, through their mass media, tried to create hostility towards immigrants and to use it to fight against the trade union demand for shorter working hours. The campaign started with the speech of the then Federal Chancellor Erhard in May 1964. He called upon German workers to work longer so that the immigrants could be sent home. The peak of the agitation was the headline in the mass-circulation BILDZEITUNG of March 31, 1966, which asked provocatively: "Do foreign workers work harder than German workers?" The climate of hostility towards immigrants was such that the headline led to a series of fights and unofficial strikes. The unions tried to counter the campaign through articles in the trade union press and leaflets distributed in factories. In some cases meetings were held to discuss the problems of the employment of immigrant workers. But no decisive steps were taken to fight against the anti-immigrant propaganda. Offensive measures like strikes or overtime bans were never even considered. The moral appeals for international solidarity were not successful in reducing hostility towards immigrants, as a series of opinion polls taken at this time show.[17] As the unions basically support the capitalist system, they were unable to show how exploitation of the industrial reserve army and the use of propaganda to divide up the workers is an intrinsic part of capitalism that can only be combatted by fighting the system as a whole. The moral appeals could have no effect on the workers, who know perfectly well that the bosses recruit immigrants to keep down wages and raise profits. In retrospect the anti-immigrant campaign of 1964-66 can be seen as the ideological preparation for the 1966-67 recession, during which the unions were just as helpless in preventing the splitting of the class and in defending immigrants' rights as they had been during the preparatory phase.

Secondly, there are industrial conflicts in which unions carry out official action to secure higher wages. In such cases, the West German employers often try to weaken the workers' front through special forms of repression against the immigrants. For example, during the rubber workers' strike in the State of Hessen in November 1967, the management tried to break the strike by threatening to expel the immigrants from the works hostels if they did not resume work immediately. At the same time they distributed a leaflet to German workers, blaming the strike on the immigrants, whom they described as "a drunken Mediterranean horde." In this case the Chemical Workers Union was able to take measures which successfully countered these attempts to split the workers, and the strike was won.[18] Frequently, immigrants who strike are threatened by the bosses with deportation and the authorities collaborate in such measures. However, the authors know of no industrial dispute in which immigrant workers have allowed themselves to be used as scabs. On the contrary, the solidarity shown in the behavior of the immigrants often leads to the removal of prejudices during industrial disputes.

Thirdly, there are industrial disputes in which immigrant workers fight against special forms of discrimination. Such struggles, which aim at combatting the oppression of immigrants, seldom receive support from the unions and the German workers, and tend more and more to take the form of unofficial strikes. Examples are the strikes at Hella in Lippstadt in September 1969 and July 1973, and at Kharmann, Ford, and Pierburg in 1973.

The Hella car components factory in Lippstadt has the distinction of being one of the few factories which played a prominent part in the strike movements of both 1969 and 1973. In both cases, immigrant workers took the lead. In 1969, 95 per cent of the workers in the northern branch works were immigrants, mainly Spanish and Italian women, graded as semi-skilled. They were paid much less than the German workers in the main works, who were for the most part skilled. The immigrants had had to sign contracts, which they could not properly understand, in their countries of origin. Wage discrimination was the original issue in the strike. In addition, demands were made concerning Christmas bonuses, which the management cut when workers had been off sick, and the length of holidays. The German workers gave the strike some verbal support but did not join in. The Metal Workers Union tried to get the immigrants back to work: the claims were justified, said the officials, but the method of an unofficial strike was not permissible. The management called in the police and the consuls of the countries of origin. The immigrant women found themselves unable to continue against this united front; they returned to work without achieving their demands.

The behavior of management and union had not changed in 1973 at Hella. The German workers were given an "inflation bonus" of 15 pfennig per hour, while the immigrants got nothing. In this way the bosses successfully split the workers, for the Germans took no part in the subsequent strike of the immigrant workers. The Metal Workers Union once again opposed the strike. The bosses called in the police and the consuls. But this time the immigrant workers had elected a militant strike committee which led the struggle. Their unity resulted in victory: an increase of 40 pfennig per hour for the lower wage group and 30 pfennig per hour for the upper one.[20]

The strike at the Ford factory in Cologne in August 1973 was to date the most important expression of workers' resistance against their super-exploitation. It also showed most clearly the gulf between the union apparatus and the immigrant workers. Ford has 34,000 employees of whom more than half are immigrants, the largest group being the 14,000 Turks. The Germans have mainly skilled or supervisory posts, as have some of the Italians. The semi-skilled work, particularly the extremely arduous and intensive assembly work on the production-line, is carried out almost entirely by Turks. Management has used the special situation of the Turks — their poverty and rural origins, the long waiting lists (about a million Turks have applied for work in Germany) at the German recruitment centers — to raise the speed of production at an unbearable level. The shop stewards and works councillors, nearly all skilled German workers, who do not understand the problems of the Turks, have done nothing to prevent this and have therefore lost the trust of the immigrants. As early as 1964, a survey carried out on behalf of the Metal Workers Union showed how great the gap between German and immigrant workers had become,[21] but no effective measures were taken to change the situation. The works council elections of 1972, already mentioned above, were another danger sign which was ignored.

The strike started when 300 Turkish workers were fired because they overstayed their holidays. The 20-day annual holiday is far too short for those who have to travel for seven or eight days to reach their families in Anatolia. The sacked workers were not replaced, making the pace of work even greater for those who remained. The result was a spontaneous strike in one department, which quickly spread throughout the works. A strike committee was elected and demands were made which at first united immigrant and German workers: a raise of 1 DM. per hour for all workers, reinstatement of the sacked workers, six weeks paid holiday, reduction of production-line and machine speeds, more workers on the line and the machines. This immigrant-led strike at a major industrial plant terrified the German bosses, and they used all the weapons at their command to break it. Together they condemmed the strike, which, they alleged, was led by foreign communist agitators. Large police forces were made ready. The BILDZEITUNG mobilized nationalist feelings with headlines about "Turkish Terror at Ford." The works council did everything possible to undermine the unity of the workers. By making concessions on pay, which was the main issue for the German workers, the management was able to divide them from the Turks. This made possible an attack on the strike leadership by supervisory staff assisted by disguised policemen. The leaders were arrested and the demoralized Turks were forced back to work by threats of dismissal and deportation. The BILDZEITUNG celebrated the event with the headline "German workers liberate their factory" (as if the factory belonged to the workers!) while the Ford management praised the works councillors for their help and their "physical courage" in fighting against the workers. Ford is an extreme example of how German trade unionists have become tools of management against the immigrants, who now have to fight not only against the bosses and against the police, but also against their own "representatives."

An important factor in the Ford strike, as in other strikes in 1973, was that the immigrants were fighting not only for higher pay but also for better working conditions, in particular for a reduction in the health-destroying work-pace on production lines and in piece-work. Traditionally, the West Germans have not struggled for such demands. Rather they have become "wage-machines" concerned only with raising pay-rates through national negotiations. In the collective bargaining and official strike in Baden-Wurtemberg in the autumn of 1973, immediately following the unofficial movement, the Metal Workers Union for the first time raised demands concerning working conditions.

To sum up, it may be said that the unions seldom take account of the special needs and interests of immigrant workers, and that the immigrants often do not feel that the unions represent them. In many cases they see the local representatives of the unions as tools of the bosses. Such problems do not concern the immigrants alone. Most shop stewards and works councillors are German skilled workers or even foremen.[22] They tend first and foremost to represent the interests of the group from which they come. It is not just the immigrant workers whose interests are neglected — the same applies to all unskilled and semi-skilled workers. Apart from immigrants, the largest group in these categories are women workers who in West Germany, as elsewhere, are considerably underpaid. This explains why the unions generally make demands for a percentage rise in wages, which corresponds to the interests of better-paid workers by maintaining differentials, but until the strikes of 1973 did nothing against piece-work and inhuman working conditions.

In the last analysis, the decision whether to form separate organizations or not can only be taken by the immigrant workers themselves. But such decisions are affected strongly by union policy. If unions are unable to represent discriminated groups, if union officials become tools of the bosses and participate in discriminatory policies, then independent organizations cannot be avoided in the long run. In the U.S.A. and South Africa, where the established unions have in part become organs of racism, the formation of independent black organizations was a necessary and correct step. Things are not (yet) so bad in West Germany; few union officials consciously serve the interests of capial; most oppose the discrimination and super-exploitation of immigrant workers, at least verbally. But if this verbal opposition is not in the near future transformed into effective policies, then there can be little doubt that a section of the immigrant workers will look for new forms of organization.

**Certainly the real political practice of the
SPD-FDP is in marked contrast to the
substance and techniques they use in
presenting themselves in their propaganda.**

The Brandt Affair and the SPD: Depersonalizing History
Wolfgang Nitsch

One should not be deceived by the apparently abrupt and dramatic transition from the peace and reform chancellor Brandt to the law and order chancellor Schmidt, who declared in an official address of May 18, 1974, that the basis for detente was to be developed by concentrating on what was economically feasible and by strengthening the military and political power of NATO. In fact, one can trace an internal, politico-structural continuity and logic in the period of the social-liberal coalition since 1969[1] — a point which will be treated in greater detail later. One can also observe certain politico-structural characteristics of the German Social Democratic Party which reveal a great deal about social democratic parties in general. These characteristics can be traced back over nearly a century and are part of a formal process of gradual integration which has led social democratic parties to defend and stabilize the capitalist social order in the advanced industrial countries of Western Europe. I am referring here specifically to the conditions and mechanisms in the permanent reproduction of the ideological base and mass membership of these parties which depends on rosy pictures of social reform and peace, popular political leaders and highly disciplined bureaucratic party machines. Needless to say, these pictures have little to do with the party's (*real*) political practice.

Indeed, one notes a certain regularity in the cycles of these illusionary programs as they become caught up in the dynamics of real contradictions in capitalist-imperialist development and as they lose their effectiveness in winning the support of the masses and legitimizing the policies of these parties within the capitalist state. For this reason we see a series of alternating phases. First, a basic platform of general policy of reform is usually projected into a more distant future, and the practice of social democracy consists either in the propagandistic intensification of the fear of crises and catastrophes among the populace or in directing this fear toward a scapegoat. Thus a law and order mentality is fostered as a means for inducing mass loyalty. This in turn is followed by a new phase which once again attempts to create illusions of peace, reform and security among the now uncertain masses.

Of course, it would be bad campaign and party psychology to allow the same political leaders to symbolize and organize the different phases of this cyclical "natural history" of social democracy, just as it would be unwise to abandon all continuity in the leadership of the party. This is because there is always a problem of integrating the various factions within the party (along with their respective mass support) no matter what the phase may be, and because these factions tend to be too one-sided and inflexible in backing either the prosperity of peace and reform or the austerity policies of law and order. In this context it is only logical that Willy Brandt, as leader of the Party, retain a significant function with respect to internal Party matters of integration and long-range planning.

These "natural" cycles of Party history are materially rooted in the conjunctural cycles of the natural history of capitalism itself — without the two necessarily running parallel in all their facets. On both levels, it is a "natural history" which takes place behind the backs of the actual participants, the entrepreneurs in business and politics, and which remains beyond the scope of their understanding. Therefore, the old romantic myths about the SPD as a party of treason and conspiracy are totally out of place — both phylogenetically, because the species "Social Democratic Party" had already cast off the last revolutionary "stowaways" by its political cooperation with the state in waging World War I; and ontogenetically, because an individual becomes intensively absorbed in the operations of blind, daily routine of pursuing a career as Party functionary. Since World War I everything has become the legitimate subject of statistical probability: for instance, how to calculate the "marginal value" of specific sources, promotional techniques, public-image making and even estimates of internal party morale.

In the postwar history of the FRG there have been three social democratic cycles:

—from the hard-line, anti-communist policy of the Cold War and the cooperation with bourgeois parties in restoring capitalist-parliamentary order in the FRG under Kurt Schumacher (1945-52) to the more conciliatory program of detente and re-unification and the re-activation of traditional social democratic policies of social reform under Erich Ollenhauer;

--from a new tough, pro-western foreign and military policy and a program of liberal market economy which also included emergency and police armament against internal anti-capitalist opposition from the time of the Godesburg Program until the Party participated in the Great Coalition with the CDU/CSU (1959-68) to the flexible and active Eastern Policy and internal reform program which was begun during the Great Coalition and continued during the small coalition directed by Brandt (roughly 1972/73);

—followed once again by a phase of somewhat intensified demarcation regarding relations with the GDR and a concentration on internal security, stability and income policies, involving the abandonment of nearly all the announced reform programs. This is a phase which had already commenced during the second half of Brandt's chancellorship.

The second and third cycles can clearly be connected to the phases of economic recession and structural crisis of 1967/8 and 1973/4; however, they are not due exclusively to these factors but are bound up with a number of developments: the changes in the global strategies of the superpowers, USA and USSR; the SPD's competition with other political parties; the ideological effects of certain long-range socio-economic structural regroupings in the so-called intermediate strata between the industrial working class and capital (the relative declassification of old and new middle strata and their relationship to the protest movement among students and intellectuals in the professions).

If Brandt's fall thus complies with the internal logic of the cyclical pattern of social democratic party history, then one can speak (in a very limited sense) of a far-reaching political change of course. Certainly the real political practice of the SPD-FDP is in marked contrast to the substance and techniques they use in presenting themselves in their propaganda. This becomes clear when one attempts to answer the question as to what the policies of this coalition have achieved up to now for the majority of workers whose interests the SPD claims to represent.[2]

Brandt's official government address of 1969 contained a flood of reform promises which included equal opportunity through educational reform, improvement in living conditions, environmental, traffic, and highway planning, tax reform to benefit the poor, profit-sharing organized by the government and co-determination for workers in industrial plants. All this was propagandistically phrased in slogans coined in the United States and passed on by the brain trusts of OECD and NATO which sang sweet songs about improving the "quality of life" for everyone and regulating economic growth to bring this about. However, by the time Brandt delivered his second official address in 1973 — in other words, long before the first official speech by his successor Helmut Schmidt — there was little talk about reform.

What really happened to the "quality of life" for workers in the FRG?

Generally speaking, the main indicators of the quality of life are revealed through the scope and type of public expenditures and services. Since 1969 the SPD-FDP coalition has been fighting on shifting fronts and without any notable success against cyclical blow-ups of the economy using spending cut-backs and special taxes (1969/70, 1973); against inflationary processes of cost-transferring (1970-74); against stagflation (1971, 1974); against the permanent crises of the world monetary system; and against the artificially generated world-wide energy crisis (1973/74). During this period it was not even possible to attain the modest level of public services achieved by the CDU/CSU administrations during postwar reconstruction from 1949 to 1966. The percentage of public investments — the yardstick for measuring any improvement in the quality of life — has fallen consistently year after year in relation to the total public expenditures and particularly in relation to the gross national product. From 1964 to 1970 "*private*" investments rose on the average roughly 6% each year, public investments only 3%. Public services have been shrinking since 1970. In 1971 they amounted to 4% less than the previous year. In 1972 and 1973 they did not even reach the reduced level of 1971.[3] With the exception of highway construction programs and the educational system, total public investment in the public sphere (social programs and facilities, public health, municipal disposal systems) has been on the decline since 1971.[4]

The government has been equally unsuccessful, at least within the limits of the available budgetary funds, at effecting any changes in its reform priorities to improve public health and environmental protection.[5] A plan for the long-range financing of the educational system was declared no longer financially feasible in May of 1974 by the state ministers of finance, who, according to the Federal Constitution, are primarily responsible for education. This plan, long overdue by any international standards, had only been passed in June of 1973 after years of in-fighting between the states controlled by the CDU and the SPD-FDP. The plan would have hiked the percentage of the budget for education and science from 4.8% (1970) to 7.6% (1985) of the gross national product, and its percentage of the total public budget from 16.9% to 22.6% (only 70% of this amount was to be spent for education in the narrower sense of the term, which excluded basic and major research projects).[6]

It could easily be demonstrated in many areas of public service that the tendencies toward stagnation and restriction are closely related to tendencies which reduce the possibilities for equal opportunity created by these public services. Thus in public health and education it was impossible to stop the growing discrepancies in service between municipal or densely populated areas and rural regions as well as the discrepancies between middle-class and working-class sections. Nor could anything be done to offset the increasingly dysfunctional effects due to the intensification of capital in certain sectors of public service (sophisticated technological systems in the area of education and health which were privately produced for profit and have little effect on the majority of patients and students). Although the census of 1970 recorded that 51% of all gainfully employed males were from the working class, the Federal Bureau of Statistics published a study in July 1974 which indicated that only 11.5% of all higher education students were working-class children. According to the same study, only 16% of all pupils were admitted into college preparatory training programs in the high school, and only 18% of these pupils came from the working-class families. Since 1969 an increasing number of disciplines at universities and colleges have restricted their admissions. Hence, in Baden-Württemberg, a state which had initiated a particularly expansive educational program in the late 1960s, 130,000 applicants out of 800,000 will be turned away between 1974 and 1978. (Fourth Comprehensive Plan for University Construction Presented by the States and the Federal Government on July 15, 1974). According to this data, at the beginning of the 1973-74 school year, the percentage of pupils transferring from general elementary schools (*Grundschule*) to college-preparatory secondary schools (*Gymnasium*) was for the first time on the decline. Moreover, the decline among working-class children transferring to college preparatory secondary schools was 9% greater than among pupils from other social strata.[7] And since the federal government intends more and more to do away with scholarship grants in favor of loans, children of working-class families who would like to attend the university will become increasingly discouraged, and the discrepancies will continue to grow.

The quality of life for wage-earners has declined under the SPD-FDP coalition not only in the sector of "public poverty," but also in the sector of "private wealth" (in Galbraith's terms). As is well known, corporations, businesses and independent professionals have no difficulty circumventing the negative effects of the measures taken to stabilize the economy (special anti-cyclical taxes, investment taxes, anti-cyclical surtaxes) by means of a number of strategies (tax manipulation, tax avoidance through exports, passing increased tax costs on to the consumers through price hikes), whereas the average wage-earner is forced to accept these taxes. This means that there is a constant transferral of the tax burden to the wage-earner paying regular withholding taxes. The withholding tax revenues rise at a rate which transcends the growth rate of the gross national product, while the rate of profit and income taxes falls below the growth rate. With the exception of the general stagnation in 1971, real corporate profit rates have risen each year, while the percentage of the real income of wage-earners during the years 1967-1973 has fallen beneath the wage rate percentage of 1965 and 1966 and has continued to drop since 1971. The income discrepancy between people who are self-employed (whose numbers are rapidly diminishing) and wage-earners has grown tenfold since 1950. While the average tax on wage amounted to 7.9% in 1965, it had risen to 13.7% by 1973, without maintaining even the level of public services for "quality of life" at the 1966 level.[8]

During the recession of 1967, the state pumped billions into cyclical programs in order to make private capital accumulation more viable. Most of the funds were made available for the railways, the postal system, and the army which contracted with private firms to supply equipment or to construct new facilities. Furthermore, the state "relieved itself" of additional billions due to a virtual strike by corporations against a higher rate of profit taxation, while the burden of paying for essential public services was steadily passed on to payers of withholding taxes. At the same time, this cyclical policy, which might well be called "class struggle from above," did nothing to curb inflation — in June of 1974 the cost of living index for a working-class family of four with average income had risen 7% above the previous year and was thus 27% above 1970.[9] Nor was it able to prevent stagflation which was a first for the FRG (at least within the context of a so-called split cycle in various sectors of the economy) or to stop an unemployment rate which is extraordinarily high given postwar developments in the Federal Republic. The unemployment rate in the summer of 1974 was roughly a half a million (2.2%) and is thus even higher than it was in 1967 (1.8%). Moreover, this could exceed 800,000 by the end of the year according to official projections (prediction of the Federal Labor Institute, cited in the *Frankfurter Rundschau,* August 16, 1974, p. 6).

The consequences of these developments should not surprise anyone. The combined effect of the stagnation of real wages and the simultaneous breakdown of public services aimed at improving the "quality of life" (according to the SPD's own propaganda) along with increased work loads and speed-ups in the slumping sectors of the economy has all led to repeated spontaneous outbreaks and protests among the union rank and file. Since the wildcat strikes of 1969 there have been other signs of growing discontent: the referendum vote on union contracts in the spring of 1973 gave a narrow victory to the metal workers against their own union; spontaneous strikes, led predominantly by foreign workers, were directed against union contract settlements of spring 1973 that did not even offset inflation; public employees held their first official nation-wide strike in February of 1974.[10] The partial success of this last strike (11% pay hike instead of the requested 15%, plus an across-the-board minimal pay raise of 170 DM per month) and its general mobilization of solidarity among those involved, served to tarnish the prestige of the Brandt government which had taken a clear-cut stand against even an 11% pay increase and against the right of public employees to strike. This chain reaction against the SPD also includes the significant drop in participation in regional and municipal elections in industrial workers' areas traditionally held by the SPD (according to an INFAS study, cited in the *Frankfurter Rundschau* on March 5, 1974).

What *is* astonishing, especially in comparison to labor movements in other Western European countries, is the limited willingness on the part of the West German labor movement in the postwar period to struggle for better conditions — when real wages are stagnating and even sinking in some branches of industry.

This fact brings us again to what has perhaps been the most important long-range and historically relevant function of major social democratic parties in general and of the German SPD within the political framework of the FRG in particular.[11] Because of its ideological history, its more recent programs, and its membership structure, the SPD has an integrative and pacifying effect on the working class which cannot be countered or matched by any other party. This is particularly true during periods of economic stagnation and recession as well as in areas and branches of the economy which suffer from structural crises. And here the role played by the SPD cannot be compared with the traditional one of the Democratic Party in its dealings with organized labor in the United States.

The influence of the SPD is mediated specifically by the following mechanisms:

1.   The intensification and reproduction of a primitive anti-communism, also among the masses of workers, which while playing upon the real political mistakes and wrongs committed by the Stalinist bureaucratic machines and their "revisionist" successors, is demagogically projected onto any anti-capitalist, or even radical reformist political activity. All this is nourished by the real latent and manifest material fears of the masses.

2.   The conscious attempt to identify the radical past of the SPD with the illusions of reform put forth by the state. Here the real socio-political achievements and improvements, for which the SPD fought on behalf of the working classes (though, to be sure, always carried out in the enlightened interests of the entire society and always supported by conservative forces) are linked to the reformist pretensions of the state. This state presents reform measures, immanent and necessary to the system, both as supposed examples or precursors of a strategic program aimed at changing the state and as if they were policies created by a neutral social state, independent of the domination of capital, which realizes the equal rights and partnership of capital and labor in a "mixed economic system" of so-called democratic socialism. (This

particular reform and state ideology can be found in the SPD's Bad Godesberg Program of 1959, the reform euphoria of the government declaration of 1969, the programmatic declarations of the Young Socialists, the youth organization of the SPD, and the draft of an SPD long-term program published in 1973).[12]

3. The close personnel and political interlocking of the leadership machine, the career and patronage structures in the SPD, the unions, city and state bureaucracies and service organizations and even the shop steward committees and workers' representatives committees elected by the workers and employees in the public and private plants and businesses. This is manifested in the considerable predominance, in terms of numbers and activity, of those nearly one million Party members employed mainly in the domain of public services. In addition, there are a number of different Party career positions held in combination by SPD members — in shop councils, the regional union bureaucracy and the local city administration. There are also the regular top-level discussions on economic and union contract policy matters between union leaders and leading SPD officials. Finally, "Working Groups for Workers' Questions" have been established which, for all intents and purposes, are limited to functionary participants within the SPD at the local and supra-regional level, while the development of rank and file working groups, provided for in the Party's constitution have consciously been neglected.

However, the SPD's objective role in the preservation of the capitalist social system is not derived from its participation in the government or in actually bringing about structural reforms necessary to the system. Indeed, the most far-reaching socio-political reforms had already been realized under Bismarck, just as they have been under Adenauer in the economically stable postwar years. And, insofar as the struggle for such social improvements included the participation of organized labor, the struggle itself often mobilized the political experiences and competency of the rank and file. The most decisive factors for this integrative function of the SPD are the state and social partnership ideologies and illusions constantly propagated among functionaries and workers by the day-to-day practice of the Party, and in part of the unions. With each reform concession fought for with the aid of the working populace which is also necessary for the maintenance of the system, the SPD creates a programmatic fanfare celebrating the far-reaching implications of these materially based reforms. Finally, the Party uses a fanatic anti-communism which emanates from real historical experience in order to confuse the situation and absorb alternatives in socio-political charity.

The concrete effects of this political function filled by the SPD in support of the capitalist system can be demonstrated in a number of areas in the history of the FRG:

—in the disciplining and pacifying influence on the labor struggles of union leaders so that union leaders renounce militancy in favor of social democratic election strategies and promises of social and tax reforms;

—in the forced political support of the SPD since the sixties for the expansion of an arms-spending equalled only in the USA (including para-military police units for "internal emergency") despite all the programs for peace and detente;

—in the SPD's active participation in watering down and eliminating the liberal, legalist-state constitutional principles and institutions (already weakened by the persecution of communists under Adenauer) and in the increasing elimination by the executive of civil rights protection for so-called enemies of the state and radicals. An instance of this occurred when the Brandt government strongly supported and reactivated the law (dating back to the Prussian monarchy) prohibiting employment in the civil service for all persons suspected of being radical, and this in turn resulted in a significant rise in the number of job refusals in schools and universities for persons accused of being radical or of belonging to communist organizations. This has been coupled more recently with the trend to expel "radicals" from the unions.[13]

The scope of political defamation, deprivation of rights, and expatriation of so-called radicals in the climate of state authoritarianism and anti-communism — contributed to by the SPD — can be seen in a final decision reached by the supreme labor court of the Federal Republic on August 24, 1972 (reprinted with a critical commentary by *Kritische Justiz,* 1973, pp. 409-416). According to this decision, workers can be legally fired if, even in their so-called spare time, they "encroach upon the interests of their employers," or in particular "discredit the professional status of their employer and the employer himself in the eyes of the public." In this specific case, a member of the German Communist Party (DKP), employed by a bank, had distributed DKP leaflets (not written by him) during an election which, in the opinion of the bank in question, were directed against the interests of the bank in that they criticized the role of the banks in the economic system. The astonishing thing about this case is not the bank's quite normal behavior in the day-to-day life of capitalism. Given the present balance of power between capital and labor in the FRG, one is more surprised at the provocative and unnecessary effort to destroy the SPD illusion of a constitutional state which supposedly guarantees the equal rights of social partners. (Compare this with Article 118, paragraph 1 of the Constitution of the Weimar Republic, at that time strongly supported by the SPD, which had been directed against any encroachment on the rights to freedom of expression and opinion no matter where the person might be employed).

In the face of the growing number of persons who now can be subjected to *legal* public defamation and who can lose their jobs and in light of the attempts by the ruling SPD government to curb the unions in spite of the impending drop in real wages, a point has been reached where union members and some functionaries close to the rank and file could question the ideology and practice of the SPD. If over a period of years, the SPD as the party in power should reveal itself incapable of achieving partial successes in maintaining the living standard of organized union workers as well as protecting them against political disciplinary measures and dismissals because of their union activities, then it is highly possible, for the first time in the history of the Federal Republic, that a union opposition might become a reality — as has long been the case in most Western European countries. If this independent movement were to have some degree of success in labor struggles, as is the case in France and Italy, and if it were to express an interest in the creation of a left-socialist political coalition, then the attractiveness of the SPD as a coalition partner for conservative parties which have no power base in the unions and hope to pacify the unions through the SPD, would probably diminish rapidly.

Given the developments we have touched upon, moralizing accusations and stories of corruption and treason which attribute the SPD leadership with nearly omnipotent, manipulative powers over the working class, are both out of place and dangerous.[14] These were the tactics of the Communist Party of Germany (KPD) in its attack on the so-called "social fascism" of the SPD at the end of the Weimar Republic. Also off target are various interpretations developed by left minority groups within the SPD, the German Communist Party (DKP) and other radical democratic groups. These divide the SPD schematically into progressive and reactionary camps; into a right-wing leadership under the influence of big business vs. a progressive left wing, opposed by the right at every turn, steadfastly initiating reforms which will change the system and promote a policy of peace and detente.[15]

Both interpretations pay too little attention to the material and mass-psychological base of social democracy and the social interests and fears of its functionaries, members and voters. In order to transform the idealized legal and propagandistic illusion of democracy based on constitutionalism and welfare — which as such is an illusion only for intellectuals — into a tangible real illusion for the majority of workers, the SPD is forced, even during a period of economic stagnation, to attempt to bring about real reform programs. At the very least, these programs seek to prevent the further decline in the standard of living of that sector of organized labor which is still employed (not the young, crippled and retired). In the same way, the SPD also must fight against the elimination of the constitutional rights of labor and the basic rights of union activities, if it does not want to lose much of its influence over the unions.

Occasionally the SPD is really forced to stand up for the life needs of its base, even when its defense of these needs is objectively anti-capitalist. On such occasions it is incumbent upon the autonomous, non-sectarian radical left — and there are only the beginnings of such a movement in the FRG today[16] — to enter into action coalitions within the SPD and with union functionaries. The illusions of social democracy and the illusions of the workers, employees and public officials about social democracy can only be broken down through concrete experience and struggle in which the masses participate spontaneously and in an organized manner.[17]

On the other hand, a great deal of what has been presented within the SPD as left policy capable of overcoming the system has to date been a necessary device of integrative ideology. As such it is a measure designed to influence the masses as well as an honest self-deception with respect to the real politico-economic laws of capitalism which others will not permit as temporary alleviations of the destructive dynamics of capital.

Whenever there are minor periods of crisis and recession which do not become world economic crises and whenever there is a strong need for integrative reform and illusions about the state in order to pacify union militancy, the social democratic mass parties will be called upon to join the government as partner. During relatively stable phases (for example, during the reconstruction phase after World War II), the liberal and conservative parties are equally as successful in gaining mass loyalty. During extremely unstable phases, the whole institutional system of constitutional parliamentarianism of union interests becomes partially or completely cancelled by conservative or fascist military regimes, unless a strong autonomous labor movement can emerge to prevent this.

4. The Soviet Union

Whatever else is true or untrue about the Soviet Union, one fact is indisputable: citizens do not control their means of production, their specific work process, or the distribution of the goods and services they produce. The workers have been discouraged from thinking about these original goals of the 1917 revolution and are in fact subjected to a counterfeit version of Marxism-Leninism. The situation has led many radicals to agree with Serge Mallet's analogy that Soviet state socialism is to true socialism what "the monsters of the paleolithic era are to present animal species: clumsy, abortive, prototypes."[1] It is precisely this failure to strive toward self-government of the masses in all spheres of Soviet life — not the persistence of classes — that constitutes the severest indictment brought by Marxists against Soviet leadership today.

In the first reading in this section, Lucio Colletti, the Italian philosopher and political theorist, examines the role and historical situation of Stalinism. Colletti draws some firm conclusions as to the fate of "socialism in one country" and strongly suggests that Russia's socialist transformation must now be characterized as degenerative or, at best, stagnant and immobilized. However, this arrested development demonstrates neither the inherent failure of socialism nor the superiority of capitalism. The fault lies with the anti-socialist behavior of the regime. Critiques of Soviet bureaucratic centralism by those who truly favor the working class achieving socialist democracy do not receive a wide hearing in the American news media. In his contribution, George Saunders is careful to separate these genuine Marxists or "neo-Bolsheviks" (or "neo-Leninists") from the more highly publicized pro-capitalist "dissidents," naive reformists, and right-wing intelligentsia.

The barriers facing any proponents of genuine ideological self-determination are treated in a discerning fashion by Isaac Deutscher. His essay focuses on the price the Soviet Union is still paying for Stalinism. A recent first-hand impression of Soviet society by members of the Chicago-based Revolutionary Union further reveals the existence of a drastic departure from the old Bolshevik vision. This selection is from their larger study, *How Capitalism has been Restored in the Soviet Union.* Finally, M. Holubenko explores some particular manifestations of Soviet working class opposition to the prevailing system. He also documents the methods employed by the bureaucratic elite to neutralize protest and exclude the working class from the political arena. One must conclude that the prospects for developing a coherent worker's opposition movement are not encouraging at this juncture. But there is strong reason to believe that the regime cannot indefinitely escape the dilemmas and contradictions of its own making. Nor should it be forgotten that "There is a strength in humanity stronger than any 'habit of submission': people's perpetual longing for justice and fraternity, the banner under which were accomplished all the revolutions of the past, and under which will be accomplished all revolutions of the future."[2]

---

[1]"Bureaucracy and Technology in the Socialist Countries," *Socialist Revolution, I,* No. 3 (May/June, 1970), p. 45, as cited by Richard Edwards, Michael Reich and Thomas Weisskopf (editors), *The Capitalist System* (Englewood Cliffs, New Jersey: Prentice-Hall, 1972), p. 4.

[2]Galanskou quoted in Tamara Deutscher, "Soviet Fabians and Others," *New Left Review* (July/August, 1970), p. 56.

The revolution which the Bolsheviks accomplished in Russia was not conceived essentially as a Russian revolution, but as the first step in a European and world revolution; as an exclusively Russian phenomenon, it had no significance for them, no validity and no possibility for survival.

The Question of Stalin
Lucio Colletti

When in November 1917 the Bolshevik Party unleashed an insurrection and took power, Lenin and his comrades were convinced that this was the first act in a world revolution. The process was started in Russia, not because Russia was considered internally ripe for a socialist revolution, but because the immense carnage of the First World War, military defeat, hunger and the deep misery of the masses had precipitated a social and political crisis in Russia before any other country. The collapse of Czarism in Febuary 1917 thus produced an uncertain and vacillating bourgeois-democratic republic, incapable of remedying the disasters of Russian society, or providing the basic necessities of life for the popular masses. The Bolsheviks, in other words, believed that their party could take power and begin the socialist revolution even in Russia, despite its secular backwardness. For the World War had confirmed once again what had already been revealed in 1905. Not merely in spite, but precisely because of its backwardness, and the sum of old and new contradictions that were interlaced within it, Russia represented both the most explosive point in the chain of world imperialism and the 'weakest link'. This link, once broken, would carry with it the entire chain, accelerating the revolutionary process in the more developed industrialized countries of Europe, starting above all with Germany.

The Premises of Bolshevism

Their objective was therefore not simply to achieve the revolution in one particular country, even a country of such gigantic proportions as the Czarist Empire, spread over two continents. Their objective was world revolution.

The revolution which the Bolsheviks accomplished in Russia was not conceived essentially as a Russian revolution, but as the first step in a European and world revolution; as an exclusively Russian phenomenon, it had no significance for them, no validity and no possibility of survival.

Hence the country in which the revolutionary process began did not interest the Bolsheviks for its own sake, its special characteristics or its national destiny, but as a platform from which an international upheaval could be launched. In these years Europe was — or seemed to be — the pivot of the world. If the revolution could spread from vast and backward Russia to triumph in Germany, Austro-Hungary, Italy, the axis of the whole globe would be shifted.

What is striking today in retracing this experience, is the intense travail and inflexible determination with which the Bolsheviks, in a relatively short period of time, distilled and selected this strategic vision. The most impressive fact here is the rigid intransigence of their refusal to make any concessions to nationalism. In the concluding years of the 19th century, Marxism had penetrated Russia not only as a foreign ideology, historically and culturally developed in Western Europe, but as an open denial of any special mission peculiar to Russia, any privileged path for reaching socialism. It is enough to recall the implacable polemics of Lenin and Plekhanov against populism. In opposition to Slavophile tendencies, which were deeply rooted in Russian culture and often took up combative revolutionary positions at the political level, the first Marxist nuclei of what was later to become the Russian Social-Democratic Labour Party did not hesitate to advocate the path of *Westernization*. The economic and social development of the country was not to be entrusted to the primordial virtues of Mother Russia. Development meant industrialization, the advance of capitalism. The only cure for the ills arising from the 'Asiatic backwardness' of Czarist Russia was Western science and technology, capitalist industrial development, which would itself engender a modern factory proletariat.

The importance of this ideological emphasis and the extent to which the entire first generation of Russian Marxists were committed to it, are documented in Lenin's monumental research dedicated to *The Development of Capitalism in Russia*. In the last decade of the century the Russian Marxists thus occupied the difficult position (which was naturally exploited polemically by the Populists) of advocating, though with radically divergent goals and perspectives, the same process of rapid industrialization that was supported by the liberal bourgeoisie.

The basic idea governing this position was that which forms the very core and nucleus of the whole of Marx's thought. The socialist revolution is a revolution made and led by the working class, a class which grows with the development of industrial capitalism itself. The socialist revolution is a complete human emancipation, but this emancipation presupposes certain historical and material conditions: not only the 'socialization of labour' or formation of the 'collective worker', not only a vertiginous increase in the productivity of labour, but also the dissolution of local and corporative limits, which can only be achieved in the framework of modern industrial production and the world market created by capitalism. In the absence of these last two decisive preconditions, Marx's whole theory itself remains in the air. For they provide both a world-wide revolutionary theatre in which the unification of all humanity, international communism, can be realized, and a revolutionary agency linked to *scientific* and *rational* work processes — the modern worker and technician.

In the first years of this century, however, Russian Marxists soon began to graft a series of specifications, and at times even modifications, onto this basic system of premises. They had to correct their sights for the specific social and political terrain in which they had to operate, contemporary Russian society, in order to make a deep impact on it and act effectively as a revolutionary force.

The first and one of the most important of these specifications was, of course, the 'Jacobin' conception of the party introduced by Lenin. In this conception, the party became a 'party of cadres' or 'professional revolutionaries', in other words a highly centralized vanguard. It is not difficult to discern the pressure, indeed necessity, exercised on Russian Marxism here by the special conditions of *illegality* in which the party was obliged to operate under the Czarist autocracy.

A second specification, or rather in this case alteration, was critical discussion of the classic Marxist schema, or at least that which had hitherto been attributed to Marx, of two epochs or phases of revolution — bourgeois-democratic and socialist — as distinct stages located in successive historical eras. The problem encountered here derived even more from the specificity of Russian conditions. However the sheer scale of the problem in this case was such that it profoundly affected the whole strategy and future of the workers' party. Given the autocratic character of the Czarist regime and the complete absence of any form of liberal constitutionalism — not to speak of the still somewhat feeble development of industrial capitalism — the Marxist party had to operate in an environment where it was universally acknowledged that a bourgeois revolution would in any event have to take place before the socialist revolution. The problem then was: what position should a Marxist party take towards this bourgeois revolution, which both promotes the further development of capitalism, and reinforces and organizes the working class?

Until about 1905, the Russian Marxists were broadly content to accept the thesis according to which socialist revolution was not possible in an economically backward country like Russia, where the industrial proletariat was a tiny minority and where no bourgeois revolution had yet taken place. In Russia, they argued, the revolution could only be bourgeois; the task of Russian social-democrats could only be that of supporting the bourgeoisie and not therefore that of carrying out their own revolution.

After 1905, however, only the Mensheviks continued to maintain this thesis. The Menshevik line, which implied either support for the liberal bourgeoisie in accomplishing the bourgeois revolution or abstention by the social-democratic party to 'keep its hands clean', was opposed by two other strategic perspectives within the Russian workers' movement during the 1905 Revolution. These two alternative perspectives were themselves counterposed: Lenin's 'revolutionary-democratic dictatorship of the proletariat and the peasantry' and Trotsky's 'permanent revolution'.

Common to both these positions, as against the Mensheviks, was their assignation of a positive and leading role to the social-democrats during the bourgeois-democratic revolution itself. The differences between them, however, were great enough to make them antithetical in other respects. Lenin thought that the party should promote a revolutionary worker-peasant coalition which would accomplish the bourgeois revolution and thereby prepare the ground for the socialist revolution; yet this process would nevertheless remain for a whole historical period a purely *bourgeois* revolution, given the preponderance of the peasantry. Trotsky, on the other hand, maintained that while the Russian proletariat ought to win the peasants and lead them in the bourgeois revolution, it would not be able to halt the process at that point. The completion of the bourgeois revolution would necessarily oblige the proletariat to initiate its own revolution in an uninterrupted process.

It is important to grasp one point: both these lines, born precisely as responses to the specific problem of revolution *in Russia,* nonetheless presuppose more or less explicitly an integration, support and completion at the international level. Removed from this global context and enclosed within the limits of Russian society at that period, they would clearly have been arbitrary and impracticable. Lenin's line would have meant summoning the proletariat to take a leading role, through the bourgeois-democratic revolution, in the establishment of a regime in which it could itself only suffer the generalized reign of wage labour and capitalist exploitation. Trotsky's line, on the other hand, would have meant advocating the uninterrupted transition from a bourgeois to a socialist revolution in a country in which the industrial proletariat represented a mere island surrounded by a limitless sea of peasants.

Nevertheless, despite their differences and limits, particularly in their 1905 versions, the force and originality of these two theses lies in the fact that they both resolutely posed the real, central *contradiction* in which the Russian party found itself: it was a party of socialist revolution in a country profoundly immature for such a revolution, yet a party born for this destination on such apparently mistaken terrain not by chance but for deep historical reasons

In grappling with this central contradiction, these two positions already implicitly contained new elements of analysis which only came to light and were adequately explained several years later, in the Leninist theory of *imperialism*. The first of these was the conviction that a revolutionary bourgeoisie could no longer exist in the 20th century: hence the inevitability of the proletariat itself leading the bourgeois-democratic revolution, where this had still to take place. This idea reclaimed and developed Marx's earlier analysis of the history of modern Germany, in which he discussed the weakness and inability of the German bourgeoisie to confront the problem of its own revolution and to break its pact with Prussian *Junkertum*. The second novel element, yet more original than the first, lay in the incipient hypothesis that the socialist revolution was not necessarily bound to break out initially in the Western heartlands of advanced capitalism, but could be set in motion from the backward East or even from zones peripheral to the metropolitan countries themselves and the nerve centres of the system. This thesis to some extent prefigured Lenin's later analysis of imperialism. It prepared the ground for what he was to call the law of 'uneven development', according to which the most explosive point in the world system is not necessarily the most 'developed', but can on the contrary be the 'weakest' link from the standpoint of capitalist industry; for despite its weakness, this link may be rich in revolutionary potential and volcanic forces, precisely because it cumulates both old and new contradictions.

Lenin's Internationalism

It has often been noted that both these theses considerably modified Marx's original conception in certain ways; the Mensheviks were only the first to point this out. However, a more considered and objective appraisal, from the vantage-point of historical distance, would suggest that despite the changes they introduced, the positions of Lenin and Trotsky not only preserved the essentials of Marx's analysis, but would be quite inconceivable apart from it. For while both of them confronted the challenge presented by history, to think through the revolutionary tasks of a Marxist workers' party in a relatively backward country, their common characteristic was a clear awareness that the upheaval which was ripening, wherever it might actually begin, could only be an *international* revolutionary upheaval — the sole adequate response to the world imperialist order. Both, moreover, emphasised that the decisive terrain on which the battle would ultimately be lost or won could only be the central countries of metropolitan capitalism — at that period this meant, above all, Germany — and its principal protagonist could only be the modern factory proletariat, which was the historical subject of the revolution for Marx.

It is crucially important to situate these points correctly and clearly, for they correspond to a historical reality — the conception which underlay the Bolshevik seizure of power in 1917 and the theory and practice of the party leadership at least until 1924. Indeed, only the Bolsheviks' conscious reference to the basic content of Marx's analysis can explain what was undoubtedly the most salient feature that characterized most of them: their intense and consistent consciousness of the 'exceptional' and in a certain sense *contradictory* nature of the tasks posed to the Russian party, as the instrument of socialist revolution in a country that was not yet ripe for it.

In this connection there is a particularly illuminating passage from Engels' *Peasant War in Germany,* which may help us to express what we have in mind: 'The worst thing that can befall a leader of an extreme party is to be compelled to take over a government in an epoch when the movement is not yet ripe for the domination of the class which he represents, and for the realisation of the measures which that domination implies. What he *can* do depends not upon his will but upon the level of development of the material means of existence, of the conditions of production and commerce . . . What he *ought* to do, what his party demands of him, again depends not upon him . . . He is bound to the doctrines and demands hitherto propounded . . . Thus, he necessarily finds himself in an unsolvable dilemma. What he *can* do contradicts all the previous actions, principles and immediate interests of his party, and what he *ought* to do cannot be done. In a word, he is compelled to represent not his party or his call, but the class for whose domination the movement is then ripe. In the interests of the movement he is compelled to advance the interests of an alien class, and to feed his own class with phrases and promises, and with the asseveration that the interests of that alien class are their own interests. Whoever is put into this awkward position is irrevocably lost.'[1]

None of the Bolshevik leadership and least of all Lenin would ever have accepted the idea that their prospects were hopeless. But it is nevertheless striking that the Bolsheviks again and again showed such a clear awareness of the *contradiction* imposed on them by history and by the development of imperialism, that — in order to master rather than suffer it — they took the only possible correct course: namely, not to ignore or conceal it, but to assume its consequences openly in their own strategy. This is the clue that explains, for example, the first acts of the Bolshevik Party in power, such as the decrees distributing land to the peasants or granting nationalities the right of self-determination, including the right to secede from the ex-Czarist Empire: both measures attacked by critics, notably Rosa Luxemburg, as bourgeois-democratic and counterproductive, serving only to create future obstacles to the building of socialism. The same awareness lies behind the travail of Lenin's thought on the nature of the October Revolution and the question of its socialist character, not only immediately after the seizure of power but also later in 1919 or 1921. This travail is supremely reflected in the very title bestowed on the new regime: 'Workers' and peasants' government'. Here the omission of Russia underlines the internationalist nature of the revolution, while a second class, never anticipated in the original theory of the dictatorship of the proletariat, appears alongside the working-class — the peasantry. His awareness of this contradiction in fact underlies virtually all of Lenin's political actions and changes of course, from the beginning to the end of his career.

The Limits of Backwardness

Today there seems to be a need, which I would not wish to dispute, for an impartial re-examination of several key points in the thought and work of Lenin. The objects of greatest contemporary concern lie, firstly, in his conception of the Party and, secondly, in the delay with which he came to appreciate the role and meaning of the Soviets, which had already emerged in the 1905 revolution. These interrogations naturally arise in the light of developments in Russia after Lenin's death. Here we discover the prophetic meaning of Rosa Luxemburg's celebrated warning in her pamphlet on the Russian Revolution: 'With the repression of political life in the land as a whole, life in the soviets must also become more and more crippled. Without general elections, without unrestricted freedom of press and assembly, without a free struggle of opinion, life dies out in every public institution, becomes a mere semblance of life, in which only the bureaucracy remains as the active element. Public life gradually falls asleep, a few dozen party leaders of inexhaustible energy and boundless experience direct and rule. Among them, in reality only a dozen outstanding heads do the leading and an elite of the working class is invited from time to time to meetings where they are to applaud the speeches of the leaders, and to approve resolutions unanimously — at bottom, then, a clique affair — a dictatorship, to be sure, not the dictatorship of the proletariat, however, but only the dictatorship of a handful of politicians, that is a dictatorship in the bourgeois sense, in the sense of the rule of the Jacobins.'[2]

It is of course true, as Lenin himself fully acknowledged, that the form of political regime realized by the October Revolution in Russia was never, even at the beginning a dictatorship of the proletariat; it was rather a *dictatorship of the party* exercised on behalf of the proletariat. Because of the existing 'low cultural level of the working masses', Lenin wrote as early as 1919, 'the soviets, which according to their programme are organs of direct administration *by the workers,* are instead organs of administration *for the workers,* led by the proletarian vanguard, not by the working masses.' In the same year, he affirmed, no less explicitly, that the dictatorship of the party was to be considered the effective form of the dictatorship of the proletariat, and he specified that 'the dictatorship of the working class is realized by the Bolshevik Party, which since at least 1905 has been united with the whole revolutionary protetariat.'

However much we may be aware of these problems, it is essential to emphasize two points: 1. These 'contradictions' in Lenin's and the Bolshevik's policies were not something marginal or fortuitous which they encountered *after* taking power. On the contrary, they represented one aspect of the basic contradiction I have already outlined: the contradiction of a party as the instrument of socialist revolution in a country as yet unripe for it. Clearly, we cannot lightly attribute this contradiction to Lenin, without simultaneously reproaching him, like the Mensheviks, for making the revolution instead of leaving Kerensky in power in the first place. 2. The brief passages cited above show that this contradiction was (almost) always *avowed* in Lenin's writings and the most lucid party texts, in complete consciousness, openly subjected to analysis and debate. This is not, as one might imagine, merely a question of form, but also a matter of content and substance: the very act of making the problem explicit simultaneously posed the question of the means by which it could be, if not solved, at least contained and mitigated. (One only has to think, for example, of Moshe Lewin's account of *Lenin's Last Struggle.*)

It seems likely that Lenin's fault lay in having too often made a virtue of necessity, adopting the means necessary for action in the *Russian* context, without always making explicit the historical and political limits, in terms of which these means were imposed and derived their validity. This could, for instance, be the case with the strongly centralized character of the party, adapted to conditions of illegality. In my view it does not, however, apply to another aspect of this theory, namely the bringing of 'political consciousness' to the working class 'from outside', which produces such scandal today among intellectual currents of ouvrierism and spontaneism.

In short, no amount of sophism can escape the essential point: given that Russia was not ripe for socialist revolution, the Bolshevik Party — small, cohesive, yet permeated with a dialectical political life to an extent not even imagined today — represented the indispensable tool for operating under *these* conditions. While it is not easy to be sure from the evidence, it must nonetheless be emphasized that the 'isolation' of the Bolshevik vanguard from the masses was never a 'choice' made by Lenin, nor even an 'effect' of his political line: it was dictated by the objective situation. One could object that in spite of general backwardness, Russia did contain several industrial centres. Deutscher has indeed observed that these industries were in certain sectors among the most modern in the world, that their 'coefficient of concentration was even higher than that of American industry at the time'. This is of course true and helps to explain why the October Revolution — unlike the Chinese Revolution which was essentially peasant in character — was a workers' revolution, which spread from the city to the countryside and not vice versa. But we must not forget the artificial origins of this industrial concentration, its implantation 'from above', its recent development, and finally, the fact that Russia remained in the last analysis a country with a vast peasant majority.

To fail to see this situation clearly means to preclude from the outset any understanding of Lenin's life and work. The Bolshevik Party, at least in the years immediately before 1917, was the expression of highly concentrated nuclei of the working class, endowed with all the qualities of discipline, organization and vanguard consciousness proper to the modern 'collective worker'; it nonetheless remained, in relation to the whole country, without a firm class base. This state of affairs, not unlike that referred to by Engels in the passage quoted, implicitly contained an objective danger, the awareness of which dominated Lenin's thought and practice. For the party, precisely in so far as it was adequate to the task of carrying out the socialist revolution, was condemned to isolation from the broad masses of backward Russian society. Hence the impulse to close itself off, to become concentrated, to make itself not only a vanguard but the depository of a political goal, relatively inaccessible because premature. On the other hand, the party had to escape from this dilemma if it was really to act as a *revolutionary force,* mobilizing the masses, rather than as a simple putschist organization.

This poses a problem that has not been sufficiently studied for some time, but which had a vital, central importance for Lenin: the problem of *consensus* — that is, the necessity for the party in accordance with the fundamental aspirations of the broad masses. A casual glance at his writings, especially those of 1917, is sufficient to reveal his continual insistence on this theme. 'The party of the proletariat cannot assume the task of introducing socialism in a country of small peasants, until the vast majority of the population has become conscious of the need for socialist revolution.' Or: 'We are not Blanquists, we do not advocate the seizure of power by a minority. We are Marxists.' 'The Commune (the Soviet of Workers' and Peasants' Deputies) does not and must not intend to introduce *any* reform that is not fully warranted both by economic reality and by the consciousness of the vast majority of the people. To the extent that the organizing experience of the Russian people is weak, we must all the more firmly build up our organizations through the work of the *masses themselves*.'

Each of the problems raised here deserves a chapter to itself which the reader must try to formulate. To start with, what I have called the problem of *consensus* is at the same time the question, essential to Leninism, of the attention bestowed on the peasantry and relations with the petty bourgeoisie as a whole. 'Russia', Lenin wrote in 1917, 'is a country of petty-bourgeois. The vast majority of the population belong to this class.' It also raises the problem of nationalities, and that of exploited colonial peoples. Finally, it bears upon the most important problem of all, precisely the one nowadays most obscured: namely, the need for the class struggle to be structured and articulated as a *political struggle,* which, in so far as it surpasses the limits of mere ouvrierism, cannot avoid coming to terms with the problem of *alliances.* Marx had already said as much in 1844: if the socialist revolution is 'a political revolution with a social essence', this essence or content is itself insufficient because it needs a *political form,* if only because 'revolution in general is a *political act'* and 'without the revolution socialism cannot be realized.'

The Meaning of Lenin's Oscillations

The attention given to winning the consent of the masses, combined with the objective gulf that isolated the party from the vast backward strata of Russian society, explains the continuous oscillations and adjustments of Lenin's political line. This was always prey to two contradictory exigencies. On the one hand, there was the need to *adhere* to the Russian situation, which meant not only that the party had to defer genuinely socialist objectives, but also that in the meantime it had to represent the only future agent and depository of these objectives. On the other hand, since Russia was also only the point of departure and temporary platform for a European or world revolution, there was a permanent need to *anticipate* a world beyond the existing state of affairs, prefiguring not only the transition to socialism but even communism itself.

This helps us to understand the ideal projection or 'leap' represented by

State and Revolution — both a 'utopian' work from the standpoint of the time and place in which it was written, and also an indispensable statement of the goals and finality of any authentic socialist revolution. Alternatively, it helps to situate Lenin's perplexity and doubts, almost at the very moment of the revolution, as to its nature and significance. Here we gain a measure of the dramatic seriousness of Lenin's Marxism, which distinguishes him from all the others — from Zinoviev, Kamenev, Stalin, Bukharin and perhaps even from Trotsky: by his very uncertainty, he emerged as the most conscious protagonist of them all. In August 1921, he wrote that the revolution from November 1917 to January 1918 had been bourgeois-democratic, that the socialist stage had only begun with establishment of proletarian democracy. But then he proposed a different periodization; the socialist stage was only reached with the class struggle of the committees of poor peasants against the kulaks. This oscillation never ceased. Two months later, in October 1921, a further periodization emerges: this time the bourgeois-democratic stage of the revolution was only completed in 1921, at the very moment when he was writing.

Behind these oscillations lay precisely the development that had been least foreseen. The decisive presupposition upon which the Bolsheviks had based their seizure of power, which would itself have more than compensated for the difficulties arising from Russia's backwardness, was slow to materialize. The revolution in Western Europe did not occur, or rather had occurred and had been temporarily defeated. From the delay attending the second wave, Lenin was forced to confront the truth that he, more than anyone else, had always known: that the economic and social foundations essential for the realization of the goals of Soviet power in Russia were almost totally lacking and therefore the dictatorship of the party was suspended in a void. With the Bolsheviks in power, the old contradiction with which the party had struggled since its birth was presented much more acutely: while Russia now had the most advanced political regime in the world, she had not even a minimally adequate economic structure to correspond to the regime. The terms of the classic formula of historical materialism on the relationship between structure and superstructure were now turned upside-down to its most stern devotees. The Mensheviks, already defeated on the battleground of historical struggle, could now brandish these very formulae against Lenin. The seizure of power in the absence of an adequate economic base; the dictatorship of the proletariat in the near absence of a proletariat, and moreover by a party in which this element was in a minority; the reintroduction of capitalism after the revolution with NEP; the preponderance of a vast bureaucratic state machine; all these added up to a body of evidence that flew in the face of doctrine as well as common sense.

Scarcely two years after *State and Revolution,* in which he had theorized the 'destruction of the state machine', Lenin had to admit with his usual frankness that not only was this machine still intact, but it remained largely in the hands of its original personnel. 'We have an indeterminate quantity of our militants at the higher levels — at the least a few thousands, at most ten thousand. However, at the base of the hierarchy hundreds of thousands of exfunctionaries whom we inherited from the Czar and the bourgeoisie are working, partly consciously and partly unconsciously, against us.'

If we add to this the civil war and armed intervention of foreign powers, the enormous difficulties faced by the Bolshevik leadership begin to emerge concretely. Within months of taking power, the Party found itself commanding an armed fortress, starved of food and besieged on all sides and even from within. To resist, it had continually to resort to even greater centralization. The masses who had supported the Bolsheviks in the first phase now fell back, decimated and scattered. The workers' battalions deserted the semi-ruined factories to march to the front.

It is scarely possible to paint the picture too sombrely; Russian society, already badly shaken by the First World War, now seemed to totter on the brink of destruction under the combined effects of physical decimation and industrial paralysis. The surviving nuclei of workers fled from famine into the countryside. The history of human progress which has always proceeded from the countryside to the city, now seemed violently to reverse itself. From 1917 to 1920, it has been observed, the urban population of European Russia decreased by 35.2 percent. Petrograd, with a population of 2,400,000 in 1916, by 1920 had no more than 740,000, while that of Moscow fell in the same period from 1,900,000 to 1,120,000.

In this situation, the revolutionary impetus reached the limits of its endurance; NEP represented an inevitable retreat. After October and the tremendous exertions of the Civil War, Old Russia, until then regarded as merely the outpost of international revolution, threw the whole weight of her backwardness into the scales. The party, suspended between an exhausted working class, a mere shadow of its past, and a peasantry anxious to profit at last from the lands granted them in the revolution, now had to face the task of bringing a bleeding and paralysed society, wholly preoccupied with food, clothing and heating, back to life. The great revolutionary goals were laid aside; political programmes gave way to everyday routine, subversive theory to traditional practice. The party was now forced to take on an omnipresent role, not only political, but administrative, social and economic. It was thus obliged to swell its ranks, not with agitators or political militants but rather with administrators who could control, manage, manoeuvre and supervise: the men demanded by this new situation.

The Genesis of Stalin

This was the moment of the greatest cleavage between the vanguard and the class which it ought to have represented. The very results of 1917 seemed on the point of vanishing. With freedom of commerce, NEP introduced measures to facilitate the revival of businessmen, merchants, and capitalists. While it benefited the peasantry, more especially rich and middle peasants, it necessarily disappointed the demands of the proletariat which had hitherto had to carry the heaviest burdens of the revolution. The most important element which defined the new situation, already emerging during the NEP period, was the definitive abandonment of the strategy upon which the revolution had been carried out. The last hope of revolution in Europe collapsed. The bourgeois order in Germany, three times on the point of its breakdown, resisted. Its victory both carried within it the seeds of Nazism and contributed to the definitive isolation of the USSR, reinforcing the trend towards retrenchment and post-revolutionary involution.

The rise of Stalin to leadership, first within the Party and then within the State, must be seen in this perspective. His importance begins to emerge with the growing bureaucratization of Party and State. But the bureaucracy in its turn developed and expanded because of Russia's extreme backwardness and isolation; it was the product of a revolution in retreat, pinned down within the frontiers of a poverty-stricken economy, dependent on an enormous mass of primitive peasants.

The change which occurred in these years, preceding and immediately following Lenin's death, proved decisive for the whole subsequent course of world history. The failure of the western revolution destroyed the strategy which had hitherto underpinned the practice of the Bolsheviks. The possibility of gradually bridging the gulf between Russian backwardness and a socialist programme, through the industrial and cultural support afforded by the resources of a socialist Europe, was now unpredictably severed. Almost at once the party found itself no longer on solid ground.

The first result of this new situation was the internal struggle within the Bolshevik leadership after Lenin's death. The rapid defeat to which the Left Opposition was fated was not the defeat of revolutionary romanticism; it was the immediate repercussion of the aborted European revolution within the USSR. Indeed it is not possible to reduce the conflict between Stalin and the Left Opposition to a series of mere struggles for power, in which Stalin, cautious and slow, used his cunning against an adversary who had shown in the Revolution and Civil war great capacity for manoeuvre, but had now mysteriously become too proud, clumsy, sure of himself. The premises of this struggle must be sought elsewhere. The first rung of the ladder which was to carry Stalin to power was supplied by the Social-Democratic leaders who in January 1919 murdered Rosa Luxemburg and Karl Liebknecht; their absence weighed heavily in the defeats of 1921 and 1923 in Germany. The remaining rungs were supplied by the reactionary wave which subsequently swept Europe, conjuring forth Mussolini, Primo de Rivera, Horthy and so many others.

Isolated and enclosed within the 'Asiatic backwardness' of Russia, the party underwent more than a mere change in strategy. The weight and inertia of the Russian historical legacy now reasserted itself over every force of change and revolutionary rupture. The re-emergent features of the old order were manifested not only in the rebirth of former ideological and institutional structures, but also, as Carr has shown, in a *national restoration*. The social forces which now re-emerged from their previous defeat to make their compromise with the new revolutionary order and insensibly to influence its course, were above all forces which reaffirmed the validity of an autochthonous tradition against foreign influences.

The cause of Russia and the cause of Bolshevism were now fused into an undifferentiated unity. This was a truly hybrid amalgam; within it the old Slavophile, anti-enlightenment tendencies soon gained an unexpected new lease of life. A complete reversal of origins now occurred. Communism, which had entered Russia with a programme of Westernization (industry, science, modern working class, critical and experimental outlook), condensed in Lenin's formula 'Electrification + Soviets', which itself contains the whole message of Marxism to the modern world, now began to be impregnated with the corrupt humours of the autocratic Great-Russian mentality.

'On his departure from us, Comrade Lenin commanded us to revere and maintain the purity of the name of party member. We swear, Comrade Lenin, that we will faithfully carry out this command! . . . On his departure from us, Comrade Lenin commanded us to safeguard, like the pupil of our eyes, the unity of our party. We swear, Comrade Lenin, that we will faithfully carry out this command!'

These lines from Stalin's famous speech at the 11th Congress of the Soviets (January 26th, 1924) measure the abyss of centuries — centuries which had witnessed Galileo, Newton, Voltaire and Kant — separating this language and mentality from that of Marx and Lenin. The tone of this 'oath', laden with liturgical solemnity, in which Stalin poses as the earthly vicar and executor of the last testament of a defunct god, allows us more easily to understand certain connections than would any amount of analysis. Above all, the links between Stalin and his bureaucratic apparatus, with its proliferation of obscure functionaries extraneous to the history of

Bolshevism and the revolution (Poskrebyshev, Smitten, Yezhov, Pospelov, Bauman, Mekhlis, Uritsky, Varga, Malenkov, and others) on the one hand, and on the other the mass party membership, which through the 'Lenin levy', the incipient purges, the massive entry of Mensheviks and remnants of the old regime, increasingly became an opaque and enfeebled body, already largely composed of devoted cyphers or straightforward political illiterates.

It is crucial to bear all this in mind in order to understand the real meaning of the banner under which Stalin was victorious, 'Socialism in One Country'. This slogan does not mean, as the legend has it, that Stalin alone, in the midst of a bewildered and confused leadership, had the courage and foresight to indicate a solution in the conditions of isolation which followed the failure of revolution in the West. In fact, there is no programme or political strategy if this is what we mean by 'solution', which bears Stalin's name. Ideas, for Stalin, were always means, or rather mere pretexts. Zinoviev and Kamenev provided him with the themes with which to combat Trotsky. Bukharin's advocacy of 'Socialism at a Snail's Pace' provided him with the basis for 'Socialism in One Country', and for his struggle against the United Opposition. Finally, the industrialization programme, conceived by the Opposition, provided him with the platform from which to destroy Bukharin, after the Opposition had already been expelled from the party.

What constituted Stalin's specific characteristic, or, if this is what one is expected to say, the element of his 'greatness', which enabled him as an individual to assume a Hegelian 'world-historical' role? It was his ability to interpret the isolation forced upon Russia — which from a revolutionary Marxist position, could only be regarded as a negative event, to be surmounted as soon as possible — as a fortunate opportunity from the standpoint of Russia's destiny as a state. This does not mean that one can simply speak of chauvinism, or even nationalism in the common sense of the term, as early as 1925 or 1926. The process was more complex. It had its roots, as Carr has acutely observed, in a certain sense of pride in the fact that the revolution had, after all, succeeded, that it had been a Russian achievement, that Russia had succeeded where other, supposedly more advanced countries had failed. For those who felt this new 'nationalist-revolutionary' pride, it was an immense pleasure to be told that Russia would lead the world, not only in making the revolution but in constructing a new economy. It was precisely his instinctive ability to interpret and represent this 'force', obscure yet palpable like all elements of so-called 'national spirit', that enabled Stalin to establish and fortify his power. 'Socialism in One Country' was above all a declaration of independence from the West, a proclamation which re-echoed some of the old Slavophile Russian tradition. It did not represent an economic analysis, programme, or a long-term political strategy. For this Stalin's intellectual qualities were quite inadequate, as were those of his advisers: Molotov, Kaganovitch, Ordjhonokidze, Kirov, Yaroslavsky, Yagoda, and later Beria, Zhdanov and so on. This declaration was something else: something for which the Marxism of most of the Bolshevik leadership, with its high intellectual level and profoundly international education, rendered them quite incapable. It was, in short, a declaration of faith in the virtue and destiny of the Russian people.

According to Carr, who is in many respects so favourable towards Stalin, it was the fusion of two characteristic elements of his personality that enabled him to express an objective process at work in the years following Lenin's death. These were: firstly, a 'reaction against the prevalent "European" model in terms of which the revolution had hitherto been conducted', in favour of 'a conscious or inconscious return to national Russian traditions'; and secondly, the abandonment of an intellectual and theoretical framework developed in the whole period when Lenin led the party, for 'a decided re-evaluation of practical and administrative tasks'.

Stalin alone, among the Bolshevik leaders, had never lived in Europe, nor had he ever read or spoken a Western language. From this standpoint his rise to power represented something that far surpassed his own personality, namely the replacement of an entire political group within the leading ranks of the party, concomitant with the adoption of 'Socialism in One Country'. Trotsky, Radek, Rakovsky, Preobrazhensky, Zinoviev, Kamenev, Piatakov, Bukharin and others were gradually removed; they were replaced by a radically different type of personnel, whose most striking features were fundamental indifference towards Marxist theory and a purely 'administrative' attitude towards major questions of political analysis and strategy. Molotov, Kirov, Kaganovitch, Voroshilov, or Kuibyshev, the men who were subsequently closest to Stalin, were like himself totally lacking in Western culture or any internationalist outlook whatever.

Carr writes: 'All the original Bolshevik leaders, except Stalin, were in a sense the heirs or products of the Russian intelligentsia and took for granted the premises of 19th-century western rationalism. Stalin alone was reared in an educational tradition which was not only indifferent to western ways of life and thought, but consciously rejected them. The Marxism of the older Bolsheviks included an unconscious assimilation of the western cultural foundations on which Marxism had first arisen. The fundamental assumptions of the enlightenment were never questioned; a basis of rational argument was always presupposed. Stalin's Marxism was imposed on a background totally alien to it, and acquired the character of a formalistic creed rather than of an intellectual conviction.'[3]

The arrival on the scene of this new political elite, which in most cases expressed a 'national-socialist' rather than international outlook, explains the new direction imposed by Stalin on the Third International — which he soon came to call 'the shop'. In the years when the Comintern was still a vital organism, involving Lenin, Trotsky and Zinoviev in feverish activity, he showed no interest in it. He began to concern himself with it only after 1924, when it had already ceased to serve the needs of world revolution and become a bureaucratic machine and an instrument for the promotion of Russian policy, or merely of his own personal designs. Henceforward, the abandonment of any internationalist perspective was complete. International prospects and goals were replaced by unscrupulous diplomatic manoeuvres with various capitalist states; the world working-class movement and its Communist parties were definitively and totally subordinated to the interests of the Soviet State. Within this State, Stalin not only showed himself to be the most 'Russian' of all the Bolshevik leaders of the older generation but violently subjugated all the other nationalities of the ex-Czarist empire (starting with his native Georgia).

The Consequences of Stalin

It would be useless to dwell upon these points any further; subsequent events have made them all too limpidly evident. The distortion and instrumentalization of the Communist International is writ large on the mediocre bureaucrats who were progressively promoted within it, while the leaderships of the various national sections were destroyed. In the postwar period these personalities appear in the satellite states at the head of the so-called 'People's Democracies'; the Beiruts, Rakosis, Anna Paukers and Georghiu Dejs, the Gottwalds, Novotnys and Ulbrichts — often pursued by popular hatred beyond the grave, or if they survived, no longer daring to set foot in their native countries. Great Russian corruption and chauvinism was sealed in Stalin's Pact with Hitler, to mention no more: even if a declaration of non-aggression was dictated by necessity, the 'pact of friendship', containing secret clauses by which the Soviet Union obtained and later kept the Baltic republics (Latvia, Lithuania, Estonia, part of Poland and Bessarabia), was not. Here we well and truly have a direct reply to Lenin's text on the right of nations to self-determination, written less than 30 years before, and the first example of 'socialist policy' at the service of state expansion and territorial annexation.

For the rest, we can grasp the general sense of the political outlook and aims with which Stalin presided over what should have been the 'Union of Soviet Socialist Republics' from actions and signs which, though ostensibly trivial, are nonetheless richly eloquent. In 1944 he dissolved the Comintern as a pledge and guarantee to the USA and Britain. In the same year, the *Internationale* was replaced by a new *national* anthem, the text of which sings his glory and greatness. In March 1946, he rebaptized the Council of People's Commissars as the Council of Ministers, a title which Lenin had always abhorred. On February 25th, 1947, he changed the name 'Red Army of the Workers and Peasants' into that of 'Armed Forces of the USSR'. At the Nineteenth Congress of the Party he suppressed the qualification of 'Bolshevik' which had hitherto designated it. He was so concerned to break any connection, even of a formal kind, which linked the postwar USSR to the October Revolution that in his speech of February 9th, 1946, speaking of those outside the Party and militants within the Party, he declared: 'The only difference between them consists in the fact that the latter are members, the former are not. But this is only a formal difference.'

This was an official sanction for the death of the Party as such. For some time already the Party had been only one instrument of absolute rule among others, alongside the various secret police organizations. A compact and congealed layer of functionaries, police, informers, flatterers and bureaucrats covered and suffocated the entire country and society. 'To flatter them Stalin gave distinctions to the small and large bureaucrats upon which his power depended': on May 28th, 1943 the personnel of the Foreign Ministry were assigned ranks 'indicated by epaulettes trimmed with silver thread with old insignia representing two interwoven palms'.[4] Distinctions and uniforms elegantly ranked all the other civil servants. In their turn, the endless swarm of petty and large functionaries, academics, pseudo-scientists and sinister bards of the regime, in order to merit these marks of flavour, put in the form of verse or 'scientific memoranda', what Tacitus simply called *ruere in servitium*: 'J.V. Stalin and Linguistics', 'J.V. Stalin and Chemistry', 'J. V. Stalin and Physics' ad infinitum. *Pravda,* which had once carried the incisive and sarcastic prose of Lenin now sang lullabies to the masses in the form of stanzas like: 'O Stalin, Great Leader of all Peoples,/ You have given birth to Man,/ You fertilize the Earth,/ You rejuvenate the Centuries,/ You are one and the same with Spring,/ You make the Lyre sing. . . ,/ You are the flower of my Springtime,/ a Sun reflected in thousands of human hearts.'. . .

The change which had occured in Russia since Lenin is demonstrated quite unequivocally by the forces and values called upon by the State during the Second World War. The spiritual energies of the country were not mobilized in the name or defence of Communism but in that of 'Russian Patriotism.' In his speech in Red Square at the moment when the Nazi armies were approaching Moscow (November 7th, 1941), Stalin appealed to the founders of the Russian Fatherland and to the great Czarist generals: 'In this war let us be inspired by the glorious example of our great ancestors, Alexander

Nevsky, Dimitri Donskoi, Kuzma Minin, Dimitri Poyarsky, Alexander Suvorov, Mikhail Kutuzov!' In October 1942 he abolished the political commissars of the Red Army and several weeks later created for officers the orders of Suvorov, Kutuzov and Alexander Nevsky. In the beginning of 1943, he issued a regulation defining the privileges of the officer caste, reintroducing several aspects of Czarist etiquette. For the Ukrainians he created the order of Bogdan-Chmelnitsky, after the name of the (historic) Ukrainian Ataman, a specialist in Jewish pogroms.[5] Finally the new national unity was sealed by a *rapprochement* with the Russian Orthodox Church. Stalin crowned the Patriarch of Moscow, permitted the re-establishment of the Holy Synod, and received the three metropolitans of the Russian Church, Sergius, Alexis and Nicolai, who greeted him as 'Father of us All, Joseph Vissarionovitch'.

From this time onwards the World War was officially designated in Russia the 'Great Patriotic War'. Under this name it ended. On the day of the Japanese surrender, Stalin addressed a message to the Soviet people: 'We have for 40 years been waiting for this day. . .'. He was of course, alluding to revenge for the Czarist defeat in the Russo-Japanese war, a defeat that had led to the revolution of 1905 and was at that time greeted as a victory by all revolutionaries. The political past of the Stalinist USSR was not, therefore, that of Bolshevism, but that of Czarist Russia.

The significance of all these aspects of Stalin's work became explicit in the climate at the moment of his death, in mysterious circumstances, in 1953. Lenin's Russia, the first bastion of the socialist transformation of the world, was now no more than a distant memory. At the moment of Stalin's death the country was a prey to the furies of obscurantism. From Moscow, there no longer resounded the summons: 'Workers of the World Unite!', but rather a call to anti-semitic persecution (the 'Doctors Plot') and the struggle to death against so called 'cosmopolitanism'.

What need is there here to revoke the Moscow trials or to speak of the systematic destruction of all the old Bolshevik cadre and militants? To record the toll of the 'purges', of the mass liquidations, of the concentration camps and deportations? Since moral indignation and horror are not effective, we must harness our hatred and trust ourselves to the power of reasoning. This cold and despotic man, whom we have attempted to describe, had more Communists on his conscience than had hitherto been exterminated by the entire world bourgeoisie; he calculated impassively the ruin of whole populations; far from the masses, under his regime the soviets born in 1917 ended as dependencies of the Ministry of the Interior. Nonetheless this man was in his own way endowed with a 'greatness' that we must in some way attempt to define, more to understand what he produced than what he was himself. The liberal English historian Carr had written: 'Stalin is the most impersonal of the great historical figures.'[6] Through industrialization, 'he westernized Russia, but through a revolt, partly conscious, partly unconscious, against western influence and authority and a reversion to familiar national attitudes and traditions. The goal to be attained and the methods adopted or proposed to attain it often seemed in flagrant contradiction . . . Stalin's ambiguous record was an expression of this dilemma. He was an emancipator and a tyrant; a man devoted to a cause, yet a personal dictator; and he consistently displayed a ruthless vigour which issued, on the one hand, in extreme boldness and determination and, on the other, in extreme brutality and indifference to human suffering. The key to these ambiguities cannot be found in the man himself. The initial verdict of those who failed to find in Stalin any notable distinguishing marks had some justification. Few great men have been so conspicuously as Stalin the product of the time and place in which they lived.'[7]

It is obvious that this judgement could have no foundation if it were not for the fact that the Stalin period also included industrialization and the great Five Year plans. Through this process Russia became the second industrial power in the world; it is undeniable that this transformation contained within it not only potentially but in real terms a liberatory content. Enormous masses of men were brought into contact with modern productive processes, technology and scientific rationality. Illiteracy was wiped out. The nationalities of Central Asia were dragged out of their nomadic past and in some sense involved in the circuit of modern life: their elementary cultural and material needs were satisfied. The mechanization of agriculture began the transformation of the *muzhik* into a worker.

The criticisms levelled at the manner in which collectivization of the countryside was achieved are both well-known and well-justified. Brutality and violence, no attempt to win consent, millions and millions of victims. Even if these criticisms had never been made, the results of this collectivization would speak for themselves: the permanent crisis of Soviet agriculture, the low productivity of labour, the still high percentage of those employed in the countryside, and Russia's import of grain supplies.

However at the root of these criticism, there may also be a cerain tendency to underestimate the 'irrationality' or at least the exceptional character of the problem which the Bolshevik party was obliged to confront and which several other Communist parties, on taking power, were later to encounter. The problem was that of the transition towards socialism in a country in which the process of *accumulation* had not yet taken place, that accumulation which in Europe was the work of capitalism and its industrial revolution.

Workers' Democracy and Accumulation

To build a socialist society means to establish *socialist relations of production*. However one interprets it, this construction is inseparable from the development of *socialist democracy,* soviet power or this self-government of the producers, in the real and not metaphorical sense of the word. On the other hand, and on the contrary, *accumulation* implies saving an extremely high quota of the national product for investment in industrial development; this means violently repressing mass consumption, violently restraining the needs of the population. It presupposes the precise opposite of democracy and of soviets: a coercive apparatus, charismatic power and the *utilization* rather than the self-regulation of the masses.

This is the problem with which Stalin was faced, or rather in the face of which the 'situation' selected Stalin. It is also substantially the problem which, *mutatis mutandis,* confronts Mao and the Chinese leadership today, whatever so many intellectuals in their naivete may suppose. Why is industrial accumulation necessary? Why is it not possible to construct socialism on the basis of small peasant production or more simply by changing men's souls, appealing to altruism, converting everyone from cormorants into doves? Why is not possible to abolish, here and now, the 'division of labour'? The innocence with which these questions are asked by so many intellectuals today is a witness of the radical destruction which theoretical Marxism has undergone in recent decades.

It is, of course, true that the reply to these questions is not contained at any particular point in Marx's work. It is only to be found on every page that he ever wrote, from first to last, starting naturally with the 1848 *Manifesto of the Communist Party* (what, the party already in Marx?). The self-government of the masses presupposes: a high productivity of labour, the possibility of a drastic reduction in the working day, the progressive combination of intellectual and industrial work in the category of the worker-technician, masses conscious and capable of making society function at a higher historical level. In short, the self-government of the masses, the rule of the proletariat, presupposes the modern *collective worker.* These conditions can only arise on the basis of large scale industry, and not of agricultural communes or production with the wooden plough.

Let us return to the thread of the discussion. Stalin's 'greatness' lay in his construction of a great State (the State which Lenin had hoped would rapidly wither away) and a Great Power. He was great in the same sense as Peter the Great. His importance belongs less to the history of the international workers' movement than to its 'pre-history', which is still being prolonged beyond all our anticipations: a history not of human emancipation but of great powers dividing the world, of *raison d'etat,* of races confronting one another and displacing class divisions, history governed by geopolitics.

In face of the enormous scale of what he built, Stalin has impressed many admirers for his realism. What do principles matter? What does it matter how people live? Does it count or decide anything? What counts is millions of tons of steel, missiles, nuclear power. Admiration for 'realism' of this kind has often led to the conclusion that 'Stalin constructed socialism' and that 'Russia is the first socialist country!'

In reality, what Stalin produced is inseparable from *the way* in which it was produced. Seventeen years after his death (an entire historical epoch!) Russia is still, more than ever, gripped by the same contradictions as in 1953. As the passage of time reveals, this is a society which cannot be reformed peacefully. Yet unable to reform itself, it is destined for deep convulsions.

How then can we characterize Soviet society? The strategic sector of the means of production is owned by the State. But State ownership is certainly not the same as the *socialization* of the means of production. Nonetheless it allows for a *planning policy* which, whatever its defects, is not only quite different from so-called 'programming' of the West, but in so far as it reduces and maintains control over the mechanisms of the market, makes it impossible to speak for the time being of a real capitalist restoration. On the other hand, to attribute to this society a so-called *basis* of socialism is equally impossible, for if the words have any meaning this 'basis' must be the socialist relations of production and exchange themselves, which clearly do not exist in Russia. A provisional conclusion — certainly not sufficient but perhaps the least unacceptable of those suggested — is provided by the formula 'society of transition', but not in the classic, original sense, in which the society of 'transition' is already a 'socialist' one. The formula in this case refers to a society half-way between capitalism and socialism and capable, therefore, of advancing or regressing. We must, moreover, qualify this definition with the proviso that in the present danger of degeneration of the Soviet state, the general laws of transition from capitalism to socialism are not expressed; instead, an exceptional and temporary refraction of these laws obtains in a country which developed from a profound backwardness, and which has for so many decades now been oppressed and stifled by a bureaucracy which often combines habits and mores of autocratic absolutism with methods of fascist extraction.

The Long Stagnation

To conclude, Stalinist and post-Stalinist Russia constitutes a long *stagnation* in the process of transformation of bourgeois society into socialist society; a repugnant stagnation which *could* be the preamble and inception of a new exploitative society. Amidst this chaos of problems, completely unforeseen by theory, in which at times everyone must feel lost and despairing, one thing at least is clear. The epoch of 'Socialism in One Country' is over; this epoch which saw the triumph of Realpolitik over 'Utopia' has in the end revealed the unrealistic side of this 'realism'. Not only has Russia emerged from the hands of Stalin afflicted with the gravest ailments, but the whole edifice of which it was for years the keystone is collapsing into fragments. The so-called 'socialist camp' is partly falling apart, partly held together by military violence and police coercion. The danger of war today does not run along the frontiers of the USSR and the imperialist world, but along the border between the USSR and People's China.

Revolutionary thought has often paid dearly for its recourse to Utopias. But in the long run Realpolitik has itself — though for opposite reasons — been revealed as a Utopia; the idea that 'moral energies' count for nothing in History, that force is everything, that force is enough to subject peoples, has been conclusively exposed. For, today this Realpolitik has failed. The policy of 'Socialism in One Country' is now shown to be completely unequal to the tasks posed by the problems arising from any 'socialist camp', that is, a community of peoples engaged in a common task of building socialism. Stripped naked, it is revealed for what it has in the meantime become: a crude disguise for the old *raison d'etat,* a theory of 'limited sovereignty', that is, for the weaker States, unlimited for the chauvinism of the most powerful State. This historical defeat of Stalinism, in all its forms, has only one positive outcome. It restores to the internationalist theory of Marx and Lenin a sense of truth and actuality. For this theory, the socialist transformation of the world was unthinkable without the determinant contribution of revolution in the West, that is in the heart of capitalism itself. Yet it must also be said that — even though the time of society is not that of individuals — theoretical Marxism today confronts a test: it is for us to decide whether it is to be merely a chiliasm, or the foreceps capable of giving birth to history.

The legacy of the Stalin era defeated
him [Khrushchev], and it still over-shadows
the Soviet scene today.

Ideological Trends in the USSR
Isaac Deutscher

. . . Khrushchev and his colleagues, the present Soviet leaders, have dealt
with the legacy of the Stalin era in a manner which could only produce
confusion and frustration. Brought up in the Stalinist school of thought, and
ever mindful of their own stake in Stalinism, they merely sought to cover up
the void by means of bureaucratic manipulations. They conducted even de-
Stalinization in a Stalinist manner. Imbued with the characteristic Stalinist
belief in the omnipotence of the trick, a belief which has with them the force
of an ineradicable superstition, Khrushchev and his collegues in the end
turned de-Stalinization itself into a trick, into a huge and elaborate essay in
deception and make-believe. They denounced Stalin's hypocrisy but sought
to protect the hierarchical structure on which it had rested. They exposed his
crimes and did what they could to conceal their own participation in them.
They discredited the "cult of the personality" but clung to the orthodoxy the
cult had epitomized. They cried out against Stalin's prodigious despotism
but were anxious to save most of his canons and dogmas. They freed the
Soviet people from his massive and ubiquitous terror but tried to keep the
body-politic in the shape it had taken on under the press of that terror. They
sought to preserve the monolith and to keep Soviet society in that
amorphous and atomized condition in which people cannot think for
themselves, express themselves, arrive at nonconformist opinions, and voice
them.

Yet, the huge trick with all the evasions, subterfuges and contradictions
did not work. Underneath the monolithic surface, deep down in the mass of
the people, and even higher up in the ruling group, ferments were released
which were bound to escape control. Some people saw through the evasions
and contradictions and began to press for a more radical and genuine de-
Stalinization. Others, especially among the bureaucracy, took fright at the
ideological drifting and called for an end to the desecration of the old idol;
many reacted simply with disgust and cynicism. Some were raising the
demand for the mitigation or abolition of various forms of administrative
controls and thought control, the demand for more freedom; while others,

again among the bureaucracy, afraid that popular discontent and criticism might arise in a flood, were anxious to close the gates. Khrushchev manoeuvred uneasily and clumsily between the conflicting pressures until he exhausted his moral credit. In 1956 he used Stalin as the colossal scapegoat for all the sins of the Soviet bureaucracy. In 1964 the bureaucracy quietly made of Khrushchev the scapegoat. But the men who took over from him inherited all his dilemmas without having any new programme or any new idea on how to resolve them. Their chief advantage over Khrushchev was that they could afford to mark time, as he could not. . . .

Khrushchev, attempting always to be all things to all men, in the end antagonized all. The crypto-Stalinists never forgave him his speech at the 20th Congress. The bureaucrats were eager to avenge themselves on him for his pogrom of the central economic ministries; and the disciplinarians resented the latitude he allowed the critics and muckrakers who exposed not only Stalin's rule but the heavy remnants of Stalinism, surviving in every sphere of Soviet life. On the other hand, to the critics and muckrakers, the liberals and the radicals, Khrushchev's benevolence was only too whimsical and deceptive. They knew only too well that every one of his liberal gestures made in public concealed many acts of repression. The writers and the artists resented his censorship and his attempts to impose on them his crude and uneducated tastes. In 1964 the anti-Stalinists and the crypto-Stalinists, the liberalizers and the authoritarians for a moment joined hands against him, each hoping to gain from his downfall. These hopes too have been frustrated. Khrushchev's successors have not identified themselves with either of the opposed groupings. They have rather tried to do what Khrushchev had done, only to do it with greater discretion and caution. They have pursued a middle line and have tried hard to keep the "extremes" at bay.

The division between the de-Stalinizers and the crypto-Stalinists, and between the liberalizers and the authoritarians, forms only part of the picture, its most conspicuous and superficial part. Overshadowed by it there is another division, largely latent and even inchoate but, in the long term, perhaps more essential, namely, the division between right, left, and centre. The reappearance of this classical division follows naturally from the cracking up of the monolith, the essential of which consisted precisely in suppressing the dialectics inherent in any live movement or party and in preventing any spontaneous differentiation of opinion, both within the party and without. The last time the Soviet Union witnessed any open struggle between right, left, and centre was in the middle and late 1920's. The present re-differentiation resumes to some extent, but only to some extent, the trends of the 1920's but it does so spontaneously, almost unconsciously, and confusedly. And in view of the change in the social circumstances and in the political context, the continuity of these trends can be only partial. That the tendency to a division between right, left and centre is at work in the international Communist movement is now clear enough, even though that division is blurred and distorted by many-sided bureaucratic manipulation, and even though each trend *tends* to be identified with a particular national interest and school of thought — the left or "ultra-left" with Maoism, the centre with predominant Soviet policy, and the right with Titoism and its multiple national varieties. However, a *tendency* towards this differentiation is discernible within each Communist party as well, even though each tries to maintain the official facade of its monolithic unity. This makes it often difficult to see and evaluate the hidden processes of division. But when the facade happens to be suddenly and dramatically blown off, as it has been in China recently, the reality of the division asserts itself. The Soviet Party is hardly more monolithic or more united than the Chinese was just before the outbreak of the so-called cultural revolution. Here and there many indications point to the submerged pattern of differentiation — I repeat to an inchoate or, at best, half-potential and half-actual division between right, left, and centre. The division cannot become fully actual as long as the groupings involved in it are not free to express themselves and formulate their ideas or programmes, for it is precisely in the process of self-expression that ideological trends and political groupings become conscious of themselves and find their identity.

I should, perhaps, clarify here to some extent my criteria and explain what attitudes I describe as "left" or "right" in the context of Soviet social life and Soviet politics at this time.

The specific crucial issues over which the divisions tend to arise are those of egalitarianism versus privilege; of workers' control, or workers' participation in control, over industry versus strictly managerial control; of freedom of expression and association versus bureaucratic dictatorship and monolithic discipline; and last but not least, of socialist internationalism versus nationalism.

. . . Trying to trace the features of the emerging political types, one is inclined to melancholy reflections about the price the Soviet Union is still paying, in spiritual and intellectual terms, for the forcible interruption by Stalinism of all open ideological and political confrontation. The level of political thinking and expression is lamentably low. The profile of a man of the right in the 1960's is simple enough. He usually defends privilege, favours wide discrepancies in scales of wages and salaries, and tends to be a Great Russian Chauvinist and power politician; he is contemptuous of the small Soviet nationalities and of such poor relations as Poles and Hungarians, but, above all, of the Chinese, against whom he will even vent prejudice. More often than not, he is an antisemite. Next to him stands a more moderate and educated man of the right, who may combine antiegalitarianism and distrust of the masses, with a certain cosmopolitanism, with an eagerness for close relations with the West, and with an intense fear of any Russian involvement in class struggles abroad or in anti-imperialist wars of liberation. Western observers often come across this political type amongst Soviet diplomats, journalists, and industrial managers; but more plebeian versions of the type also abound.

The man of the Soviet Left is more often than not an intellectual, a philosopher, sociologist, or party historian; but he may also be a worker at the factory bench. He criticizes the present distribution of the national income, the wide wage differentials, and bureaucratic privilege. He attacks — sometimes even in public — the secrecy with which the earnings of the various "income groups" are surrounded, and presses for a radical narrowing of their discrepancies. He favours shorter working hours in the factories and demands better and wider educational facilities for working class children. That pressure on all these points has been effective is evidenced by the concessions which the ruling group has again and again had to make in regard to them. This new egalitarianism, inherently hostile to the Stalinist tradition, is also critical of the social implications of the new economic policy, with its heavy emphasis on profitability and the "laws of the market". The man of the Left recalls that Socialism has aspired and should still aspire to transcend gradually the laws of the market, not by means of rigid bureaucratic direction, but by a rational economic policy and the producers' participation in control over the economy. In ideology and politics, the elements of the Left seek to pick up the threads of the revolutionary tradition where Stalinism broke them, and restore the true history of the revolution and of Bolshevism, for they feel that only if the ground is cleared to the end of the rubble of Stalinist legends and myths, will a new socialist consciousness develop in the people. In foreign affairs men of the left try to grasp the significance of recent social-revolutionary events in the world, of Cuba and Vietnam, and of China's internal conflicts; and they attempt to relate these to Soviet policy. They are, no doubt, perturbed by the decline of international solidarity in the USSR and by the quasi-isolationist mood that characterizes both official policy and the popular frame of mind.

I do not undertake, I don't think anyone can undertake, to judge the relative strength and weight of these opposed currents of thought and feeling. Even the characterization of the types is, of necessity, fragmentary and patchy. Yet it is based on the internal evidence of the events, and on a wide range of philosophical, economic, sociological and literary indications. These are the hidden or half-hidden conflicting pressures under which, I think, Soviet policy finds itself and by which it is to some extent shaped. Official policy is, of course, centrist, cagey, and is trying to keep at a safe distance from the extremes or to reconcile the contradictions. But in the long run the basic trends seem more important: they are likely to become more effective as time goes on; they make up the submerged bulk of the Soviet iceberg.

The two patterns of the ideological and political division, the division over Stalinism and the conflict between right and left are not coincidental. They overlap and produce cross-currents. Among the adherents of de-Stalinization there are some with a rightist and others with a leftist bias. In the early years after Stalin, Khrushchev sought to rally the support of both wings; and therein lay his strength. In his later years, his own policy showed a markedly rightist bias in both domestic and foreign affairs. This circumstance undoubtedly brought a measure of discredit upon de-Stalinization. Occasionally, it lent colour to the Maoist accusation that, by undermining the Stalinist orthodoxy, Khrushchev released or stimulated latent reactionary forces, within the Soviet Union as well as without, in Eastern Europe, in Hungary, Poland and elsewhere.

Thus, paradoxically, the opposition to de-Stalinization, which at first came only from a rather narrow conservative bureaucratic milieu, found itself gradually strengthened by a spreading disappointment with various aspects of Khrushchevism. Seeing that de-Stalinization in Khrushchev's policy was, in his last years, associated with antiegalitarianism, with a virtual wage freeze, and agricultural failure, and further with the Russo-Chinese feud and the disintegration of the Soviet Bloc, quite a few people inclined towards egalitarianism and internationalism became fearful of the implications of Khrushchevism. Critical, well-informed observers reported, for instance, in the years 1963 and 1964, the spread of something like a spontaneous, nostalgic Stalin cult among Soviet factory workers, a mood which expressed itself in biting popular witticisms contrasting some of Khrushchev's failures with Stalin's wisdom and foresight. "Do you know what was the greatest of Stalin's crimes?" went one popular joke, "it was this, that he did not lay up a stock of grain that would last us longer than five years of Khrushchev's rule". What a paradox! Who would have thought in 1956 that anyone in the Soviet Union would only a few years later look back nostalgically to the Stalin era.[1] But this was, in fact, the outcome of half-hearted, hypocritical and "rightist" de-Stalinization. One consequence of that state of affairs — one would like to hope an ephemeral one — is that the progressive, anti-Stalinist intelligentsia found itself frequently isolated from the mood in the working class. Another is that before the recent uproar and commotion in China, Maoist criticism struck more chords in the Soviet

Union than Soviet officialdom was ready to admit.

Seen against this background the task of Khrushchev's successors has not been an easy one. They were not well equipped to deal with the conflicting trends and cross-currents. They represent — in this respect the Maoists are right — Khrushchevism without Khrushchev. When they turned against their former leader, they held that his policies had been basically correct, but that he had distorted and compromised them by his temperamental outbursts, eccentricities, and excesses. There was a grain of truth in that, but not more. Khrushchev's behavior became increasingly erratic as his policies were leading him into an impasse. He tried to get out of it by alternate overemphatic gestures of conciliation and by aggressive vituperation, by attempts to ingratiate himself with his opponents at home or abroad, and by loud fist-banging or shoe-banging.

There is, in any case, a curiously repetitive logic in all this. It had been Khrushchev's strongly-held view that Stalin's policy had, over many years, been basically correct until Stalin spoiled everything by his morbid lust for power and his excesses. Khrushchev, as it were, appealed from the latter-day insane Stalin to the alleged sanity of the earlier Stalinism. Now Brezhnev and Kosygin react in the same way to Khrushchevism. They seek to rescue it from Khrushchev's latter-day distortions.

They began by moving on tiptoes and trying to hush discordant voices around them. There were to be no further drastic exposures of Stalinism, no more talk about the terrors of the concentration camps of the past; but there was to be no rehabilitation of Stalinism either, and no repudiation of the Twentieth and Twenty-second Congresses. There was to be no further liberalization; but neither was there to be any drastic curtailment of Khrushchev's semi-liberal reforms. There was to be no more voicing of egalitarian demands — the emphasis was and is on incentive payments and rewards; but neither was there to be any campaign against the egalitarians. In foreign affairs, Kosygin and Brezhnev decided to put an end to personal diplomacy a la Khrushchev, but reasserted their faith in his interpretation of "peaceful coexistence". They tried to restore the unity of the Communist parties and to mend the bridge with China; but they are not willing to make any concessions of substance to the Chinese. Kosygin's first journey, on assumption of the office of Prime Minister, was to Vietnam and China; but since this journey yielded no positive results, Moscow decided to lapse into silence over China, a silence which it maintained for about two years. To undo the harm that Khrushchev had done to Vietnam, by declaring just before his downfall that the Soviet Union had no interest in defending Southeast Asia, his successors reaffirmed Russia's interest in that area: but they have been rather careful in doling out aid to the North Vietnamese and the "Viet Cong". At the twenty-third Congress, Kosygin and Brezhnev declared that the Soviet aid to the Vietnamese amounted to half a billion roubles, a negligible sum compared to the many billion dollars spent by the United States on the war in Vietnam. In a word, theirs was to be the good old middle-of-the-road Khrushchevism, not the one drifting more and more to the right, Khrushchevism without Khrushchevian excesses, Khrushchevism combined with silence, which is golden, and with wait and see.

It seems that the waiting game is drawing to a close. Brezhnev, Kosygin, and their colleagues are discovering that Khrushchev's "excesses", distortions, and drifting were not accidental or caused merely by his temperamental disposition. The point is that one cannot be afraid of radical egalitarian and of democratic socialist and internationalist trends indefinitely without lapsing into bureaucratic conservatism and drifting to the right. Brezhnev and Kosygin are indeed finding it more difficult to maintain a cautious, non-committal, centrist position. The conflicting pressures from right and left have been mounting, even if right and left are not any organized groupings but more or less diffused tendencies and moods.

And so, after an interval of silence, all controversies are resumed, even though they are as a rule conducted behind closed doors. But there they are conducted with a vehemence of which the echoes reaching the Soviet public or the Western World give only a faint idea. Egalitarian and antiegalitarian voices are heard again, even though the former are muffled, and speak less openly than the latter. And in the background one can discern the renewed, though unfocused, discord between nationalism, and, on a different level, the clash between various interpretations of peaceful coexistence.[2] On all these issues, official policies are slowly but perceptibly drifting again to the right. . .

Ivan Yakhimovich:
"Stalinism no, Leninism yes."

Samizdat: Voices of the Soviet Opposition

George Saunders

The political development of the Soviet Union from its birth in 1917 has passed through three phases: the formative period of the first workers' state, under the Bolshevik leadership of Lenin and Trotsky, from 1917 to 1923; the rise and consolidation of the bureaucratic caste under Stalin's personal dictatorship from 1924 to his death in 1953; the post-Stalin decades from 1953 to the present. One of the most remarkable features of the post-Stalin years has been the emergence — and the endurance under extremely adverse conditions — of an articulate, if diverse and disorganized, opposition to the powers that be in the USSR. This antibureaucratic opposition heralds a new chapter of political progress in the second most powerful country in the world.

The difficulties in assessing the present political opposition movement in the USSR are obvious. The official press, controlled by the privileged bureaucracy, with its monopolistic hold on power, hardly gives reliable information. First-hand interviews from those of oppositionist views are hard to come by — even if not in jails, camps, or "special" psychiatric hospitals, they are not likely to speak freely with foreign reporters, because of the ever present police threat. And of course the capitalist press and intelligence agencies can be expected to distort or suppress what information they do get. The best source to judge from is samizdat.

Samizdat is a Soviet term coined by post-Stalin dissidents for the old Russian revolutionary practice, from the days of the czarist censorship, of circulating uncensored material privately, usually in manuscript form — nonconformist poetry and fiction, memoirs, historical documents, protest statements, trial records, etc. The name "Samizdat" — Self-Publishers — is an ironic parody of such official acronyms as "Gosizdat" meaning State Publishers (short for Gosudarstvennoe Izdatelstvo). More colloquially, one

From "Introduction," to *Samizdat: Voices of the Soviet Opposition* by George Saunders (Editor), copyright © 1974 by Monad Press and reprinted by permission of the publisher.

might translate samizdat as the Do-It-Yourself Press. The message is clear: "If the bureaucrats won't print it, we'll get it around *ourselves.*" Today's samizdat has post-October antecedents as well as prerevolutionary ones — in the private printing and circulation of manuscripts done by the Left Opposition in the twenties and thirties after it was denied the use of the party's printing facilities (the "illegal" printing and circulation of its program was one of the charges that led to the expulsion of the Left Opposition).

In the late twenties and early thirties many Left Opposition documents passed from reader to reader by the same methods that today are called samizdat. Here is how Trotsky described the fate of his 1927 "Letter to the Bureau of Party History": "It circulated from hand to hand in the USSR. In hundreds of copies, either retyped or copied by hand. Single copies, often inexact, filtered abroad. Translations of them appeared in several languages." How contemporary this description sounds! It could refer to any of dozens of samizdat documents of recent years.

The fact is that samizdat is nothing more than the revival, whether conscious or not, of the methods used by the opponents of the Stalin bureaucracy in the period before all vestiges of criticism were stamped out by mass terror.

Even in the early thirties, when most Oppositionists were in prison or exile, their political documents were passed around. Moreover, as late as 1932, they were able to smuggle materials out to be published in the Russian-language *Bulletin of the Opposition,* edited by Trotsky. (In one case, a lengthy theoretical tract, written on cigarette paper in microscopic lettering, was mailed out in a matchbox.) And at the Verkhne-Uralsk "isolator" (a prison) the political prisoners circulated their own manuscript publication, "The Militant Bolshevik" (*Voinstvuyushchiy Bolshevik*). Its issue no. 2 was reprinted in the Russian Bulletin no. 27 (March 1932).

In fact, like the *Chronicle of Current Events* today, the *Bulletin of the Opposition* in 1929-32 found its way into the USSR and "passed stealthily . . . from hand to hand, eagerly read and commented upon even in Stalin's entourage. . . . If only readers in the West had, in the early 1930s, paid more attention to the Letters from Exile from various 'isolators' and camps [reprinted in the *Bulletin*], the 'revelations' of Khrushchev, *The Tales of Kolyma* or the story of Ivan Denisovich would have been much less startling." (*Times Literary Supplement* [London], November 23, 1973).

There is a key difference, of course. The unauthorized circulation of Opposition literature in the thirties was part of the last resistance to the Thermidorian undertow in the Soviet Union fostered by the international recession of anticapitalist revolution. This rise of samizdat, its steady spread, and the deepening politicization in post-Stalin Soviet society are part of a worldwide revolutionary upswing.

The struggle for socialist democracy in the Soviet Union in recent years has centered around samizdat to a great extent. Most of the trials have been aimed at intimidating dissidents involved in producing or circulating uncensored literature. The most prominent figures among the oppositionists have relied on the samizdat network in their battle for free speech, freedom of the press, and basic democratic rights. . . .

Is there any connection between the Left Opposition destroyed in the purges of the 1930s . . . and the "democratic movement" in the Soviet Union today? This is a highly important question for Soviet history and politics.

The Left Opposition was led by a group of prominent Bolsheviks who had played major roles in the October Revolution, civil war, and construction of the Soviet state. Its ranks consisted largely of a younger generation that had fought in the revolution and civil war. In the twenties these young people remained the most active, devoted, and internationalist-minded of the young Communists, both workers and students.

By contrast with the Left Opposition of old, the best-known Soviet "dissidents" today are not veteran party leaders or revolutionary-minded Marxist activists. Writers like Aleksandr Solzhenitsyn, Andrei Sinyavsky, Yuli Daniel, Lidia Chukovskaya, and scientists like Andrei Sakharov and Zhores Medvedev, highly publicized by the mass media in America and the West generally, give the impression that most of Soviet dissent today is centered in literary and cultural circles and among some of the "technical intelligentsia" of Moscow and the main Russian cities. However, more radical forms of dissent, and expressions of discontent among the masses, definitely exist, though they have received far less attention.

Throughout the Stalin and post-Stalin eras, there has been a continuing tendency for radical opposition to crop up among students and workers, not least of all among the nationally oppressed. The conditions of bureaucratic rule, as well as the surviving traditions of the Bolshevik revolution and of true Marxism and Leninism, have guided such tendencies toward ideas and activities often closely parallel to those of the Left Opposition. (One expression of such "neo-Bolshevik" trends, the circle consisting of Grigorenko, Kosterin, and their friends — which was closely linked with and influenced the "democratic movement" — has even received considerable publicity.). . .

Likewise, protest actions in the USSR involving large numbers of workers and members of oppressed nationalities have occurred rather often in the past two decades, although Western public opinion is not nearly so aware of those as of similar outbreaks in Eastern Europe.

Without denying the importance of the ferment in the upper intellectual establishment of the Soviet Union, or the courageous role of the most prominent dissidents, this essay attempts to acquaint the reader with the more radical, often "neo-Bolshevik" groupings, especially among the youth, and the instances of mass outbreaks that have occurred in the Soviet Union, even though detailed information is often lacking.

A look at the opposition currents that grew up among Soviet youth in the last period of Stalin's rule (1945-53), shows that militant anti-Stalinist struggle soon revived in spite of the destruction of most of the old Opposition cadres. Several clandestine youth organizations appeared in the early forties which had arrived "independently" at positions very close to Trotskyism. We say "independently" in quotes because it is impossible to know where the ideas came from that finally took shape in underground student groups functioning in several major cities.

But before looking more closely at the opposition groups of the early postwar period, a review of the background to their struggle is necessary.

The years 1938 and after saw the final defeat of the Spanish revolution, the Munich agreement, the Stalin-Hitler pact, and the opening of World War II. Simultaneously, inside the USSR, the bloody purges of 1936-38 subsided into a more "normalized" routine pattern of repression and execution.

The Nazi invasion of the Soviet Union in June 1941 precipitated a new crisis. In the face of the disastrous early setbacks of the Nazi-Soviet war, Stalin was forced to release many of his prisoners — those who were able to serve the defense of the workers' state more effectively than Stalin's old cronies in charge of Soviet defense, incompetents like Budenny and Voroshilov, who were set aside by late 1941. (Not all of Stalin's revolutionary prisoners, however, were allowed to participate in the fight. Many of the surviving Oppositionists volunteered for duty, but some were immediately executed and others assigned to suicide missions.)

The war also produced new droves of prisoners for the camps, the generation of the "Ivan Denisoviches." Anyone who had been captured by the Germans or exposed to the West became suspect and was jailed. In addition, many military personnel who, like Solzhenitsyn, fought to defend the Soviet state, but were caught expressing criticism of Stalin's calamitous misleadership, were sent to the camps, if not shot outright.

Political life went on in the society, beneath the surface. And in the camps, all the most politicized elements were gathered. There, even if in tenuous and distorted ways, and despite the murderous conditions, the revolutionary heritage passed on to new generations.

In the postwar years, antibureaucratic moods and struggles grew stronger. After a slight relaxation in 1945-46, Stalin introduced a new reign of terror — a brutal anti-Semitic campaign in which the cream of Soviet Jewish culture was exterminated; a campaign against "bourgeois nationalism" aimed particularly against the newly assimilated territories of the Western Ukraine, Western Byelorussia, the Baltic republics, and Moldavia. All who resisted the policy of Russification in those areas — or any other non-Russian areas of the Union — were likewise purged for "bourgeois nationalism," even if they were Communists, as the 1972 letter by Latvian CP members has shown.

Stalin's ferocious intensification of terror in the postwar period culminated in the notorious Doctor's Plot. Several Jewish doctors who attended top leaders in the Kremlin were accused of planning to poison their eminent patients. Here anti-Semitism, one of Stalin's long-time devices, was combined with plans for generalized terror, arrests, and executions on an unparalleled scale.

Stalin's timely death in 1953 interrupted the plans for the massive Doctor's Plot purge. His heirs dropped the whole scheme, cleared the accused physicians, and began a whole series of reforms and concessions to mass discontent that finally peaked in the "de-Stalinization" revelations of the twentieth and twenty-second congresses.

Behind the ferocity of the terror in Stalin's last years stood an insoluble crisis of the system — economic, social, and political strains that reflected the persistent pressures of imperialism and the impossibility of building "socialism in one country." In the face of U.S. imperialism's postwar expansionist drive, and the U.S. nuclear threat, the inefficient Soviet bureaucracy, with its swollen military apparatus, continued to employ only military-diplomatic methods and intensified political repression, once again showing its hostility to a revolutionary internationalist strategy based on socialist democracy.

The Stalin regime incorporated the East European buffer states, according to its military-diplomatic perspective, with no regard for the special conditions or national feelings of the incorporated nations. Its arbitrary Russian chauvinist, military-bureaucratic methods provoked the Tito split in 1948; and to prevent similar developments in other East European countries, the Stalinist police then engineered show trials against "Titoites and Trotskyites" (i.e., unreliable local CP leaders) throughout Eastern Europe.

The same cold war pressures, and military-bureaucratic responses, led the Kremlin high command to introduce a five-year plan with impossible targets that once again brought Soviet agriculture to a state of crisis, causing famine in the countryside just as forced collectivization had done in the early thirties.

These pressures and crises continually regenerated opposition from below. The police-bureaucratic management of the economy, and the unproductive approach to the domestic and international problems of state drove thinking people, especially the young, to revolutionary conclusions. In the Western Ukraine and in Lithuania, Russian chauvinism and the bureaucratic establishment of Soviet power led to guerrilla resistance involving tens and hundreds of thousands against the Stalin regime.

Against the social and historical background outlined above, the significance of the revolutionary underground groups known to have emerged in the 1945-53 period is better understood. An echo of the Bolshevik-Leninist tradition reappeared in them, and they foreshadowed the "neo-Bolshevik" or "neo-Leninist" groupings of the post-Stalin period.

Revolutionary Underground Groups of 1945-53

The most detailed description of the political ideas of dissident Soviet youth in the early postwar years is given by Brigitte Gerland, in her memoirs of life at Vorkuta in 1948-53, published as "Vorkuta (1950-53): Oppositional Currents and the Mine Strikes." Most interesting is the fact that a neo-Leninist group, numbering some hundreds of students at major universities in Moscow, Leningrad, Kiev, and Odessa arrived at a program very close to that of the Left Opposition, even though, as Gerland believes, "the young Leninists had no contact of any kind with the old Opposition."

Many of these young Leninists had been children of "enemies of the people," i.e., their parents had been prominent in the party, government, and military but had been purged in 1936-38. (Stalin had feared the potential challenge to his apparatus from the entire older generation of revolutionists from October and the civil war years.)

"The whole movement is said to have started in 1948 from a discussion between five Moscow University students on the long-banned poetry of Boris Pasternak, in which the idea is developed that spiritual freedom is incompatible with social justice," Gerland relates in her book on Vorkuta published in Germany in 1955. In response to the pessimism prevalent all around them and expressed in Pasternak's poetry, the students resolved to find "a way of making room for spiritual freedom in a collectivist society by decentralization of state power."

This episode is a remarkable forerunner of events to come. The struggle for greater freedom of literary and cultural expression became a major feature not only of the anti-Stalinist movement under Khrushchev (and around Pasternak's poetry then, as well as other "unapproved" literature) but also in the struggles in Eastern Europe for socialist democracy.

Program of the "Lenin's True Work" Group

The program these orphans of the "generation of 1937" developed, called Istinny Trud Lenina (Lenin's True Work), paralleled that of Trotskyism in many ways. Gerland quotes from it and describes it in full in her memoirs of Vorkuta. Briefly, it advocated political revolution to replace the bureaucracy with full Soviet democracy, based on soviets (councils) in every plant and collective farm. These councils were to be elected by the workers and peasants by secret ballot, with all council members subject to immediate recall by the voters. Instead of salaried professionals there would be committees of workers and peasants to carry out administrative tasks. The standing army — whose officer caste had generally proved to be a mainstay of the privileged bureaucracy — was to be replaced by a workers' and peasants' militia (an idea paralleling a proposal by Trotsky in the early twenties).

"Bourgeois democracy, . . . parliamentary forms, and the capitalist economy of the West had little attraction for these young people thirsting for social justice," Gerland stressed in her book.

On the international level, they decisively rejected the dogma of "socialism in one country." They asserted that the transition to communism "can be achieved only by the working classes of all countries, acting in common, in a revolution embracing the whole world." The Istinny Trud Lenina (ITL) supporters were also convinced that "the world revolution was impossible without a world Communist party, leading the proletariat in the struggle."

The consistency of Bolshevik-Leninist line they had reached is strikingly apparent not only on the question of international revolution but also on the question of *nationalities policy* within the sphere of postcapitalist society. Here they opposed the military-bureaucratic methods, the bureaucratic supercentralism, and the Russian chauvinist policies of the Kremlin, not only in relation to non-Russian nations within Soviet borders but also toward the nations of Eastern Europe where capitalism had been abolished. Insofar as the Kremlin's postwar annexations (Western Ukraine, Western Byelorussia, the Baltic states) violated national self-determination, the young Leninists condemned them.

Other Neo-Leninist Groups

The ITL was not the only neo-Leninist grouping to have its origins among young Communists affected by the purges. The "Lenin Group," an underground youth organization that was discovered and smashed by the secret police in 1947, is another group that had its origins in a reaction against the purges, if only a delayed one.

Less is known about the "Lenin Group" than about the ITL but its origins are indicated in its program, which was described in an anonymous "Letter to Stalin" that apparently circulated in the USSR before 1947. The author of the letter was a young Communist who had gone along with the purges of 1936-38, because the Soviet Union had seemed the "only rampart of the forces of progress in the world" at that time, encircled by world capitalism and threatened by fascist invasion. In that atmosphere the purging of the Old Bolsheviks and all oppositionists had been tolerated because the external threat appeared to make monolithic unity imperative.

Once the war had been victoriously concluded, however, and the Soviet state was no longer isolated and encircled, the anonymous author of the letter, this once-loyal Stalinist, revived many of the very criticisms made by the purged opposition: The bureaucracy has become a privileged caste, ever more estranged from the working masses, an aristocracy that ruins agriculture and disorganizes industry. The letter writer even predicted that Stalin's successors would disavow him in order to maintain their bureaucratic power!

The groups we have named are not the only ones known to exist in the early postwar period. One of the most interesting was a clandestine organization in the camps in 1947-48, made up of veterans of the war against the Nazis, that took the name "Democratic Movement of the North of Russia." Its composition reflected the fact that Stalin's camps had been swelled by Soviet soldiers arrested during and after the war. Whole units cut off and surrounded by Germans in the first period of the war, after fighting their way back to their own lines, would find themselves arrested on charges of desertion or treason — all in order to cover up for the bureaucracy's own disorganization of the army by wiping out the top military leadership in the purges and failing to prepare for the invasion.

Veterans like the ones organized in the secret Democratic Movement of the North of Russia staged a desperate revolt in 1948. Seizing their guards' weapons, they tried to take a town in the vast Norilsk labor-camp region, east of the Urals. The effort failed, and they fled toward the mountains — reportedly over 2,000 strong — but were annihilated by the Kremlin's airpower. A similar revolt apparently occurred in the eastern Siberian region of Kolyma, according to the Soviet writer Varlam Shalamov, whose *Notes from Kolyma* have circulated in samizdat and been published outside the USSR.

All-out mobilization of the forces of the bureaucratic machine managed to break up such opposition groups and crush the isolated revolts of 1948-53.

But as the strains and tensions persisted, the bureaucracy finally had to take a new tack. With Stalin's death, they began a relaxation. But this encouraged the rebels in the camps to organize strikes that were partly successful — and incidentally were strengthened by the example of the East Berlin workers' revolt of June 1953. Although the regime smashed the strikes, it also was forced to grant some concessions. New strikes kept breaking out through 1954 and 1955, until finally a general amnesty of political prisoners was granted and the camp system partly dismantled. Thus the stage was set for the twentieth congress and the official repudiation of Stalin by his heirs and former henchmen.

Bolshevik Traditions and the National Question

Nationalities policy has always been a central index of the struggle between revolutionary internationalist tendencies and bureaucratic-reactionary ones in the Soviet Union. It was one of the key issues that caused Lenin to break with Stalin in late 1922 and early 1923, and to prepare an all-out fight against bureaucracy in the party and government. Lenin's illness and death meant that the first step in that fight — removal of Stalin from the post of "general secretary" because of his great-power chauvinism and abuse of authority — was not carried through.

Stalin retained and augmented his power and the bureaucratic, Russian-centralizing tendency he represented grew stronger as the general trend of reaction deepened. Stalin imposed his great-power chauvinist concept upon the USSR in spite of the struggle by the Left Opposition and revolutionary elements in the national republics to fight for implementation of Lenin's policy, as adopted by the 1923 twelfth party congress.

The Left Opposition carried on Lenin's struggle for a correct nationalities policy, and the 1927 *Platform of the Left Opposition* raised eleven demands on this question. It is a significant fact that "a larger proportion" of Trotskyists "than in other parties were members of national minorities," as Joseph Berger observes.[1]

The defeat of the Left Opposition and the strengthening of the narrow, Russian-chauvinist bureaucracy's stranglehold on the party, government, and economy in the early thirties meant an end to whatever progress in Ukrainization, Turkification, and so on, had actually been achieved in the twenties under the impact of Lenin's fight and the best Bolshevik traditions. Ivan Dzyuba in his *Internationalism or Russification?* describes the crude brutality with which Stalin in 1932-33 cut short the highly positive Ukrainization program — a term that Dzyuba says is still mentioned only in whispers to this very day. Thousands of prominent figures in the cultural life of the Ukraine were slaughtered in a blood purge of the Ukrainian Republic promoted by Stalin, several years before the infamous unionwide blood purges of 1936-38.

But the complexities and difficulties for the Soviet state and for the course of world revolutionary developments in general caused by the national question did not disappear even with Stalin's attempts to wipe it out physically. The coming of World War II brought Soviet expansion into the Western Ukraine, Western Byelorussia, and the Baltic republics. In the postwar period, Soviet influence dominated most of Eastern Europe, and under Stalin's direction played a major role in Iranian Azerbaidzhan, Mongolia, Manchuria, Korea, and in relation to the Chinese and Vietnamese revolutions. These and similar events continually placed the Russian-centered, narrowly chauvinist Kremlin bureaucracy in conflict with the national aspirations and needs of masses of people, often moving in revolutionary directions.

The bureaucratic-military approach of the Stalinist bureaucracy in overturning capitalism in the Western Ukraine and the Baltic republics drove peasants in those areas to organize guerrilla warfare against the Stalin regime. It is of great significance that the neo-Leninist youth group that evolved at Vorkuta in the late forties and early fifties, arriving at positions close to those of the old Left Opposition, should have found the national differences with the Ukrainian and Baltic guerrilla veterans to be the most difficult problem in coordinating a fight against the regime. The fact that they were able to ultimately forge an alliance with those "national" elements was also of enormous significance, and was clearly the key to the substantial gains won in that fight.

The revolutionary socialist tendency among the postwar Ukrainian guerrillas was significant. A major tendency in the Ukrainian Partisan Army (UPA), which survived into the early fifties, based its struggle on an anticapitalist and anti-Stalinist program in favor of socialist democracy.[2]

The post-Stalin period, and the half-hearted "de-Stalinization" concessions, created an opening in which the struggle for national rights could reassert itself. On the one hand this was spurred by the continuing policies of Russification pursued by the bureaucratic regime — Stalin's heirs remained true to his program in that respect. On the other hand, the total non-Russian population, by the 1970 census, was threatening to turn the dominant Russian nation's majority into a plurality.

The revival of struggle against Stalinism around the national question was most dramatic in two areas: the new "cultural" opposition in the Ukraine; and the linkup between neo-Leninist oppositionists in Moscow and the struggle for "rehabilitation" of nationalities deported wholesale by Stalin during World War II. (Entire populations had been accused of collaboration with the Nazis.)

The present collection cannot do justice to the complexity and variety of the national question in the Soviet Union today. But some of the uncensored materials from the USSR show that it is an explosive issue. The struggle for a correct revolutionary policy on this issue, uncompromisingly opposed to Russian chauvinism, as Lenin's example showed, is of vital importance in the struggle against the bureaucracy. All "neo-Leninist" tendencies must grapple with this problem and solve it correctly. In fact, on the central problem of mobilizing masses of people into a struggle against the bureaucracy and for a political revolution to institute socialist democracy, the national grievances have thus far produced the nearest thing to mass movements in which the more conscious elements, coming first from the ranks of the intelligentsia and party, have been able to find a common voice with the workers and peasants.

"De-Stalinization" and the Upsurge of 1956

We come now to the watershed between two periods of Soviet history — Stalin's death. "De-Stalinization," made official at the twentieth congress (1956) with Khrushchev's denunciation of Stalin, created a new situation for opposition elements in the struggle against bureaucratism and for socialist democracy, a framework in which certain legal opportunities became available. This is by no means to imply that the bureaucracy could or wished to, reform itself out of existence, as some thought or hoped. The bureaucracy's "de-Stalinization" was not self-motivated, but a *concession* to mass pressure — and it grudgingly conceded as little as possible. Khrushchev and his apparatchiks tried to retain maximum control over the process by which the worst excesses of the Stalin era were halted while the basic structures of the Stalin system were retained. (Soon Khrushchev's accomplices would restore the Stalin figurehead — though on a much smaller scale.)

How much leeway was there for antibureaucratic oppositionists in this new situation? Despite Khrushchev's claim that there were no more political prisoners, the repression continued. And it took the form of savage violence by the terrified police regime whenever mass movements began to get "out of hand." But day-to-day repression was modified and pulled back; the bureaucracy tried to adopt a more legalistic form, to be less obviously high-handed. A certain level of grumbling, or mild dissent, was allowed — within limits — as long as it did not become coherent, vocal, organized, or massive.

Thus, in the post-Stalin era, some critical ideas could be expressed, without running the risk of harsh reprisals. The possibility of fighting one's case in court and appealing for public support even opened up. Some oppositional ideas found an avenue of expression — especially when couched in the regime's own terminology: "the cult of personality," "overcoming harmful vestiges of the past," restoring "Leninist norms in the party and state," observing "socialist legality." In the worst periods under Stalin, extreme clandestinity had been required. In the post-Stalin situation, by contrast, rebels against the system could more easily hear about one another, establish contact, hold discussions, make their ideas known, if only in disguised and allegorical fashion.

Another important new feature of the post-Stalin situation was its world context. There was some relaxation of border controls. Information from abroad entered more easily. At the same time, divergent currents arose within "official" world Communism, even in "fraternal" countries -- lands that were no longer jumping-off points for imperialist invasion, where "bourgeois ideology" could no longer be said to prevail. If certain ideas -- or a certain status as "independent" socialist republics — were permissible in the case of Yugoslavia or Poland, then why not for individuals or nations within the USSR? This heterogeneity and multipolarity in the world Communist movement continues to play a significant role to the present day.

The initial response to de-Stalinization was explosive — reflecting the high pressures that had built up among the masses. The East Berlin uprising and the Vorkuta and other labor camp strikes in summer 1953, and then on a greater scale, the uprisings in Poland and Hungary in October-November 1956, were like the first rush of steam through a half-opened valve.

The Polish and Hungarian workers' revolts raised the specter of political revolution, which could have replaced the bureaucratic caste with workers' democracy and institutions of self-management. The uprisings came very close to succeeding; they were prevented only by the repressive forces thrown in by the Kremlin and the lack of revolutionary leadership at the head of the insurgent masses.

This high point of antibureaucratic revolt had reverberations inside the Soviet Union itself. Mass protests were reported in some areas, such as the ancient Lithuanian city of Kaunas. During the Hungarian events entire Soviet military units, sympathetic to the rebels, had to be pulled out of Hungary; there were also reports that Soviet railway workers refused to run military supply trains in for the repressive forces.

These turbulent developments were reflected in the reappearance among Soviet youth of a strong "neo-Bolshevik" current, with ideas close to those of the Left Opposition. Clandestine neo-Leninist groups, strikingly similar to the ITL of the late forties, were once again reported from Moscow student circles.

It is worth taking a closer look at the neo-Bolshevik currents of 1956-57, for similar groupings have been consistently reported throughout the sixties and into the seventies.

Neo-Bolsheviks of 1956-57

At Moscow University in November 1956, students at a compulsory session on Marxism-Leninism began to bombard the professor with questions about the suppression of the Hungarian revolt, refuting his apologies with — quotations from Lenin! The Lecturer was forced to leave, and the class was dismissed. The next day a Communist Youth (Komsomol) meeting was called to discuss the "shameful" incident. The student audience again took over the meeting from their official leaders, converting it into a solidarity demonstration with the Hungarian workers and drawing analogies between the regimes in Hungary and the USSR. Despite expulsions and other reprisals against hundreds of student activists, open protests continued for a while. Similar student meetings were reported in Leningrad (where there was also a demonstration supporting the Hungarian workers, held in front of the Winter Palace) and in other major Soviet cities, including in Central Asia, as well as in the Komsomol of the Moscow army garrison.

A dramatic first-hand description of the student turbulence in Moscow at that time has been given by David Burg, pseudonym of a Soviet exile now living in Britain who was a student at Moscow University in the period 1951-56.

"In 1956-57, after the XXth Party Congress," Burg writes, "opposition elements within the institutes and universities began to wage an open battle against [the] Komsomol leadership. They sought, first of all, to gain freedom of criticism and expression, and second to introduce a degree of intra-Komsomol democracy that would make the Komsomol a truly representative organization with an honestly elected leadership. Freedom of expression was in fact gradually achieved at that period by a kind of procedure of protestation, and extraordinarily sharp critical comments were heard more and more commonly at meetings. At the same time, illegal and semilegal student journals with such characteristic titles as *Heresy* and *Fresh Voices* began to appear; they discussed art and ideology, ridiculed socialist realism, and attacked the local Komsomol leaders. . . .[3]

Burg estimates that between one-third and one-fourth of the student body evinced open political discontent during "the thaw of 1956." The attitude of the rest of the students toward the political avant-garde was "sometimes sympathetic, sometimes uncomprehending, but rarely hostile."

It is worth noting that demands for the rehabilitation of the major defendants of the purge trials were widely raised by the student protesters.

Burg also comments that previously unmentionable names like Trotsky and Bukharin began to be mentioned, and that the open and semi-"legal" tactics of 1956 were supplemented in some cases "by the creation of illegal political groups that had far-reaching political aspirations. In the history faculty at the University of Moscow, for example, a group of some ten to fifteen graduate students and young research workers printed and distributed leaflets directed against Khrushchev personally and the party dictatorship generally, and calling for the establishment of Soviet democracy and a return to the 'Leninist line.' " This apparently refers to the group around the history students Krasnopevtsev and Rendel; the group was eventually discovered and broken up by the secret police in summer 1957; most of its members were arrested and sentenced to harsh prison terms. This group reflected the predominant view among student oppositionists. "The leaflets issued by clandestine groups," Burg reports, "generally expound the neo-Bolshevik line, as did the history students at the University of Moscow."

The neo-Bolshevik line was reported the strongest of the three main political currents among Soviet students at that time. Burg describes these three viewpoints in some detail. They were, to use his terminology, the "neo-Bolsheviks" (or "neo Leninists"), the "liberal socialist," and the pro-Western "antisocialists."

Burg's account is confirmed by a description in the German socialist youth paper, *Junge Gemeinschaft*, of November 1957: "The oppositional youth consider themselves Marxists, but they feel that the present Soviet social order does not correspond to Marxist ideals. They seek a genuine Marxism and have therefore turned to the pre-Soviet period and to the twenties. . . . They consider the purges of 1937 as an annihilation of the true leaders of the Revolution by Stalin's bureaucratic clique — as a kind of Thermidor."

The program of the "neo-Bolsheviks" of 1956-57 was remarkably similar to that of the Istinny Trud Lenina group of 1948-53, and to that of the original Bolshevik-Leninists destroyed in the purges. They advocated: retention of the planned economy with workers' control of industry and the transformation of the collective farms into real cooperatives managed by their members; political power in the hands of democratically elected and genuinely representative soviets; an end to persecution of dissenters; and free discussion of all interpretations of Marxist thought, as well as freedom of discussion in science and art. The neo-Bolsheviks, according to Burg, did not favor a multiparty system, but rather full internal democracy within the Communist Party. They also opposed introduction of market mechanisms into the economy, believing these would lead to inequality.

Their attitude toward the major centers of world capitalism in particular is worth noting. "The neo-Bolsheviks," reports Burg, "usually argue that while the West is politically freer than the USSR, the Soviet economic structure is more progressive because it is no longer under capitalist control. All that remains to be accomplished, therefore, is the modification of the political structure to prevent the consolidation of power in the hands of a new exploiting class. In contrast, the West is still faced with the problem of wresting economic power from a strongly entrenched bourgeoisie." This is exactly the kind of distinction, it should be noted, that Trotsky drew with the characterization of *political* rather than *social* revolution for the bureaucratized workers' state.

The second political tendency that Burg describes is that of the "liberal socialists" whom he likened to Mensheviks under changed historical circumstances. They do not think a return to October is possible or desirable; instead they favor introducing market-type modifications in the economy and a Western-style parliamentary democracy. Their ultimate goal is individual political freedom, defined rather narrowly. In general, the "liberals" fear revolution and advocate gradual reform as a near-universal solution. They tend to have illusions about life in advanced capitalist societies and a concomitant inability to see the Soviet working class as the potentially mighty force that could topple the bureaucracy.

The openly procapitalist "antisocialists" are the third tendency Burg describes. They tend to think in more simplistic terms: Whatever they dislike in their environment they attribute to evils inherent in the system of planned economy; whatever they wish for but do not have, they believe that capitalism, private property, a "free economy," could provide. According to Burg, this attitude was found more frequently among the *technical intelligentsia* — students at engineering, technical, and similar schools.

Such divergences of viewpoint among oppositionist elements developed further in the Khrushchev and Brezhnev eras. Roy Medvedev in his 1970 book *On Socialist Democracy* described similar currents in the late sixties.

The upsurge of 1956-57 was beaten down, and thousands of student oppositionists swelled the population of the camps and prisons for politicals.

Clandestine Neo-Leninst Groups Since 1956

Andrei Amalrik, a dissident historian now serving a prison term under very harsh conditions, wrote a brief account of the rise of what he calls "the democratic movement" in his well-known essay, *Will the Soviet Union Survive Until 1984?* In it he refers to a number of underground organizations which,"despite the secrecy surrounding their trials," have become known since 1956. Besides the Krasnopevtsev-Rendel group, he mentions the

Leningrad group that published *Kolokol* (The Bell) in 1964-65. *Kolokol* had been the name of one of the clandestine journals that appeared in the 1956-57 period in Leningrad, apparently of neo-Bolshevik viewpoint. Its title was taken from Herzen's famous anti-czarist emigre publication of the mid-nineteenth century. The later *Kolokol*, of 1964-65, was put out by a group called the Union of Communards, which based its Marxist program on Lenin's *State and Revolution*. It was presumably a revival of the 1956-57 publication.

Clandestine, usually "neo-Leninist" groups have continued to exist or come into being as a regular feature of Soviet political life. Little first-hand information about them has become available. The exceptions are the group around Kosterin and Grigorenko in 1968 and the Ukrainian group of 1960-61, called the Union of Workers and Peasants of the Ukraine.

The bureaucracy surrounds such groups with the strictest secrecy because it fears them the most. Sometimes the only information about them appears as a few lines or a few paragraphs in *The Chronicle of Current Events*.[4]

In the late fifties and early sixties several clandestine organizations appeared in the Ukraine. These groups were especially significant because workers were involved.

There have been reports that a clandestine organization of young neo-Bolsheviks played an important role in mass strikes and protests by workers in the Donbas region in 1962. One report, although unverified, described students in a role strikingly reminiscent of the one played by the young Leninists in the Vorkuta strikes, even including collaboration with "Ukrainian nationalists."

"In June of 1962, an uprising occurred in Novocherkassk. There a large part of the population joined in a massive demonstration [against price increases on meat and dairy products] that was brutally suppressed. Almost helpless in cases like this the military was forced to call up reinforcements. But even these additional troops allegedly refused to fire into the crowd after the commanding officer shot himself in front of their eyes. Accompanied by tank units, the MVD [internal security] troops . . . finally put an end to the mass demonstrations. According to unofficial reports, several hundred people were killed.

"The insurgents in the Donbas region [where a wave of protest strikes had occurred] reportedly considered . . . the demonstration in Novocherkassk unsuccessful mainly because they rebelled there without the consent of the strike organization offices in [nearby] Rostov (on the Don), Lugansk,

Taganrog, and other cities. This would confirm rumors and reports concerning a headquarters for organized opposition in [the] Donbas and also explain that a planned co-ordinated demonstration didn't develop because of tumult breaking out over the price increases before final preparations could be made. (*The agitation was supposedly instigated for the most part by students and intellectuals, abetted by a few Ukrainian nationalists.*)" [Emphasis added — G.S.][5]

Mass Discontent — the Power Behind the Opposition

The oppositional activities of the intellectuals and students have usually been the first to reach our ears. This is not only because they are harbingers of the movements in the depths of the working class, but because they are more articulate and have easier access to means of publicity. In fact, however, they draw inspiration and courage from the mood of the workers and the knowledge that they have the support of the workers. Behind the continual reappearance of clandestine revolutionary grouping in the USSR stand the much broader, general discontents of the masses, especially the hostility of the workers toward the privileged bureaucracy. Such feelings are widespread and just below the surface.

As the economy becomes more complex, as the consumer demands of the ever larger, more educated and confident working class (50 million strong) become greater, the privilege-seeking bureaucrats are under more and more pressure to produce efficiently. But the total monopoly on decision-making, which the bureaucracy needs to protect its privileged position, necessarily means inefficiency. For in the planned economy, full, democratic self-management by the workers is ultimately the only way the economy can function to the optimum.

It is against this background of the economic and social crisis of the bureaucracy that the student and intellectual protests of today must be seen.

There have been literally hundreds of occasions in the last decade when the Soviet working class has broken out into open protest, often in the form of violent spontaneous outbursts. "It is interesting to note," one observer writes, "the speed with which these outbursts develop and how quickly they spread if the bureaucracy fails to contain them by cordoning off the city in which they occur." He goes on to describe working class protests in several cities. In Kiev the striking workers of the hydro-electric plant "actually organized mass meetings which were addressed by their own elected representatives, and where the bureaucrats who tried to address the workers were physically evicted from the platform. The strike was about housing shortages. But during demonstrations which the workers organized, banners were raised calling for 'All Power to the Soviets'."[6]

In this action and others, it is the women who receive on the average 50 percent of men's wages and still bear the burden of housekeeping, cooking, and shopping, who have felt the shortages more acutely than the men and have taken the initiative to protest.

Another example of such outbreaks was the one that occurred in Temir-Tau, Kazakhstan, where a strike began in October 1959 involving several thousand young women and men at a metallurgical center under construction. This was the region where the Karaganda network of Stalin-era labor camps had functioned. The Khrushchev regime, instead of shipping people off to labor camps, applied various kinds of pressure, including appeals to youthful idealism to get workers out to such remote industrial areas. At Temir-Tau they were stuck living in a tent colony without sanitation facilities or adequate supplies. On October 3, some fifty young workers began a demonstration, including expropriation of goods from stores. When the police interfered, the number of rebels grew to over fifteen hundred, barricades were set up, and the police chief and director of the tent colony were seized. On October 4, troops from Karaganda arrived but were disarmed by the rebels (apparently by fraternization tactics). The rebels took over the whole town. Only on the evening of October 5 did reinforcements — special detachments of security police — suppress the rebellion, after cordoning off the city.

At the March 1960 congress of the Communist Party of Kazakhstan, a few months later, the new party secretary Kunaev, who had replaced his predecessor Belyaev in January, laid the blame for these explosive events on "the scornful attitude of the director of the tent colony toward the living conditions of the workers."

Many other specific instances of such explosions have become known, despite the secrecy with which the bureaucracy tries to hide them.[7]

Dissident author Andrei Amalrik has given a valuable firsthand impression of the mass moods behind these outbreaks, though he qualifies his assessment with the observation that "no one, not even the bureaucratic elite, knows exactly what attitudes prevail among the wider sections of the population." (*Will the Soviet Union Survive. . . ?*)

Writing during the period 1966-69, Amalrik used the rather apt term "passive discontent" to summarize his impression of popular attitudes. Mass discontent was not at that time directed against the regime itself, in Amalrik's opinion, but against certain *aspects* of conditions in society.

"The workers, for example, are bitter over having no rights vis-a-vis the factory management. The collective farmers are resentful about their total dependence on the kolkhoz [farm] chairman. . . . Everybody is angered by the great inequalities in wealth, the low wages, the austere housing conditions, the lack of essential consumer goods, compulsory registration at their places of residence and work, and so forth."

The slow rise in the standard of living, Amalrik felt, had neutralized popular anger but not removed it. If such improvement stopped or was reversed, explosions of mass discontent would follow. He speculated that fear of such an explosion had induced the regime not to introduce a big price increase in early 1969, but to let creeping inflation go on instead. The regime learned a lesson in 1962, he argued, when Khrushchev's raising of meat and dairy prices had sparked the series of strikes and mass protests we have referred to earlier.

In a 1970 television interview Amalrik spoke further on the discontent among the masses. "[There is] a great deal of dissatisfaction on account of the wide discrepancies in wage levels, extreme annoyance at the existence of special closed shops and stores, in which ruling elite are able to buy goods which cannot be bought in the ordinary shops, and with other ways in which the nation's wealth is unfairly distributed."

"The workers are discontented because of their low wages, high work quotas, and the efforts to force them to stay at their workplaces. The farm workers are discontented also because they are forced to remain at one place of work and [because of] their very hard working conditions. Some people are discontented at having so little money; others because there is nothing to spend it on."

The possibility of "passive discontent" erupting into strikes and revolts in reaction to unpopular economc measures was clearly demonstrated in the USSR's neighbor Poland in December 1970. In response to sharp price hikes on food, fuel, and other essentials, dockworkers in Gdansk, Gdynia, and Szczecin went on strike. Police attempts to repress the strikers led to large-scale street fighting and the spread of strikes to other areas. Only the resignation of Gomulka and the concessions introduced by his successor Gierek, above all a rescinding of the price increases, brought the situation under the regime's control again in early 1971. And since then the Polish workers have remained combative, asserting increasing independence.

If the lesson of Novocherkassk in 1962 was not enough, that of Poland in December 1970 clearly influenced the Brezhnev regime in the USSR. In March 1971, at the twenty-fourth Soviet party congress, a plan for increased consumer goods supplies and other guarantees of improved living standards for the Soviet population received a great deal of emphasis, largely due to the Polish events and the concomitant wildcat demonstrations in the Soviet Union for better living conditions and better consumer goods.[8]

From "Cultural" Opposition to Political Opposition

After the 1956-57 upsurge among students and intellectuals, the late fifties and early sixties saw a relative decline of overt protest as many of the more militant dissidents were expelled from universities or other institutions and sent off to labor camps, and as articulate opposition elements that remained turned to less explicitly political activities. A broader, more diffuse, more "culturally" oriented ferment among young rebels then arose. It was permitted a semilegal existence: though constantly harassed by "selective" arrests and trials, it was not crushed completely. That was how Khrushchev's "thaw" developed, with a relative relaxation of censorship and a partial alliance between the regime and liberal elements in the "cultural" establishment. And alongside them emerged the unofficial, privately circulated literature of the "cultural opposition," evolving gradually, growing more and more daring.

At first, unauthorized student publishing ventures were concerned mainly with literature and arts. They criticized or parodied official "socialist realism" and reproduced literary works that departed from the official school in order to express real attitudes and feelings, not those dictated from on high.

The loose, unstructured phenomenon of the "cultural opposition" — spontaneous public readings; the passing around of a piece of poetry or other writing among friends, etc. — with time became more widespread and systematic, developing into the social phenomenon of samizdat, a regular network by which uncensored material was duplicated and passed around to the interested audience.[9]

The vague ferment in the rebel circles that produced and read underground literature gradually became more organized, focused, and political, especially around the time of Khrushchev's ouster, in 1964-65. This was a time of growing discontent, not only among the more politicized intellectual layers, but among the masses of workers. There were reports of strikes and slowdowns, for example, at an automobile plant in Moscow, that apparently contributed to the decision to replace Khrushchev with the bureaucratic team of Brezhnev-Kosygin.

An example of the trend toward greater organization and coherence among literary dissidents in 1964-65 was the formation of a loose organization called SMOG. (The acronym has been variously explained.)

Like their hero, Mayakovsky, the SMOGists wanted to break from conventionalism and had revolutionary impulses: "Today we have to fight against everything from the Chekists [secret police] to the bourgeoisie, from ineptitude to ignorance," said one of their manifestos. The idea of forming SMOG groups apparently caught on among young rebels in many parts of the Soviet Union. While the movement was centered in Moscow and Leningrad, there were also reports in 1965 of SMOG groups that put out uncensored newsletters in the Urals, Odessa, and "southern Russia."

In April 1965, on the anniversary of Mayakovsky's death, SMOGists organized a "literary-political" meeting, as they described it. About a thousand young people turned out to hear SMOG speakers demand recognition from the official Writers Union, and the right to discuss ideas freely and to set up their own press. Among the SMOG demands was freedom for figures like Vladimir Bukovsky and Joseph Brodsky.[10]

The new wave of rebel youth in the post-Stalin period look back with strong affinity to the native revolutionary tradition, starting with the Decembrists and ending with Lenin and the October Revolution. They are also quite curious about and sympathetic to the post-October leaders who opposed Stalin.

Both the trend toward greater organization and the increased political interest in revolutionary traditions were reflected in the formation of the Ryleev Club in June 1964 by young rebels of the SMOG circles, in particular, Evgeny Kushev and Vladimir Voskresensky. This organization was interested in social criticism as well as literature, and claimed to stand in the tradition of the Decembrist secret society, the Society of the Russian Word, which had been led in the 1820s by the poet and Decembrist leader, Kondraty Ryleev. They accordingly published a samizdat journal called *Russkoe Slovo* (Russian Word) in July 1966.[11] Many of its articles were devoted to investigating and describing the lives and experiences of nineteenth-century revolutionaries, and relating these to the struggle of young rebels in post-Stalin Soviet society.

A similar undergound journal of 1964-65 was *Tetradi Sotsial-Demokratii* (Notebooks of Social Democracy). Kushev was also one of its editors, and the same circles of rebel youth and literary-cultural dissenters contributed to it. Like *Russkoe Slovo,* the *Notebooks* editors were interested in bringing relevant interpretations of revolutionary traditions to the rebel youth of the sixties. But unlike *Russkoe Slovo* the *Notebooks* dealt mainly, not with the Narodniks and Decembrists — if we judge by its title — but with the Marxist wing of the nineteenth-century revolutionary movement.[12]

As part of its exploration of the early Marxist traditions in Russia, the magazine found itself defending that anathema of anathemas, Trotsky, against an official attack in the Soviet press of 1965, which it did fairly ably in its eighth, and apparently final, issue.

It was undoubtedly to circles of rebel youth like the producers of these publications that the anonymous author of the "Memoirs of a Bolshevik-Leninist" addressed himself when he produced his samizdat account in the mid-sixties.

The appearance of journals like *Russkoe Slovo* and *Notebooks of Social-Democracy* (and the more clandestine journal of the Union of Communards in 1964-65) marked a trend from broader "cultural" concerns toward specifically political ones. At the same time, the young rebels were getting to know older, more "hardened" elements, who had spent years in the camps and were making their influence felt in a society that was increasingly interested in politics.

Just to mention some of the names of these returnees from the camps is to indicate their political impact on the youth: Solzhenitsyn, whose stature has become comparable to that of Tolstoy; Lev Kopelev, a writer whose analysis of Stalinism, written for the Austrian CP magazine *Tagebuch*, led to his expulsion from the CPSU in 1968; Evgenia Ginzburg, an old Communist, whose *Journey into the Whirlwind* is a samizdat memoir of Stalin's purges; A.V. Snegov, an unreconstructed anti-Stalinist who in open discussions at the Institute of Marxism-Leninism in 1968 denounced Stalin's counterrevolutionary policies in the Spanish Civil War and in Germany on the eve of Hitler's takeover; Aleksei Kosterin and Pyotr Yakir, whose experiences in Stalin's camps and role in the post-Khrushchev protest movement are well known and documented.

The early and middle sixties were a time when many memoirs by Old Bolsheviks and oppositionists telling the truth about the revolution, the twenties, and Stalinism began to circulate. It was people of that pre-Stalin generation who joined with young rebels in early 1966, on the eve of the twenty-third congress, to demonstrate in Moscow against the rumored plans to "rehabilitate" Stalin at that congress.

The ferment of the early sixties, stirred by veterans returning from the camps, affected not only advanced sections of the youth. Inside the CP, in the ranks of the bureaucracy itself, older members were having their thinking shaken up, or were feeling that their previously restrained critical views could get a hearing with the relaxation of police controls (Grigorenko was one of these). New "reformist" elements also were brought into the CPSU after 1956, in an effort at cooptation. Roy Medvedev and Ivan Yakhimovich are examples of the youth, filled with hopes of antibureaucratic reform, who joined at that time. Others, such as Lev Kopelev, Evgenia Ginzburg, and Aleksei Kosterin were readmitted.

Later, after the 1968 protest movement, most of these individuals found themselves outside the party again.

The Rise of the Public Protest Movement
(1965 to the Present)

A brief resume is needed here to clarify the forces giving rise to the new stage — the so-called "democratic movement."

After the defeat of the Hungarian revolution, the intensity of student protest, which had given rise to groups like that of Krasnopevtsev-Rendel at Moscow University and the first publication of *Kolokol* in Leningrad, subsided.

The bureaucracy accompanied arrests and trials with the explusion of several thousands from universities and from the party (loss of career possibilities) and by a strident campaign to "straighten out the ideological front."

For the moment it seemed that the possibility of action from below was closed off. Although a radical current continued to engage in underground organizing and publishing, and thus prefigured samizdat, these young underground editors and poets of the late 1950s (Galanskov, Ginzburg, Bukovsky, Delone) were not the dominant trend. The main disposition in the 1958-62 period was to wait for the promised reforms from above, in the belief that the bureaucratic dictatorship would liberalize itself. The criticism of Stalinism that the twentieth congress had made legitimate seemed to offer a "normal" way to restore the Soviet democracy of Lenin's day. It also seemed that improvements in living standards would be made available to the masses. The legal "cultural opposition" appeared, centered around Tvardovsky's *Novy Mir,* as did the "legal" rebel poets Yevtushenko and Voznesensky.

By 1962 and 1963 those illusions were becoming tarnished. The failure of Khrushchev's economic policies brought a sudden halt in the improvement of living standards; the price rises on basic foods, provoking strikes and protests in the summer of 1962, came only a few months after Khrushchev promised that "communism was being built" within the borders of the USSR after the consummation of socialism.

Even before Khrushchev fell in October 1964, a hardening on the "ideological front" began, accompanied by a rehabilitation of Stalin and a continuous counterreform aimed against the most advanced sectors of the intelligentsia and the anti-Stalinist Communist militants (among the youth as well as the Old Bolsheviks).

This counterreform which is still in progress, cut short the illusory belief in the re-establishment of Soviet democracy from above. As early as 1963 one of the leading figures in the new Communist opposition in the USSR, former Major General Pyotr Grigorenko, thought of constituting an underground

Bolshevik organization, reflecting the loss of confidence in Khrushchev-type "liberalization."

In 1965 the Brezhnev-Kosygin regime decisively stepped up the counter-offensive with the arrest of Sinyavsky and Daniel, samizdat authors who were typical of the semilegal circles of "cultural ferment" in Moscow; the arrest of dozens of anti-Stalinist Ukrainian intellectuals for reaffirming the national cultural traditions and opposing Russification; and in Leningrad, the arrest of the leaders of the Union of Communards, editors of *Kolokol.*

But in response to this official hardening, 1966 and 1967 saw a new flowering of opposition in protest against the Sinyavsky-Daniel trial and, in the Ukraine, against the imprisonment of dissident intellectuals. That is, the move toward tighter controls sparked a more intensified resistance. Out of this developed a more politicized samizdat, reflecting a network of thousands, the most active elements of which became central figures in the "democratic movement." A movement of open, public protest in behalf of democratic rights began which has been the center of attention into the early 1970s.

For all the severity of the Brezhnev "counterreform," the worst forms of the Stalinist dictatorship have not been restored, and it is unlikely that they will be, because of the changed relationship of forces between the masses and the bureaucracy. But the gradual retracting of concessions that the masses had won through struggle in the 1953-62 period stimulated the developing vanguard, the more conscious elements among the youth, the workers, the intelligentsia, and the party rank-and-file, to resist. These elements became convinced that they had to take a stand; the reimposition of the repressive police regime had to be prevented at all costs. Thus rose the opposition which chose to act *in the open,* not just underground, but to appeal to the population at large.

The tactic adopted by this opposition was to take the text of the 1936 constitution and demand all the freedoms that it guaranteed; to declare that it, the opposition, was adhering to law and that the bureaucratic authorities were the violators. This initial tactic was politically well founded, because the aspiration for Soviet democracy is undoubtedly the chief common denominator of the various layers in opposition, and of the different ideological currents within what is now given the name "democratic movement."

This tactic is also consistent with the basic political logic of the most consistent elements among the new opposition who approach fundamentally the same point of view as that held by the Left Opposition. That is, it regards Soviet society as a social structure resulting from the October Revolution and denies that Stalinist terror is the product of October or of Leninism.[13]

The proof is that Stalin had to destroy the Bolshevik Party and exterminate the entire generation that led the revolution in order to consolidate his power. The opposition focuses its attacks on the phenomena of bureaucratic degeneration and considers the establishment of full democratic freedoms for all the workers and citizens under the socialist constitution as the central aim of its struggle. Stalinism appears to the new oppositionists primarily as the violation of legality; they do not always detect or point out the institutionalized material privileges of the bureaucracy.

The struggle against the arbitrariness of today, by the same logic, is related to the struggle against past injustices. Hence the great importance attached by the new opposition to resisting the rehabilitation of Stalin, to calling for posthumous condemnation of Stalin as a criminal and full rehabilitation for all his victims.

Inevitably the rise of the antibureaucratic political revolution in the Czechoslovak Socialist Republic in 1968 met with a sympathetic response among the rebellious Soviet intelligentsia. The trend toward establishing the norms of socialist democracy in the state and party was the main aspect of the Prague Spring and directly corresponded to the central concern of the Soviet oppositionists. These oppositionists, isolated, poorly informed, if at all, about the changes that had been occurring in the relationship of forces on the world scale in recent years, participated indirectly, through Czechoslovakia, in the worldwide phenomenon of youth radicalization and a new rise in international revolutionary struggles.

Besides these events, with Czechoslovakia being the strongest impulse, there were some more basic causes that stirred the new opposition to public political action in the Soviet Union.

During the postwar period, when the Soviet economy, ravaged by the war, was being rebuilt, the borrowing of Western industrial technology still characterized much of Soviet industry. There was unquestionable progress in the top-priority fields of armaments, aeronautics, and space. But behind that, a structural crisis appeared. The decline in economic growth rates was one symptom. In early 1970, Brezhnev himself revealed a serious decline in agricultural production and delays in the rise of labor productivity. The regime even flirted with the idea of calling for a full discussion of economic problems. (It was at that time that Roy Medvedev, Sakharov, and Turchin submitted their document on the relation of democratization to the economic difficulties.)

The essence of the crisis is that Soviet society — with a bureaucratically degenerated regime fastened onto a society in transition between capitalism and socialism — is threatened in most fields by the consequences of the absence of both workers' democracy and democratically centralized self-management by the producers.

In *The Revolution Betrayed,* Trotsky wrote that "under a nationalized economy, *quality* [or higher productivity] demands a democracy of producers and consumers, freedom of criticism and initiative — conditions incompatible with a totalitarian regime of fear, lies, and flattery.... Behind the question of quality stands a more complicated and [elaborate] problem which may be comprised in the concept of *independent, technical* and *cultural creation.* The ancient philosopher said that strife is the father of all things. No new values can be created where a free conflict of ideas is impossible. . . . The dictatorship of the proletariat opens a wider scope to human genius the more it ceases to be a dictatorship. Socialist culture will flourish only in proportion to the dying away of the state. In that simple and unshakable historical law is contained the death sentence of the present political regime in the Soviet Union. Soviet democracy is not the demand of an abstract policy, still less an abstract moral. It has become a life-and-death need of the country."

This impasse of the system is manifested in many ways — among them, the lag in research and technical innovation in some key fields, such as computers; the striking disparity between the high level of technological development in some areas and the mediocre living standards of the masses; the multiplication of waste and loss in production and distribution; the tension around access to university education; and the increasing disproportions in employment.

The courage shown by the new oppositionists in openly espousing their aims is a reflection of this social crisis. They sense that they can win sympathy and support. Individual promotion through education no longer seems available to millions of sons and daughters of workers and collective farm peasants. Not only individuals but entire social layers feel there is no way out. Although the increasing levels of repression are aimed at cauterizing such feelings, they are nevertheless bound to become increasingly articulate.

There is still a very wide gap, however, between the minority of courageous oppositionists and the large masses. This is not only the result of the break in continuity between the older Bolshevik generation and the present-day mass of workers — the result of the bureaucracy's conscious massacre of the cadres of the entire revolutionary generation. It is also true that Marxism has been seriously discredited in the eyes of the masses by the bureaucracy, which has debased it to the status of a state religion. The prolonged isolation of the politically inactive masses from the international labor and revolutionary movements has served further to aggravate the situation.

This explains the pronounced confusion of wide layers among the intellectuals and in the populace at large — and the wide range of viewpoints that have emerged, from Slavophile and semifeudal nostalgia to Communist trends quite close to revolutionary Marxism.

Within the prosocialist democratic movement the political spectrum is still quite varied. A right wing may be seen in Academician Andrei Sakharov, advocate of convergence between Western "democracy" and Soviet "socialism," who does not seem to understand many central issues of the world revolutionary movement and who shies away from any involvement of the masses in democratization, unless strictly limited and controlled.

The left wing in the democratic movement is represented by those like the former farm chairman Ivan Yakhimovich, whose call is "Stalinism no, Leninism yes." The most outstanding representatives of this current so far have been Pyotr Grigorenko and the late Bolshevik writer Aleksei Kosterin.

In a certain sense the funeral of Kosterin constituted the first public opposition rally in the USSR since the Left Opposition demonstrations of 1927.

The oppositionists are still a small minority, fighting from a weak position. The regime has opened an offensive against them, especially since January 1972, determined to destroy the civil rights groups that tried to establish an open existence. In the same way the police did destroy the organization in the city of Vladimir that claimed the right to "legal" existence — the Independent Youth for Socialist Democracy — and has broken up and tried several large neo-Marxist youth groups, in Gorky, Samara, Saratov, and again in 1971, Leningrad. Even more, the regime made it a central objective to stamp out the regular underground publications, particularly the *Chronicle of Current Events* in Russia and *Ukrainsky Visnyk* in Ukraine. For the moment, it has apparently succeeded in that aim.

Although the antibureaucratic opposition assumes a much larger scale among some of the non-Russian nationalities — and has been able to win some concessions from the bureaucracy as a result — and although there is a certain level of popular sympathy with the oppositionists, still the regime is able to physically break up the initial formations of these groups.

How large is the democratic movement? And how much support does it have? Its activists have been variously estimated at from several hundred to a couple of thousand.

Besides those who protest openly there are certainly many more who sympathize silently. The ups and downs of repression and relaxation also, obviously, affect the number who will openly associate themselves with the protest movement.

What is the social composition of the movement? What social layers, if any, does it base itself on? What chance does it have to win mass support, to become a force that can influence or change policy in the Soviet Union?

It is rather obvious that most of the protesters come from the ranks of the intelligentsia — that is, people with professional training and a higher education. A good number were party members, usually a prerequisite for a "good job." Many worked at institutes or were teachers or technicians, or worked at publishing houses.

There is nothing unusual in this. Most revolutionary movements have started in layers of society which have had the leisure time and interest or sensitivity to ideas and social problems to become aware of the need for change before the mass of the population began to stir. An odd feature of the Soviet movement is that students have made up a relatively small proportion so far. Although some of the best-known figures began their oppositional activities in the student milieu in the late fifties, during the sixties the students as a whole remained quiescent. One reason is that it is extremely difficult to get into a university or institute of higher education. Only a small percentage of those who apply are admitted — after a series of extremely rigorous exams. Thus, there is a strong tendency not to rock the boat and lose the rare career opportunity of university admission. One of the first steps the regime takes against dissenters is to have them fired from their jobs or, if they are students, expelled from their university. The extremely limited access to higher education, especially in comparison with the high number of secondary school graduates, has up to now apparently had a dampening effect on student participation in the civil rights movement. But this is a factor that in the future could turn from a deterrent into an explosive protest issue.

Amalrik draws some conclusions from the high proportion of intellectuals, "academics," and "specialists" from the layer of "new scientific and technical personnel" in the protest movement. These social types, in Amalrik's view, are the "least capable of purposeful action." While the "middle class" of technicians and specialists is "capable of comprehending the principles of personal freedom, rule of law and democratic government . . . needs those principles, and provides the emerging Democratic Movement with its basic contingent of supporters, the vast majority of this class is so mediocre . . . and [even] its intellectually most independent members are so passive that the success of a Democratic Movement based on it seems to me to be gravely in doubt."

Amalrik holds that the movement's base in a part of the "middle class" leaves it too weak and too ridden by contradictions to be able to engage in a real struggle with the regime. Can it, he asks, find a broader base of support among the masses?

That is a central question. And the answer depends in part on what policies the democratic movement adopts, and which of the tendencies within it can learn to mobilize the masses. In the present stage, since 1972, as the Brezhnev regime resorts to the harshest repressive measures used since Stalin's purges, it is too early to say what the final outcome of the effort to create a public movement for democratic rights will be. The full impact of the 1965-73 phase of struggle, which may have ended with the trial of Yakir and the apparently successful suppression of *Ukrainsky Visnyk* and the *Chronicle of Current Events,* cannot yet be assessed. The protest movement may prove to have had more deep-going effects than are immediately evident. Certainly a new turn and change of tactics is dictated for oppositional elements, as the Nixon-Brezhnev detente, and the harshest repression for a generation, create a new and contradictory situation.

Regardless of the momentary ups and downs, however, the general perspective remains unpromising for bureaucratic rule. As the young Communist Ivan Yakhimovich said in 1968, "The genie is at large and cannot be confined again."

We asked him if he was a communist, a member of the CPSU. He roared with laughter and said, "No! I'm not a communist. I'm a worker!"

Report of a Recent Visit to the USSR
Revolutionary Union

Editor's note: the following is a report of a member of the Revolutionary Union who visited the Soviet Union for three weeks in June, 1974 as part of a delegation of political economists from the United States.

When our delegation met with officials or university economists at the various "Friendship Houses" or elsewhere, we always introduced ourselves as radical political economists, including communists and Marxist-Leninists

---

The selection "Report of a Recent Visit to the USSR" is reprinted from Red Papers 7: How Capitalism Has Been Restored in the Soviet Union and What This Means for the World Struggle, available from the Revolutionary Communist Party, USA, P.O. Box 3486, Merchandise Mart, Chicago, IL 60654.

and also other progressive people united in the work of making revolutionary change in the U.S. We said we had come to the Soviet Union to learn what we could about the economy and the society more generally, to bring back what lessons we could. NOT ONCE DID ANYONE PICK UP ON THIS. No one asked, "How's it going?" or "What problems do you face?" or in any way indicated interest in that conception of what we were about.

On the contrary, we met cynicism. Two particular examples stand out. In Moscow, some of us had a long discussion with Alexander Bikov, a high level government economist specializing in trade relations and development in South Asia. After he described the Soviet view of peaceful coexistence and East-West trade, he was asked how the crisis of imperialism and prospects for revolutionary movements in the U.S. entered into the Soviet picture. *He laughed.* He said we were being simplistic, that the Soviet Union was "not dealing with a corpse", and that it was idle to "speculate" about when revolutionary changes might develop. "Will it be next week? In fifty years? Tell me, when do *you* think it will be?" he grinned.

Meeting with members of the Armenian Academy of Sciences in Yerevan, the Armenian capital, the question of impeachment of Nixon came up, as it did in most discussions. The Soviets said that Nixon would not be successfully impeached. We laid out a view of the crisis of imperialism and the consequent political and ideological crisis which requires a restoration of confidence in the bourgeois state among the U.S. people. They said it was a "good class analysis", and added that "the bourgeoisie will surely win. The bourgeoisie will surely fool the American people."

This cynicism was matched by a widespread careerism with respect to the Party. We asked students and others we met why they wanted to join the Communist Party, and the answer invariably had to do with a desire to "be the director", "be a professor instead of an assistant so that I can do the work I'm interested in", be in positions of power, make more money or travel abroad. Party members also said the same thing. One sociologist openly said that he joined the Party because "if you're smart you know what way the wind is blowing and you play the game. I want security when I get older, and being a professor will give me that."

A group of children 12-15 years old was at a beach we visited in Kiev. We asked them what they wanted to do when they grew up, and they all answered doctor, engineer, director, etc. No one wanted to drive a truck, build housing projects, or anything like that. We learned that anyone with advanced training, in engineering or other fields, is not *allowed* to be a production worker because that would be a "waste" of the State resources that went into the training.

Everyone complains about the bureaucracy, including Party people, who acknowledge the problem. Stories of bribery and corruption are regular, but not specific. We heard that Georgia and Armenia are particularly well-known for shady deals. Land for a private dacha (country home) can evidently be purchased for a 3% bribe to a local official. Our delegation had no direct dealings with the bureaucracy because our tour guide was the go-between, but we learned that we got tickets for the circus which was "sold out", after a ball point pen and a U.S. political button were given to the box-office clerk, together with the money for the tickets. In Kiev, I was told that for a large bribe, nationality on passports can be changed to something other than Jewish.

Pilfering and appropriation of State resources for private use came to our attention as well. Late at night, buses (a kind not used for regular public transportation) can be hailed on the street, and the driver will take you across town for a ruble (1.34), which he keeps. We were told that someone had picked a bed of tulips and sold the flowers, was arrested and sentenced to five years in jail. The same person who told us this was proud of the stero he had built for his apartment, using components stolen by himself and his wife from the electronics enterprises where they work as engineers. He said that kind of thing is common. (He played Carole King, Simon and Garfunkle and Aretha Franklin records, as well as some Russian folk dances and Russian rock 'n' roll and "big band" music.)

Western influence in music is great, even in Armenia. Young people are very interested in a variety of U.S. and British groups — Creedence Clearwater, Kris Kristofferson, the Beatles and others. The radio stations play a lot of rock and pop music, either U.S. or Russian imitations. In the evening, on Yerevan's Lenin Square, loudspeakers play "Billy Joe McAllister Jumped Off the Tallahatchie Bridge", and in the morning a hideous arrangement of "Hernando's Hideway", for organ and 1001 Strings, comes over the hotel loudspeaker.

In every city we visited, we were approached by young people wanting to buy blue jeans, other clothing or chewing gum. I was offered 12 rubles for a pair of jeans, which I later learned often sell on the street for as much as 70 rubles. Occasional offers for currency exchange (two rubles for a dollar, and sometimes as high as four rubles) came along or in connection with interest in blue jeans. Some young Australian tourists told me that they had been offered hashish for sale on four different occasions on the Nevsky Prospekt, one of the main streets of Leningrad. In Moscow, the going price for prostitution is 5 rubles a trick, with business centered at the posh downtown hotels.

Western currency gains special importance in connection with the so-called "hard currency shops." These stores carry Soviet and imported goods, principally for tourists, but also for any Soviet citizen with Western "hard" currency. Prices are given in rubles, but rubles are not accepted as currency in these stores. The price is converted into whatever currency one has, at official exchange rates. Most of the displayed goods are gift-type things, but one can also buy shoes, clothing, television sets and other appliances and even automobiles.

Although almost all of the goods in these shops are available in regular Soviet stores, there is often a big price advantage, especially on alcohol and expensive goods. For example, our guide was preparing to buy a car in a hard currency shop for 1000 rubles which costs 5500 rubles to a person without hard currency. Television sets sell for about 40% of the regular cost. Soviet citizens have legal access to foreign currency if they work abroad and are paid in foreign currency, if money is sent to them by relatives abroad, if they receive royalties from sale of publications abroad, and possibly in some other ways. Our guide, for example, worked for two years in the Soviet embassy in Washington and brought back a considerable amount of dollars which he was allowed to keep as hard currency in a special type of bank account.

Before leaving for the USSR, the delegation decided not to change money except through official banks and exchanges. Towards the end of the trip, it came out that several delegates had been exchanging money with our guide, sometimes at the official rate, sometimes 1:1. Some of us felt that these transactions should stop, and raised the issue at a group meeting.

The three CPUSA members of the delegation took the lead in opposing reversal. They made several interesting arguments. "Did you come here to teach morality?" "It is not a *lot* of money" ($100-200). "Those of you who exchanged money are already guilty so you better keep quiet." "The only time you need receipts to get out of the country is if you have more money leaving than you had coming in." "What's the matter, didn't you ever do anything illegal in the U.S.?" "It wasn't illegal because the guide says guides are authorized to change money in emergencies outside of banking hours." In a narrow vote, it was decided "not to make waves."

* * *

Everywhere in the Soviet Union memory of WW 2 is kept alive. There are monuments, museums, movies and TV shows (documentary and fictional drama). In each restored room of the Summer Palace, there is a photograph of the room as it was left by the retreating Nazis. Older people who fought in the war are proud of their participation and the role of the USSR. A bus driver in Kiev told me that he had fought in Brno, Dresden, and Berlin, and an old man some of us met in a small village on the edge of Moscow said he fought in the Leningrad Blockade and took off his shirt to show the scars.

The Soviet people certainly have cause for pride and remembrance. Over 20 million Soviet people died during the war. When the Western capitalist powers finally got around to opening a second front in Europe in 1944, five out of every six German divisions were on the Eastern front, and the invasion was still very nearly thrown back. Leningrad was under siege for 900 days, and over 500,000 people there died in that period, mostly of starvation. Kiev was 80% destroyed, but resistance was never-ending, as in Stalingrad and all over the country.

Out of all this, the war is preserved by the social-imperialists only to put forth the line that "war is hell", that only madmen want war (covering over the difference between just and unjust wars), that war must be avoided at all costs, etc. All the political and military lessons are gutted out, and pacifism is upheld. This, of course, is necessary to bolster the revisionist line on peaceful coexistence, peaceful transition to socialism, and Stalin.

Stalin is not mentioned, even in the most obvious opportunities. For example, Armenia now has an extensive system of irrigation and hydroelectric plants along the Razdan River, utilizing the resources of the large Sevan Lake. Our Armenian guide told us that the projects were begun in 1939 and completed in 1950, but never mentioned Stalin. Instead the guide mentioned a telegram Lenin sent in 1920 to the Central Committee of the Armenian Party recommending the development of Lake Sevan for irrigation and hydroelectic power. Stalin's role in building socialism and conducting class struggle in the 1920s and 1930s is also never discussed.

An Armenian historian I spoke to explained that Stalin is not discussed because "it would be very disruptive," and that it is now irrelevant to have the whole debate over Stalin because it doesn't bear on the immediate tasks of building socialism through the increase in productive forces. He said that on the one hand, the Chinese are using the question of Stalin to attack the current Soviet leadership and divide them from the development of socialism in the USSR, and on the other hand the Western powers use Stalin to generate anti-communism. I asked why a principled defense of Stalin was not the best response in this situation, and he repeated that it would be irrelevant and "very disruptive." He added that many people in the Soviet Union are more favorable to Stalin than the official line, as he himself seemed to be. When pushed further on Stalin, the historian repeated that it would be disruptive and irrelevant to have the debate, since the 20th Congress documents had already been discussed, and there was no sense repeating the whole thing now.

* * *

The outrageous and distorted Soviet view of China came out in a number of conversations and publications. Although it was never laid out fully all at once, the main points amount to this: China was doing well and developing under the guidance of the Soviet Union until 1960. Then, the Chinese leadership expelled Soviet technicians and embarked on the petty-bourgeois course of self-reliance. This had its roots in the national chauvinism of China, which wants to dominate the world and the socialist camp in particular. Self-reliance divorced China from aid from the Soviet Union and from "guaranteed markets" for Chinese goods in the Soviet Union. Without Soviet aid and markets, China has stagnated economically and is incapable of developing productive forces as the basis of building socialism and moving to communism.

Being cut off from the real basis for socialist construction (growing productive forces), the Chinese have been forced to concoct "metaphysical solutions" to socialist construction, such as stress on the subjective factor (the slogan "men are decisive, not machines" is a prime example in the revisionists' views of Chinese "metaphysics") and a deepening stress on self-reliance. To divert the Chinese people from the hardships of life, the CPC leadership has embarked on international adventurism, stirring up trouble on the Soviet border and meddling in European Security Conference preparations of the USSR.

These "metaphysical approaches" are creating worsening conditions in China and leading the Chinese leadership to make wilder and wilder attacks on the USSR and Marxism-Leninism. These "left deviations" from Marxism-Leninism stem from the national chauvinism of the Chinese, and from the petty-bourgeois peasant base of the CPC. Hopefully in the future, the Chinese will come to their senses and realize the correct Marxist-Leninist path, especially after the current leadership dies.

The Soviet revisionists' line on China is drawn out further in their comparison of the prospects for India and China. A. Bikov, the "expert" on Asia who laughed at our question about revolutionary developments in the U.S., declared that India clearly had better chances for development and progress for its people than China. After explaining that China had cut itself off from Soviet aid and markets, making it impossible for China to develop productive capacity, he said that India had chances for progress because it was "open to American and Soviet influence."

I was surprised by the openly reactionary character of this line, having expected more subtlety than an equation of U.S. and Soviet influence as progressive forces in the Third World.

The Soviet revisionists try to justify their entire line with the "theory of productive forces." This theory says basically that social relations cannot change until the material basis for these changes has been laid in the organization and level of production, and severely downgrades the role social relations play in socialist construction. The CPSU cannot totally ignore social relations and their importance as a basis for development of productive forces. But they restrict their attention to the most narrow possible interpretation, saying only that socialist relations of production already exist in the Soviet Union because there is no private capital, no privately employed labor, and therefore no bourgeoisie. What remains, they claim, is to take advantage of the opportunities now opening up for expanding production. *The present emphasis is entirely on increasing productivity, expanding enterprise profit, and reorganizing and consolidating (concentrating) productive capacity to expand output as rapidly as possible. They say that it will be possible to advance the socialist consciousness of the Soviet people only when material production advances, especially in the consumer goods industries.*

These ideas came out most clearly in a long discussion we had with one CP member, the only one we met who seemed to be seriously interested in figuring out how to make socialism and communism in the Soviet Union. He said that at the present time, the Soviet people do not control the social institutions. This, he said was the other side of the problem of bureaucracy and careerism, which he saw as major problems in Soviet society holding back the development of communism and "Soviet socialist man." To solve the problem, he said it is necessary to improve the people's living standards and to educate people to Marxism-Leninism so they will learn the socialist and communist ideology of cooperation and sharing.

Ideological study, he continued, becomes sloganeering and empty in the absence of material advances for the people. Moral incentives amount to exhortation, which can be used effectively for only a limited period of "revolutionary enthusiasm", long since passed in the Soviet Union. In the long run, one must return to the material basis of progress, production itself. Material incentives for workers (bonuses, opportunities for vacations at special resorts, etc.) should be emphasized, but there is an important role for moral incentives in the form of "socialist emulation."

"Socialist emulation" campaigns operate all the time. In factories and universities, one sees pictures of the best workers and students prominently displayed, and it is considered an honor to be chosen. But even the socialist emulation boils down to productivity, since the "best" students are the ones with the highest grades in their courses, and the "best" workers are the ones who produce the most or most contribute to production through innovative ideas about technique. This is the direct result of the idea that building socialism amounts to increasing production, which sets the terms of the "moral" as well as the material incentives.

Some of us in the delegation disagreed with this "strategy" for developing "Soviet socialist man" by pointing out that socialism and socialist consciousness develop in struggle against capitalism and bourgeois consciousness, not in a mechanical development of production plus "education." We said that it would be more useful to look at the bureaucracy and careerism in the Soviet Union as reflections of the fact that capitalism has been restored there.

A fundamental law of development and dialectics is that change and progress occur through the struggle of opposites, and that society develops through class struggle. This way of looking at the question seemed to mystify the CPSU member (it was certainly not a problem of translation or some other purely language problem), who responded that there was no bourgeoisie in the Soviet Union, and therefore there was no class struggle of an antagonistic nature. He agreed that in capitalist countries, communists developed in the class struggle, but that in a socialist country, where there was no privately employed labor and therefore no bourgeoisie and no material basis for bourgeois ideology or class struggle, new forms of developing communism had to be discovered.

When one divorces the building of socialism from class struggle, many problems arise. Take, for example, the question of incentives. The problem is traditionally posed as a choice between material and moral incentives. But this is a misleading way of posing the differences. Socialist incentives involve the application of *class consciousness* to production and every other problem, whereas bourgeois incentives involve competition and division among people, each striving for individual attention or advancement.

Class consciousness is not a moral question. Class conscious solutions to production *do* advance the needs and interests of working people, but the individual grasps the solution not principally because of his or her *particular individual* interest, but because of the interest of the class as a whole, through which the individual's interests are best served. It is certainly a good thing for class conscious activity to guide the development of society, but that doesn't make it a "moral" question. It is a question of scientifically and correctly assessing the needs of the period, summed up out of the experiences and needs of the people, preparing a plan or program to meet those needs *in a way which will advance the class consciousness of the people so that they themselves will be more effective instruments of socialist construction,* and then winning people politically and ideologically to the plan or program.

Socialism certainly involves the expansion of production and the development of productive forces. But this is the result of revolutionizing the relations of production through the everdeepening class conscious control of the working class over production (and all other aspects of society).

The theory of productive forces has led to the separation of ideology and class consciousness from the everyday work of production and social organization. By reserving ideology for the narrowest and most general statements (socialism is good, co-operation is good), the actual planning and carrying out of production in the Soviet Union is based on pragmatism and the principles of efficiency and profit. This is reflected further in the attitude of many Soviet students that political education is a separate subject, removed from the "practical" methods required for the solution to the pressing problems of the society. It has also led to the generally low level of political and ideological awareness.

The political and ideological leadership of the Soviet Union, the CPSU, through the theory of productive forces, effectively belittles class consciousness by restricting class antagonism to the narrowest conception of legal property relations. This denies the material force of ideas and bourgeois ideology, denies the great variety of ways in which capitalist relations can be introduced to contradict socialist relations, and denies the richness and generality of class struggle which is the essence of socialist construction.

The CPSU agrees (reluctantly) that China is a socialist country and that India is a capitalist country. But the theory of productive forces justifies the CPSU position that a capitalist country, India, has greater potential for progress and development than a socialist country, China. This abandonment of class struggle and acceptance of capitalism is further reflected in the CPSU policies towards India, which is to support the ruling (and ruling class) Congress Party, while maintaining the Communist Party of India (CPI) as an instrument to sidetrack and even denounce class struggle, as for example in the recent strike of railroad workers in India, in which 7000 militants were arrested. . . .

* * *

Within the Soviet Union, we had limited contact with minority nationalities, visiting Kiev in the Ukraine and Yerevan in Armenia. Each of the fifteen Soviet Republics has its own language, and schools are generally conducted in that language, with Russian as a voluntary second language. The everyday language of commerce and cultural life is the local language, although Russian is the official language everywhere. Local art and handicraft, dance, song and music are preserved in the schools and in popular culture.

The language of instruction through the university level is the local language, but the language of the most important prestigious Soviet institutes and universities, concentrated in Moscow and Leningrad, is Russian. Admission to these institutions is done according to competitive examination, which must be taken in Russian. While visiting Moscow University, we had a special guide who spoke no English, and so our regular guide translated our questions and her answers. When we asked about the proportion of students enrolled from minority nationalities, our regular guide told us that was too technical a question, and refused even to translate it.

During Stalin's time, there was a policy of favoring poorer regions and republics, where there was a large concentration of minority nationalities, with compensatory investment funds to aid in national development and diversify the economic base of the country as a whole. We did not get a clear sense of current policy in this regard on our tour, and got no new data on investment trends by region or republic. But two articles in a recent issue of *Slavic Review* (Vol. 31, No. 3, September 1973) give some information.

David Hooson writes that "The doctrine of equalization of economic development retains much of the ideological appeal of fifty years ago, but is being applied to the outlying parts of the Russian Republic (Siberia) rather than to other peripheral republics." (p. 553)

In "Some Aspects of Regional Development in Soviet Central Asia", Ann Sheehy reports that "the development gap between the Central Asian, and also Azerbaijan and Kazakh, republics and the rest of the country expressed in national income produced per capita increased throughout the decade" of the 1960s, reversing the historical trend towards equalization. She says that in 1965, per capita income in the Central Asian republics was 62% of the all-union average. These reversals are occurring despite *planned* targets of more equalization.

Sheeny relies on Soviet newspapers and journals to document increasing frictions between the people of the minority republics and Russia itself. In the 1960s, Uzbeks challenged the rapacious Russian use of Uzbeks natural gas, and insisted on retaining more for local development. Disputes over training of technical workers have increased as "the development of industry has outstripped the training of local workers" in recent years. When a factory is set up in a minority republic, Russian workers are imported to take the skilled and even unskilled jobs. Sheehy provides the following data on the influx of Russian population in selected areas of economic development:

1959-1970 Increase In Russian Population in Selected Areas

Area	Increase in Russian Population	% Increase
Bukhara Oblast (natural gas, gold)	60,000	124
Kzyl-Orda Oblast (Tiuratum Space Complex)	42,000	83
Guriev Oblast (oil)	77,000	128
Russian population increase (entire country)		13

The factories are run in the Russian language, which greatly limits the number of local workers who can get jobs in them. "At the 1970 census only some 15-20% of Uzbeks, Tadzhiks, Turkmens, and Kirghiz claimed to have a good command of the language." (p. 561) Local people do not want to move out of the countryside into "Russianized" towns and factories.

* * *

Why does the CPSU raise the bourgeois theory of productive forces to a principle in their polemics against China's socialism? Why does the Soviet Union propagate national chauvinism and racism?

These wrong and bourgeois ideas are reflections of the essentially capitalist nature of present Soviet society. Bourgeois ideas also exist in socialist countries, preserved by those who want to restore capitalism and defeat the working class. In socialist China today, the class struggle against bourgeois ideas and methods of organization continues under the leadership of the Chinese Communist Party, which expects the struggle to continue for many decades.

But while bourgeois ideas have existed in the Soviet Union throughout its history, the situation today is qualitatively different from the period of socialism in the USSR. Today bourgeois ideas are official policy, and open struggle against them is not allowed. Revisionism, the interpretation of Marxism-Leninism which denies class antagonism and class struggle, has in recent years become official doctrine, in line with the recent restoration of capitalist relations of production in the Soviet Union.

The Soviet revisionists, of course, hotly deny that the Soviet Union is a capitalist country, and many people don't see how it is possible that the first socialist country could now be capitalist. The Soviet Union is capitalist because the class that produces things in the Soviet Union does not control what it produces, does not control how it will produce, and does not control how the product should be distributed. Instead this control is effectively in the hands of state planners and managers in factories and farms, aided by technical experts and the trade union leadership.

We are used to thinking of capitalism in terms of individual capitalists, competing to one degree or another and each owning individual means of production. In the Soviet Union, there are examples of individual private entrepreneurs, as reported in a number of quotes from *Pravda* given in the pamphlet "Khrushchev's Phoney Communism", published by the Foreign Languages Press in Peking. But this form of capitalism is not the chief feature of modern Soviet capitalism, because capitalism was recently restored after the means of production had already basically been completely centralized under socialist state control. In these particular historical circumstances, bourgeois rule takes the form of *state capitalism*.

The planning apparatus still exists, and some of the decentralization tried under Khrushchev has recently been reversed. But in our discussions with enterprise managers, two important features of the planning process came out. First, all plans originate at the enterprise level, and are then submitted to higher authorities for review. In no case were we told of an example where higher authorities altered the submitted plan in any important respect.

Secondly, enterprises are allowed to keep one-third of their after-tax profits for reinvestment *outside the plan;* i.e., managers are free to invest profits in expanding capacity or buying up other plants in the same branch of industry (conglomerates are not allowed) in any way that seems most profitable. Any productive capacity built or acquired then comes under the plan for production, but these plans again originate with the enterprise. So even with the planning apparatus inherited from socialism, some essential features of capitalism have emerged as part of the process of expanding capital.

Within the Soviet Union, there are a number of social conditions which are well advanced over the U.S. and many other capitalist countries. Housing is relatively cheap, costing less than 10% of the minimum wage for a new apartment. Mass transit is in general very good within cities, although inter-urban travel is more backward. The cities are clean, and medical care is free and generally available. Supporters of the Soviet Union often point to these accomplishments as proof of the existence of socialism.

There are two problems with this. First, much of the transportation, housing, and medical programs were established while the USSR was still a socialist country, and their continued existence is a reflection of that history and not necessarily a result of current initiative. Secondly, and more important, the conditions of housing, etc., are not the *decisive* characteristic of socialism. Many capitalist countries have good subway systems (France, England, Canada), and a number have well developed social welfare programs to subsidize housing, medical care, etc. Socialism is distinct from capitalism on the basis of production relations, whether or not the working class controls production and all aspects of society, exercising dictatorship over the remnants of exploiting classes and waging relentless class struggle against them.

On this ground, the Soviet Union fails the test. Enterprise managers can hire and fire labor in response to profit requirements at their own discretion. There are "joint production conferences" in which labor and management representatives sit down to determine the method of plan implementation, but it is indicative of the power relations that we never were allowed to talk with workers in any factory. Instead, we always met with the enterprise director and a trade union official.

The director was always in charge of the meeting, answered almost all of the questions, and set the tone of the interview. In our contacts with workers on the street and informally, we asked what role ordinary workers had in formulating plans and building socialism. We heard a variety of answers, but they all boiled down to what one transport mechanic said in Kiev: "It's very simple. The workers work." The work force is told what the production targets are by the management, and encouraged to accomplish the goal by the management and the trade union officials.

* * *

The rise of modern Soviet state capitalism is very different from the history of other capitalist countries. It has emerged with highly developed and centralized productive capacity and the need for markets and raw materials on a large scale. Because the USSR was the first socialist country, it also had close economic, political and military ties with a number of countries in East Europe and the Third World, and enjoyed great prestige among progressive people all over the world. When socialism was reversed and capitalism restored, these ties and prestige were the basis for extensive foreign interventions which amount to a very powerful imperialism.

Like any imperialist power, the USSR seeks to integrate the political and economic life of other countries around its own needs, placing itself at the hub of an international network of markets, treaties, and trade agreements. It seeks hegemony in its own "sphere of influence", treats its "allies" as secondary and dependent states, and tries to expand its "sphere of influence" at the expense of other imperialist powers, especially the U.S.

But Soviet imperialism is conducted under the guise of socialist ideology, with talk of international solidarity and the responsibilities of one socialist country to the peoples of other countries. Soviet imperialism is socialist in words, but it is capitalist and imperialist in essence, which is why it is called "social-imperialism."

The particulars of Soviet social-imperialism are varied and require more detailed study, although information gained on the trip confirmed and somewhat elaborated the general outline of Soviet control. It is clear, for example, that the countries of East Europe, the COMECON and Warsaw Pact countries, are linked in a subordinate way to the hub of the Soviet economy under the cover-up slogan "international socialist division of labor."

The Soviet Union seeks to integrate the plans of the East European economies into its own import and export requirements. The manufacture of buses and other transportation equipment in Hungary, for example, is directly tied to Soviet needs and markets, and changes in those needs have been reflected in a redirection of Hungary's output. This was "explained" to us in the Soviet Union with the view that it would be senseless, after all, for the Hungarians to produce things for which there was no market.

When Czechoslovakia sought to expand its trade relations with West Europe and the U.S. in 1967 and 1968, in an attempt to diversify its international contacts and become less dependent upon the Soviet Union, the country was openly invaded and militarily suppressed. At the time, the USSR did not try to hide its displeasure at the proposed reduction in trade and economic integration between the USSR and Czechoslovakia, and this attitude was repeated again in discussions with trade officials and economists on the trip. At the same time, the Soviet Union seeks *for itself* much greater trade ties and markets with the West.

The method of providing "foreign aid" to underdeveloped countries is again indicative of social-imperialism. In India, for example, the Soviet Union enters into contracts with the Indian government to aid in constructing productive facilities. In negotiating the contracts, the Soviet Union agrees to supply from its own production a certain amount of materials needed for construction in India. In return, India will repay the loan (with interest) by shipping to the Soviet Union a part of the output of the new facility, together with shipments of traditional Indian products. The prices at which these material goods are valued are sometimes world prices, sometimes prices specially negotiated in the contract.

For example, if the Soviet Union aids in the construction of a cement factory, it will ship to India some steel and other goods used in building the factory, and in return India will ship cement to the Soviet Union. In negotiating the contracts and deciding what kinds of projects to support, the Soviet officials pay attention to the export requirements of Soviet production, and also to the import needs anticipated for future growth. It finances those projects in underdeveloped countries which "fit" into the Soviet economy. Soviet officials quickly add that these projects also materially aid the underdeveloped country by providing jobs and a more advanced level of productive forces, a view remarkably similar to what Gulf Oil Co. says about its operations in Angola.

Many people concede that the Soviet Union has raised revisionism to a principle, but still see the USSR as a progressive anti-imperialist force in the world because it "aids" Cuba and provides arms to certain Third World national liberation struggles. The Soviet Union provided no aid at all to the Cuban war against Batista, and struck up relations with Castro only after the U.S. imposed an embargo and economic boycott. These relations quickly resulted in the positioning of military bases and Soviet-controlled missiles in Cuba in 1962, and in an economic dependence of Cuba on the USSR. Cuba remains today a basically one-crop economy (sugar), which the USSR buys up in exchange for political and ideological support from Castro and the possibility of extending its influence throughout Latin America. The Soviet Union may not need all the sugar it buys from Cuba, but it certainly needs Castro's voice in defense of social-imperialism at international conferences of Third World countries, such as the recent meeting in Algiers.

We know from our experience with U.S. imperialism that foreign relations and economic ties are complex and often cannot be analyzed in strict dollar terms for any particular country. U.S. involvement in Vietnam had more to do with global strategies for containing national liberation movements and China than it had to do with particular resources available in Vietnam. Social-imperialism also has a broad strategy, that of "peaceful transition", "peaceful coexistence", "peaceful competition", and "international division of labor." All of these things gut class struggle out of national and international affairs, deny the "relevance" of revolution and seek to place countries throughout the world at the disposal of the USSR.

The Soviet Union provides arms to some national liberation movements, *once those revolutionary struggles are well underway* and can no longer be ignored by a country claiming to be socialist. But the arms are *sold,* not given, and wherever possible the USSR uses its political influence to mute the struggle. This can be seen in its policies of peaceful transition in Chile, and its program for negotiation with Portugal in Mozambique and Angola, combined with the strikebreaking activity of the Communist Party in Portugal itself.

* * *

The social-imperialism of the USSR comes into conflict with the imperialism of the U.S. and other monopoly capitalist countries. The search for markets, raw materials and political control — the extension of Soviet spheres of influence — is colliding with U.S. interests in Asia, Europe, the Middle East, Africa and Latin America. This rivalry is not at all about the independence of other countries, but concerns which big power will have supremacy in the world.

When the U.S. replaced England as the major power in Iran or Egypt, the change did not give those countries independence. Soviet attempts to replace the U.S. as the major power in India hold no promise of independence for India. For the Indian people, the USSR does not represent a path to national liberation, even though Soviet activity there does not weaken U.S. and British imperialism. Only the Indian people, organized and united around the Indian working class and consciously opposed to all imperialism, can win independence and build socialism, relying first and foremost on themselves.

The Soviet Union holds out the hope for peace. In a pamphlet entitled "Why We Need Disarmament" (by Igor Glagalev, Novosti Press 1973), the backward notion that "the danger of war remains since the imperialist powers persist in their arms drive" (p. 54) is advanced to support the idea that peace can come through disarmament. If only we can get the imperialists to give up their weapons, then there will be no war. Wonderful. We are aware that "A number of measures to limit arms and bring about disarmament have been taken by some countries since the 24th CPSU Congress. This shows that the forces of peace are stronger than those of war and aggression." (p. 52)

For all this talk, the Soviet military budget, and that of the U.S. and other imperialist countries, continues to grow each year. And this must be, because military power and wars arise out of imperialist rivalries for markets and political hegemony, not out of the evil minds of some munitions makers and legislators who can be outvoted by an aroused people. Stalin said, "To eliminate the inevitability of war, it is necessary to abolish imperialism." But of course Stalin is out of favor now, and this quote and the class stand it represents do not appear any longer in the official line of the CPSU.

The danger of world war is in fact increasing, not decreasing. The rivalries among imperialists, especially between the U.S. and USSR, are growing deeper. Whether in the Middle East, in the Mediterranean, India/Pakistan or Latin America, these two superpowers are involved behind the scenes in military adventures, coups, and all-out war. These conflicts in turn come from the difficulties and near-panic of U.S. imperialism, challenged everywhere by rising national movements, increased competition from Europe and Japan, and also from the recent appearance of the Soviet Union as a major imperialist power hungry for markets and hegemony of its own. Both WW 1 and WW 2 grew out of similar conditions of rapid realignment and attempts by newly emerging imperialist powers (especially Germany) for world power.

One of the most important lessons of Marxism is that capitalism operates according to laws which function independently of people's wills. We find our freedom and make progress within the bounds of these laws of social development, not by making up fantasies and trying to realize them. No amount of resolutions for peace can change the basis of imperialist wars, or remove the reality of current growing rivalries among imperialist powers, especially between the U.S. and USSR. As the Chinese point out, either revolution will prevent world war, or world war will give rise to revolution.

Within the Soviet Union itself, the situation is extremely difficult for the working class and its allies. Internal control over media, political organization, trade unions, etc., is very great, and opposition is a difficult task. As visitors, we didn't get any direct sense of organized opposition, although in some cases there was indication that people opposed current policies. The writings of Marx and Lenin (but not Mao) are freely available and many older people remember socialism first hand. These conditions provide the basis of progress against capitalism. But Marx and Lenin are claimed by the Soviet capitalists and turned around to justify capitalist restoration, national chauvinism, etc.

The difficulty this poses for communist forces is reflected in an exchange some us had with an older bus driver in Kiev, who pretty much summed up the whole impression we got in the USSR. He was telling us proudly about how he fought to defeat fascists in WW 2, naming all the major battles he was in. We asked him if he was a communist, a member of the CPSU. He roared with laughter and said, "No! I'm not a communist, I'm a *worker!*"

The threat of working class protest has become a dominant fact in the political life of the Soviet Union.

The Soviet Working Class: Discontent and Opposition
M. Holubenko

The Soviet bureaucracy uses formidable methods to subdue and atomize the working class, scientifically track it down, and destroy every embryonic form of its opposition. But as we peer beneath the bureaucratic lid imposed on Soviet society, we perceive that the class struggle, supposedly destroyed forever, continues on its way. This article is an attempt to chronicle that struggle, to analyze some of its forms, and to evaluate its prospects for the future.

A number of points must be made at the outset, relating to problems of

"The Soviet Working Class: Discontent and Opposition," by M. Holubenko, *Critique* (Scotland), Spring, 1975, copyright © 1975 by *Critique* and reprinted by permission of the publisher.

analyzing working class opposition. The major and most obvious is that because of a rigorous censorship, the Soviet press is silent on outbreaks of working class discontent.[1] Secondly, *samizdat* has yielded little on the question of working class opposition. *Samizdat,* which now reaches the West in well over 1,000 items a year, is written mostly by 'liberal' or right-wing intelligentsia, and reflects the concerns of that intelligentsia. It is quite possible that there exists a small body of left-wing *samizdat* which takes up broader social questions, but no such material has yet reached the West, or if it has, it is not publicized. Finally, what is surprising and lamentable is the fact that, although the central contradiction of Soviet society is that between the working class and the bureaucracy, one is hard pressed to find a single article on the Soviet working class, let alone the question of its opposition, written by a Marxist in the West. Soviet sources, although silent on the question of opposition, do contain a great deal of information about other aspects of the working class. Journals, statistical handbooks, and law codes, if analyzed by a Marxist, can provide a fairly good picture of the structure of the working class, its living conditions, and the factory regime. On the basis of such an analysis one can begin to make meaningful statements about possible areas of tension, working class attitudes, etc. It is not amiss in a socialist journal to make a plea for some serious work on the working class from those in Soviet studies holding left-wing political views.

Social Control

An analysis of working class opposition must begin with a discussion of the mechanisms of social control specific to the USSR. Without such an analysis it is difficult to understand why working class opposition takes the form that it does.

The nature of the Soviet Union as a society renders its mechanisms of social control radically different from those operating in a capitalist society. The abolition of the market and of unemployment in the Soviet Union, in the *absence of a workers' democracy,* meant that the only effective sanction against the working class at the disposal of the bureaucracy was repressive administrative controls at all levels of the enterprise. Soviet enterprises are teeming with administrative personnel whose sole function consists of controlling, observing and verifying the activity of workers. Without the threat of unemployment, of a reserve army of labour, this administrative-repressive apparatus had to be created to 'stimulate' workers to perform. Such an apparatus is not an accidental aspect of bureaucratic power; it is the sole mechanism at the disposal of the regime for 'disciplining' the working class.

Also, unlike a capitalist society, the privileges of the ruling group in the Soviet Union are not based on bourgeois property relations. Rather, they are allocated through a juridical-administrative procedure, the precondition of which is the monopoly of political power. The social inequality produced in this fashion is not mediated by market relations, and all the mystifications that go with it, operating at the level of civil society. There exists no 'invisible hand' which distributes wealth and determines the social structure, but only the very visible hand of the bureaucracy. In short, the very nature of the Soviet Union is such that social relations are highly transparent.

The recognition of social relations is also facilitated by the highly centralized nature of decision-making. This centralization makes possible a rather accurate pin-pointing of the source of power and the cause of privilege. It is the central political apparatus in Moscow which determines all important questions in the country, and this is recognized by everyone. Thus the workers of the Kiev Hydro-Electric Station, for example, when pressing their claim for an improvement in housing conditions, appealed directly to the Central Committee of the CPSU — knowing well that it is there that real decisions are made.

The centralization of political and economic decision-making means that the economic demands of workers at factory level are in reality also demands on the central political apparatus. Therefore the ramifications of making economic demands in the USSR are infinitely greater than in capitalist countries.

If the privileges of the ruling group are transparent and if this group lacks the 'invisible hand' of the market behind which to hide, neither does it possess a mystifying ideology. The official ideology in the Soviet Union does not serve to legitimize the ruling group's privileges and power over society. The official ideology is in sharp contradiction with the existing social structure. The ruling group is saddled with an ideology which teaches the non-legitimacy of its existence. In this respect the Soviet ruling group is in a unique position among all privileged groupings in history.

Because of these (and other) factors, the Soviet ruling group is in a very unstable position, and the Soviet Union is an inherently unstable society. Social control cannot operate in resolving conflicts 'normally' or 'naturally' at the level of civil society; the state does not preserve a semblance of neutrality, but intervenes constantly to penetrate and smash civil society.

To maintain social control, the ruling group sustains a massive apparatus of repression designed to reduce the population to a state of inertia. However, the very existence of such a massive police apparatus is proof of the chronic instability of the regime: it shows that social control cannot be achieved in civil society, but requires the constant intervention of the state.

The fundamental principle of the state's intervention is that all significant interaction between individuals and groups must be mediated by the state and its organizations. Activity which cannot be mediated must either be reduced to a minimum or suppressed. It is not only unmediated political activity which is at stake, but spontaneous human interaction itself. In a post-capitalist society, where the economy is not autonomous, the state's penetration of society is more thorough than under any previously existing social system. The result is that no society in human history has been atomized as Soviet society is today.

The apparatus of repression penetrates society to keep it in an amorphous and atomized condition, and to deprive the individual of meaningful group solidarity without which any form of action is inconceivable. Thus, if the Soviet working class has appeared to remain passive, this is above all because of the weight of the repressive apparatus.

The principal effect on the working class of this form of social control is to atomize and individualize its protest. The working class is unable to organize itself into genuine trade unions or other autonomous organizations. Instead, it must work in the context of a factory regime where every worker must carry a labour book which registers his work record, and without which he cannot find employment, and where the widespread use of piece-rates divides the workers and forces them to compete with one another. Under these conditions, most of working class opposition must be expressed through individual acts of despair: alcoholism, 'hooliganism', absenteeism (resulting in high rates of labour turnover), extremely shoddy production, and industrial sabotage. Working class opposition in the Soviet Union is expressed principally through so-called 'deviance' and 'social problems'.

Of all the forms of 'deviance', drunkenness is the most prevalent outlet for frustration. Alcoholism has reached such chronic proportions that a series of decrees were passed in 1972 in an unprecedented struggle against drunkenness. While alcoholism is a major expression of working class discontent, it was used in the past as an important means of controlling the Soviet working class and for raising revenues under Stalin. (For example: organizing vodka kiosks outside factory gates.) Today the situation has changed. In an effort to raise labour productivity, the regime had initiated a campaign against alcoholism, but has had little success. In fact, according to some observers, alcoholism has become more widespread since the turn of the decade following the dashing of hopes raised by Khrushchevism. Given the absence (for the moment) of other outlets, the 'butyl'ka' will continue to play its role.

There are other important consequences for working class opposition resulting from the mechanisms of social control specific to the Soviet Union.

One of the most noticeable features of the existing strike pattern in the USSR is the fact that they tend to occur frequently in the periphery, that is, in the areas removed from the central Moscow-Leningrad region. Secondly, strikes taking place in the periphery tend to be much more violent.

Concerning the frequency of strikes in the periphery: there are perhaps three major reasons for this. The most important is undoubtedly the fact that the peripheral regions suffer much more from shortages of all kinds. Also, these regions are less easily penetrated by the secret police, especially the non-Russian republics. Thirdly, the regime knows that as long as it remains in full control of the commanding strategic centers, the periphery can pose no serious threat. A strike in Magadan (there may have been hundreds for all we know) will not shake the world, a major strike in Moscow could. There is, therefore, much greater scope for spontaneous working class protest in the peripheral areas.

This pattern of opportunity for working class protest poses serious consequences for the future development of the Soviet working class movement. It means that those areas of least strategic importance, where the working class is bound to be at a lower political and cultural level, are presented with the most favourable possibilities for open opposition. However, the lower political and cultural level existing here must also mean that these opportunities will not be used to the full.

The situation can be formulated in the following way: the larger the factory, or the closer it is to a major center, or the closer it is to a major road or boulevard, then, the more intensive will be the surveillance of it. It is not only the economic importance of a factory which determines the extent of its surveillance, but also its strategic political importance.

If a strike breaks out in a factory of strategic importance, the regime is extremely flexible. This explains why strikes in the major centers do not have the same violent character as strikes in the periphery. Once a strike breaks out in a politically strategic factory, the regime will, uncharacteristically, meet workers' demands with lightening speed in order to contain the strike and defuse it as quickly as possible. To react with savage repression against a mass of workers in the center is to risk an escalation of the struggle in the strategic heartland. It is also more difficult to keep the strike a secret from the domestic and foreign public. Neither does the regime react to strikes with lock-outs or shut-downs — typically capitalist tactics intended to defeat the workers into dragging out the struggle. In the USSR, to force thousands of angry workers into the streets by a lock-out is to create fertile conditions for the creation of autonomous political life. Of course, if swift concessions do not defuse a strike, then repression is quick and brutal.

A recent strike in Kiev, the third largest city in the Soviet Union, is perhaps the best known example of the regime's flexibility when faced with a strike situation in a politically strategic factory. In May 1973, thousands of workers at the machine-building factory on the busy Brest-Litovsk Chausee went on strike at 11:00 a.m., demanding higher pay.[2] The factory director immediately telephoned the Central Committee of the Communist Party of Ukraine (C.P.U.). By noon, a member of the C.P.U. Politburo arrived at the factory to evaluate the situation. He met a delegation of workers and immediately promised to fulfill their demands. By 3:00 p.m. the workers were informed that their salaries were to be increased, and most of the top administrators of the factory were dismissed. (It is important to note that the local population, according to this report, attributed the success of this strike to the fact that it had an organized character, and that the regime was afraid that this strike might develop into a 'Ukrainian Stettin'.)

Even in a politically strategic factory, the regime is flexible only when faced with a *mass show of force*. Vis-a-vis individual workers, the regime behaves in an altogether different fashion. If an individual worker is seen to be making an attempt at organizing a protest by stirring-up workers, repression is hard and swift. There are certainly no show trials; that is reserved for intellectuals. It is extremely dangerous for workers to organize themselves clandestinely in such factories. In Moscow in 1970, for example, reports circulated that several 'troublesome' workers from a number of factories simply vanished in a series of preventative arrests and were never heard from again.

If a strike does break out in any factory, the first objects of attention for the KGB inquiry are the 'instigators' of the protests. These will fall victim to repression after the strike has ended. By then, the surge of solidarity will have subsided and the KGB can do its work without interference. Vladimir Bukovsky, the Russian dissident, tells of the fate that befell one strike organizer:

> "Another of my friends in the mad-house was, for example, a French communist of Rumanian origin who had lived for more than 10 years in Marseilles and who came to the Soviet Union to learn, to see what communism was like in practice. He went to work in a footwear factory in Moldavia and worked there a long time. But he was displeased that the workers there received such low wages. He told his workmates that they ought to fight for better pay — they went on strike, he was arrested and declared insane. In the hospital he just couldn't understand what had happened to him, how communists could do such things. For him communism and the struggle for a better life were more or less the same thing — he just couldn't understand. Towards the end of his stay he really began to go out of his mind, it seems to me, because he was telling everybody that the Soviet Government was under the influence of the Vatican."[3]

If a strike is to be in any way organized under conditions of severe police repression, the organizing has to be done in deep clandestinity. This is the reason for the seemingly thorough spontaneity of Soviet strikes. There have been several strikes, however, where even the most rigorous KGB investigation failed to find 'instigators'. What probably happens in these cases, is that the situation, having already reached boiling-point, a few exemplary actions, such as leaving a work bench or dropping a tool, are enough to trigger a strike.

Strikes and other forms of protest: The Khrushchev Period

Under Khrushchev, the rate of wage increases was slow, there were several pay cuts, and one dramatic increase in the price of meat and dairy products. Khrushchev dangled the promise of the consumer society and when this could not be fulfilled, there was deep resentment in the working class. The atmosphere of the Khrushchevian 'thaw' meant that this resentment was bound to take a more open expression. For the first time in several decades, anger coming from the depth of society boiled over into strikes and other open forms of protest.

During the 1956 thaw, there were many stormy meetings in factories connected with the 20th Party Congress at which even members of the Politburo (then the Praesidium) were howled down as representatives of the "new wealthy".[4] In the autumn of 1959, popular discontent mounted as pay cuts were announced, and this combined with continuing food shortages, drove the discontent to take violent forms in several places. The riots at the Temir-Tau metallurgical complex in Kazakhstan are one well documented example.[5] According to sources in Moscow, similar demonstrations occurred in Kemerovo, the center of the Siberian industrial basin of the Kuzgas, in early January, 1960.[6] Again, in 1961, working class protest erupted, this time in response to Khrushchev's currency reforms.[7]

The biggest and most widespread explosion of working class discontent occurred in 1962. Nothing on a similar scale has occurred since then. The June 1st, 1962, announcement of price increases on meat and dairy products was greeted everywhere throughout the Soviet Union with demonstrative anger. Sit-down strikes, mass protest demonstrations on factory premises, street demonstrations, and in several instances in many parts of the Soviet Union, large scale rioting occurred. Evidence at hand speaks of such occurrences at Grosny, Krasnodar, Donetsk, Yaroslav, Zhdanov, Gorky, and even Moscow itself, where reportedly a mass meeting took place at the Moskvich Automobile Factory.[8]

It was in the Donbas region, and in particular in the city of

Novocherkassk, that the struggles of 1962 took their sharpest form. The noteable feature of the Novocherkassk explosion was the speed with which it engulfed the working class. Another feature of these events was the role played by women. In the Soviet Union, women are almost totally employed, but in the low paying jobs, and therefore receive, on the average, half the male salary. It is women who do the overwhelming bulk of domestic chores, it is they who do the queuing, and it is they who are among the first to respond to food shortages and price increases . . . The third important feature was the active involvement of students and youth. In Novocherkassk, 16,000 young people lived in municipal dormitories in appalling conditions.[9] It was they, together with women, who took initiatives in the town center. The fourth feature of the Novocherkassk events is the very high level of violence. Here authorities did not make concessions, but brought out the militia instead. Finally, the Novocherkassk riots showed the relative unreliability of local police and troops stationed in the locality. To quell the riots, special internal security troops had to be flown in.

There are several accounts of the Novocherkassk riots. The riots seem to have been started by two events: firstly, by the action of workers at the Budenny Electric Locomotive Works on the outskirts of the city, and by a crowd primarily led by women from a textile factory, and secondly, from a student gathering in the city center outside the party headquarters. It is perhaps of some interest to quote one of the most interesting accounts of this important event of Soviet working class opposition.

". . . In June 1962, meat prices to the consumers were increased. Grumbling and discontent which became general soon crystallized into action. At the Budenny Electric Locomotive Works, employing several thousands, the management lowered the rates on piecework. The news had the effect of an electric shock on workers who were already dissatisfied with their miserable living conditions and a hopelessly inadequate diet.

A group of employees from one of the shops sent a delegation to the management to protest against lowering of the rates. No one would meet them. This increased the tension and more people began to gather from other shops. A train, passing on a railway that ran in the vicinity was stopped. Someone began sounding the locomotive whistle and then the factory sirens. This brought large numbers of workers from other shifts. The mood of the crowd was ugly.

Soon the militia arrived but was driven off. Then soldiers appeared in armoured cars, followed by tanks, and occupied the shops. The crowd did not disperse, but increased as employees of the new shifts arrived. (The shops worked on a three-shift system) The following morning several thousand workers, who had remained at the locomotive works all night, began to march on Novocherkassk, which is located on a tributary of the Don River. In order to enter the town they had to cross a bridge which was blocked by soldiers.

In the meantime another mass of people (mostly women and students — M.H.) had already gathered in the central square of the city before the building of the local committee of the party, which was guarded by formations of the KGB armed with automatic weapons. The city secretary of the party appeared and began to address the crowd. Some tried to shout him down; others hurled objects at him. Suddenly the KGB detachment opened fire into the crowd. Shooting also began from other directions. In one area, when soldiers were ordered to fire, one officer pulled out his party membership card, tore it up, and then shot himself. Many soldiers refused to obey the command.

According to reports, at least several hundred were killed. Martial law and a curfew were imposed, troops and tanks patrolled the streets and the area was completely sealed off ... This was accompanied by house to house visits of the KGB agents, mass arrests and secret trials. Many soldiers and officers were courtmartialed. In the meantime, several members of the Central Committee of the CPSU, among them Kozlov,[10] Polyansky and Mikoyan, came to Novocherkassk to pacify the population."[11]

The protest in Novocherkassk was one of many that occurred in the Donbas region. In one account, it is suggested that the strike movement in the Donbas had succeeded in establishing a regional strike committee which was planning coordinated protest on a regional basis. If true, this is a fact of overwhelming importance. According to this account:

"The insurgents in the Donbas region reportedly considered . . . the demonstrations in Novocherkassk unsuccessful because they rebelled there without the consent of the strike organization offices in Rostov (on the Don), Lugansk, Taganrog, and other cities. This would confirm rumours and reports concerning a headquarters for organized opposition in the Donbas and also explain that a planned co-ordinated demonstration didn't develop because of tumult breaking out over the price increases before final preparations could be made . . . "[12]

Strikes and other forms of protest: After Khrushchev

The majority of strikes and other forms of working class protest which have come to light since the fall of Khrushchev, occurred in response to three basic issues: a) low wages — in particular a sudden drop in bonuses or in wages due to revised work norms announced by factory management; b) food and consumer goods shortages; c) inadequate housing. There were, of course, major disturbances in Kaunas, Bilhorod, Tashkent and Frunze which were in response to national oppression. But these and other instances cannot be dealt with in this article. Suffice it to say that strikes and other forms of mass protest raising national demands, that is, directly political demands, are particularly dangerous for the regime. Also of great importance are the solidarity strikes with the December 1970 revolt of the

Polish workers on the Baltic coast. These were reported to have taken place in Kaliningrad, Lvov, and in some cities of Byelorussia.[13] But the overwhelming majority of known strikes have been in response to a direct attack on the living standards of the working class brought about either by a) a management decision to cut bonuses, raise work norms and thus cut wages, or b) frequently occurring in conjunction with the former protests over food shortages.[14]

There was a very noticeable increase in the occurrence of strikes beginning in late 1969/early 1970, and strikes have continued fairly regularly to the present day. Between the fall of Khrushchev and the end of 1969, news of only one significant strike has come to light. This was in 1967, when thousands of workers at the Kharkov Tractor Factory walked out.

The apparent relative absence of strikes between 1964, and 1969-70, can be explained by looking at the wage policy of the Brezhnev-Kosygin leadership. During its first five years in power, the leadership courted popularity and was much more generous to workers on the question of wages than Khrushchev had been. Since 1969, however, a determined effort has been made to return wage increases to the modest level of the Khrushchev period. Low growth of wages continues to characterize the policy today, and one can therefore expect strikes to continue and intensify. Indeed, there is some evidence to suggest that the regime expects the same and has consequently taken a series of preventive measures. This will be dealt with later; let us first examine some of the most significant outbreaks of working class protest since 1969.

The most important disturbances in this period took place in Dnipropetrovsk and Dniprodzerzhinsk in the heavy industrial region in southern Ukraine. In September 1972, in Dnipropetrovsk, thousands of workers went on strike, demanding higher wages and a general improvement in the standard of living. The strikes involved more than one factory and were repressed at a cost of many dead and wounded. However, a month later in October 1972, riots broke out again in the same city. The demands: better provisioning, improvement in living conditions, and the right to choose a job instead of having it imposed.[15]

Unfortunately, this is the extent of the information available on an event which was undoubtedly an important working class mobilization.

Fortunately, because of the existence of a recent *samizdat* document, a good deal more information is available on the riots which occurred in Dniprodzerzhinsk, a city of 270,000, several kilometers from Dnipropetrovsk.[16] The riots in Dniprodzerzhinsk were sparked off by an incident concerning the militia. Specifically, the militia arrested a few drunken members of a wedding party, loaded them into a police wagon, and drove off. Minutes later, the police wagon crashed and the militia (who themselves had been drinking) concentrated on saving themselves, leaving the arrested to burn to death in the wagon which exploded. The assembled crowd marched in fury to the city's central militia building and ransacked it, burning police files and causing other damage. The crowd then marched to the Party headquarters where the person 'on duty' ordered the crowd, with threats, to disperse immediately. The crowd surged forward and attacked the Party building, whereupon two militia battalions opened fire. There were ten dead, including two militia men killed by the crowd. The Dniprodzerzhinsk riot is an example of the strained social relations in the Soviet Union — an example of how an apparently small incident can spark off a major event which far surpasses the importance of the incident itself.

Examples of strikes which have occurred over wages since 1969:

— strike at the Kiev machine-building factory in May, 1972 (already mentioned).

— a strike in Vytebsk, in the city's largest factory, February 1973. It occurred after a 20% drop in wages brought about by new work norms for skilled workers. The strike lasted for two days until the KGB ordered the factory director to restore the wages. The KGB apparently tried to track down the instigators of the strike, but could find none.

— at Kopeyske, in the Cheliabinsk oblast, at the Kirov factory, 1971. In this the largest equipment factory in the USSR, the KGB was reported to have arrested the strike organizers.

— in Sverdlovsk oblast, at a large rubber plant, 1969. A strike broke out following a 25% drop in salary with the introduction of the 5 day work week, and a further drop in salary with the introduction of new wage norms. The situation was aggravated by the shortages of meat and dairy products which in turn resulted in 4 to 5 hour queues for consumers.

— strikes were reported in Vladimir in early 1970. These lasted for one or two days and occurred simutaneously in more than one factory.

— scores of work stoppages on construction sites were reported in Moscow and Leningrad in the winter of 1973.

Strikes in response to food shortages are much more of a threat to the regime because they raise an issue affecting the entire working class, including white collar workers, and not just workers of single factories. One strike over this issue was particularly important because it was relatively highly organized. This was the three day stay-at-home strike in Krasnodar, Kuban. In a novel form of protest, the majority of workers refused to go to the factories until decent consumer goods and foodstuffs arrived in the stores. A variant of this tactic was used by women in Gorky, later in 1969. Women working at an armaments factory walked off the job stating that they were going to buy meat and would not return to work until they had bought enough of it. And again in late 1969, workers in Sverdlovsk went on strike raising the threatening egalitarian demand of food rationing, claiming that at least this would ensure an equal distribution of food for everyone.

The best known example of a strike on the question of housing occurred in the settlement attached to the Kiev Hydro-Electric Station in 1969.[17] Organized on a geographical basis, involving all those living in the settlement, the strike showed a high level of organization. It also has the distinction of being the only industrial action to be reported in the *Chronicle of Current Events,* the clandestine journal of the intellectual opposition. This is how the strike was reported in the *Chronicle:*

> "In mid-May 1969, workers at the Kiev Hydro-Electric Station in the village of Beryozka met to discuss the housing problem; many of them are still living in prefabricated huts and railway coaches despite the authorities' promise to provide housing. The workers declared that they no longer believed local authorities, and decided to write to the Central Committee of the Communist Party. After their meeting the workers marched off with banners carrying such slogans as "All Power To the Soviets!". KGB men drove up in veterinary vans and were greeted with shouts of "What d' you think we are? Dogs?!". Remonstrating with the crowd, the KGB men tried to whip up feelings of 'class hatred' towards one of the active participants in the affair, retired Major Ivan O. Hryshchuk, by pointing out that he was on a good pension, so what had he got to kick up a fuss about? Hryshchuk agreed that his pension really was undeservedly large — indeed he had already been donating it to a children's home for two years. Moreover, he earned his living by honest labour, unlike the KGB men.
>
> The next day there was an official meeting at which some of the speakers tried to blacken Hryshchuk, but by the time they left the platform they had been literally spat upon by the workers. The workers sent a delegation to Moscow with a letter signed by about 600 people on their housing problem. At the end of June, Ivan Hryshchuk was arrested in Moscow. The workers wrote a new letter, this time demanding his release as well . . ."[18]

Finally, there have been strikes reported, the immediate causes of which are not known. For example, a group of Moscow dissidents calling themselves the Citizens' Committee of Moscow issued a statement, in July 1970, calling for industrial action to bring down the regime, and spoke of strikes in Leningrad and Moscow.

The strikes mentioned in this article are but a partial list of those that have come to light in the West. However, they are representative of the strikes that have taken place. There is little doubt that information on only a small number of the strikes that occur reaches the West.

The strikes, localized events in most cases and raising limited demands, cannot signify the existence today of a real mass movement of the working class. What the strikes do show, however, is that the working class, terrorized into passivity under Stalin, is slowly recovering its strength. "The workers", as Amalrik has pointed out, "are bitter over having no rights vis-a-vis the factory management. The collective farmers are resentful about their total dependence on the kolkhoz chairman . . . Everybody is angered by the great inequality in wealth, the low wages, the austere housing conditions, the lack of essential consumer goods, compulsory registration at their places of residence and work, and so forth."[19] The discontent, although profound, is for the time being not directed clearly at the bureaucratic regime as such, but against certain aspects of the regime. Today's strikes are but skirmishes in the unfolding class struggle.

The threat of working class protest has become a dominant fact in the political life of the Soviet Union. Although the working class cannot pose its solutions (as yet) to the economic and social crisis of Soviet society, the threat of its protest has limited the options of social and economic policy of the bureaucracy. (It was the threat of an explosion of working class discontent that discouraged the regime from introducing major price increases in early 1969, and which induced them to allow creeping inflation to continue instead).[20] In considering economic reforms, the timidity of bureaucracy in moving towards the mark with its inevitable attack on security of employment, is above all because of a fear of the working class.

Other Evidence of Rising Working Class Discontent

Because the regime has taken a series of measures to strengthen its apparatus against the threat of rising discontent, there is a clear indication that it is aware of growing social tension. Since 1965, and especially since 1967, many new organizations have been established to reinforce the police and special agent departments. The power of the police has widened, the number of policemen greatly increased and professional security officers, night-shift police stations and motorized police units set up. Futhermore, a series of new laws has been put into effect to "strengthen the social order in all fields of law". Ordinances, decrees and laws such as the one passed in July 1969, which emphasised the suppression of dangerous political offenders, mass riots and the murder of policemen,[21] reflect a new emphasis on 'law and order'. There is also the unprecedented promotion of KGB security chiefs to positions in the central and republican politburos. The promotion of

Andropov, the KGB Chairman in the Ministerial Council of the USSR, to full membership in the Politburo of the CPSU — an honour last accorded to Beria — is well known. But what has received far less publicity is the promotion of KGB heads to either full or candidate members of republican party politburos in Byelorussia, Azerbaidzhan, Tadzhikistan, Uzbekistan, Kirgizia, Georgia, Moldavia, and Ukraine. In addition, the new party leaders of Armenia and Azerbaidzhan are both ex-high officials of the KGB. This development reflects the regime's awareness of a maturing social tension — a situation which must increase the importance of security organs. Hence the promotion of their chiefs to the highest bodies so as to have proper political control and to effect the most efficient political integration of these organs.

Finally, on the question of growing working class discontent, there is a rather rare and very revealing survey of workers attitudes taken at the locomotive plant in Voroshilovgrad reported in *Izvestia*.[22] The survey has the important virtue of comparing responses in 1973 with responses obtained from a similar survey in the same plant in 1968. One sees, therefore, the change of attitudes over time. The survey shows that two thirds of those polled at the factory were dissatisfied with their wages. Five years ago, among the same group, 54% of the workers said they were not happy with their pay. At the same time, the researchers writing in *Izvestia* admitted that the workers seemed to be unhappy about the country's slow progress in providing the desired consumer goods. An even higher proportion of the workers polled, 71% in both 1968 and 1973, said their working equipment was poor. In 1973, 70% also said health conditions at the plant were poor, compared with 65% in 1968. 57% were dissatisfied with the production quotas set for the enterprise, and two thirds were dissatisfied with the standard of productivity in the plant. "The equipment is outdated", workers told the pollsters. "The plant needs a basic reconstruction. New technology is introduced too slowly." In addition, 78% of the workers were unaware that the government had initiated a management reform programme, designed to make Soviet industry more efficient, and to lead to higher productivity and pay. Almost all workers knew that the factory had failed to meet its 1973 production quota, because, as a result, they had failed to receive their so-called 13th month's salary — a month's wages as a bonus.

Wages

If dissatisfaction with wages is growing, it is for good reason. The average monthly wage in the USSR was 135 rubles in 1973. But the average monthly wage hides more than it reveals; one must know the distribution of wages, and this the State seems to regard almost as a military secret. For industrial workers, male and female, in the first half of 1973, the *average* gross earnings were 143.14 rubles. But to get at the average take-home pay, one must take into account income tax and other deductions (13.61 rubles). So, the average monthly take-home pay was 129.53 rubles for industrial workers.

But even these salaries are meagre if one takes into account the poverty line established by Soviet researchers in the 1960s. A Soviet researcher writes "... at the present time (1966-70) for a typical worker's family of four people" (i.e. mother and father working, two children at school), "a little over 200 rubles [a month — M.H.] is needed to satisfy their *minimal* requirements..." [my emphasis — M.H.].[23] That is, a little over a per capita income of 50 rubles in the family is still required to provide for minimal requirements. Some recently published results of family budgets indicate that poverty, in the terms set by Soviet researchers, represents the conditions of a sizeable part of the Soviet working class.

One survey covering some 10,000 workers of all kinds in Leningrad (1961-65) showed that 40% of their families had not reached the per capita income of 50 rubles a month.[24] And Leningrad, it must be remembered, is a privileged city when compared to other centers. A study published by a Soviet economist revealed that among workers and white collar families in the USSR, as a whole, over 30% were by Soviet standards poor.[25] A 1967 handbook of Soviet labour statistics showed that over 20% of workers employed in the highest paid sector, the construction industry, were below the poverty line, and over 60% of those in the low paid textile and food industries were under the poverty line.[26]

The average wage increase in 1973 was 3.7%. (*Izvestia*, 26.12.1974.) This is a small increase, and was in any case partially offset by inflation. There are some who claim that the annual increase in retail prices has wholly offset the increase in wages. This is an exaggeration, but there is no doubt that inflation has hit hard. Of course, Soviet inflation does not occur in the same way as inflation under capitalism. Retail prices are raised not by marking up the price of goods outright, but by reclassifying the same article under a new grade of goods or under a new trade mark, and selling the item for a higher price. It seems on the surface that a new or improved product has appeared. In reality, it is the same product under a new name or category with a higher price. The old product at the cheaper price, is still technically available — that is, it is still listed on the books. However, it is not to be seen on the shelves. Recently, meat has been particularly affected by this re-labelling procedure.

As mentioned earlier, there is a deliberate government policy of attacking wages. This was clearly foreseen in the current Five Year Plan. Automatic wage increases are being reduced, and the wage system is to focus more sharply on the task of increasing labour productivity. To quote an official economic report: "In the current five-year plan only half of the wage increases will derive from the introduction of the new basic wages, salaries and other conditions of pay; while the other half will be received by workers and office employees in production performance."[27] But, in the absence of a trade union to defend the interests of the working class, wage-rises lag considerably behind the rise in labour productivity.

An article in a Soviet journal gives a rather clear indication of this.[28] Going back to the years 1951-60, one sees that although labour productivity rose by 7.4%, the average wage increase rose only by 2.6%. Between the years 1961 and 1965, labour productivity rose by 4.6%, wages again by 2.6%. But between 1966-70, labour productivity rose by 5.7%, wages by 5.0% — reflecting the better deal for workers that Brezhev-Kosygin introduced during the consolidation of their leadership following Khrushchev's fall. If one looks at the wage increases of that period, for each individual year, one sees that there were no fewer than three years in which the growth of wages exceeded the growth of productivity (1966-68). This ended abruptly in 1970. In 1970, labour productivity rose by 7.0%, wages by 4.4%. Moreover, in 1971, the Soviet worker received only one third as much in rubles for each percentage point of productivity growth as in 1968, and for 1972 he got half as much, and in 1973 it was roughly the same as in 1972 — labour productivity went up by 6.0%, while the average wages rose by only 3.7%.

The average wage increase of 3.7% in 1973, if looked at closely hides a real attack on earning power of the working class. The large portion of the increase in the average wage was accounted for by a) an increase in the official minimum wage, from 60 to 70 rubles a month, and b) an increase in incentives in the Far North and Siberia. It is clear that workers in the industrial heartland got little or no increase in pay during 1973. Furthermore, if one takes inflation into account, it is quite conceivable that the economic situation for many workers has remained unchanged.

The Economic Reforms and the Working Class

The effort to increase labour productivity is the *leitmotif* of the current Five Year Plan and of the economic reforms. As the possibilities for developing Soviet industry extensively, e.g. by building new plants and increasing the labour force, began to be exhausted, this problem was posed in an acute way. Inevitably, there arose the problem of diminishing effectiveness of capital investment and decreasing growth rates of labour productivity. The increase in labour productivity, however, can be brought about in two ways: by introducing new and improved technology, or by improving the efficiency of workers using the old machines. The problem posed by the introduction of new technology meant that considerably more emphasis was going to be placed on the other alternative — making the worker more efficient by increasing his tempo of work, changing assembly line techniques, employing 'new scientific management', and releasing redundant labour.

Soviet labour productivity is extremely low in comparison with capitalist countries, not only because of the poor equipment, but also because of the high proportion of workers performing no useful function in the factory, and the low motivation to work. It is calculated, according to Soviet sources, that around 10% of the existing labour force could be dismissed without affecting production.[29] In fact the Shchekino experiment showed that dismissals, and the subsequent redistribution of wages of those dismissed to the surviving labour force, brought about a rather significant increase in productivity. The Shchekino experiment has now been extended to 700 enterprises. But, according to Soviet law, workers cannot be released without alternative employment being provided. (There is some evidence which suggests that, in fact, some enterprises have found a way to circumvent the law *de facto* by offering alternative employment in Siberia, where of course no worker wants to live.) Factory managers would, of course, like to have the firm right of dismissal, knowing that without this right economic reforms will grind to a halt. But the central political authority, fearing the possible results of such a move, is resisting this.

Security of employment is one of the last conquests of the October revolution not to have been taken away from the working class. To make any economic sense, it would have to be removed on a wide scale, and this would provoke a major revolt of the working class. Some *Izvestia* reports on Shchekino (1.7.69. and 28.6.69.) noted workers' dissatisfaction on being released — and this in a situation where all were found re-employment with another branch of the same factory in the same locality. A more serious case of working class anger is to be found in an alleged strike of port workers in Odessa who stopped work in solidarity with dockers released as a result of the rationalization of labour.

The inefficiency of Soviet workers and their unenthusiastic performance on the job, has been commented on *ad nauseam* by Soviet specialists. The fact of the matter remains: the right not to work hard at the factory is one of the few remaining rights which the Soviet worker holds. The Soviet worker will resist and "carry on a clandestine economic struggle", as one Soviet dissident put it, against all efforts to intensify the work pace.[30]

The regime has been making a concerted effort to increase labour productivity by a more intense organization of work. Today, almost every third worker is employed on an assembly line. As this proportion increases, a new area of tension opens up between the regime and the working class.

As Soviet research has shown, the discontent of the Soviet working class with assembly work is growing. This discontent is expressed in large labour turnovers as in many capitalist countries. In Sweden's Volvo plant in 1969, the turnover of labour each year reached 52%, and in Italy at Fiat, absenteeism was running between 12-30%.[31] Soviet figures are comparable. At the Lenin Komsomol Automobile Plant in Moscow, the annual turnover among assembly-line workers was close to 40% in 1972.[32] Investigations at the Likhachev Automobile Plant in Moscow, and the Volga Automobile Plant showed similar results.[33] The same article showed that, at a Moscow machine-building plant, labour turnover among assembly-line workers, is 3 to 4 times greater than the factory average.

Soviet specialists analyzing the discontent of assembly line workers attribute the cause to the fact that the modern factory worker tends to be better educated and hence more demanding about working conditions than before. The Soviet worker, like his Western counterpart, is no longer content to perform monotonous, sterotyped operations at a conveyer belt. But the Western worker does have a big advantage over his Soviet counterpart; he has a trade union which can fight measures, such as speed-ups. The Soviet worker has no way of striking back in an organized fashion; his response is individualized.

Détente and the increased trade with the West, in particular the large scale importation of Western plants, will aggravate the problem. Mario Dido, the Secretary of the CGIL, Italy's Communist Party dominated labour federation, had some very interesting comments to make on this question. He made them after visiting the new Soviet automobile plant which the Fiat firm built in Togliattigrad. Dido complains that, without consulting the Italian trade unions, the Soviet leaders have imported one of the most sophisticated and advanced capitalist factory-organizations. Dido said:

> "The entire project has been carried out on the basis of plans prepared and supervised by Fiat technicians . . . not only the technical equipment but also the organization of work is of the Fiat type . . . it is important to distinguish the administrative organization . . . whether with regard to working conditions or the absolute priority given to productivity from that of the Turin plant . . . At Togliattigrad . . . they have adopted not only Western machines but also Western systems of organizations. To have a minimum of equilibrium, however, such a system presupposes at the very least the existence of a strong trade union force. But at the present moment such a force does not exist, either in the Soviet Union or in the other countries of Eastern Europe."

When asked what disturbed him most about Togliattigrad, the C.P. labour leader replied that it was hearing the Turin boss say that "the trade union demands are unjustified, since even the Soviet leaders in Togliattigrad pay no attention to them."[34]

New Management Techniques and Not So New Ones

If the Soviet bureaucracy is relying more heavily on the West for technology, it has also been very busy studying Western management techniques, capitalist labour psychology and industrial sociology — all in an effort to learn the capitalist secret of labour management. *Izvestia* (11.10.1970) writes: "Modern methods of management forged in the business world, bring new stimulants to the human factor". *Literaturnaya Gazetta* (10.1.1968) writes: "The science of management is on the order of the day ... The science of management of men in a socialist society and the science of of managing men in a capitalist society are two opposing phenomena in their ends and substance. But it would be totally unreasonable to ignore the experience of capitalism in this sphere, it would be irrational from the economic point of view not to utilize this experience." *Izvestia* (17.10.1970) carries this a little further: "In the capitalist countries, the effectiveness of management increase much quicker than in socialist countries due to the hypertrophy of commercial services, and enormous expenses consecrated to advertising and competition. However, statistical evidence expresses a tendency common to all industrial countries.

Literaturnaya Gazetta (24.5.1972) published a long article about a pilot experiment designed to improve "the relations between the leaders and their subordinates" and create "a smoother psychological climate". The article stressed the importance of "prevention of conflicts" by a management staff trained in psychology. The experiment elicited great interest from other factory managers. To satiate this interest, the factory manager where the experiment was carried out codified in shortened form the principle findings. His second recommendation was: "One has to know how to address subordinates. A silent worker always represents an enigma and is a difficult subject for management. But it isn't any less important to stop at times a subordinate who talks more than he should."

If the psycho-sociological insights of 'advanced management techniques' do not help in controlling the 'human fact', there is an alternative. *Izvestia* (9.7.72) points out in a long article signed jointly by the manager and the Party Committee Chairman of the Moscow Brake Factory that: "functionaries of the police visit the factory systematically. They conduct inquiries on violations of the legal order in our factory". They report further: "The staff of the Sverdlovsk district prosecutor have verified the state of labour discipline in our factory. They presented the management with a report . . . and we took appropriate steps." *Pravda* (29.7.1972) writes of a similar not-so-modern management technique: "The staff of the Ministry of the Interior and the courts visit quite frequently the labour collective. Functionaries of the police take a very severe position towards those who violate the legal order."

A more novel approach to solving 'conflict situations', one applied to political oppositionists and now proposed for factories, was outlined in *Pravda* (28.8.1971). The writer asks the question: "Why not include a psychologist in the management in large factories. Working hand in hand with social organizations, this will contribute greatly towards the prevention of various conflicts." Carrying this line a little further was a *Literaturnaya Gazetta* article (26.7.1972). The journalist reports: "A psychiatrist told me: give me the possibility of examining all the personnel of any enterprise and I will always discover people who need my care. And in effect, why should it be excluded that certain members of each enterprise shouldn't have the perfectly justifiable advantage of consultations when they are blamed for something, when their premiums are lowered, or something similar?"

The frantic search for new technique is not a solution to the fundamental contradiction of Soviet society — that existing between the bureaucracy and the working class. The contradiction arose because the bureaucracy substituted its dictatorship for the dictatorship of the proletariat. This contradiction can only be resolved by the seizure of power by the working class, organized democratically through Soviets. Whether or not the re-entry of the working class into the political arena in the very near future is on the agenda is difficult to predict. Certainly, the transformation of the country's social structure, the strengthening of the social weight of the proletariat, has created conditions which place the working class in a much stronger position to carry out this task than at any other period in the history of the Soviet Union. The central core of the proletariat, the machine building and metal workers, increased from 8,842,737 in 1959 to 15,008,515 in 1970; chemical workers from 1,290,000 in 1959 to 2,451,000 in 1970, etc. In the meantime, the agricultural labour force declined from 33,930,000 in 1959 to 22,724,000 in 1970. Furthermore, the transformation of the countryside, where one no longer has a peasantry but an agricultural proletariat, has given the urban proletariat powerful allies in the countryside.[35]

The educational and cultural level of the Soviet workers has increased and with this have come new expectations. But perhaps the most important factor is that, with the end of primitive accumulation and with the dramatic decline in social mobility over the past two decades, there has arisen for the first time in the Soviet Union a large *hereditary* proletariat. A hereditary proletariat raises the cultural level of the working class and the consciousness of itself as a social force. It is this proletariat which will lead the working class into the political arena — this time with redoubled force.

NOTES

Great Britain

The Fateful Meridian

[1]A. Gramsci, *Note sul Machiavelli,* pp. 22-23.

[2]Karl Marx, *Letter to the Labour Parliament* (1854).

[3]Marx's very logically minded view of class relations in Britain is like his view of the Constitution, which in 1855 he thought was on its last legs. Soon, he wrote, "the mask will be torn off which has hitherto hid the real political features of Great Britain . . . England will at last be compelled to share in the general social evolutions of European society." It was Marx's misfortune to be living in the least revolutionary society of the time, and he had little interest in British illogic or the static formulae of British conservatism. This is perhaps why he could write so much more profoundly about France, even at a distance, than about the Britain round about him. It was the economic rationality of Britain which appealed to him, the underlying socio-economic revolution wrought by capital; not the conservative sheath in which this process had been compressed. His relative indifference to the latter (understandable in an intelligence which sought above all for laws of revolutionary motion) has had a general, little-explored effect of the whole development of Marxist thought, and was to prove particularly unfortunate in Britain itself. There, Marxist political movements obviously could not afford the same indifference; but there was little they could turn to in Marx's own writings to help them develop a concrete critique.

[4]C. B. Macpherson, "Edmund Burke," *Transactions of the Royal Society of Canada,* 3rd series (sect. 2), 1959, vol. LIII, pp. 19-26.

[5]Edmund Burke, *Reflections on the French Revolution* (Worlds Classics), p. 271.

[6]Burke, *ibid.,* pp. 94-95 and p. 83.

[7]John Rae, *Life of Adam Smith* (1895), pp. 387-88.

[8]G. K. Lewis, "The Metaphysics of Conservatism," *Western Political Quarterly,* vol. VI (1953), pp. 730-31.

[9]S. T. Coleridge, quoted in *The Political Thought of Samuel Taylor Coleridge,* ed. R. J. White, p. 96.

[10]N. J. Annan, "The Intellectual Aristocracy of the 19th Century," in *Studies in Social History,* ed. J. H. Plumb (1955), p. 244.

[11]*Ibid.,* p. 243. Hence the extraordinary importance of education in British society, and the distinctive form which educational ideals assumed there (as a formation of "character," of total personality, rather than of the intellect). Apart from religion, no other subject seemed more important to the Victorians. Hence, too, the quite exceptional role of childhood generally, as exemplified by the prominence of the child in 19th century literature, and the profusion and popularity of children's literature in Britain and, even more significant, of the "child's book" which is actually read by adults, and remains a living part of adult culture).

[12]N. J. Annan, *ibid.,* pp. 285-86.

[13]*George Eliot's Life,* ed. J. W. Cross (1885), vol. I, p. 432.

[14]Thus, Gramsci too was perfectly aware of the importance of "direct fellow-feeling," but never thought it made doctrines less important. In 1922 he wrote to his wife: "How many times have I wondered if it is really possible to forge links with a mass of people when one has never had strong feelings for anyone . . . to love a collectivity

when one has not been deeply loved oneself, by individual human creatures?" (*The Life of Antonio Gramsci, Giuseppe Fiori*, p. 157).

[15]B. Willey, *Nineteenth Century Studies*, p. 205.

[16]E. Shils, "The Intellectuals of Great Britain," *Encounter*, April 1955.

[17]William Morris, "How I became a Socialist" (1894), quoted in Edward Thompson, *William Morris* (1955), p. 63.

[18]B. E. Lippincott, *Victorian Critics of Democracy* (1938), p. 47.

[19]J. A. Hobson, *John Ruskin, Social Reformer* (1898), p. 193.

[20]J. A. Hobson, *ibid.*, p. 185.

[21]Walter Bagehot, *The English Constitution* (1964 ed.), pp. 248-49,

[22]Walter Bagehot, *ibid.*, pp. 85-86.

[23]W. L. Burn, *The Age of Equipoise* (1964), p. 58.

[24]E. Bulwer-Lytton, *England and the English* (1833), p. 32.

[25]Robert Owen, "Address of Mr Owen to the Agriculturists, Mechanics and Manufacturers, both Masters and Operatives, of Great Britain and Ireland," in the *Cooperative Magazine*, 1827.

[26]Bronterre O'Brien, quoted in Edward Thompson, *The Making of the English Working Class* (1963), p. 803.

[27]F. Engels, *Anti-Dühring* (1954 ed.), pp. 290-91.

[28]J.F.C. Harrison, *Robert Owen and the Owenites in Britain and America: the Quest for the New Moral World* (1969), p. 196.

[29]Sidney and Beatrice Webb, *History of Trade Unionism*, p. 148.

[30]F. Engels, *Socialism, Utopian and Scientific* (Marx and Engels, *Selected Works*, 1968 ed., pp. 430-31).

[31]Andre Breton, *Ode to Fourier* (1948), English translation by K. White, 1969.

[32]Marx, article from *Vorwärts* (1844), in Karl Marx: *Selected Writings in Sociology and Social Philosophy*, ed. Bottomore & Rubel.

[33]A. R. Schoyen, *The Chartist Challenge*, p. 96.

[34]Royden Harrison comments on this event: "The victory of 10th April was of a different order from that suggested by *The Times*. The Chartists had not 'raised the signal of revolution' nor had they 'made the challenge.' The Government had not foiled a bid for revolution, but had skilfully manoeuvred the Chartists into a position in which it could represent itself as having done so. The workmen's party had paid the penalty which any party is likely to pay if it organizes for peaceful purposes while talking academically about the right to make a revolution in the last resort. Instead of this being a threat which the Government anticipated with dread, the Government took the initiative and anticipated the threat. It used the threat to push its opponents into a false position from which they could extricate themselves only by acting up to the intentions ascribed to them, or by going through the humiliating experience of climbing down without ever having climbed up. This was a situation from which the leaders of the British working class proved unable to disengage themselves in 1848 or again in 1926." (*Before the Socialists: Studies in Labour and Politics 1861-1881*, p. 79). The technique was employed again, and again led by *The Times,* in the great student-led demonstration against the Vietnam War, in October 1968. Again, for weeks, beforehand London was depicted lying in ruins at the hands of a revolutionary mob; and again, when the gathering dispersed peaceably at Hyde Park, the tone of comment changed instantly to one of sneering contempt and smug derision at the "failure" of the march to destroy the British Constitution and burn down Whitehall.

[35]R. W. Procter, *The Barber's Shop,* quoted in W. L. Burn, *op. cit.*

[36]J. Gallagher and R. Robinson, "The Imperialism of Free Trade," in *Economic History Review,* 2nd series, vol. VI, No. I (1953).

[37]Gallagher and Robinson, *ibid.,* p. 11.

[38]Sir J. Seeley, *The Expansion of England* (1883), pp. 354 and 89.

[39]F. Engels, letter of August 11th, 1881.

[40]F. Engels, letter of September 12th, 1882.

[41]V. I. Lenin, *Imperialism, the Highest Stage of Capitalism*, sect. VIII.

[42]A. L. Morton and C. Tate, *The British Labour Movement*, p. 148.

[43]E. J. Hobsbawm, "The Labour Aristocracy in 19th Century Britain," in *Labouring Men.*

[44]A. C. Pigou, *Memorials of Alfred Marshall*, p. 105.

The Failure of the Socialist Promise

[1]R. Miliband and J. Saville, "Labour Policy and the Labour Left," in their jointly edited *The Socialist Register 1964* (New York, Monthly Review Press, 1964) pp. 152-3

[2]Barratt Brown, M. *From Labourism to Socialism* (Nottingham, Spokesman Books, 1972), pp. 59-60

[3]A. Rogow (and Shore, P.) *The Labour Government and British Industry* (Oxford, Basil Blackwell, 1955), p. 179

[4]*Ibid.*, p. 176.

[5]Raymond Williams, *The May Day Manifesto 1968* (Harmondsworth, Penguin, 1968) p. 124.

[6]R. Miliband, *The State in Capitalist Society* (London, Weidenfeld and Nicolson, 1972), p. 155.

[7]Williams, *May Day Manifesto 1968*, p. 120

[8]T. Nairn, "The Nature of the Labour Party," in P. Anderson (editor), *Towards Socialism* (London, Fontana, 1965), p. 196.

[9]Anderson, "Problems of Socialist Strategy," in his *Towards Socialism*, p. 237.

[10]The call for the "gamble" to be attempted is very persuasively argued in J. Goldthorpe *et al., The Affluent Worker in the Class Structure* (Cambridge University Press, 1969) pp. 192-5.

[11]Nairn, "The Nature of the Labour Party," p. 179

[12]R. Skidelsky, *Politicians and the Slump* (Harmondsworth, Penguin, 1970), p. 112.

[13]E. Dell, *Political Responsibility and Industry,* (London, Allen and Unwin, 1973) p. 137.

[14]M. Foot, *Aneurin Bevan, Volume I 1897-1945* (London, Four Square Illustrated, 1966), pp. 130-1

[15]A. Bevan, *In Place of Fear* (London, Heinemann, 1952), pp. 6-7.

[16]F. Brockway, *Inside the Left* (London, Allen and Unwin, 1942), pp. 201 and 222-3.

[17]Foot, *Aneurin Bevan, Volume I 1897-1945*, pp. 227-8.

[18]Anderson, "Problems of Socialist Strategy," p. 236.

[19]Above, p. 31.

[20]H. Wilson, *The Labour Government: a Personal Record* (London, Weidenfeld, and Nicolson and Michael Joseph, 1971), pp. 128-9.

[21]R. Prentice, "Lessons of the Labour Government: not socialist enough," *Political Quarterly*, vol. 41 (2) April-June 1970, p. 149.

[22]J. Saville, "Labourism and the Labour Government," in R. Miliband and J. Saville (editors), *The Socialist Register 1967* (London, Merlin Press, 1967), pp. 56-7.

France

Socialism in France?

[1] *Programme commun de gouvernement du parti communiste et du parti socialiste,* introduction by Georges Marchais (Paris: Editions Sociales, 1972), referred to hereafter as *PCG.*

[2] *PCG,* p. 90.

[3] *PCG,* p. 98.

[4] These last two points represent a major concession on the part of the Communist Party, which has been traditionally hostile to NATO and the Common Market. No doubt the general détente between the Soviet Union and the United States inspired this concession to a Western-oriented international strategy. The provision concerning NATO and the Warsaw Pact now fits in with Soviet intentions. Continued cooperation with the Common Market may seem incompatible with the pursuit of socialist policies in France, but I think it would be easy to exaggerate the problems. No provisions of the Treaty of Rome forbid extensive nationalizations and social measures in member countries. There has been some intermingling of capital in Europe, especially in the form of German investments in neighboring countries, but there does not seem to be any general trend toward massive concentration of international capital. In fact, as Serge Mallet pointed out some years ago, the fall of trade barriers may encourage aggressively nationalistic economic policies rather than the reverse. This has been especially true of France, which, under a socialist government, would hold no new terrors for its European partners in this respect. In short, the Common Market does not appear to be a latter-day Congress of Vienna, poised to suppress social progress throughout Europe. It is much too weak to be a major threat to leftward movement in the region at this time.

[5] *Le mouvement étudiant entre la lutte contre l'exploitation du prolétariat et la critique de la société de consommation.* The American reader should understand that neither this text nor the preceding one constitute moralistic attacks on individuals for holding "middle class" jobs. The point is a political one: to understand why *in fact* during the May Events those who had such jobs were capable of criticizing the repressive content of their work and demanding its transformation, even in some cases abolition, in a socialist society.

[6] Rosa Luxemburg, "The Mass Strike, the Political Party and the Trade Unions," in *Rosa Luxemburg Speaks* (New York: Pathfinder Press, 1970), p. 185.

[7] *PCG,* p. 72.

[8] *PCG,* p. 56.

[9] NACLA, *New Chile* (Berkeley, 1972), p. 130.

[10] *PCG,* p. 173.

[11] *PCG,* pp. 114-15.

The May Events

[1] Regis Debray, *Revolution in the Revolution* (New York: Monthly Review, 1967), p. 98.

The State in Capitalist Society

[1] G. Lefranc, *Histoire du Front Populaire,* 1965, p. 131.

[2] *Ibid.,* p. 146.

[3] For which see *ibid.,* part 3.

[4]J. Baumier, *Les Grandes Affaires Francaises,* 1967, p. 35.

[5]The point is also relevant to the foreign policy of the government, and notably to its attitude to the Spanish Civil War. It supplied some military equipment and aircraft to the Republicans, but resisted all demands for greater help to them. This failed to appease the Right, and further helped to divide and demoralise the Left.

[6]D. M. Pickles, *The French Political Scene,* 1938, p. 130.

[7]Lefranc, *Histoire du Front Populaire,* p. 141. For a perceptive discussion of this distinction in Léon Blum's thought, see C. Audry, *Leon Blum ou la Politique du Fuste,* 1955.

[8]See, e.g., P.M. de la Gorce, *De Gaulle entre deux Mondes,* 1964, pp. 339ff.; for the political collapse of the "classical Right" after Liberation, see, e.g., Rene Remond, *La Droite en France,* 1963, pp. 243ff.

[9]See., e.g., Charles de Gaulle, *Memoires de Guerre, vol 2, L'Unite, 1942-1944,* 1956.

[10]Quoted in B. D. Graham, *The French Socialists and Tri-partisme 1944-1947,* 1965, p. 48.

[11]De Gaulle, *Memoires de Guerre,* vol 3, pp. 274ff.

[12]*Ibid.,* p. 276.

The Movement for Self-Management in France

[1]This discussion derives from a larger work, "Revolutionary Trade Unionism in France: Goals and Constraints in the French Democratic Confederation of Labor (CFDT) in Grenoble" (unpublished Ph.D. dissertation, The University of Michigan, 1975). I would like to thank Valerie Bunce and Jack Thomas for helpful comments on an earlier draft of this discussion. As well, I express gratitude to Roy Pierce, Samuel H. Barnes, Samuel J. Eldersveld, Joel Samoff, and Charles Tilly, who guided me through the project itself.

[2]There are two other French trade unions of note: (1) the General Confederation of Labor (CGT), which claims 2 million members and is closely identified with the Communist Party; and (2) Workers' Force (FO), a "socialist" union which split off from the CGT in 1948 in opposition to the latter's Communist leanings; FO claims about 500,000 members. It should be noted that these membership figures are only a very rough approximation. Union membership in France, compared with the United States, is haphazard; the closed shop is proscribed by law, and union "members" come and go at will.

[3]The Unified Socialist Party (PSU) should also be mentioned as part of the *autogestion* movement; however, recent defections of its top leadership to the Socialist Party have weakened its effectiveness. The PSU has normally gained about 3 percent of the vote in National Assembly elections.

[4]Gilles Martinet, in *Le Nouvel Observateur* (June 9, 1973), pp. 28-29.

[5]The CFDT had its origins in the Catholic labor movement, having been known officially from its founding in 1919 until 1964 as the French Confederation of Christian Workers (CFTC). Until 1945 it generally followed the conservative social doctrine of the Church — recruiting only Christian workers, seeking collaboration with management, and so on. After World War II, however, a young generation of Catholic militants who had fought alongside Communist Party and CGT members in the Resistance began to challenge the conservative leadership of the CFTC. The main grievance of this insurgent group (called the "minority" within the union) was that the union's leadership had served largely the interests of Catholic, white-collar workers (by far the largest group within the CFTC), while neglecting the much larger number of blue-collar industrial workers. By 1961 the "minority" had gained a majority of voting members and elected one of its leaders General Secretary of the CFTC. Three years later, union members voted to drop the Christian reference in the union's name, and the new CFDT began seeking an ideology and strategy consonant with its new identity as a secular, anti-capitalist trade union.

For a full account of the rise of this "minority" within the CFTC, see Gérard Adam, *La CFTC, 1940-1958* (Paris: Armand Colin, 1964).

⁶For a full discussion of setting and research methods I employed, see Smith, *op. cit.*, pp. 10-19.

⁷For a good description of May 1968, see David Goldey, "A Precarious Regime: The Events of May 1968," in Philip M. Williams, *French Politicians and Elections, 1951-1969* (Cambridge: Cambridge University Press, 1970), pp. 226-260.

⁸Quoted in Albert Detraz, *et. al.* (eds.), *La CFDT et l'autogestion* (Paris: Editions du CERF, 1973), pp. 76-77.

⁹Pierre Dubois, *et al., Grèves revendicatives ou greves politiques?* (Paris: Editions Anthropos, 1971), pp.93-159.

¹⁰The following discussion of the CFDT's program represents my distillation of a number of union position statements as well as summaries by other observers. See, for example, Albert Detraz, *et al.* (eds.), *op. cit.*; "Planification démocratique et autogestion," special issue of *Syndicalisme Magazine* (official CFDT publication), No. 1279a (February, 1970); *La CFDT* (Paris: Editions du Seuil, 1971); Everett M. Kassalow, "The Transformation of Christian Trade Unionism in France," *Journal of Economic Issues,* Vol. VIII, No. 1 March, 1974), pp. 1-39.

¹¹Political action, the CFDT recognizes, is also important in bringing about change, and the union seeks to support mobilization campaigns, as well as certain electoral campaigns, by left political parties. However, the CFDT refuses to align itself with any particular party or group. The CFDT's stance with regard to "control" reforms and the union's political role has often come under sharp attack from the CGT. The CGT holds that priority in its struggle must be given to political conquest by a government of the Left; the union's responsibility is to defend workers' immediate interests in the workplace, wages and working conditions for example. As long as capitalist forces hold political power, the CGT claims, proposals for increased worker control over production represent reformism of the worst kind, as workers would assume not only some measure of control over production, but also responsibility for maintaining the capitalist order.

¹²Albert Detraz, *et al., op. cit.*, p. 37.

¹³See Daniel Mothé, "Où va la CFDT?," *Esprit,* Vol. 39, No. 5 (May, 1971), pp. 1046-1048; Jean-Marie Dupont, "La CFDT après sa révolution culturelle," *Le Monde* (May 29, 1973), p. 20.

¹⁴Michel Crozier, "La participation des travailleurs à la gestion des entreprises," *Preuves,* No. 93 (November, 1959), p. 54.

¹⁵See, for example, Serge Mallet, "L'après-mai: grèves pour le controle ouvrier," *Sociologie du travail,* Vol. VII, No. 3 (July-September, 1970), pp. 309-327.

¹⁶Jacques Capdevielle and Jean-Pierre Oppenheim, "Les luttes sociales en Europe: les conditions et les perspectives," *La Nef,* No. 51 (April-June, 1973), pp. 7-32.

¹⁷Michelle Durand and Yvette Harff, "Panorama statistique des greves," *Sociologie du travail,* Vol. XV, No. 4 (October-December, 1973), pp. 356-375.

¹⁸Daniel Mothe, *op. cit.*, p. 1044.

¹⁹For a discussion of differences between the "spontaneity" and "vanguard" models, see Paul M. Sweezy, "The Nature of Soviet Society," *Monthly Review,* Vol. 26, No. 6 (November, 1974), pp. 1-16.

²⁰Sabine Erbès-Seguin, in Pierre Dubois, *et al., op. cit.*, p. 306.

²¹*Liaison* (bulletin of CFDT departmental union of Isere), No. 8 (November, 1970), p. 2.

²²"French Labor Relations: A Functional Analysis," *Yale Law Journal,* Vol. 82, No. 4 (March, 1973), p. 810.

²³Gérard Adam, *et al., La negociation collective en France* (Paris: Editions

Ouvrieres, 1972).

[24]Guy Caire, *Les syndicats ouvriers* (Paris: Presses Universitaires de France, 1971), p. 568.

[25]As mentioned, the CFDT organizes nationally only about 5 percent of the work force; in individual plants it is frequently outnumbered more than two to one by the CGT.

[26]James O'Connor, *The Fiscal Crisis of the State* (New York: St. Martin's Press, 1973), pp. 40-63; Stanley Aronowitz, "Trade Unionism and Workers' Control," in Gerry Hunius, *et al.* (eds.), *Workers Control* (New York: Vintage Books, 1973), pp. 62-106.

[27]*New York Times* (March 25, 1975), p. 14.

[28]Obviously a principal constraint "outside the plant" to the achieving of self-management would be the implacable resistance to such a system on the part of the state, employers, and, one may assume, a lot of citizens without direct interests at stake but fearful of drastic social change. Without in any way assuming this problem away, I shall turn my focus instead on the internal organizational problem for the CFDT of mobilizing and coordinating its own resources in seeking self-management.

[29]See Smith, *op. cit.*, pp. 104-153.

[30]Peirre Dubois, *et al., op. cit.;* David Jenkins, *Job Power* (Baltimore: Penguin Books, 1973), pp. 134-154; Ronald Inglehart, "The Silent Revolution in Europe: Intergenerational Change in Post-Industrial Society," *American Political Science Review,* Vol. LXV, No. 4 (December, 1971), pp. 991-1017.

Federal Republic of Germany

Twenty-Five Years of the Federal Republic

[1]cf. Hartwich, *Sozialstaatspostulat und gesellschaftlicher status quo* (Cologne and Opladen, 1970), pp. 64 ff. Contains further references.

[2]cf. Huster et al., *Determinanten der westdeutschen Restauration 1945-1949* (Frankfurt, 1972), pp. 44 ff.

[3]cf. Grosser, *Deutschlandbilanz: Geschichte Deutschlands seit 1945,* 4th ed. (Munich, 1972), pp. 100 ff.

[4]For the effect of economic interests on American policies in Europe after 1945 see: Joyce and Gabriel Kolko, *The Limits of Power: The World and the United States Foreign Policy, 1945-1954* (New York, 1972); David Horowitz, ed., *Big Business und Kalter Krieg* (Frankfurt, 1971); Ernest Mandel, *Die EWG und die Konkurrenz Europa — Amerika,* 6th ed. (Frankfurt, 1972), esp. pp. 6-33.

[5]cf. Huster, pp. 42 ff.

[6]For the structure of American policies in Europe after 1945 see: David Horowitz, *Kalter Krieg, Hintergründe der US-Aubenpolitik von Jalta bis Vietnam,* 2 vols.

(Berlin, 1969); William Appleman Williams, *Die Tragödie der amerikanischen Diplomatie* (Frankfurt, 1973); Czempiel, *Das amerikanische Sicherheitssystem 1945-1949: Studie zur Außenpolitik der bürgerlichen Gesellschaft* (Berlin, 1966).

[7]For the structure of American policies in Germany after 1945 see: Hartwich, esp. pp. 61-117; Huster, esp. pp. 9-68; Hans Schwarz, *Vom Reich der Bundesrepublik: Deutschland im Widerstreit der außenpolitischen Konzeptionen in den Jahren der Besatzungsherrschaft 1945-1949* (Neuwied and Berlin, 1966); Gibmel, *Amerikanische Besatzungspolitik in Deutschland 1945-1949* (Frankfurt, 1971).

[8]cf. Huster, pp. 47 ff.; Harwich, pp. 66 ff.

[9]cf. Huster, pp. 72 ff.

[10]cf. Huster, p. 41

[11]cf. Schwarz, p. 81; Huster, pp. 59 ff.

[12]cf. Wolfgang Abendroth, "Bilanz der sozialistischen Idee in der Bundesrepublik Deutschland," *Antagonistische Gesellschaft und politische Demokratie,* 2nd ed. (Neuwied and Berlin, 1972), pp. 429 ff.

[13]Abendroth, p. 449.

[14]Abendroth, p. 438.

[15]cf. Abendroth, pp. 436-444.

[16]Wiltraut Rupp-von Brünneck, "Einführung in die Verfassung des Landes Hessen und in das Grundgesetz," *Verfassung des Landes Hessen und Grundgesetz für die Bundesrepublik Deutschland,* 27th ed. (Bad Homburg, 1973), p. 22.

[17]Eberhard Schmidt, *Die verhinderte Neuordnung 1945-1952* (Frankfurt, 1970), pp. 150 ff.; Ute Schmid and Fichter, *Der erzwungene Kapitalismus* (Berlin, 1971), esp. pp. 23-30.

[18]cf. Huster, pp. 214 ff.

[19]Printed in Huster, pp. 424 ff.

[20]cf. Huster, p. 220.

[21]Printed in Huster, pp. 429 ff.

[22]For the policies of the SPD in the postwar period see Huster, pp. 120 ff.

[23]Kurt Schumacher, "Aufgaben und Ziele der deutschen Sozialdemokratie," a lecture at the SPD party conference in Hannover in May 1946, printed in Huster, p. 369.

[24]Quoted by Huster, p. 132.

[25]cf. Kurt Schumacher, pp. 369, 370.

[26]Hartwich, pp. 57 ff.

[27]cf. Huster, pp. 154 ff.

[28]cf. Huster, pp. 160, 161: Hartwich, pp. 92 ff.

[29]cf. Soergel, Konsensus und Interessen: eine Studie zur Entstehung des Grundgesetzes für die Bundesrepublik Deutschland (Stuttgart, 1969), pp. 77 ff.; Huster, pp. 168 ff.

[30]Printed by Huster, pp. 388 ff.

[31]cf. Eberhard Schmidt, pp. 173 ff.

[32]cf. Huster, pp. 175 ff.

[33]See the proclamation of the Central Committee of the KPD of June 11, 1945, printed by Huster, pp. 356 ff.

[34]cf. Schmidt and Fichter, pp. 40 ff.

[35]cf. Abendroth, pp. 450 ff.

[36]cf. Hartwich, pp. 61-117.

[37]For the putting into law of the program of "social free enterprise" see Hartwich, pp. 119 ff.

[38]For the concept see Janossy, *Das Ende der Wirtschaftswunder: Erscheinung und Wesen der wirtschaftlichen Entwicklung* (Frankfurt, n.d.); For a concretization of

Janossy's initial treatment cf. H. M. Hutter and G. Nahr, *Aktuelle Grenzen kapitalistischer Entwicklung in der BRD: Zum Problem von Rekonstruktionsperiode und Wachstumstrategie* (Starnberg, 1971).

[39]cf. *Statistisches Jahrbuch für die Bundesrepublik Deutschland 1953* (Stuttgart und Cologne, n.d.), pp. 548, 549.

[40]cf. *Statistisches Jahrbuch 1953*, p. 549.

[41]cf. *Statistisches Jahrbuch 1953*, p. 551.

[42]For an analysis of the background of the "economic miracle" see: Henry C. Wallich, *Triebkräfte des deutschen Wiederaufstiegs* (Frankfurt, 1955); Theodor Prager, *Wirtschaftswunder oder keines?* (Vienna, 1963); Kurt Pritzkoleit, *Gott erhält die Mächtigen: Rück-und Rundblick auf den deutschen Wohlstand* (Düsseldorf, 1963); Grosser, pp. 264-319.

[43]For the wording of the Soviet note of March 10, 1952 with the draft of the peace treaty see H. von Siegler, *Dokumentation zur Deutschlandfrage*, III (Bonn, 1961), pp. 138 ff.

[44]For the notes of the three powers in response to the Soviet Union on March 23, 1952 see H. von Siegler, pp. 140 ff.

[45]cf. Paul Noack, *Deutsche Aubenpolitik seit 1945* (Stuttgart, 1972), p. 57 ff.

[46]This is the subtitle of the collection by Gustav Heinemann, *Verfehlte Deutschlandpolitik* (Frankfurt, 1966).

[47]cf. Fritz Krause, *Antimilitaristische Opposition in der BRD 1949-1955* (Frankfurt, 1971).

[48]See the speech by Herbert Wehners of June 30, 1960, "Verhandlungen des Deutschen Bundestages, 3. Wahlperiode," pp. 7052 ff.

[49]cf. Hans Karl Rupp, *Auberparlamentarische Opposition in der Ära Adenauer: Der Kampf gegen die Atombewaffnung in den fünfziger ahren* (Cologne, 1970).

[50]Kurt Pritzkoleit, *Das kommandierte Wunder* (Vienna, 1959), p. 775.

[51]cf. Grosser, *Deutschlandbilanz*, pp. 162-164.

[52]On the "Spiegel affair" see Jürgen Seifert and Alfred Grosser, *Die Spiegel-Affare*, 2 vols. (Olten, 1966).

[53]cf. Leibfried, *Die angepabte Universität* (Frankfurt, 1968), pp. 7 ff; Joachim Hirsch, *Wissenschaftlich-technischer Fortschritt und politisches System* (Frankfurt, 1970); Altvater and Huisken, *Materialien zur politischen Ökonomie des Ausbildungssektors* (Erlangen, 1971).

[54]cf. Ernest Mandel, *Die Deutsche Wirtschaftskrise: Lehren der Rezession 1966/1967*, 3rd ed. (Frankfurt, 1969); Huffschmidt, *Die Politik des Kapitals* (Frankfurt, 1969).

Workers and Trade Unions in Post-War Germany

[1]See A. Pietre, *L'économie allemande contemporaine, 1945-1952,* Paris (1952),p. 65.

[2]Michael Balfour, *Viermachte Kontrolle in Deutschland,* Dusseldorf (1959),p. 23.

[3]L.J. Edinger, *Post-totalitarian leadership: Elites in the German Federal Republic,* in: The American Political Science Review, LIV, (1960).

[4]J. M. Vincent, *West Germany — The Reactionary Democracy,* in: The Socialist Register, ed. by R. Miliband and J. Saville, London (1964) pp. 68-81, here p. 69.

[5]There are no available figures for the preceding period, however we can safely say that they were still lower. In 1949, the index of real wages had risen to 87.5% (1938 = 100). See A. Pietre, *op. cit.,* p. 615.

[6]United Nations, Dept. of Economic Affairs, *Economic Survey of Europe since the War* (U.N. Economic Commission for Europe, Research and Planning Division) Geneva (1953),p. 73.

[7]Pietre holds that the figure two million for prisoners of war is too low, *op. cit.*, pp. 57-58. The number of disabled, of which 75% suffering disability of 30% or more their 23-25.

[8]See *Die Eingliederung der Flüchtlinge in die deutsche Gemeinschaft*, Report of the Federal Ministry on the refugees, presented to the Federal Chancellor, Bonn, 1951, pp. 23-25.

[9]D. Rodnick, *Post-War Germans*, New Haven (1948), p. 4.

[10]H. Schelsky, *Wandlungen der deutschen Familie in der Gegenwart, Stuttgart* (1954), pp. 136-7, writes: "The materialistic and self-centered attitude noted in the past and so complained of today, toward public affairs and the State, is probably a consequence of the disappearance of the tendency to identify with a social or State 'whole', with the need for order and life of a collectivity."

[11]In some cases the Western occupation powers also put down the trade union demands for *Mitbestimmung* and socialization with the threat of cutting off food supplies. In this regard, see also the attitude of the trade unions on the Marshall Plan, *Die Gewerkschaftsbewegung in der britischen Besatzungszone, op. cit.*, p. 137 ff.

[12]V. Agartz, *Wirtschafts und Steuerpolitik, op. cit.*, p. 8.

[13]This fatal attitude manifested itself most clearly in the position taken by the unions on the dismanteling of factories by the Allies. While on the one hand they pointed out the "tense situation" and the "serious agitation of the population," on the other, they rejected all recourse to an active struggle. "In no case, can the unions carry out an active struggle against the dismantling of the factories. The trade unions cannot take on semi-military duties. Only the insane can suggest such a thing." *Die Gewerschaftsbewegung in der britischen Besatzungzone, op. cit.*, p. 154.

[14]See Daniel Lerner, *Sykewar*, New York (1949), pp. 114-115.

[15]See these indications in Balfour, *op. cit.*, p. 91.

[16]*Gruppenexperiment, ein Studienbericht;* elaborated by F. Pollock Frankfurt/M (1955), p. 337. See also *Institut für Sozialforschung: zum politischen Bewusstsein ehemaliger Kriegsgefangener, Forschungsbericht*, Frankfurt/M, 1957.

[17]*Gruppenexperiment, op. cit.*, p. 482.

[18]Institut fur Demoskopie. *Das Dritte Reich. Eine Studie uber Nachwirkungen des Faschismus*, Allensbach (1949), p. 11.

[19]Quoted from W. Hennis, *Die Entnazifizierung in der deutschen Nachkriegspolitik*, Frankfurt/M, 1954, p. 184.

[20]A. Grosser, *L'Allemagne de l'Occident, 1945-1952*, Paris (1953), p. 109.

[21]See O. Stammer, "Wider den Sozialen Defaitismus," in *Gewerkschaftliche Monatschefte*, I, 1950, p. 492-498, and K.P. Schulz, *Die Wurzeln des sozialen defaitismus*, in *ibidem*, II, 1951, p. 2-7.

[22]See W. Abendroth, in *Neokapitalismus, Rustungswirtschaft, Westeuropaeische Arbeiterbewegung*, Frankfurt/M (1966), p. 110.

[23]Quoted from M. Balfour, *op. cit.*, p. 89.

[24]*Ibid.*, p. 224.

[25]See T. Pirker, *Blinde Macht*, Vol. I, p. 55.

[26]H. W. Richter, "Der Sieg des Opportunismus" in *Der Ruf*, ed. H. Schwab-Felisch, Munich, 1962, p. 295.

[27]Rolf Badstubner, *Restauration in Westdeutschland, 1945-1949*, Berlin (1965), p. 134.

[28]Second Regular Federal Congress of the DGB, Berlin 1952, Acts, p. 162.

Decentralisation of Power in the Federal Republic of Germany

[1]From: *Imperialismus der BRD*, Frankfurt 1971, p. 145. Cf. Jaeggi (1973), p. 71.

[2]The figures relating to the legal control of capital give, of course, only a vague

impression of the economic power of the large companies. Small companies which are legally independent will in fact often depend totally on the favour of the big companies for their continued existence. This is probably true, for example, of many of the 30,000 firms which supply goods to Siemens, or the 23,000 suppliers of Krupp, or 17,000 suppliers of Daimler-Benz. Cf. Schafer/Nedelmann (1969), vol. 1, p. 54.

[3]Cf. Huffschmid (1972), p. 144.

[4]*Ibid.*, p. 146ff.

[5]Cf. Francis-Poncet (1970), p. 177; Stamokap (1973), p. 58; *Jahresgutachten* 1971, ch. IV.

[6]As the banker, Hermann Josef Abs, the man who, above all others, personifies the post-war concentration of economic power in the hands of the few, put it (on a different occasion): 'it will be impossible in the long run to maintain the private economic system of the Federal Republic close to the Iron Curtain, unless we succeed in binding a few million West Germans, as shareholders, more closely to this system'; *Der Spiegel*, 18-2-1959, quoted by Müller in Schäfer/Nedelmann (1969), vol. 1, p. 35.

[7]The largest general meeting of shareholders ever held in Europe. Cf. Francois-Poncet (1970), p. 150.

[8]Siebke J., *Die Vermögensbildung der privaten Haushalte in der Bundesrepublik Deutschland*. Cited in Jaeggi (1973), p. 69.

[9]There has also been a movement for codetermination, or "participation" in other spheres, particularly in the universities, where the question is one of the controversial points in the proposed *Hochschulrahmengesetz*. But our main concern here is with economic power.

[10]The definition of this term is to be that given in the *Betriebsverfassungsgesetz* of 1972 (*Bundesgesetzblatt* 1972, *Teil* 1, pp. 13 ff.); according to this law (§5(3)) '*leitende Angestellte* are those who (1) 'have the right to employ or dismiss workers working in the firm or department of the firm, or (2) have plenipotentiary powers or power of attorney, or (3) are themselves responsible for duties, which, because of their importance for the running and development of the firm are regularly entrusted to them on the basis of their special experience and knowledge.'

[11]An agreement between the coalition partners on both codetermination and capital formation policy was announced in January, 1974 (published in "Presse-und Informationsamt der Bundesregierung," *Bulletin*, 30 January 1974). In both areas, but especially in the capital formation plan, the SPD have made significant concessions to the FDP. In the field of capital formation, the most important concession made by the SPD is that the funds raised will not be administered centrally. Instead, they will be administered by a number of companies (*Vermögensanlagegesellschaften*) which will be specially created by public and private credit institutes in the form of private companies (*Gesellschaften mit beschränkter Haftung*). Each certificate holder will have the right to choose which of these companies is to administer his share of the fund: thus the companies will have to compete with one another for funds. The resulting need to invest profitably will presumably be of decisive importance in the administration of the fund. Of the investment policy of these companies, it is said only that it should not lead to distortions of competition on the capital market. Their cash is to be invested in shares and, beyond that, they may finance public or private investments by means of fixed-interest bonds. Two-thirds of the seats of the supervisory boards of these companies are to be given to representatives elected indirectly by the certificate holders. It should be clear from the analysis in the text that the abandonment of the idea of a central fund deprives the proposed legislation of much of its interest.

The concessions made by the SPD on codetermination are not as far-reaching. It is proposed that the new law would apply to all companies with more than 2000 employees (the *Montanmitbestimmungsgesetz* would continue to the coal and steel industry, and the *Betriebsverfassungsgesetz* to smaller firms). If the proposal is accepted, the Supervisory Board of these companies will have twenty members, ten representatives of the shareholders and ten representatives of the employees. Of the ten employees representatives, seven will be employees of the company and three representatives of the trade unions. Of the seven — and this is the most important concession to the FDP — at least one must be a salaried employee (*Angestellter*) and one a member of the senior salaried staff (*leitender Angestellter*). All the employees' representatives will be elected by a committee of electors, themselves elected separately by the workers, the salaried and the senior salaried staff. There will be no "neutral member" in the Supervisory Board. In the event of an equal division of votes, the chairman could be given the casting vote if the majority of both sides agree. Unless otherwise agreed by two-thirds of the members, the Chairmanship of the Board will alternate between the two groups. There is no provision that any member of the Management should be appointed only with the agreement of the employees' representatives, i.e. there is no equivalent of the *Arbeitsdirektor* under the MBG. If one argues, as the SPD have in the past argued, that members of the senior salaried staff (*Leitende Angestellte*) would identify with the interests of the shareholders, then it would seem that, notwithstanding the complex election procedures, the SPD have in fact abandoned the principle of "parity," which was intended to be the basis of the whole reform. The argument in this essay, however, suggests that this will make little difference in practice.

The coalition compromise has, however, been strongly criticised by both parliamentary parties, and especially by members of the SPD. It thus remains uncertain whether it will form the basis of eventual legislation.

[12]Deppe *et al.* (1972), p. 147.

[13]*Ibid.*, p. 147.

[14]Cf. Deppe (1972), ch. IV.

[15]Probably the effect of such a fund would not be very different from the effect which IRI has on the Italian economy.

[16]Mandel (1971), p. 163.

[17]Some of which we have already mentioned above.

Immigrant Workers and Trade Unions in the Federal Republic of Germany

[1]For a fuller treatment of these problems see: Stephen Castles and Godula Kosack, "The Function of Labor Immigration in Western European Capitalism." *New Left Review* (73, July 1972).

[2]Gienanth, "So schnell geht nicht," in *Der Arbeitgeber* (March 20, 1966).

[3]For further details see: Stephen Castles and Godula Kosack, *Immigrant Workers and Class Structure In Western Europe* (London, 1973), pp. 167 ff and 430 ff.

[4]The example of the Swiss unions shows what happens when unions all too obviously collaborate with the bosses and betray the interests of the workers. There have been hardly any official strikes in Switzerland since 1937, when the unions made an "industrial peace" agreement with the bosses. The result is that the unions are rapidly losing membership. In particular the unions, due to their nationalistic policies, have been unable to organize most immigrant workers. Today these unions are being increasingly ignored, even by the bosses.

[5]See Walther Muller-Jentsch, "Entwicklungen und Widerspruche in der westdeutschen Gewerkschaftsbewegung," in *Gewerkschaften und Klassenkampf, Kritisches Jahrbuch '73* (Frankfurt, 1973), p. 150 ff.

[6]See the D.G.B. publication: "Die deutschen Gewerkschaften und die auslandischen Arbeitnehmer" (Frankfurt, November 21, 1971), pp. 9-10.

[7]*Ibid.*, p. 1

[8]Vostand der I. G. Metall, *Beratungsbericht zu den Fragen Gewerkschaft und Auslandische Arbeitnehmer* (Frankfurt, February 5, 1970), p. 13.

[9]Ernest Piehl, "Gewerkschaften und auslandische Arbeiter," in *Gewerkschaftsspiegel*, No. 1/1972, pp. 19 ff.

[10]I. G. Metall, *Schnellinformation Uber das Ergebnis der Vertrauensleutewahlen 1973.* Vertrauensleute are roughly comparable with shop stewards and are elected every three years for a whole industry at once.

[11]These figures indicate the degree of representation of immigrants, but do not mean that shop stewards are elected only by specific national groups. Stewards, like works councillors, are of course elected by the whole work force in a factory or department.

[12]Works councils can be elected in every West German enterprise with more than 10 employees. They are elected by all employees (not just union members) and have various social and legal functions as laid down in the Works Constitution Law of 1972.

[13]According to the size of the enterprise, a certain number of works council members are released from work (on full pay) to carry out their duties. Obviously, those released have far more opportunity of representing their colleagues than those who have to go on working.

[14]I.G. Metall *Ergebnisse der Betriebsratswahlen 1972,* p. 10 and p. 13.

[15]For a fuller discussion see: Castles and Kosack, *Immigrant Workers...*, pp. 152 ff.

[16]See I. G. Metall, *Die Auslanderwelle und die Gewerkschaften* (Frankfurt, 1966).

[17]See for instance: "Institut fur angewandte Sozialwissenschaft," *Deutsche und Gastarbeiter* (Bad Godesberg, 1966), DIVO Reprasentativerhebung February 1966, DIVO Pressendienst.

[18]F. Dobler, "Der Streik in der hessischen Gummiindustrie im November 1967 unter besonderer Berucksichtigung der 'Dunlop' Hanaux" (Hanau, 1968).

[19]See Castles and Kosack, *Immigrant Workers...,* p. 159.

[20]See *Klassenkampf* (Frankfurt, September 27, 1973); *Kommunistische Volkszeitung* (2, September 12, 1973); *Der Spiegel* (September 3, 1973).

[21]Institut fur angewandte Sozialwissenschaft, *Arbeiter — Vertrauensleute — Gewerkschaft,* (Bad Godesberg, 1964).

[22]Rainer Riehl, "Der Aufstand der Angelernten," *Klassenkampf* (October 28, 1973).

The Brandt Affair and the SPD: Depersonalizing History

[1]For a survey of this issue, see also Karl D. Bredthauer, "Aspekte des Regierungswechsels in Bonn," *Blätter für deutsche und internationale Politik* (June, 1974), 559-568.

[2]See Dirk Ipsen, "Reformgerede und harte Arbeit," and Michael Siebert, "Die Ideologie in der Krise" in *SPD und Staat* (Berlin, 1974).

[3]*DIW-Wochenberichte* 39:8 (1972), 68; 39:45 (1972), 389ff.; 40:21 (1973), 209-210; as cited in *SPD und Staat,* p. 110.

[4]*DIW-Wochenberichte* 40:24 (1973), 209-210.

[5]See *Jahresgutachten des Sachverstandigenrates,* 220 (1973); also, U. Rouge and G. Schmieg, *Restriktionen politischer Planung* (Frankfurt am Main, 1973), pp. 183-214.

[6]See *OECD at Work for Science and Education* (Paris, 1972), p. 35.

[7]Cited in *Frankfurter Rundschau* (June 20, 1974), 18; and (July 5, 1974), 19.

[8]A Blechschmidt, *Löhne, Preise und Gewinne 1967-73 Materialien zur Lohn Preis-Spirale* (Lampertheim, 1974), pp. 94 ff; also, *Materialien zur Lebens-und Arbeitssituation der Industriearbeiter in der BRD* (Frankfurt am Main, 1972).

[9]Prediction of the Federal Labor Institute as cited in *Frankfurter Rundschau* (August 10, 1974), 6; price index prepared by the German Federal Bureau of Statistics, as cited in the same issue of the *Frankfurter Rundschau,* 6.

[10]See *Spontane Streiks 1973: Krise der Gewerkschaftspolitik* (Offenbach, 1974); and *Gewerkschaften und Klassenkampf: Kritisches Jahrbuch* (Frankfurt am Main, 1973).

[11]See *SPD und Staat: Geschichte, Reformideologie, "Friedenspolitik"* Berlin, 1974); Margaret Wirth, *"Sozialstaatsillusion und aktuelle Krise,"* Links (May, 1974).

[12]See *Langzeitprogramm: Entwurf eines Ökonomisch-politischen*

Orientierungsrahmens fur die Jahre 1973-85, 5 vols. (Bad Godesberg, 1972/1973).

[13]See "Kampf um den Unterricht," *alternative* (April-June, 1974), particularly; Ulrich K.Preuss. "Die politische Aechtung legalen Verhaltens," 52-55; also Ulrich K. Preuss. "Klassenjustiz und politische Prozesse," *Der lange Marsch* (April, 1974), 11-14; *Radikale im offentlichen Dienst; Eine Dokumentation* (Frankfurt am Main, 1973); *Wortlaut und Kritik der terfassungswidrigen Januarbeschlusse* (Cologne, 1972).

[14]For a history of the social fascism propaganda of the KPD and a critique of its revival by dogmatic Marxist-Leninist circles in the FRG, see Niels Kadritzke, "Reformismus als 'Sozialfaschismus,' " *Probleme des Klassenkampfs* 11/12 (1974), 59-90.

[15]See Jurgen Haarer, "Zur Typologie und Definition sozialdemokratischer Politik," *Blätter für deutsche und internationale Politik* (June, 1974), 569-581; and *Wie links durfen die Jusos sein?* (Reinbek, 1974).

[16]On this point, see Horst Mewes, "The New German Left," *New German Critique* 1:1 (Winter, 1974), 22-41. For further information consult the following magazines: *Probleme des Klassenkampfes* (Erlangen) and *Der lange Marsch* (Berlin).

[17]See Oskar Negt, "Don't go by Numbers, Organize According to Interests, Current Questions of Organization," *New German Critique* 1:1 (Winter, 1974), 42-51.

Soviet Union

The Question of Stalin

[1]F. Engels, *The Peasant War in Germany,* (Moscow 1956).
[2]R. Luxemburg, *The Russian Revolution* (Michigan 1961), pp. 71-72.
[3]E. Carr, *Socialism in One Country,* (Penguin 1970), p. 196.
[4]J. J. Marie, *Staline,* (Paris, 1967).
[5]J. J. Marie, *Staline,* (Paris, 1967).
[6]E. Carr, *Socialism in One Country,* p. 192.
[7]E. Carr, *Socialism in One Country,* pp. 201-202.

Ideological Trends in the USSR

[1]In January 1968 the literary monthly *Oktyabr* published a poem by Feliks Chuyev expressing hope and belief that after some time Stalin's name would again be honoured and respected by the Soviet people.

[2]This was, of course, said a few months before the crisis in the Middle East and the Arab-Israel war of June 1967. A few days after that war *Krasnaya Zvezda* wrote that it was perhaps time to revise the official Soviet conception of "peaceful coexistence." (Footnote added by author, July 1967).

Samizdat: Voices of the Soviet Opposition

[1]Berger was a founder of the Communist Party of Palestine who lived in the USSR, doing Comintern work, and knew the Trotskyists well in the twenties and thirties, including in the camps and prisons.

[2]For details on that program, especially as reflected in the anticapitalist and anti-Stalinist Ukrainian paper *Vpered,* see "The Future of the Soviet Union" (an interview

with W. Wilny, a young Ukrainian emigre and supporter of *Vpered*), and "Inside the Soviet Union — Interview with Two Ukrainian Refugees" (Wilny and A. Babenko, an emigre Ukrainian Old Bolshevik, also a supporter of *Vpered*), in *Fourth International* (New York), May-June 1951, pp. 77-84, and September-October 1951, pp. 156-60 respectively.

[3] *Daedalus,* Summer 1960.

[4] For documentary materials on the Ukrainian group, see *Ferment in the Ukraine* (New York: Crisis Press, 1973). Other groups that have become known are: The "Young Workers' Party of Alma Ata," in Kazakhstan; the "Russian Socialist Party," which distributed leaflets in Leningrad calling on workers to launch a general strike; the "Party of Non-Party Workers Struggling for the Restoration of Socialism;" the "Struggle Committee for Socialist Democracy," which put out a leaflet in Moscow in August 1970 protesting the appearance of a bust of Stalin at the Lenin Mausoleum and calling for an all-out struggle for socialist democracy on a Leninist basis; the "Democratic Union of Socialists;" a group of seven "neo-Leninists" around the Leningrad engineer Dzibalov, arrested in March 1971 and tried in January 1972; the 1968-69 "Union of Independent Youth" of the town of Vladimir — an attempt at a legal organization fighting for socialist democracy based on the constitutional guarantee of "freedom of organization" (its leader, the young worker Vladimir Borisov, was arrested, forcibly confined in a mental hospital, and driven to suicide). In the late fifties and early sixties several clandestine organizations appeared in the Ukraine. The "United Party for the Liberation of the Ukraine" and the "Ukrainian National Committee" were two organizations in the Lviv region composed mostly of industrial workers. Two members of the UNC were shot, after being arrested, allegedly for planning terrorist attacks; the remainder had their death sentences commuted to long prison terms.

Another group, the Ukrainian National Front, functioned in 1965-67. Sixteen issues of its uncensored publication, *The Homeland and Freedom,* appeared before the group was uncovered by the police and broken up.

[5] Cornelia Gerstenmaier, *Voices of the Silent* (New York, 1972), pp. 97-98.

[6] Ted Harding, "Opposition Currents in the Soviet Union," *Intercontinental Press,* September 17, 1973.

[7] Other examples of recent mass actions inside the Soviet Union include a building trades strike in Moscow in 1960; a dock workers' strike in Odessa in late 1961; a strike at the Eletrosila power plant in Leningrad, apparently in 1963; a strike for lower prices that reportedly involved over 100,000 workers in Kharkiv, in the Ukraine, in autumn 1967, which won its demands; a mass demonstration by Crimean Tatars in Chirchik, Uzbekistan, on Lenin's birthday in April 1968 (one of many mass demonstrations by this nationality, demanding the right to return to its native region and have its own autonomous region, abolished by Stalin, restored to it); and the demonstrations involving thousands in Kaunas, Lithuania, in May 1972 to protest Russification and demand independence for Soviet Lithuania. Other cities where protest demonstrations over food and other shortages occurred in the sixties include Archangel and Murmansk (reported dock strikes), Gorky, Ryazan, Volgograd, Kriviy Rih, Donetsk, Zhdanov, Tashkent, Omsk, and Vladimir.

[8] Samizdat historian and gradualist dissenter Roy Medvedev explained this development in a very interesting way, reporting incidentally on a number of additional mass protests of recent occurrence. "The fact that pressure 'from above' can to some extent modify the policies of the 'high ups' is shown by the Twenty-fourth Congress of the CPSU. Many of the important social programs and plans for a more rapid rise in living standards for the workers, which were announced in two reports at the congress, were adopted even before the congress itself. These promises and programs looked quite different before December 1970 in the first variants and drafts of the Directives and the Official Report. Here, undoubtedly, effects were felt from both the Polish events of December 1970 and from certain wildcat demonstrations by workers in our own country who were dissatisfied with the difficult living conditions and the frequent interruptions in supplies of meat and dairy products (such

demonstrations, as far as know, took place in Ivanovo [Central Russia], Sverdlovsk [Urals], Gorky [on the Upper Volga], and several other cities" (*On Socialist Democracy* [Amsterdam, 1972], p. 376).

[9]On December 23, 1955, the Soviet youth paper *Komsomolskaya Pradva* complained about an uncensored publication bearing the title *Fig Leaf (Figovy List)* that was being circulated at the University of Vilnius (in Lithuania). The same newspaper referred three times in 1956 to uncensored journals appearing at educational institutions in the Leningrad area with names like *The Blue Bud (Goluboy Buton), Fresh Voices (Svezhie Golosa),* and *Heresy (Yeres).* In Moscow, an uncensored publication called *Culture (Kultura)* was reported.

These initial unauthorized student ventures were apparently concerned above all with literature and the arts — that is, they criticized or parodied official "socialist realism" (which might better be termed "bureaucratic romanticization"). They reproduced literary works that departed from the official school in order to express real attitudes and feelings, instead of those dictated from or approved on high, including satire and criticism with political implications

In the early sixties, uncensored literary-cultural publications like Ginzburg's *Syntax* and Galanskov's *Phoenix* proliferated. Usually these were collections of literary pieces that had circulated separately. In the Moscow samizdat milieu of those years, there was a monthly called *Cocktail,* three issues of a journal entitled *Siren,* and another publication, *The Seasons.* In February 1963 *The Lantern* was issued, *Bomb* in March 1964, *Workshop* in October of the same year, and in August 1965, *Neck,* as well as several issues of *Sphinxes* in 1965.Meanwhile, dissident literary circles in Leningrad circulated a publication called *Anthology of Soviet Pathology* in 1963 and another anthology of the same name in 1964.

[10]For Bukovsky, see note 77 of text. Brodsky was a nonconformist Leningrad poet whose 1964 trial for "parasitism" gained international notoriety.

[11]The *Russkoe Slovo* founded a hundred years earlier had been a legal journal of the revolutionary-democratic Narodnik movement of the 1860s.

[12]The Marxist opponents of populism, of course, used the name Russian Social Democratic Labor Party until World War I.

[13]Even observers hostile to Leninism have noted this feature of most currents in the Soviet dissident movement. Abraham Rothberg, for example, in his *Heirs of Stalin* (New York, 1972), commented on Pavel Litvinov's declaration at the 1968 trial in which Litvinov was sentenced to penal exile for demonstrating against the Kremlin's invasion of Czechoslovakia. "The prosecutor says also that we [demonstrators] were against the policies of the party and government but not against the social state system. Perhaps there are people who consider all our policies and even our government's mistakes to be the result of our state and social system. I do not see it this way. And I do not think the prosecutor himself would say this. For then he would have to say that all the crimes of the Stalin era resulted from our . . . system."

Rothberg comments: "[Such a] fundamental criticism of Soviet life and institutions [i.e., equating Stalinism with the postcapitalist social system itself] was almost everywhere avoided like the plague, by regime spokesmen and dissidents alike. Ironically [this line] was almost 'Trotskyist'; it called Stalinism a 'distortion' instead of seeing it as a direct outgrowth of the Revolution, the institutions imposed on the Soviet Union by the Bolsheviks, and the character of the Bolshevik leadership and of the Russian people."

Gerstenmaier too observes that the "majority of the dissident intellectuals and artists of the 1950's (and *even thereafter*) did not fight the Communist system, but rather, a privileged caste, which had taken advantage of this system to pursue its own personal power. The political views of the [majority of] rebels can be described as 'neo-Leninist' inasmuch as they acknowledge the basic precepts of Leninism and the goals of the October Revolution" (*Voices of the Silent,* p. 93).

The Soviet Working Class: Discontent and Opposition

[1]An interesting comment on the way in which Soviet workers themselves view the Soviet press was provided by a survey of 25,000 *Izvestia* readers. Commissioned by *Izvestia* on its 50th anniversary, and carried out by the Siberian section of the USSR Academy of Sciences, the survey surfaced to public attention in an article by Tolkunov, the *Izvestia* editor. The survey revealed that only 32% of workers, 22% of women, and 21% of collective farmers were satisfied with the newspapers' portrayal of their work and living conditions. "A serious and alarming observation," was Tolkunov's comment on the results of the survey. Tolkunov's remedy for the situation was: to expand the letters column of the newspaper. (*Izvestia,* 14 March 1967).

[2]*Suchasnist,* No. 12, 1973, p. 119 (Munich).

[3]*Survey,* No. 77, 1970 (London).

[4]Robert Conquest (ed.), *Industrial Workers in the USSR* (London, 1971), p. 11.

[5]A detailed account of the riot appears in John Kolasky's *Two Years in Soviet Ukraine* (Toronto, 1972), pp. 190-91. Based on reports he gathered while in the Soviet Union, Kolasky writes, "As construction of the enterprise began, young workers were brought in, especially from the western regions, first of all Ukraine, Belorussia, and Moldavia. But there was nowhere to house them and accommodation was provided in tents. Dissatisfaction developed rapidly over a number of basic issues: wages were much lower than those promised when workers were recruited and lower than those of foreign Komsomol brigades from other countries such as East Germany and Poland: there was a great shortage of commodities, both clothing and food: drinking water was in short supply: summers were plagued with intense heat and furious sandstorms . . . the lack of food supplies set off a mass protest movement in September, 1959. A group of youths tore down a small kiosk. Soon thousands of others began wrecking shops, setting fires and looting warehouses. When the militia was ordered out, the rioters routed it, marched on the (police) station, caught the chief and hanged him. The director of the construction site, who was intensely hated for his indifference to the workers' plight, was also killed . . . To quell the riots soldiers were flown in. The result was the massacre of at least several hundred young people, many of them Komsomol members, and the arrest of many others, some of whom were later sentenced to death."

[6]M. Tatu, *Power in the Kremlin* (London, 1969), p. 115.

[7]Vladimir Azbel, a recent Soviet emigrant writing in "Two years in Siberia" (*Research Bulletin,* Radio Liberty, Munich, August 28, 1974, p. 7) mentioned meeting, in a remote Siberian kolkhoz, workers from Rostov-on-Don who called a strike in protest against the currency reforms. One of Azbel's friends, an organizer of this strike, was sentenced to 10 years in prison, and upon his release in 1972, was condemned to exile in this village.

[8]*Problems of Communism,* No 1, 1964, p. 36.

[9]Tatu, *op. cit.* The presence of students and youth provided the regime with a convenient, albeit not very original, explanation for the Novocherkaask events — "youth hooliganism." This is how the local Novocherkassk newspaper, *Znamya Kommuny,* obliquely referred to the event after several weeks of stony silence.

[10]*Pravda,* June 9th, 1962, reported Kozlov's presence in the city. An Oblast Committee plenary session was held in his presence. *Pravda* reported in reference to the riots that "Certain Party organizations have weakened their ties with the masses and fallen down on their ideological didactic tasks," (quotes in Tatu, *op. cit.*).

[11]Kolasky, *op. cit.,* pp. 191-92. Kolasky is a former member of the Canadian Communist Party sent to the USSR on Party scholarship to study in Kiev for two years at the Higher Party School. In his book he reports other instances of working class protest: a strike of port workers in Odessa against food shortages and a strike at a motorcycle factory in Kiev for similar reasons in 1962. In 1964, a few days prior to May 1st celebrations, leaflets distributed under the sponsorship of "The Voice of the People" appeared in several Kiev factories. These leaflets contained the following

slogans: "To the Peoples of the Soviet Union!," "The Party Has Degenerated," "Control over the Party," "Power to the Soviets."

[12]Cornelia Gerstenmaier, *Voices of the Silent* (New York, 1972), quoted in G. Saunders (ed.) *op. cit.*, p. 31.

[13]The only source for this report is *Hsinhua Press Service*, Peking, January 9, 1974.

[14]Approximately one third of the average Soviet workers' salary is composed of bonuses; therefore, cuts in bonuses appear as a major cause of strikes.

[15]*Rouge*, June 8, 1973, Paris.

[16]*Ukrain'ske Slovo*, 23 March, 1973, Paris.

[17]A full account of this strike is given in *Critique* No. 2.

[18]Peter Reddaway, (ed.), *Uncensored Russia* (London, 1972), pp. 290-1.

[19]Andrei Amalrik *Will the Soviet Union Survive . . .?* quoted in G. Saunders (ed.), *op. cit.*

[20]G. Saunders (ed.) *op. cit.*, p. 31.

[21]*Vedomosti Verkhovnovo Sovieta SSSR*, 16 July, 1969, Moscow.

[22]Quoted in *International Herald Tribune*, Feb 11, 1973.

[23]A. P. Volkov, quoted in M. Matthews, *Class and Society in Soviet Russia* (London 1972), p. 82.

[24]*Ibid*, pp. 84-90.

[25]*Ibid.*

[26]*Ibid.*

[27]Quoted in *International Herald Tribune*, Feb. 11, 1973.

[28]B. Bukhanevich, "The Relationship Between the Growth of Labour Productivity and Wages," *Voprosi Ekonomiki*, No. 8, August, 1972.

[29]See H. H. Ticktin's article in *Critique* No 1.

[30]D. Panin, quoted in R. Medvedev, "Problems of Democratization and Détente," *New Left Review*, Jan.-Feb. 1974.

[31]*Financial Times*, July 10, 1973.

[32]*Molodoi Kommunist*, No. 10, 1972, p. 58.

[33]*Ibid.*

[34]*L'Espresso*, Rome, 26 September, 1971.

[35]*Itogi Vsesoyuznoi Perepisi Naselenia 1970*, Vol.6.

CREDITS

From "Decentralization of Power in the Federal Republic of Germany," by John Holloway in *The Failure of the State* by James Cornford (Editor) copyright © 1975 by Croom Helm Ltd., reprinted by permission of the author, editor, and publisher.

From "Immigrant Workers and Trade Unions in the German Federal Republic," by Stephan Castles and Godula Kosack, *Race and Class,* copyright © April, 1974, and reprinted by permission of the authors and *Race and Class.*

From "The Brandt Affair and the SPD," by Wolfgang Nitsch, *New German Critique* Fall, 1974, copyright © 1974 by *New German Critique* and reprinted by permission of the publishers.

"The Question of Stalin," by Lucio Colletti in *New Left Review,* May-June, 1970, copyright © 1970 and reprinted by permission of *New Left Review.*

From "Ideological Trends in the USSR," by Isaac Deutscher, in *The Socialist Register 1968* by Ralph Miliband and John Saville (Editors), copyright © 1968 by Merlin Press. Reprinted by permission of Monthly Review Press.

From "Introduction," to *Samizdat: Voices of the Soviet Opposition* by George Saunders (Editor), copyright © 1974 by Monad Press and reprinted by permission of the publisher.

The selection "Report of a Recent Visit to the USSR" is reprinted from Red Papers 7: How Capitalism Has Been Restored in the Soviet Union and What This Means for the World Struggle, available from the Revolutionary Communist Party, USA, P.O. Box 3486, Merchandise Mart, Chicago, IL 60654.

Red Papers 7 was originally published by the Revolutionary Union which has since gone out of existence with the formation of the RCP, USA. The book sought to prove that the USSR was a socialist state throughout the period of Lenin and Stalin, but was transformed into a new capitalist, imperialist power after Khrushchev's seizure of power in 1956.

"The Soviet Working Class: Discontent and Opposition," by M. Holubenko, *Critique* (Scotland), Spring, 1975, copyright © 1975 by *Critique* and reprinted by permission of the publisher.